PERFORMANCE ANXIETY

Sport and Work in Germany from the Empire to Nazism

GERMAN AND EUROPEAN STUDIES

General Editor: Jennifer J. Jenkins

MICHAEL HAU

Performance Anxiety

Sport and Work in Germany from the Empire to Nazism

UNIVERSITY OF TORONTO PRESS
Toronto Buffalo London

Toronto Buffalo London
www.utppublishing.com

ISBN 978-1-4426-3062-8

(German and European Studies)

Library and Archives Canada Cataloguing in Publication

Hau, Michael, author
Performance anxiety : sport and work in Germany from the empire to Nazism / Michael Hau.

(German and European studies ; 25)
Includes bibliographical references and index.
ISBN 978-1-4426-3062-8 (cloth)

1. Sports – Political aspects – Germany – History – 20th century. 2. Sports – Social aspects – Germany – History – 20th century. 3. Work – Government policy – Germany – History – 20th century. 4. National socialism – Germany – History – 20th century. I. Title. II. Series: German and European studies ; 25

GV611.H39 2017 796.0943'09041 C2016-903844-0

University of Toronto Press acknowledges the financial assistance to its publishing program of the Canada Council for the Arts and the Ontario Arts Council, an agency of the Government of Ontario.

Canada Council for the Arts | Conseil des Arts du Canada

Funded by the Government of Canada | Financé par le gouvernement du Canada

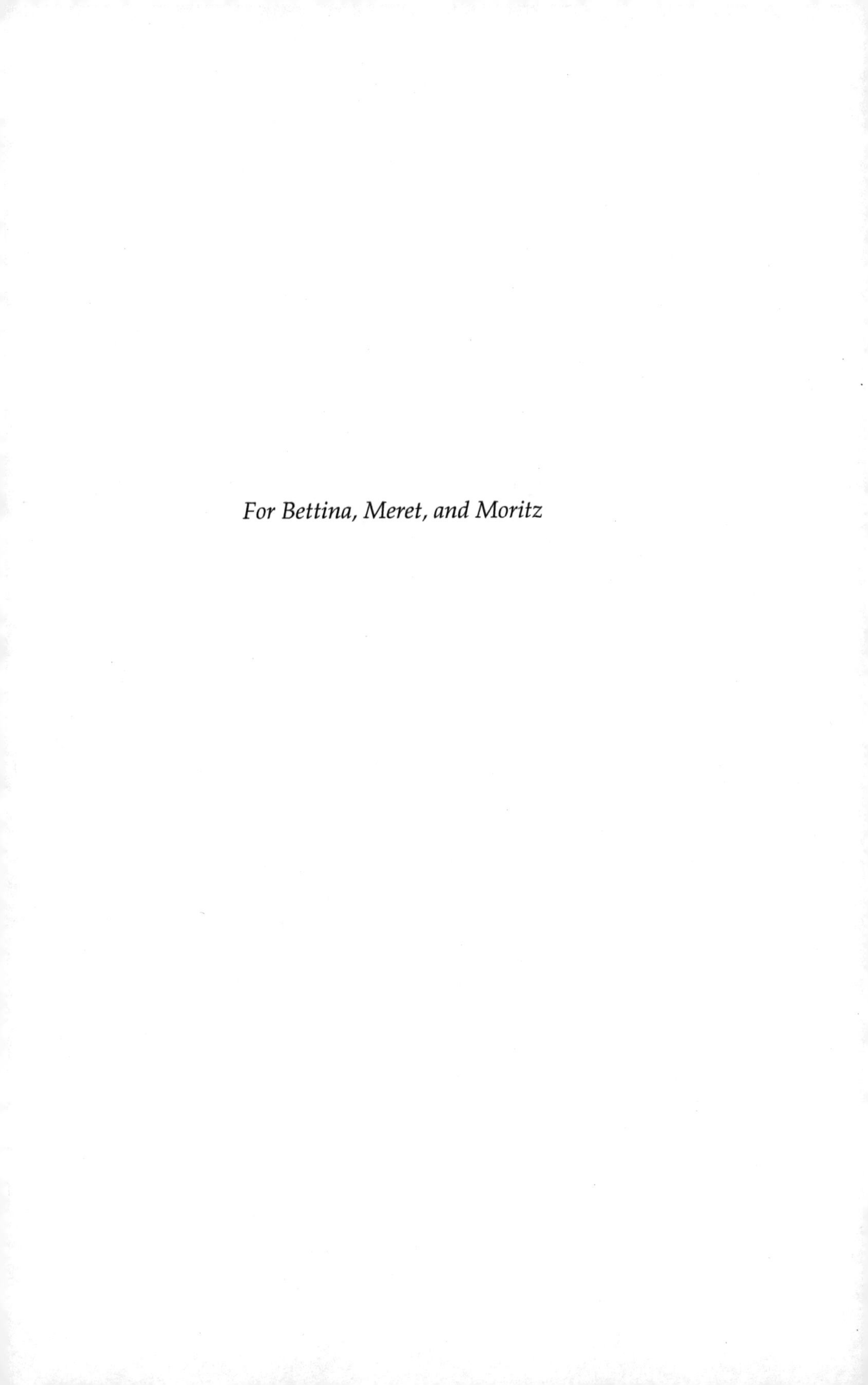

For Bettina, Meret, and Moritz

Contents

Illustrations

Acknowledgments

Employees of major corporations are quite familiar with performance targets, performance assessments, and performance management strategies developed and implemented by senior executives. Academics at Australian universities share some of these experiences. I do not know whether this is the reason many of my colleagues have become interested in my work but I have greatly benefited from their critical engagement with my ideas. I would first of all like to thank David Garrioch, who commented on the entire manuscript and suggested the title *Performance Anxiety*, a condition that is not only familiar to many scholars but, as this book shows, also to those who more or less successfully try to manage the performance of others.

Many scholars at Monash and elsewhere have commented on the manuscript or individual chapters and have provided valuable criticism over the years. I would like to thank Bain Attwood, Barbara Caine, Adam Clulow, Franz-Josef Deiters, Axel Fliethmann, Leah Garrett, Reto Hofmann, Julie Kalman, Ernest Koh, Cameron Logan, Helmut Maier, Paula Michaels, Clare Monagle, Maria Nugent, Seamus O'Hanlon, Susie Protschky, Gideon Reuveni, Richard Scully, Noah Shenker, Beatrice Trefalt, Corinna Treitel, Christina Twomey, Angelika Uhlmann, Tim Verhoeven, and Christiane Weller. Some of the early ideas that informed this book were first discussed at two panels of the annual meetings of the American Historical Association in 2005 and 2006, which included historians Geoff Eley, Mark Roseman, Chad Ross, and Ina Zweiniger-Bargielowska. I would like to thank them and the audience members for their engaging criticism. A panel at the 2007 meeting of the German Studies Association in San Diego provided further feedback. I am grateful to Kathleen Canning and Thomas Kühne for their invitation.

Hans-Jörg Rheinberger provided me with the opportunity to stay at the Berlin *Max-Planck-Institut für Wissenschaftsgeschichte* during the early stages of the project in 2005, which enabled me to do some important preliminary research on the book. I am also grateful to the anonymous readers of the manuscript, Richard Ratzlaff, the editor at UTP, for his efficient handling of the referee process, Frances Mundy for managing the final stages of the production, and Dilia Narduzzi for the copyediting.

The help of many archivists and librarians who have given me support during my research in Germany and Australia is also greatly appreciated. I thank Jenny Casey and Beth Pearson from the Monash University library for organizing the scanning of many of the images. I would also like to acknowledge the firms or their legal successors that gave me permission to see their records, especially the Bayer Corporate Archive in Leverkusen (which also allowed me to use the title image) and most of the companies with relevant records in the *Wirtschaftsarchiv* Baden-Württemberg in Stuttgart-Hohenheim. Unfortunately not every firm was so forthcoming. The Voith GmbH in Heidenheim refused access to their Nazi period files on the "Performance Competition of German Companies."

I would also like to thank friends who have taken some interest in me and my ideas in one way or another. Herbert Hildebrandt and Hubert Wondrak for reacquainting me with Swabian ways; Al Mask, Jason Moritz, Don Oberdorfer, and Mark Perkins for memorable if rare encounters; Sierra Bruckner and Rudolf Kräuter for being long-standing friends from my Iowa and Berlin years respectively; Sabine Schäfer for putting up with my regular stays in Berlin; and Andrew Cossen, David Foerster, and Heike Manet for introducing us to the Australian bush. I am also grateful to my parents Alfred and Heidrun Hau for providing support over many years. My children Meret and Moritz had to put up with the gestation of this work for their entire lives and they must be happy that it is finally finished. The book is dedicated to them and my wife Bettina Wachsmuth for their welcome disruptions and love.

Parts of chapter 2 were published previously as Michael Hau, "Sports in the Human Economy. '*Leibesübungen*,' Medicine, Psychology, and Performance Enhancement during the Weimar Republic," *Central European History* 41, no. 3 (2008): 381-412. Reprinted with permission of Cambridge University Press.

All translations from German into English are mine unless otherwise noted.

Early research for this this project was partially funded by an Australian Research Council Discovery project grant (DP 0558404) for 2005 and 2006.

Abbreviations

AGMPG	*Archiv für die Geschichte der Max-Planck-Gesellschaft* (Archive for the History of the Max Planck Society)
AHU	*Archiv der Humboldt Universität* (Archive Humboldt University)
AWI	*Arbeitswissenschaftliches Institut* (Work Science Institute of the DAF)
BABL	*Bundesarchiv Berlin-Lichterfelde* (Federal Archive Berlin-Lichterfelde)
BAV	*Bereit zur Arbeit und Verteidigung* (GDR Sports Badge)
BCA	Bayer Corporate Archive
BDM	*Bund Deutscher Mädel* (League of German Girls)
BSG	*Betriebssportgemeinschaft* (Company Sport Community)
CULDA	*Carl und Liselott Diem Archiv Deutsche Sporthochschule Köln* (Carl and Liselott Diem Archive German Sport University Cologne)
DAF	*Deutsche Arbeitsfront* (German Labour Front)
DHfL	*Deutsche Hochschule für Leibesübungen* (German University for Physical Exercise)
DINTA	*Deutsches Institut für technische Arbeitsschulung* (German Institute for Technical Work Schooling)
DRAFOS	*Deutscher Reichsausschuss für Olympische Spiele* (German Reich Committee for Olympic Games)
DRAL	*Deutscher Reichsausschuss für Leibesübungen* (German Reich Committee for Physical Exercise)
DSB	*Deutscher Sportbund* (German Sport League)
DSBA	*Deutsche Sport-Behörde für Athletik* (German Organization for Athletics)

DT	*Deutsche Turnerschaft* (German Gymnasts)
GDR	German Democratic Republic (East Germany)
GE-SO-LEI	*Gesundheitspflege-Soziale Fürsorge-Leibesübungen* (Health Care, Social Welfare, and Physical Exercise)
GG	General Government
GTO	*Gotov k trudu i oborone* (Ready for Work and Defence, Soviet sport badge)
GWS	*Gesellschaft für deutsche Wirtschafts- und Sozialpolitik* (Society for German Economic and Social Policy)
HJ	*Hitlerjugend* (Hitler Youth)
HSAS	*Hauptstaatsarchiv Stuttgart*
IOC	International Olympic Committee
JDB	*Jungdeutschlandbund* (Young Germany League)
KdF	*Kraft durch Freude* (Strength through Joy)
KWBK	*Kriegsberufswettkampf* (War Vocational Competition)
KWIA	*Kaiser-Wilhelm-Institut für Arbeitsphysiologie* (Kaiser Wilhelm Institute for Work Physiology)
(NS)RBL	*(NS) Reichsbund für Leibesübungen* (National Socialist Reich League for Physical Exercise)
OgW	*Organisation der gewerblichen Wirtschaft* (Corporate Organization of Business, Nazi period)
OND	*Opera Nazionale Dopolavoro* (National After Work Organization, Fascist Italy)
PHfL	*Preussische Hochschule für Leibesübungen* (Prussian College for Physical Exercise)
RAG	*Reichsarbeitsgemeinschaft der Behörden- und Firmensportverbände* (Umbrella organization for company sport during the Weimar period)
RAL	*Reichsakademie für Leibesübungen* (Reich Academy for Physical Exercise)
RBWK	*Reichsberufswettkampf* (Reich Vocational Competition)
RGI	*Reichsgruppe Industrie* (Corporate Organization of Industry, Nazi period)
RK	*Reichskuratorium für Jugendertüchtigung* (Reich Board for the Fortification of Youth)
RKW	*Reichskuratorium für Wirtschaftlichkeit* (National Productivity Board)
SD	*Sicherheitsdienst* (Intelligence service of the SS)
SOPADE	Reports of the Social Democratic Party in Exile
WCI	*Wirtschaftsgruppe Chemische Industrie* (Corporate Organization of Chemical Industry)

ZA *Zentralausschuß für Volks- und Jugendspiele* (Central Committee for People and Youth Games)

ZAK *Zentralkommision für Arbeitersport und Körperpflege* (Central Commission for Worker Sport and Physical Care)

PERFORMANCE ANXIETY

Sport and Work in Germany from the Empire to Nazism

Introduction

In 1943, Robert Ley declared that "performance (*Leistung*) is the only measure for the rank and social order among men."[1] Ley was the leader of the "German Labour Front" (*Deutsche Arbeitsfront* or DAF), the largest mass organization of the Nazi regime, which was responsible for turning workers into politically reliable and productive members of the national community. In his statement the Labour Front leader referred to two major concerns of Nazi social and economic policy. On the one hand, he called for a rise in work performance to prevent a collapse of the home front as in 1918. In the view of many Nazi leaders, Germany was engaged in a permanent struggle for survival, making it necessary that Germans were physically fit, prepared to serve in the military, and committed to their work. The Second World War would be the ultimate test for the German "People's and Performance Community" (*Volks- und Leistungsgemeinschaft*), which the regime propagated. On the other hand, Ley articulated a promise of social opportunity: every racially acceptable male citizen should be able to compete for social advancement and move into leadership positions based on his individual performance.

Yet, Nazi officials were far from being the first ones in German history to call for an increase in national fitness and productivity. From the 1890s, promoters of physical exercise encouraged people "to strengthen their physical powers in the interest of their health and the preservation of their working power."[2] In this book, I examine the longer-term history and the social and cultural significance of *Leistung* in Germany by looking at the ways in which German elites promoted sport, competition, and fitness in order to raise people's productivity and will to work. As early as the nineteenth century, performance or *Leistung* was (and one might argue still is) a key concept in German social, cultural, and political debates. It can refer to extraordinary accomplishments in many areas of human activity – be it art, literature, music, scholarship, work, or sport. The term can be translated as achievement, as in a task well done, but it can also refer to competitive performances in sport and to productivity and efficiency in the workplace.

My analysis focuses on performance enhancement *through* sport rather than *in* sport. I examine the significance of *Leistung* in German society by examining discourses about sport in several different social settings and political contexts, and I show how these were tied to changing ideological understandings of society from the late nineteenth century to the end of the Second World War.[3] As the title suggests my work deals with anxieties about performance. But my main emphasis is not so much on the anxieties of white- or blue-collar workers themselves, which were caused by performance pressures in the workplace. Instead I focus on the ways in which, from the 1890s to the 1940s, members of the German elites articulated their worries about the unreliability and lack of performance of the German workforce, and discuss the strategies they proposed to introduce to deal with these problems.

University professors, military officers, business people, and political leaders expressed concern about the poor health and productivity of the German population, which threatened the nation's standing and even survival in the modern world. Before the First World War, they advocated gymnastics and sport to increase the productivity and efficiency of the German imperial nation state. When in turn that war shattered Germany's imperialistic ambition, concerns about the health and productivity of the German population were expressed with even greater urgency. Consequently, the Weimar years witnessed a widespread promotion of sport to restore the performance capacity of the German populace by creating healthy citizens who were willing to work and stayed off the welfare rolls. The basic assumption behind these efforts was that sport would not only promote physical fitness but also a positive psychological performance-orientation that could be applied in the workplace. In Nazi Germany, such approaches were taken to an extreme. The regime gave unprecedented support to sport in its mass organizations and promoted sport in the workplace in order to foster performance-orientation and productivity, and to ensure political commitment to the racial community (*Volksgemeinschaft*). At the same time, the regime introduced vocational and workplace competitions to turn labour into a kind of sport to increase people's joy in work.

While my study owes much to the history of sport, it is only tangentially concerned with the kind of issues that are commonly the focus of sport historiography. I am not preoccupied with the history of the German sport and gymnastics movements, specific sport disciplines and their training practices, the careers of particular sport officials and their involvement with Nazism, or high profile sporting events such as the Olympic Games of 1936, even though I discuss aspects of these matters.[4] Moreover, while I deal with selected episodes of the history of the German sport sciences and sport pedagogy, I aim to move beyond an intellectual history of these scientific and scholarly disciplines to consider ideological and cultural implications of discourses about sport and related practices.

During the Weimar Republic and the Nazi period there was widespread fascination with the performance of elite athletes. Soccer, cycling, and boxing became spectator sports for mass audiences and the accomplishments of Germany's best athletes induced many people to take up a sport for themselves. The popular interest in athletic accomplishments and mass sport (understood in the sense of the German term *Breitensport* as sporting activities to improve the fitness of the general population) was embraced also by the elites who came to regard it as a promising social technology. As I argue, scientists, scholars, sport and government officials, as well as many employers, looked to sport as a tool for social and political interventions in the service of several interrelated goals. The promotion of mass sport was intended to guarantee the health and productivity of the working population. Hence sport was a central part of a discourse about what the Austrian social philosopher and economist Rudolf Goldscheid has called "human economy" (*Menschenökonomie*). In contrast to eugenics or racial hygiene (*Rassenhygiene*), with its assumptions of hereditary determinism and its emphasis on encouraging the reproduction of the fit and discouraging the reproduction of the unfit, *Menschenökonomie* focused on environmental factors that determined whether people could develop their physical and mental potential to the fullest. In this context, many saw in sport a promising tool for enhancing people's performance capacity, not only because it was thought to benefit physiological health, but because it was held to be character building. Advocates of *Menschenökonomie* called for the systematic development of human resources through a rational fostering of human working power. They wanted to ensure that the productive potential of every individual was fully developed – both for the benefit of the individuals and for society as a whole.[5]

From a physiological point of view, mass sport was thought to prevent damage to and exhaustion of the "human motor" while also strengthening its working capacity.[6] Researchers of sport and work physiology tried to figure out both the potential and the limits of the physical performance of humans in order to establish the parameters of performance enhancement. From a psychological point of view, the hedonistic aspects of sport were also considered important. The fun and enthusiasm generated by sport – so the argument went – made it possible for people to overcome mental fatigue and enhance their performance at work. "Strength through Joy" (*Kraft durch Freude*) was the name of the leisure organization of the German Labour Front, which promoted mass sport during the Nazi period, but the slogan could have been endorsed by advocates of mass sport during the Kaiser reich and the Weimar period.

While I examine the use of sport in what Marxists would call the reproduction of people's working power, I try to take my analysis a step further. Drawing on studies originally inspired by Michel Foucault's work on biopolitics, governmentality and technologies of subjectivation, my goal is to analyse sport practices and discourses as ways to change working people's ideas about themselves and their role in German society.[7] As I will argue, the invocation of the performance principle through sport was meant to persuade Germans to see themselves not as members of particular social classes but as responsible and willingly productive members of the German "People's Community."[8]

Since the late nineteenth century German liberals liked to encourage a sense of civic responsibility among young workers, because they believed it would support social cohesion. In his examination of Prussian debates about youth care (*Jugendpflege*) before the First World War, historian Edward Ross Dickinson has pointed to the liberal impulse in debates about youth education that aimed to increase the "working capacity" and the "joy in work" experienced by young males through the promotion of continuing education, sport, and exercise. In avoiding the appearance of compulsion and state tutelage, Dickinson claims, liberal-minded reformers looked to integrate working class youths into the productive community with promises of training, higher living standards, and upward social mobility. According to this liberal progressive vision, young workers were encouraged to develop the virtues and self-discipline for self-governance and responsible citizenship.[9]

Such technologies of subjectivation, Nikolas Rose has argued in turn, play an important role in liberal democratic societies that depend on the self-government and responsibility of their citizenry to function.[10] This may be true, but there is nothing inherently democratic in such technologies. Authoritarian and totalitarian governments also fostered such technologies to encourage their citizens to become loyal and willingly productive members of the nation. In the German case, the rise of the socialist movement after 1890 posed a serious challenge to the project of integrating the working class into the nation state. Neither indoctrination through the formal educational system nor authoritarian inculcation of discipline in the course of compulsory military service seemed to slow the rise of organized socialism or temper its threat to the social order. State-supported youth care was conceived as an attempt to address this problem differently by influencing young male workers who had just left school but who had yet to experience the educational "benefits" of military service. Continuing education and organized leisure activities, including sport, were to be put into the service of creating healthy and disciplined citizens who accepted the social order and were committed to their work. While young women were for the most part excluded from such activities before 1914, this changed during the war when authorities realized that they had to mobilize women's productive capacities more fully.

From the late nineteenth century, representatives of the German political, social, and academic elites saw sport as offering a way to change workers' attitudes and self-understanding while guaranteeing their physical fitness and working capacity at the same time. Exercise and sport were promoted as means to strengthen the physical basis for the military power of the Empire while also building the productive capacity of the population. Enhancing the "defensive power" (*Wehrkraft*) and the productive power of the Volk (*Volkskraft*) were the most important goals of these efforts. But the collapse of the Empire in 1918 did not mean that this project came to an end. Rather, it was simply given a somewhat different emphasis in a republic that faced the challenge of restoring national health, fitness, and productivity after the human losses caused by the war. With the end of conscription and the reduction of the German army to one hundred thousand men, concerns about *Wehrkraft* suddenly seemed much less important than those about the productive health of Germans and the German economy. As before the war, people worried about the competitiveness of German industry on the world market, but now this anxiety was compounded by concerns about the social, economic, and hygienic consequences of the war. Debates about the promotion of military fitness (*Wehrertüchtigung*) only resurfaced in a major way during the Depression of the early 1930s in the context of conservative attempts to overcome obstacles to the authoritarian transformation of the political and social system.

After 1933 the Nazi regime aimed to change the nature of social relations not by redistributing productive assets and wealth but by radically revamping people's understanding of themselves and their roles and responsibilities as members of the German racial community. The regime promoted sport to encourage people's performance-orientation in all areas of community life. Sporting attitudes were meant to validate the performance principle in the workplace. This connection was institutionalized through the "Reich Vocational Competitions" (*Reichsberufswettkämpfe*) in the 1930s. Propagated as the "Olympics of Labour," the annual ritual of the competitions promoted community spirit as well as performance-orientation in the workplace. Young men and women were urged to see themselves not in terms of their social class background, but as valued productive members of the community, regardless of whether they were unskilled, semi-skilled, or skilled manual workers, or whether they worked in white collar or professional occupations.

While work was to become a sport, sport was considered serious work targeted at transforming people's subjectivities. The attempt to rework people's sense of self went hand in hand with the promise of meritocracy – at least for men. In denouncing the limiting effects of poverty and social disadvantage, regime officials claimed that there were unprecedented social and professional opportunities for young males from all social backgrounds, provided they proved their willingness to perform and make sacrifices for the racial community. For all this, the Nazi regime was not an "accommodating dictatorship" that redistributed social benefits to its citizenry.[11] Even for those people who were considered racially acceptable, social entitlements were tied to their willingness to work and support the political goals of the regime.

Sport and discourses about sport, I argue, are tied to ideological perceptions of social relations in German society. To appreciate this connection it is helpful to think about sport as a part of social regimes of subjectivation. By this I mean the nexus of strategies developed and promoted by members of the German elites (including medical professionals, sport officials, government bureaucrats, employers, and leaders of the Nazi regime) intended to shape people's self-understanding. As sociologist Ulrich Bröckling has argued, the power of such strategies lies in their ability to communicate to people an unquestioned knowledge or "truth" about themselves, and the logic of their actions and their social relationships.[12] They are embedded in particular world views and articulate specific expectations about how people should see themselves, their society, and how they should conduct themselves. In this respect they fulfil ideological functions that are reinforced by ritual enactments and the distribution of social rewards. When Hitler personally received the national winners of the "Olympics of Labour" each year, the regime symbolically underscored its claims about the dignity of manual labour and the meritocratic nature of the new Germany – a place where people's class background was irrelevant for social advancement because, as in regular sport, the only thing that counted was performance.

Efforts to change people's self-understanding can be described as a form of ideological work in which shifts in emphasis in discourse are designed to change meanings and understandings of social relations.[13] This kind of work extends beyond the written, oral, or visual propagation of ideas and world views to include social practices and rituals. Sport, for example, conveys particular ideas about people's selves and the society they live in. Far from simply justifying existing social hierarchies and values, this type of ideological work was productive and transformative: it exhorted people to see themselves as members of a community that offered new possibilities of social recognition and advancement.[14] In the case of Nazism, officials urged people to see themselves as part of a privileged racial community, judged not by their social background but by their contribution – *Leistung* – to the community.

The Nazi promotion of a racial community of productive citizens was a response to class-based understandings of society. For much of the early twentieth century, the socialist movement encouraged workers to see themselves as part of a social class with particular class interests and a historical mission to transform Germany into a socialist society. The alternative culture of German socialism, with its own extensive networks of leisure, gymnastics, and sport associations, tried to reinforce such self-understandings.[15] As historians have noted, such subjectivities, and the social milieus that nurtured them, were challenged by the emergence of non-socialist forms of entertainment and mass culture, including mass sport that operated outside the framework of a distinctly proletarian subculture.[16] Pierre Bourdieu has noted that subjectivity is an essential aspect of class formation,[17] but the reverse is also true: changing subjectivities and by extension technologies of subjectivation are important for the unmaking of historically specific understandings of social class. This process is particularly evident in the Nazi regime's attempt to transform people's self-understanding from members of social classes with separate interests to citizens or members of a racial community with common interests.

Sport, gymnastics, and other types of exercise were not only meant to condition the body, they were supposed to work through the body to shape people's attitudes and values. Nazi mass organizations such as the Hitler Youth, the paramilitary SA (*Sturmabteilung*), and the Labour Front looked to sport as a way to form the ideal Nazi citizen or "people's comrade."[18] The Hitler Youth subjected its charges to regular sport competitions in addition to testing their commitment to Nazi *Weltanschauung*.[19] In collaboration with the Hitler Youth and employers, the Labour Front promoted company sport as part of its vision to create a community of producers independent of people's income and profession. In the formal educational sector, sport education assumed a more central role as well. By 1937, compulsory physical education in secondary schools was increased from two hours to five hours per week, fulfilling a long-standing demand of the German sport movement.[20] In addition, students at university were required to meet minimum physical performance standards before they could re-enrol after three semesters.[21] The centrality of Nazi sport discourse is indicative of its wider importance for the transformation of people's subjectivity. Sport was promoted to foster attitudes of performance-orientation and the "preparedness for combative commitment" (*Einsatzbereitschaft*) in the workplace, which furthered the militarization of work and social relations. Individual commitment and "team orientation" (*Mannschaftsgeist*) were promoted with reference to the wartime myth of military comradeship (*Kameradschaft*) – a male-dominated community working towards a common goal in the face of hardship and adversity.

While the Nazi regime greatly expanded previously existing efforts to shape people's minds and souls through sport, the ideological, political, and economic contexts in which these technologies were deployed had changed. Economic productivity was an even greater concern for a regime that mobilized for war. The social and economic austerity necessitated by the rearmament drive was accompanied by calls for self-denial, asceticism, and personal sacrifice in the service of greater performance for the community. People who could not perform in the workplace, or refused to do so, were denounced as work-shy and hereditarily inferior antisocials and faced persecution by the security apparatus of the regime. Active participation in Nazi performance drives, whether in conventional sport or in vocational competitions, helped to demarcate the boundaries between productive members of the people's community and allegedly non-productive social outsiders.

Nazi performance discourse was tied up with Nazi racial ideology and anti-Semitism. By subjecting themselves to regular fitness assessments, racially acceptable Germans could demonstrate their political commitment to the racial community, which the regime tried to build. In Nazi Germany, *Leistung* was overdetermined in that performance-orientation was presented as a racial trait that so-called "racial aliens" and other "community aliens" lacked. As in other social contexts, Jews were ostracized and expelled from German sport clubs and excluded from sporting competitions with other Germans.[22] The same was true in regard to performance rituals such as the Reich Vocational Competitions.

The racist assumptions of Nazi discourse about sport became even more evident during the war. In occupied Poland, sport served as a means of building a sense of community among members of the master race ruling over a hostile population. High-ranking officials like the Governor of Warsaw, Ludwig Fischer, saw in sport a technology for exercising discipline over the disparate and diverse group of German occupiers as well as a means to build new German cultural institutions in the East. Regime officials placed a lot of faith in the transformative power of sporting rituals until the very end. Back in the Reich, the revival of the Reich Vocational Competitions as "War Vocational Competitions" (*Kriegsberufswettkämpfe*) during the first half of 1944 attested to the regime's belief in the mobilizing powers of sport discourse and practice.

After 1945 *Leistung* remained an important ideological concept in German social and political discourse. Many West Germans liked to describe the Federal Republic of Germany as an open "performance society" (*Leistungsgesellschaft*) in which inherited social and economic privilege mattered less than in previous periods of German history, a self-image that referenced similar arguments made during the Nazi period. In East Germany, the communist leadership promoted the performance principle in the workplace to boost productivity and build the first socialist state on German soil. Yet, though sport was promoted in both postwar societies to improve the general fitness of the population, there were important differences from the body-centred pedagogical projects of the Nazi period. Most importantly, sporting references played a comparatively minor role in the different performance ideologies that emerged in the two postwar Germanys.

To a large extent my research is based on published and unpublished sources from government and Nazi officials, sport functionaries, and business managers. I also discuss the research and recommendations by medical and psychological experts, work scientists, and engineers who suggested the ways that sport could be used to make people more productive. While I rely on a wide range of published sources, much of the research is based on materials in business, university, city, state, and national archives. The *Carl und Liselott Diem Archiv* (CULDA) at the *Deutsche Sporthochschule* in Cologne, which holds the papers of Carl Diem (the most important German sport official in the first third of the twentieth century) provided important sources on the history of sport science and the public promotion of sport. The extensive holdings of the *Bundesarchiv* in Berlin-Lichterfelde, with its files from various government ministries, public institutions, and Nazi organizations such as the German Labour Front, were crucial as were sources from state and company archives. Where possible I have discussed the impact the extensive discourse on performance enhancement and Nazi performance campaigns had on the workforce with reference to the SOPADE reports by the Social Democratic Party in exile, the SD reports (Security Service of the SS), and scattered information from a number of archives, but the main focus of my work remains on the anxieties of German elites and their attempts to engineer political loyalties and performance mentalities among the workforce and the citizenry more generally. In doing so, I analyse historical understandings of the relationship between social class and citizenship as well as cultural and political assumptions about gender, work productivity, social mobility, and political obligations.

My work traces the history of performance enhancement through three different political regimes. The opening chapter discusses how representatives of the Wilhelmine establishment advocated state support for sport in order to foster the productivity, civic responsibility, and military fitness of the German population. Chapter 2 focuses on the Weimar period and examines how health professionals, sport officials, and governments at all levels looked to sport to restore the health and fitness of the German population after the carnage of the First World War. During this period of time, sport was seen as a means to foster people's sense of civic responsibility and will to work. Many employers supported company sport in order to change workers' attitudes to their work and to build a community of producers free of social conflicts.

The three subsequent chapters deal with the Nazi period. As I show, Nazism seized on existing elements of sport discourse and practice in order to increase social cohesion and work productivity. Chapter 3 discusses how the regime used sport to change people's self-understanding as members of a racial community. All Nazi organizations put a premium on education through sport in an attempt to create performance-oriented subjects committed to the values of the Nazism. Before 1933, many employers promoted sport to foster loyalty to the company community (*Werksgemeinschaft*), but during the Nazi period the performance ideology implicit in sport discourse served wider political purposes: it aimed to prepare the ground for a militarized understanding of sport and work in service to the Aryan racial community.

As I demonstrate in chapter 4, a militarized conception of national community and work was also reflected in the regime's attempt to turn work into sport through the Reich Vocational Competitions. A key incentive for increased vocational performance was the meritocratic promise of upward social mobility for those who could demonstrate exceptional skills and performance commitment.

In the final chapter, I consider campaigns to increase performance during the war. Regime officials in general and Labour Front officials in particular were so convinced of the efficacy of their promotion of sport that propaganda about sport continued unabated during the first three years of the war. After the military disasters of Stalingrad and Kursk, workplace competitions were revived to combat war weariness and declining work discipline. But as I will show, there remained a significant gap between the Nazi regime's ambitions for total psychological mobilization and people's capacity or willingness to comply with its campaigns for *Leistungssteigerung*.

There are two prominent themes cutting across the book. The first concerns gender. By emphasizing the need to increase the fitness and competitiveness of the population as a whole, advocates of performance enhancement moved away from older bourgeois ideas that insisted on women being shielded from physical exertion, competition, and paid work. This process started during the Empire, accelerated during the Weimar Republic, and continued into the Nazi period. Regime officials mobilized women in vocational and regular sporting competitions and emphasized fortifying them for the double or triple burden of household, motherhood, and paid work. There were few objections to the mobilization of women in the interest of greater work productivity as long as these demands were balanced by acknowledgments of the importance of women's domestic and reproductive roles.

The other issue concerns the relationship between *Leistung* and disability. The German discourse on fitness and productivity raised questions about how to treat people who had become incapacitated as a result of civilian injuries or war wounds. While there was never much tolerance of people who were considered lazy, work-shy, or shirkers of military duty, attitudes towards people with physical disabilities differed. Physicians, sport officials, and military officers turned to sport and physical exercise to raise or restore the fitness of physically impaired or disabled apprentices, workers, and soldiers. During both world wars seriously injured soldiers raised questions about the social and political status of people with physical disabilities. The Nazi regime had to be particularly concerned about how it presented the fate and prospects of disabled soldiers in a political situation in which underperformers or *Minderleistende* were easily denounced as "inferiors" or *Minderwertige*. In analysing the relationship between notions of productivity, disability, sport, and rehabilitation, I will show how authorities negotiated tensions and contradictions inherent in German performance discourse.

Chapter One

Wehrkraft and *Volkskraft*: The "Human Economy" and Performance Enhancement during the Empire

On the occasion of the thirteenth Congress for People's and Youth Games in 1912, its chairman Emil von Schenckendorff explained why sport and exercise had become an essential part of modern life. Like many of his contemporaries, he blamed the social and economic conditions of an industrialized and urbanized society for people's declining health and fitness.[1] "*The value of a firm physical preservation of strengths* moves more and more into the foreground of public interests, where the haste and drive of the time, the influences of ... big city life and the industrial centers, the long banishment in office, workshop, and factory ... has a health damaging impact on the body." Many of these factors, he claimed, could not be changed but training of the will and exercise of the body would make it possible to turn people into "healthy, resistant high performance tool[s]" who could cope with the challenges of modern life.[2]

Schenckendorff, a member of the central leadership of the National Liberal Party and deputy of the Prussian diet, was the founder and chair of the Central Committee for the Promotion of People and Youth Games (*Zentralausschuß für die Förderung der Volks- und Jugendspiele/ ZA*). The ZA functioned as a political pressure group that lobbied local, state, and national governments to lend their support to physical exercise and sport. Its membership consisted of a cross-section of mostly liberal elites. Among them were left-liberal and national-liberal politicians like Schenckendorff, physicians, professional educators, university professors, military officers, and city and state officials. Founded in 1891, the ZA pursued a hygienic and political-pedagogical agenda. Gymnastics and sport, in particular team sports, were meant to increase the health and physical fitness of young working people in the cities.

In this respect its activities complemented the goals of social hygienic reformers who wanted to improve the health of Germany's working population. But the promotion of physical fitness was only one of its aims. The ZA also looked to sport as a strategy to shape the subjective predispositions of young people in the cities. It believed that physical activity should play a role in forming the character of working youths, helping to turn them into responsible citizens who were willing to work and support the existing social and political order.[3]

By the time Schenckendorff gave his speech, the ZA could be satisfied with its achievements. By 1914 more than fourteen thousand sport teachers had been trained by the state. Sport was taught in most advanced and primary schools and it started to become part of the training of new army and navy recruits. The ZA also had played a role in the formulation and passing of the 1911 Prussian youth care decree, which provided considerable state resources for sport and other organized leisure activities for young people.[4] By promoting healthy bodies and strong characters, exercise and team sports were supposed to fortify urban youths against the political attraction of socialism as well as against the sexual and commercial temptations of the cities.[5] Healthy young people with strong characters would benefit the nation state in two ways: by enhancing the Reich's "people's strength" (*Volkskraft*), which was the source of the nation's "defensive strength" (*Wehrkraft*) and "work capacity." What mattered according to such a view was less the size of the population but what the medical professor and promoter of modern sport Ferdinand Hueppe called the "quality of the [human] material."[6]

At the beginning of the twentieth century, ideas about the economic value of human life gained currency among German elites who worried about the performance capacity and work commitment of German workers. Schenckendorff's and Hueppe's respective choice of words is revealing: "high performance tool" and "quality of the material" point to an instrumental understanding of human beings as resources that had to be preserved, used, and refined for the benefit of military strength and the productivity of the nation state. Maintaining people's working ability meant paying attention to the adverse effects of industrialization and urbanization on the human constitution. In 1908, the Austrian economist and philosopher Rudolf Goldscheid coined the term "*Menschenökonomie*" for his system of "human economics." Goldscheid denounced the "outrageous waste of humans" (*unerhörte Menschenvergeudung*) of modern times that was based on the erroneous assumption that "man is an abundant good." *Menschenökonomie* was the attempt to minimize the waste of human material in an effort to maximize human productivity. According to Goldscheid, this preservation could only be achieved through interventions that improved social conditions in such a way that they were conducive to the healthy upbringing of people. Goldscheid was a socialist and pacifist and as such he was politically quite distant from someone like Schenckendorff, a national-liberal promoter of human fitness. Yet both shared assumptions about the desirability of social interventions, be they improved general living conditions for the working classes or greater opportunities for exercise, in order to improve human well-being and productivity.[7]

Anxieties about the preservation of human working power and performance were also reflected in the debates of European work scientists and physiologists who were worried about the long-term impact of fatigue and exhaustion on productivity. Effective utilization of human resources was the rationale behind the founding of the Kaiser-Wilhelm Institute for Work Physiology in Berlin in 1913. The purpose of the institute was to apply insights from modern physiology to industrial and occupational hygiene.[8] Its director, Max Rubner, advocated for raising the performance of the population through "rational nutrition," an approach to food that provided for workers' nutritional needs within the constraints set by their income.[9] The goal of such scientific endeavours was to find the most efficient and productive uses of available human resources in the service of national productivity without compromising the long-term productivity and health of workers. In this way, as historian Anson Rabinbach has put it, "the science of work contributed to a new constellation of knowledge and politics devoted to conserving the energy of the social corpus."[10]

In twentieth-century Germany, the promotion of sport became one of the most important biopolitical technologies for increasing human performance. By biopolitics I mean all political and social initiatives that claimed to improve the health, productivity, and efficiency of the population. German biopolitics wanted to improve the hereditary health of the nation through eugenics and, at the same time, promoted fitness and productivity through welfare, education, sport, and exercise.[11] In the view of its advocates, sport improved not only the physical condition of people; rather, through the fortification of people's wills, it built strong, performance-oriented, self-reliant characters who willingly contributed to the productivity of the nation.[12] As the first section of this chapter will demonstrate, much of the ideological groundwork for these kinds of performance enhancement strategies was laid before the First World War – when physical exercise started being understood as a biological and social technology that had the potential to increase military strength and economic productivity.

In the second section I will examine how advocates of mass sport responded to the war, which in their view had taught important lessons about human endurance and performance. Advocating the systematic scientific study of sport and gymnastics, promoters of exercise argued that insights could be gained about the enhancement and upper limits of human performance. Such lessons, they claimed, were important for the physical and psychological rehabilitation of the German nation, which had to develop and utilize human resources for its biological and economic recovery in an efficient and rational manner.

The final section will look at one practical aspect of such rehabilitation efforts: the use of sport to reintegrate disabled soldiers into German society. While rehabilitation was concerned with the individual welfare of soldiers, the rationale behind such efforts was also economic. The productivity of severely injured and disabled soldiers was to be restored in order to keep down welfare and disability pension costs, which were seen as a crippling burden on the German economy. This objective was a logical extension of a view that judged physical impairment and disability in terms of their economic consequences. Rehabilitating physically disabled people meant turning "recipients of charity into tax payers," as Konrad Biesalski, the founder and medical director of Berlin's largest rehabilitation centre for physically disabled children, the Oskar-Helene Home, had already put it in 1907.[13]

I. *Wehrkraft* and *Volkskraft*: Physical and Social Fitness before the First World War

In Imperial Germany, "English sports," as a new type of physical activity that emphasized competition, became a pastime for a growing number of people.[14] The popularity of sporting activities challenged advocates of older, more established forms of physical exercise such as German gymnastics (*Turnen*), which had promoted the physical and military fitness of the nation since the early nineteenth century.[15] After 1890, sport also received the endorsement of the elite of Imperial Germany including the ruling house of Hohenzollern. With a view to the military fitness of coming generations, sport and gymnastics were to create a "strong generation," as Emperor Wilhelm II put it on the occasion of an

1890 school conference. Such high-ranking official support enabled the German sport movement and its German Reich Committee for Olympic Games (*Deutscher Reichsausschuß für Olympische Spiele/DRAFOS*) to make a successful bid for the 1916 International Olympic Games in Berlin. In 1913, the Kaiser personally attended the opening of the new Olympic stadium in Berlin-Grunewald and he publicly endorsed the sport movement.[16] Additionally, in 1914, on the occasion of the fifteenth Congress for People's and Youth Games in Altona, he welcomed the ZA's initiatives for mass sport and expressed his "joy about the development of our nation through sport."[17]

As historian Christiane Eisenberg has pointed out, sport, with its emphasis on competitiveness, performance, and records, accorded well with the values of self-made men and the upwardly mobile middle classes of Wilhelmine Germany.[18] But the growing popularity of sport among the middle and upper classes also laid the groundwork for the spread of sport as a wider mass phenomenon. In contrast to the repetitive and formalized exercise routines of German *Turnen*, sport, and in particular team sports like soccer, emphasized the playful and hedonistic aspects of exercise that younger people found more attractive. These attributes made sport a promising pedagogical instrument. Promoters of sport believed that physical exercise had a wholesome effect on the character of young people by endowing them with self-confidence, determination, a will to work, and community spirit. The latter was valued because it seemed to provide a way for overcoming class conflict. If sport promoted a sense of community, sport advocates believed, it would foster social cohesion among Germans from different social classes. For Carl Diem, president of the "Berlin Sport Club" (BSC) and the German Organization for Athletics (*Deutsche Sport-Behörde für Athletik* or DSBA), sport clubs mitigated the social estrangement between social classes. His own club, he claimed, included workers with a simple primary school education, artisans, university students, lawyers, officers, and three princes of the House of Hohenzollern, all of whom allegedly participated in the same leisure activities on an equal basis. In Diem's view, his club was a model for society at large. Its diverse membership demonstrated how social cohesion and a sense of national community could be forged through communal sporting activities.[19] But as historian Ralf Schäfer has shown, Diem's ideological vision of social integration contrasted with the reality of Wilhelmine class society as it manifested in his own club. While it is true that the BSC had a diverse membership, the club's departments tended to reproduce social divisions. The club had different departments for secondary school students (*Gymnasien* and *Realschulen*), apprentices, and young commercial employees. This segregation was justified by the difference of interests despite the participants being the same age. There was also an academic department for university students and an officers' department.[20]

In a country that was witnessing the meteoric rise of a socialist workers' party – in 1912 the SPD became the strongest party in the Reichstag – the promotion of social cohesion ranked high on liberal and conservative agendas.[21] While it was certainly possible to envisage socially integrative aspects of sport, there was also a contrary vision. During the time of the Empire and the Weimar Republic, worker sport became an integral part of a socialist alternative culture that used sport and other leisure activities, such as hiking and singing, to foster class consciousness. The workers cycling union "Solidarity," the "Worker Gymnastics League" (*Arbeiter-Turnerbund*), and, from 1912, the "Central Commission for Sport and Physical Care" (*Zentralkommision für Sport und Körperpflege*) were parts of an alternative working class culture that resisted the integrationist efforts of conservative and liberal promoters of gymnastics and sport.[22]

Older scholarship has identified social-integrationist or social-disciplinarian motivations for German welfare and hygiene policies directed at workers and the poor.[23] While this scholarship has pointed to important elements of modern welfare states (for example, attempts to create a healthy and disciplined workforce adapted to the demands of an advanced industrial economy), it is too simplistic to reduce social welfare initiatives to instruments of social control. Social hygiene efforts for maternity and infant health; campaigns against alcohol abuse, tuberculosis, syphilis, and other infectious diseases; and measures to promote youth welfare might well serve as vehicles for social discipline, but such campaigns also addressed real issues that were of concern to their target population as, for example, Larry Frohman has shown in his work on infant and maternity health centres.[24] Such studies have pointed to the ambiguous nature of biopolitical initiatives. While public health and welfare campaigns often aspired to change people's attitudes and behaviour, which could be read in terms of social-disciplinarian intent, they also responded to tangible needs, attitudes, predilections, and desires of people. This is also true for fitness campaigns. Wilhelmine and Weimar promoters of mass sport demanded better opportunities for what they considered wholesome leisure activities for young people and adults. In doing so, they addressed the real needs and desires of the people living in the rapidly expanding urban centres of Wilhelmine Germany. But because games and sporting competitions appealed to people's desire to play and have fun, they were also a useful vehicle for the promotion of physical fitness and social usefulness. Seen in this way, sport as a form of seemingly purposeless hedonistic play and sport as a utilitarian social technology were not mutually exclusive. Rather, one was a precondition of the other.[25]

In 1910, the Prussian Culture Ministry held a conference to discuss plans for the physical and moral education of Germany's youth. Participants included gymnastics and sport officials such as Diem as well as representatives of the ZA. After the conference the culture ministry declared the support of physical exercise and love of the homeland (*Heimat*) important public tasks. At the end of 1911, the "Young German League" (*Jungdeutschlandbund* or JDB) was inaugurated, and its affiliated organizations had about seven hundred and fifty thousand members by 1914. It united bourgeois and conservative youth and sport organizations in an attempt to promote patriotism, exercise, and promilitary attitudes among German youths. Its chair, the retired general staff officer and Field Marshall Colmar Freiherr von der Goltz, was convinced that in modern wars nations needed to draw on the capacities and powers of everyone. Therefore, young people had to develop a sense of responsibility for their own physical performance capacity.[26] The chief publicist of the JDB was Diem, who had moved to the centre of an organizational network that promoted mass sport through sport clubs and state-sponsored youth care.[27]

While the promotion of military fitness was an important concern for liberal and conservatives members of the Wilhelmine establishment, increasing people's work capacity and work morale were seen as equally important, since they were the foundation for Germany's economic strength and military capability. "The powers of the healthy body are the foundations and tools of fruitful work and victorious deed in peace as in war. Therefore, permanent training through physical exercise is a task for self-preservation, a national duty," an official proclamation of the Zentralausschuß declared in 1913.[28] An executive board member of the ZA, Hermann Raydt, emphasized the close importance of civilian fitness for the economic future of Germany. People should "not forget that everything we do [promoting exercise] ... will also have a heavy impact on the *peaceful competition* ... among nations" (emphasis in the original). In his view, such sacrifice of time and money for the nation's health was "the best capital investment." Ensuring the fitness of young people would save millions in social, invalidity, and health insurance costs while productive and tax-paying workers saved local governments on poor relief and other social expenses.[29]

Liberal politicians used the rhetoric of the ZA when they demanded greater public recognition for the benefits of sport and gymnastics. In a 1911 Reichstag debate, the deputy of the Liberal People's Party (*Freisinnige Volkspartei*), Willi Cuno (mayor of the city of Hagen and not to be confused with the future chancellor of the Weimar Republic Wilhelm Cuno), argued that sport and German gymnastics provided a unique means to bridge differences between military and civil society. Like the ZA, he advocated national education through physical exercise. A strong and healthy youth would not only serve the needs of the army but German society in general. It would "benefit our industrial development; because if the working capacity of our industrial workers is extended for a couple of years, this is not only a direct benefit for industry ... but the burdens of our social legislation" would diminish as well. "This is the purpose of physical education through gymnastics, games, and sport; it serves not only the army, but the entire development of our German people."[30]

The ZA, as an influential pressure group close to the national-liberal as well as the progressive variant of German liberalism, used its political influence at the state and municipal levels to push for the establishment of athletic playgrounds for Germany's youth. It often cast its demands as a necessary investment in Germany's economic future. In 1895, the ZA and the German Gymnasts (*Deutsche Turnerschaft/DT*) launched a joint appeal to German municipalities to provide more public spaces for team sports, outdoor games, and exercise. Providing such spaces would further public welfare and guarantee a big return: "The sums which you raise for [urban playgrounds] are truly invested well, [since] they carry rich interests for each individual as well as for the community through a profit in health, freshness, joy in being creative (*Schaffensfreude*), and working capacity."[31] Building athletic playgrounds for endangered urban youths was not just a German phenomenon. In the United States there was a national playground movement that promoted sport as a way to turn immigrant and poor urban youths into productive members of American society. In fact, the ZA took some inspiration from – and at the same time served as a model for – the lobbying initiatives of the American playground movement.[32]

Physicians and other sport advocates promoted exercise as an instrument of preventive hygiene for male youths who had left primary schools but were yet to be called up for military service. A writer in the ZA journal "Body and Mind" argued that preserving and strengthening the constitutional health of young people through exercise was a form of "racial biology" that created an "organic Volk bulwark" within the nation. Such a system of youth care signaled a "new era of biological prophylaxis against the health damages and dangers of the developmental age," and it also opened up new ways for the "regeneration of the physically inferior fraction of the nation."[33]

In 1911, mass sport received an official boost from the Prussian government. In order to promote the "physical and moral strength" of endangered youth, the Prussian culture and education minister August von Trott zu Solz issued a decree on youth care that encouraged sport and gymnastics associations, as well as church and private welfare associations, to develop leisure, welfare, and educational activities for male youths. The decree called upon teachers and school, state, and municipal administrations to support and coordinate such efforts through local committees (*Stadt- und Ortsausschüsse für Jugendpflege*) and district committees (*Kreis- und Bezirksausschüsse*). In order to defuse popular suspicions, the ministry explicitly advised the committees to avoid the term "youth welfare" (*Jugendfürsorge*) because "people often erroneously understand this as forced education (*Zwangserziehung*)."[34] Apprehensions about social-disciplinarian agendas were of course not without foundation. Prussian youth care was aimed at creating performance-oriented subjects capable of resisting the temptations of socialism: "a physically fit, morally virtuous youth filled with community orientation and fear of God, love of home and fatherland." It was supposed to bolster and supplement the educational efforts of the traditional authorities in the lives of young people, namely, parents, schools, employers, and masters of apprentices, without raising concerns about traditional Prussian authoritarianism.[35]

At the same time, this government decree recognized the needs of young working people as "a natural desire for entertainment and joy" and acknowledged their "wish for self-determination." Since the division of labour and the working conditions in modern factories made it difficult for young people to find meaning and "joy in work," their leisure activities had to provide them with meaningful experiences that did not endanger their physical and moral well-being. As Prussian authorities realized, youth care activities were most effective if they respected young people's "urge for freedom" and avoided anything that smacked of school discipline. *Leibesübungen* of all kinds figured prominently in the catalogue of Prussian youth care activities, because officials believed that they provided wholesome educational effects without compromising people's desire for autonomy. In the view of Prussian state authorities, military fitness, loyalty to the existing political order, and social discipline were important outcomes of youth care. But as historian Edward Ross Dickinson has argued, it would be a mistake to interpret such efforts exclusively in terms of an antiliberal and reactionary agenda. Sectors in the Prussian government, in particular the trade ministry, pushed for a more liberal educational agenda that fostered the creation of an informed, skilled, and competent citizenry by creating opportunities for working class youths.[36] This was not that different from the position taken by progressive liberal Reichstag deputies such as Willi Cuno who tried to promote social cohesion by appealing to the self-interest of workers.[37]

Most of the efforts promoting fitness targeted men. There were conservative limitations on the provision of youth care that reflected the limited citizenship rights of women who could not vote and who, despite some reforms, had fewer educational and work options.[38] The Prussian youth care decree restricted state funding to activities that benefited male youths. Female youths were allowed to use facilities financed under the youth care scheme but only if this was possible without any state subsidies.[39] On the one hand, these restrictions reveal that Prussian authorities associated lack of discipline and threats to the social and political order with men who needed to be steered away from socialism towards more "wholesome" leisure activities. On the other hand, they demonstrate how government officials equated worker productivity with the paid employment of men, despite the fact that a growing number of factory and white-collar workers were women.[40]

Schenckendorff had been consulted in the preparations for the youth care decree, but this does not mean that the ZA agreed with the constraints on women's participation.[41] Ferdinand August Schmidt, medical professor at the University of Bonn as well as deputy president of the ZA, thought that the restrictions on women were a mistake. Girls needed exercise as much as boys, because they were weaker and more likely to get sick. In contrast to some people who thought that women's natural weakness ruled out serious exercise, Schmidt saw women's constitutional weaknesses as conditions that they had acquired and that could be overcome through gymnastics and sport. Consequently he argued that social legislation, factory regulations, and "active physical care" were necessary to combat the negative effects of working-class women's paid employment in factories or as home workers. Schmidt and the ZA were concerned about young women's productivity and reproductivity. They were not motivated by concerns about women's rights. This is evident in their attack against the bourgeois feminist movement: "Instead of holding congresses about whether it is better for girls to go to a modern *Realgymnasium* or traditional *Gymnasium* [German elite secondary schools] or whether it is necessary to increase the oversupply of physicians and lawyers who are almost unable to find a living with female lawyers or physicians, it would really be better if our women would care about the physical and moral well-being of our girls from the common people."[42] The social benefits of women's sport lay in women's health, productivity, and reproductive capacities, which is why "the best women's movement is the movement of women," as another physician put it.[43] These attitudes reflected concerns about the biopolitical consequences of women's factory employment and its long-term consequences for working class families, a new social question, which according to historian Kathleen Canning marked "the female body ... as a new site of intervention for the moralizing and regulatory regimes of industrial paternalism and social reform."[44]

The ZA's Committee for the Fitness of the Female Sex declared that "the strength of the woman is of the same significance for the nation as man's." Consequently they argued that girls should have at least three hours of exercise and one afternoon for team sports and games per week. Exercise should become "a most widespread custom among the female sex." All girls should learn how to swim and young women should continue with exercise after they left school. Therefore, the committee called for significant financial support from the state and local governments. "The costs of [women's] exercise have the same significance for the nation as those sums that ... are spent for the German army."[45] Investments in the fitness of girls were considered negligible compared with the return in benefits that materialized in increased "working power" and a "stronger tax base."[46]

In reality, there were many fewer sporting opportunities for girls than for boys and many cities spent much less money on girls' activities. In 1912, Berlin spent more than five times the money on sport activities for boys. There were eleven playgrounds for boys but only six for girls. In many cities, gender segregation meant that public swimming pools had designated swimming times and girls and women were disadvantaged in this respect as well.[47] Among private associations the disparities were not much better. In 1912, only 17 per cent of all German gymnastics associations had women's departments. The Prussian youth care decree that earmarked $1 million Reichsmark for boys' activities in 1911 and $1.5 million in 1912 further increased gender disparities. In this situation, the fact that young women did not share in the alleged hygienic benefits of military service lent even more urgency to calls for better sporting opportunities for women.[48]

Dorothea Meinecke, a member of the aforementioned ZA committee on women's fitness, explained that women's fitness was important because the burden to raise productive citizens fell on them: "*Married women were called upon to give life to a healthy resistant race* (*Geschlecht*) *and to influence this life in such a way that physical, mental, and moral health are capable of creating true national welfare* ... in other words the state needs ... healthy mothers for the preservation of the nation" (emphasis in the original). Because the nation was threatened from without as well as within, Germany had to draw on the full potential of her human resources, which meant that "the existing intelligence in all social classes has to be retrieved and utilized" and women needed to keep fit to play their part in this mobilization. In Meinecke's view, the improvement of women's fitness was an essential part of biopolitical initiatives that safeguarded the productivity of the nation by raising healthy offspring. But since "large circles of women are forced to earn their living," their fitness was also important for productivity in paid work outside the home.[49]

In many ways, the Prussian youth care decree simply reflected wider social assumptions about gender roles and citizenship. While men's physical fitness was tied to expectations about their military service and their work productivity, the promotion of women's fitness was considered less important by state authorities despite a growing number of voices that expressed concerns about the health and fitness of women workers. The medical doctor Alice Profé, the most prominent woman physician promoting women sport before the First World War, denounced the disparity in sporting opportunities for boys and girls during the ZA's Heidelberg congress in 1912. In contrast to people like Ferdinand August Schmidt, who were exclusively concerned about the preservation of the human capital of the nation, Profé invoked notions of justice and citizenship rights which were denied to women: "Joy, strength, and health" were goods for the entire people, but "until now the German woman ... has remained empty-handed after their distribution."[50] Women often worked in industry sectors like the textile industry where their jobs demanded that they worked long hours on machines that imposed health-damaging unnatural postures, they received less pay for the same performance, and they had to cope with the double burdens of household and paid employment. "Everywhere we find … developments detrimental to [women's] health, which earlier – because of lower demands on their performance capacity – were not quite so disastrous as today, where life demands competent work from them."[51] In Profé's view, physical competence demanded that women play the same sports as men. Their exercises were meant to emphasize strength and performance and not the "so-called gracious movements" considered feminine by men.[52] While it is significant that there were both men and women who demanded more equal sporting opportunities for women, before the war their efforts yielded limited results. Only the mobilization of women during the war and the collapse of the political and social order in 1918 would slowly change that.[53]

Concerns about *Wehrkraft* and *Volkskraft* owed much to the notion that Germany was in a permanent struggle with other imperialist nation states for resources and markets. Such perceptions supported nationalist myths about a special working ability and working ethos that distinguished industrious Germans from subjects in their colonies, citizens of other nations, the "work-shy," and vagrants within the German Reich. Historian Sebastian Conrad sees "a parallel structure of educational projects" in the metropolis and the colonies, which aimed at making people productive by educating them through and for work. In this context, "education for work" was part of a bourgeois cultural mission that distinguished the colonial and domestic savages from the civilized.[54] Claims about a particular German industriousness and work ethic became common during the late nineteenth century.[55] Even by the early 1860s, the conservative cultural critic Wilhelm Heinrich Riehl claimed that national character was revealed through attitudes towards work and that "Germany was *the* nation of work." According to Riehl, Germans worked for work's sake and not for the sake of profit, which distinguished them from Americans or Jews.[56] In this line of thinking, the capacity and willingness to work constituted the difference between the responsible and respectable German, who worked for the community, and the ethnic or racial other, who was only interested in material gain. This notion would become a staple of radical *völkisch* and Nazi thought about work and performance.[57]

While the conservative Riehl had been rather sceptical about the prospects of industrial modernization, in Wilhelmine Germany the national mythology about a particular German work ethic was reconciled with the managerial demands of the rapidly industrializing nation state facing strong economic competition.[58] Germany's lack of natural and human resources made it all the more important that her population was kept fit. In 1913, the newly appointed professor for social hygiene at Munich University, Ignaz Kaup, insisted that the Germans, as a people living primarily from the fruits of its own labour (*Arbeitsvolk*), needed to explore all its "sources of physical and mental and hence economic performance capacity."[59] As one of the speakers at the fifteenth ZA congress in June 1914 put it: "Only from a physically healthy and fit youth can emerge those men and women on whose shoulders the future of Germany rests secure. Our fatherland will have to defend its world significance (*Weltgeltung*) in heavy fighting, be it the fight with weapons or the no less difficult fight against new competitors on the world market, against new nations which demand their place in the sun with the unbroken strength of their youth."[60] The fear of imperialistic competition and geostrategic encirclement, which was so prevalent among national liberal and conservative Wilhelmine elites, is cast here in terms of a biopolitical problem: the alleged need to develop and strengthen the human resource base of Germany.[61]

Wilhelmine discourse on population policies focused on quantitative and qualitative aspects. Germany's declining birth rate from the late nineteenth century onwards and the debates on possible pronatalist counterstrategies have caught the attention of contemporaries and historians alike.[62] Increasingly, however, biopolitical arguments came to focus on issues of population quality and its implications for national productivity. As the broader concerns about national fitness demonstrate, the emerging eugenics movement in Germany is but one example of this qualitative turn in German biopolitics. In this debate, the quality of the "human material" was not only discussed in terms of heredity, but in terms of the impact of exercise and other environmental conditions on human fitness.

The views of Kaup are particularly instructive here. An active mountain climber, soccer player, and rower, he became one of the most tireless medical advocates of mass sport during the late empire and the Weimar Republic.[63] Like Goldscheid, Kaup thought in terms of the economic value of human life and he advocated social improvements such as shorter working hours and vacations for youths to prevent damage to their fitness. He distinguished between people on the basis of their productivity and economic value for the nation, which is why he devoted much of his career to the assessment of the "improvement or worsening of the human material." He was interested in a more comprehensive measure of national health and performance capacity. All children and youths should be assessed at crucial periods in their lives; for example, when they entered and left school and when they took up work. These assessments would complement the physical assessments of military recruits.[64]

According to Kaup, military fitness was a reliable indication of the physical and mental fitness of young men, but data about "the generative power of young mothers" were also needed to arrive at a comprehensive assessment of the population. What was most important for an accurate measure of the economic performance capacity of the nation was the average "length of the life period in gainful employment." In Kaup's view it was wrong to calculate this from the start of people's employment until their deaths, as many statisticians did, because this often included long periods of non-productive invalidity before death. He painted a bleak picture of a country overwhelmed by a growing number of work invalids of all ages with pension entitlements (due to Germany's system of pension, health, and disability insurance), which put a burden on its productivity.[65] Contemporary physicians who worried about the abuse of social entitlements by patients, in particular those who claimed to suffer from work-related mental disorders such as neuroses, hysteria, and neurasthenia expressed similar concerns.[66]

Despite the improvements in urban hygiene and social welfare, which, as Kaup acknowledged, had lowered mortality rates, he could not see significant advancement in terms of the "physical and mental freshness" of young people. Like many of his colleagues in the ZA, he attributed this absence of general fitness to the lack of open spaces for sport and games in German cities. He claimed that in England, where there were many such spaces, 80 per cent of students had a good physical constitution, whereas in Germany there were only about half as many.[67] This situation was worrying because people's physical condition was, in his view, a much more important indicator of productive capacities than mortality and morbidity statistics. Since there were no civilian statistics about the physical condition of youths, Kaup relied on data from the medical inspections for young recruits from 1902–3 to 1908–9. This information pointed to an alarming trend. The percentage of youths who were fit for military service had declined progressively during the period from 57.8 of those examined to 54.1. The situation was worse for those born in cities (a decline from 54.3 to 48.9 per cent) compared to those born in the countryside (a decline from 60 to 57 per cent). The worst data came from big cites such as Berlin. In 1910, only 27.6 per cent of those examined were considered fit for the military. While Kaup and his colleagues in the ZA were certainly troubled about the decline in military fitness as such, it needs to be stressed that Kaup's main concern here was not the decline of fitness for the army but the implication of this for the productivity and economic performance of the nation state. To put it another way: unhealthy and weak recruits indicated the deterioration of the quality of human resources more generally.[68]

In many ways German anxieties about the declining fitness and performance capacity of young workers were similar to concerns expressed by members of the British elites who were alarmed by the results of the fitness examinations of British army recruits for the Boer War. While a 1904 government report by the Interdepartmental Committee on Physical Deterioration rejected the idea that there was widespread physical deterioration, public anxiety about the "physical efficiency" of the working class led the committee to recommend anthropometric surveys to assess the physical state of the population. In addition to systematic medical inspections of school children, the committee emphasized the benefits of playgrounds, gymnastics, and physical education of boys and girls.[69] In 1906 and 1907 government education acts encouraged the provision of school meals for poor children and authorized education administrations to "make arrangements ... for attending to the health and physical condition of children educated in public elementary schools."[70] This process happened in the context of what historian Zweiniger-Bargielowska has described as a "thriving culture of patriotic leagues and organizations" (Robert Baden-Powell's Boy Scouts movement being the most important one). They all promoted increased physical fitness as a duty of good citizenship in the service of the British Empire.[71]

In Germany, the military recruitment data seemed to show that the physical condition of recruits had declined everywhere, but the situation seemed to be particularly bad in the cities where adverse environmental conditions such as long working hours, living arrangements, nutritional deficits, alcohol, and tobacco abuse exacerbated it. But Kaup was not one of those conservative critics of industrialism who argued for a return to an agrarian society.[72] In his view, there was little that could be done in the short term to change the reality of modern work and living arrangements. What remained as a matter of urgency was the "far-reaching physical toughening up of youths." Kaup's diagnosis justified the agitation for more playgrounds for young people. In a 1908 memorandum to the Prussian House of Deputies, the ZA had already pointed out that about four-fifths of all youths between fourteen and eighteen grew up without regular exercise.[73] To address this issue, the ZA, the German Gymnasts, and a number of sport organizations demanded an extension of the system of "compulsory continuing education schools" (*Pflichtfortbildungsschulen*) for young workers and apprentices. These schools should provide a minimum of two hours of physical exercise per week as part of their curriculum for students who went to work after attending basic primary schools (the so-called *Volkschulen*) but had not yet served in the military.[74] Such demands were quite realistic because they complemented the above-mentioned promotion of youth care by the Prussian government. A legal revision of the system of commercial regulations made it possible for Prussian authorities to demand the introduction of these schools from local governments. It also allowed for an extension of the system for young girls working in commerce and industry. These measures were not enough for the ZA, though, because the regulations did not specifically mandate physical exercise and excluded young people working in agriculture and young women working as domestic servants.[75] By 1910, only about 33 per cent of male youths attended such schools in Prussia; the percentage for girls must have been much lower.[76] But in June 1914, the ZA's campaigning for compulsory exercise in continuing education schools received official support from the Prussian minister of trade and commerce; the minister recommended to all administrations responsible for these schools to make gymnastics a mandatory subject.[77]

In addition to promoting sport and gymnastics in schools, the ZA demanded shorter working hours on Saturday – as well as vacations – so that young people could pursue fitness activities in their leisure time. While more leisure and resting time for young workers might initially impose some costs on employers and the health insurance system, those costs were always presented as a worthwhile investment in human resources. Kaup thought that the expenses could be easily recovered through the reduction of sick days, which amounted to considerable savings. According to one calculation, a large company sickness fund in Berlin would be able to cut the number of sick days per member from twenty-two to about eight (which was considered normal). This would save 20,000 RM per year and guarantee a healthy, permanent workforce. Overall, millions in healthcare benefits and invalidity pensions could be saved each year. Additional savings accrued through higher survival rates among young workers. If raising a young unskilled worker cost about 3,000 RM, excluding expenses for welfare benefits and schooling, a premature death meant that these expenses were entirely wasted.[78]

The growing significance of sport in public policy debates coincided with the emergence of sport-related research. In 1911, a scientific section at the International Hygiene Exhibition in Dresden gave a comprehensive overview of sport and sport research in the German Empire.[79] The exhibition was organized by leading sport scientists in collaboration with the ZA. Like the ZA, it emphasized the pedagogical and economic benefits of exercise. To promote sport among the five and a half million visitors to the Dresden hygiene exhibition, a number of high profile sporting events were conducted in conjunction with it; for example, there were soccer games. The Scottish champion Glasgow Celtics took on a team from Dresden, the final of the German soccer championship was played out between Victoria Berlin and VfB Leipzig, and the German national soccer team played against Austria. Other events included the finals of the German track and field, wrestling, and weight lifting championships, as well as world championships in the latter two sports.[80]

At the time, it was not unusual to have high profile sporting competitions in conjunction with major exhibitions. For example, the 1900 and 1904 International Olympic Games in Paris and St. Louis were held during world fairs. Whether such sporting contests helped to publicize exhibitions or vice versa is an open question, at least in the case of the Dresden event.[81] While they were meant to entertain, the organizers of the sport exhibition certainly hoped that the competitions would entice people to take up sport themselves. They had great expectations of the wider social and hygienic benefits of exercise. Sport would fortify the body against infectious diseases and increase the physical performance capacity of people. They also saw a close connection between sport and work sciences, claiming that the hygienic dangers of the workplace were very similar to those encountered by athletes who subjected their bodies to extreme exercise. In their view, exercise was important for work performance in many ways. A rational selection of specific exercises could compensate for the negative health effects of one-sided physical labour. Youths in particular could be prepared for their "future life tasks" (*künftigen Lebensaufgaben*) through systematic exercise.

Raising people's "performance capacity" (*Leistungsfähigkeit*) included mental performance levels: "The education for the nimble mastering of muscles means, however ... a development of the performance of the brain; in particular those sections of it in which the conscious impulses for activity take place in which what we call quick thinking, decisive action is produced."[82] Physical exercise involving competition or collaboration between several people was seen as an exercise of those "mental performances," which were of particular importance for success in practical life. Schools should not confine themselves to the communication of positive and directly applicable knowledge, but should "train the mind for all possible unforeseeable tasks of the future." Sport was to play a crucial role in this training, because it was "an irreplaceable means of mental schooling," on a par with other subjects. The organizers lent some urgency to their call for performance enhancement by pointing to other "cultural nations," such as England and the United States, whose superiority "in the many struggles of practical life, in industry and commerce, but also in some fields of science" was in large part due to the fostering of "mental endowments" through various forms of physical exercise.[83]

As Noyan Dinçkal has pointed out, the sport exhibition also promoted sport as a means to enable people to cope with their work lives. Modern life was presented as a permanent struggle, which fatigued both body and mind and shortened people's life expectancy. People who wanted to advance professionally had to make sure that they achieved the "highest degree of performances ... mobilization of full strength and dexterity, [and] perpetual alertness."[84] Sport was presented here as a technology of the self for people who desired to maximize their own "personal efficiency" in their daily lives.[85] Seen in this light, sport was not just promoted as a managerial tool to influence the behaviour of socially dependent workers and youths, even though that was central to the liberal and conservative agendas of various levels of government and the ZA. Sport also offered people a means to refigure themselves into performance-oriented subjects, a transformation of the self that promised enhanced abilities to cope with the challenges of their professional and personal lives.[86]

The successful sport exhibition gave a major impetus to the sport sciences in Germany. In 1912, the first scientific sport congress was held in the Thuringian town of Oberhof, bringing together some of the leading German scientists working on sport-related issues. The congress led to the formation of the Reich Committee for Scientific Research on Sport and Physical Exercise, whose existence was cut short by the war.[87] Like the sport exhibition of the previous year these attempts demonstrated a keen interest to promote the general fitness and hence productivity of the nation state through sport. In this way sport and the sport sciences became increasingly entangled with biopolitical projects to enhance German national strength.

Some of the new research interests in extreme physical performances were similar to existing lines of research by work physiologists who examined the relationship between work performances, energy expenditure, fatigue, and exhaustion. In this type of research, sport was conceived as a form of physical labour. Researchers examined physiological and anatomical changes during rest and various sporting and working activities. Often they were less concerned with performance enhancement than with clarifying the effects of physical activity on the body in order to be better able to diagnose overexertion. A good example of this approach is the work by the director of the physiological institute at Berlin Veterinary University, Nathan Zuntz, who was considered one of the most renowned researchers on the impact of exercise on the human body. Similar to his more famous Italian colleague, Angelo Mosso, he researched the limits of human endurance in high altitude experiments in the Italian Alps.[88]

Zuntz, one of the organizers of the Dresden exhibition, warned of the risks overexertion in exercise posed to health. He spoke from experience, because he himself had suffered from severe altitude sickness during one of his expeditions to the Monte Rosa, the second-highest peak in the Alps. These dangers made it necessary, in his view, to establish the limits of physical performances and closely supervise intrepid youngsters who might be incapable of maximum performances for reasons of health. Otherwise the reputation of sport would suffer in the eyes of parents who might still be afraid that sport could harm their children. Before the war such cautious – almost defensive – approaches to the promotion of sport were the rule.[89] But the war would change this. Calls for the total mobilization of the population raised new questions about the limits of human endurance and performance capacity.

II. War and National Performance: Sport and Sport Research during the War

The First World War had a profound impact on German civilian life. For many of those who were not drafted, the war meant longer working hours, malnutrition, and a radical curtailment of leisure activities. Mobilization disrupted the activities of German gymnastics and sport clubs. As more and more male members of such clubs were drafted into the army, the number of sporting competitions was drastically reduced and some sport federations lost most of their members. Gymnastic halls and club homes were turned into military barracks and hospitals and, as the war dragged on and the nutritional situation of the population worsened, athletic fields were often used for the production of food. A number of public sporting competitions were staged as entertainment and diversion for the home front, though, which attests to the continued popularity of sport.[90]

The army primarily judged sport in terms of its usefulness for military performance. Supporters of the ZA, the DRAFOS, and sport officials like Diem had long praised the contribution of sport to the *Wehrkraft* of the nation.[91] At the same time, a number of army officers pushed for the greater recognition of sport as a means to train soldiers. Their efforts paid off. In 1910, track and field exercises were officially integrated into the army-training program. This change was not only due to the growing public significance of sport. It was also a result of the recognition that modern warfare demanded a new type of soldier who was capable of acting independently in small fighting groups or alone. Compared to German gymnastics with its regimented mass exercises, sport training with more individualized exercise regimes was considered to be more suitable for these purposes.[92] One of the officers who pushed for a greater recognition of sport within the army was Walther von Reichenau, who in 1913 accompanied a group of German sport officials to the United States. The group, which also included the new DRAFOS general secretary, Diem, visited the US to learn about the American sport system with a view to the German preparation for the 1916 Olympic games. Reichenau, who would later become one of Hitler's most notorious generals, summarized the lessons of the journey for military training. In his view, sport could endow soldiers with "a character of steel, an indomitable will" that allowed them to act under "immense tension." Therefore sport was an excellent preparation for the demands of modern battle.[93]

Reichenau was but one of several junior officers who were enthusiastic sportsmen and who promoted sport in the army of their own accord. The war further increased the acceptance of sport within the armed forces. Sporting activities often arose from local initiatives by officers and unit leaders who had been active gymnasts and athletes before the war. High-ranking military commanders often supported these pursuits because of their positive impact on discipline and morale. In the staging areas behind the Western front, individual and team sports became popular pastimes for soldiers preparing to return to the frontline. As historians have pointed out, soldiers' sporting experience during the war was also one of the drivers for the expansion of the sport movement during the Weimar Republic. Soccer was popular with soldiers as well as with military authorities who believed that soldiers could improve their physical fitness and recover psychologically by voluntarily engaging in recreational activities. Sport also promised relief from the rigidity of military discipline and hierarchy because, on the sport field, such things allegedly did not matter.[94]

Whether common sporting experiences contributed to bridging social and cultural gaps between officers and rank and file soldiers to a significant extent remains doubtful. The rhetoric of "people's community" (*Volksgemeinschaft*) and "comradeship" (*Kameradschaft*) that allegedly transcended military ranks and social differences did not necessarily reflect the underlying reality of social relations in the army. The rhetoric might also be read as a reaction to significant tensions within the army. Diem, for example, who served as a staff officer, was scathing in his criticism of officers who abused their power to obtain personal privileges and lived in luxury while regular soldiers were lacking provisions.[95] It is also no accident that after the outbreak of the German revolution soldiers' discontent found a dramatic expression in symbolic degradations of officers who were stripped of their rank insignia.[96]

During the war civilian promoters of sport did not tire of emphasizing that sports were crucial in order to ensure the military fitness of youths. A crucial impetus came from private sport and gymnastic organizations, which used the lessons of the war to promote exercise as a social technology with the authorities. In January 1917, the DRAFOS vice president Ulrich von Oertzen declared that as long as "our enemies run up against the iron wall of German resistance power (*Widerstandskraft*) ... we help ... to make the adolescent youths militarily resistant and strong, so that they can step into the gaps and help to force the enemy to their knees."[97] To achieve these goals, the DRAFOS drafted a national law that would have made physical education mandatory for male youths before they entered the army. As the DRAFOS saw it, the key challenge in formulating the law was to ensure that young people would not see sport as a "heavy fetter" but as a "joyful gift" because, in this way, "physical education will bear fruit beyond the mandatory years."[98] The DRAFOS pointed here to one of the core dilemmas of utilitarian and pedagogical approaches to sport. Sport was seen as an ideal instrument for mobilizing people's enthusiasm for performance enhancement, in particular if people experienced it as a form of play, as a purposeless, hedonistic activity. But making sporting activities mandatory threatened to negate their alleged psychological benefits.

As the war dragged on, German sport leaders began to think about the role of sport during the postwar era. In their view, the human losses were so tremendous that sport had to play a crucial role for the recovery of national health and strength. As Oertzen put it: "When the bells ring in the German peace, then our iron duty commences, to re-erect with all strength what the war has destroyed, to heal the wounds of German national strength struck by the war." The groundwork for this task had to be laid during the war, because "a healthy, well-trained body is the precondition for our great future," and only sport ensured long-term fitness into old age.[99] Youths were to develop "strength of will, courage and manly attitude," while adults would regain "joy, working power, and love of live."[100] Therefore, it wasn't only military fitness on the agenda. During peacetime the "wealth of the nation" demanded "the physical strengthening of our race beyond school and military time. Physical exercise must become a common good and a way of life (*Lebensgewohnheit*) for everyone."[101] The ZA concurred with this dual emphasis on military and civilian fitness. Already in 1915, it pushed for the "Reich Youth Defensive Law" (*Reichsjugendwehrgesetz*) that emphasized the need to develop human performance capacity to the fullest for the benefit of war as well as the peacetime economy: "The state which knows how to form the physically and morally most outstanding human material, will stand supreme in war as in cultural and economic life and win the palm of victory. More valuable than the best cannons and the best ammunition is man."[102]

In 1915, the War Ministry's office for exemptions from military service developed guidelines for the military and civilian deployment of men. People who were physically or psychologically unfit for active military duty could still be declared "usable for work" (*arbeitsverwendungsfähig*) and put to work in industry. In 1916, efforts for the effective mobilization of human resources culminated in the passing of the auxiliary service law, which tried to optimize the allocation of human resources to industry and the military.[103] But these efforts could not resolve the problem of acute labour shortages. High-ranking military physicians drew their own lessons from this and looked for ways to compensate for Germany's inadequate human resource base. In early 1918, the Chief of Army

Sanitary Services, General Staff Physician (*Generalstabsarzt*) Otto von Schjerning, pointed out that after the war Germany needed new forces for the "peaceful as well as military competition between nations." This meant "substitutes for the fallen, substitutes for the maimed and damaged movement and sensory organs, substitutes for the enormous loss of births." For Schjerning it was not the conclusion of a peace treaty that decided victory or defeat: it was the ability to "compensate [for] ... losses of *Volkskraft* and *Wehrkraft* in the shortest time period after the war," which was why he welcomed all efforts to promote youth games and sport. He also announced the Emperor's intention to create a military research institute for the physiology and hygiene of gymnastics and sport. Germany's defeat prevented the realization of such a military institute, but the plans demonstrate official acceptance of the claim that sport and sport science could serve as instruments for the biopolitical reconstruction of Germany's population. The founding of the German University for Physical Exercise (*Deutsche Hochschule für Leibesübungen/DHfL*) in 1920 was driven by similar considerations.[104]

In early 1917, the DRAFOS was renamed German Reich Committee for Physical Exercise (*Deutscher Reichsausschuß für Leibesübungen/DRAL*). This change reflected the altered agenda of the organization whose leaders believed the International Olympic Games had become impossible for the foreseeable future because of the war. Thus, the national Olympic committee had to be transformed into a national sport and gymnastics association that promoted physical exercise for the health and fitness of the entire nation.[105] According to Diem, "physical exercise [is] a citizen's virtue (*Bürgertugend*)" but the promotion of physical fitness required close collaboration between private citizens' organizations such as the DRAL and the state. According to this vision, the DRAL was to remain an independent private organization whose activities would nevertheless be sanctioned by the state.[106] The war had forced the state and the individual to the "highest unfolding of their forces" and required the mobilization of the special talents of each individual. At the same time, the state had to ensure that people remained fit for a longer period of their lives, which Diem described as "aging earlier and remaining young longer." By this he meant that people should develop their adult performance levels earlier in their lives and preserve them into old age.[107]

The left-liberal Reichstag deputy Ernst Müller-Meiningen also expressed his hope that state authorities would further acknowledge the contributions of private gymnastics and sport associations working to raise the level of national fitness, since these efforts were in the state's own interest.[108] For such visions, the 1911 youth care decree could serve as a model because this empowered church associations, gymnastics and sport clubs, and other private organizations to promote fitness and social cohesion through leisure activities and sport. These visions also pointed to the future: in the corporatist system of the Weimar Republic, the state often recognized initiatives from civil society and provided official support for the private associations that backed them.

The war also placed new demands on the fitness of women whose labour power was badly needed by industry: "Everyone has to bring out his best so that an individual can perform the work of 20 or 30," one advocate of women's fitness declared.[109] Sport was also advocated as a means to instil military-style discipline into young women through a compulsory period of national service. Directed at women who left school, one such proposal emphasized the benefits of gymnastics. In controlling the movements of their bodies women would discipline their minds and gain self-mastery. The "physical, mental firmness (*körperlich geistige Straffheit*)" that was fostered by physical exercise taught women discipline and gave them "*Haltung*," a bearing commonly associated with the disciplined masculinity of soldiers. For young women who for some reason could not do compulsory national service, the proposal demanded that they join a gymnastics or sport club and exercise at least once a week.[110]

While plans for a women's service year or compulsory exercise did not materialize, they tell us something about shifting attitudes towards women, who now were expected to keep fit in order to hold their own in formerly masculine domains of work. As a result of these changing expectations, financial support for youth care was extended to young women and girls with many clubs offering gymnastics in return for state funding.[111] At the same time, women who supervised youth care activities for young girls were offered training courses as supervisors for team sports and games.[112] Advocates of women's sport hoped that exercise would mobilize and discipline young working women. They thought that such positive effects would also carry over into the period after the war when women were expected to play a significant role in the economic and biological reconstruction of "national strength and health."[113]

During the war sport leaders expressed ideas that would become a central rationale for the promotion of sport during the Weimar Republic. Weimar sport officials such as Theodor Lewald and Carl Diem promoted sport as part of a biopolitical project of national recovery that would heal the wounds of the people's body and ensure its fitness and productivity in the long run. If the war had struck deep wounds into the people's body, the war experience could also serve as guidance for overcoming the national trauma. In Diem's view, the war showed what astonishing feats people could achieve and demonstrated people's performance potential in adversity. In future it was the task of science to determine "performance goals and performance limits for different ages, constitutional classes, and sexes."[114]

Strengthening the people's body was an absolute necessity, as Diem explained in October 1918, less than a month before the armistice: "We will urgently need an increase in our physical strength, because the war was a negative selection whose consequences one cannot easily overestimate. To compensate for the loss of blood of those of high value (*Hochwertiger*) in the interest of our future world importance, we will have to introduce very decisive measures." Among these initiatives he did not mention eugenics, which was an increasingly popular idea among medical professionals and government officials who looked to biopolitical solutions for what they considered Germany's qualitative population problems. Like these people, Diem wanted to restore and improve the value of the population, but instead of focusing on people's heredity he emphasized better hygiene and living conditions and, most importantly, physical exercise. The desire for *Leibesübungen* had to be instilled into boys and girls from an early age and become a lifelong habit. Increasing the fitness of the masses was also crucial for fostering the optimum performances of athletes on the higher end of the performance scale.[115]

To foster national fitness, Diem renewed calls upon the state and municipalities to provide sporting facilities and create laws that encouraged mass participation in sport. Only with their help would "the heavy wounds struck by this war heal. The German race will be insuperable."[116] While these laws would have a mandatory component for youths, young people would be free to choose any sporting activities they liked among the many sports offered by German sport clubs. This voluntary aspect was meant to ensure that sporting enthusiasm was carried into adulthood while also guaranteeing "the physical strengthening of the people after the hemorrhage of this war."[117] According to the DRAL, the provision of sporting opportunities for everyone but especially for youths was key to any practical population policy that aimed at the preservation of human resources: "We cannot afford the luxury of handing over the strength and life of youths to consumption in coffee houses for the masses, beer halls, and dubious amusement venues. A healthy economic plan for national expenditure of energy precludes such a waste of the highest good of the people."[118]

For this biopolitical project it did not matter whether people favoured competitive sports or the more traditional German *Turnen*. While tensions between the advocates of these different types of *Leibesübungen* continued, leading to sometimes bitter conflicts during the Republic, there was an overall consensus that exercise of some type would have to play a crucial role in the recovery of the German national body. The most efficient and healthy forms of exercise were yet to be determined either through practical experience or sport science, the latter finding an institutional place at the DHfL during the Weimar period.[119]

Plans for the DHfL ultimately emerged from initiatives of the DRAL. In February 1917, the DRAL stated that one of its goals was to determine scientifically the hygienic effects of exercise.[120] In the following year a Committee for Scientific Research (*Ausschuß für wissenschaftliche Forschung*) was formed to examine "the laws and limits of human performance and growth enhancement through the different forms of physical exercise and ways of life compatible with exercise." The research was to include all age groups and both sexes. The first focus were the "laws of performance enhancement" in terms of increased strengths of muscles, organs (especially the heart), the nerves and senses, the will, and mental characteristics. This list shows that sport advocates assumed that exercise was a means to enhance physical and psychological performance in many areas of modern life, not just sport. The mutual effect of physical work and mental work was of particular interest.[121]

The next major research emphasis was to examine the limits of performance enhancement: the causes and signs of physical and mental fatigue, fatigue curves (*Ermüdungskurven*) during short and longer exertions, and the causes and signs of overexertion were some of the matters to be investigated. Related to this was the question of how sport should be integrated into the workdays of school children, and mental and physical workers. During the Weimar years many of these issues were important research areas for sport and work physiologists who were worried about physiological overexertion and the harm this could cause in a working population, which was already weakened by the war and subsequent social crises. These shared research interests between the sport and work sciences would provide a common intellectual ground for collaborations between the DHfL and the Kaiser Wilhelm Institute for Work Physiology (see chapter 2). Other research emphases cited by the Committee for Scientific Research included anthropological work on physical growth through exercise, developmental anomalies, performance curves for different ages, and the influence of different habits of life (e.g., nutrition, drugs, and sex) on performance capacity.[122] Not all of this comprehensive research program would become a reality, but it anticipated much of the research agenda of the DHfL that would be founded two years later with the help of the Reich government. Most importantly, however, these plans point to the ways in which sport and exercise could be turned into a social technology for human resource development and performance enhancement. If the nation's biological substance had suffered serious damage during the war and immediate postwar era, eugenics, social hygiene, and welfare promised various kinds of remedies for social disadvantage, disease, and lack of fitness. In combination with sport and exercise these measures were part of a qualitative vision of biopolitics that aimed to restore the productive health of German citizens.

III. Sport and the Productivity of the Maimed

The war exacerbated concerns about the declining productive capacity of the German population by raising the specter of a large number of permanently disabled men. Physically disabled soldiers as well as soldiers suffering from war neuroses and hysteria threatened to impose an unbearable burden on Germany's social insurance system. Combined with the severe labour shortages during the war the mounting casualties fuelled a push to rehabilitate seriously impaired soldiers in order to reintegrate them in the workforce. In the case of soldiers with war neuroses, who often exhibited debilitating symptoms such as uncontrollable shaking, paralysis of one or several limbs, muteness or deafness, military psychiatrists came up with a range of therapeutic measures including hypnosis or electroshock therapy. Rejecting the idea that these conditions were in any way somatic, psychiatrists like Max Nonne and Fritz Kaufmann used such therapies as technologies of suggestion. As historian Paul Lerner has shown, these medical interventions were not used for their physical and physiological effects – even though they often worked through people's bodies as in the case of electroshock therapy – they targeted the mind. In changing people's "false" ideas about their conditions, they tried "to convert the will to remain disabled into the will to recover" in order to restore their working capacity.[123]

The existence of a large number of disabled veterans reinvigorated debates about the preservation of human resources and the restoration of people's performance capacity. People were increasingly judged by the economic contributions they made to the German war effort and the more productive they were the more they were valued. The extent to which assumptions about the economic value of human life had become acceptable becomes apparent in an article published in the ZA journal *Body and Mind*. The author, the renowned liberal Protestant theology professor at the University of Kiel, Otto Baumgarten, expressed his satisfaction with the fitness of German youths whose excellent physical and nervous strength had helped to offset the numerical supremacy of Germany's enemies. Nevertheless, Germany's difficult situation demanded renewed efforts to mobilize all remaining human reserves and preserve the physical strength of the Volk. This included the "wonderful care for cripples which has emerged during the war," which made sure that "whatever can be used for the construction (*Aufbau*) of the nation ... [will be] be protected from decay." These efforts "brought even half and quarter forces (*halbe und Viertelskräfte*) to a position where they can serve the whole." While these were "people of lesser value" (*Minderwertige*), Baumgarten rejected the notion that one could go too far in "the care for broken, crippled, half and quarter forces" because "the number of cases in which crippled, partially incurable, inferior, psychopathic persons can still be restored to a productive life ... is far larger than one can assume beforehand."[124]

During the war, exercise and sport emerged as important elements in the rehabilitation of injured war veterans. In army hospitals, so-called medico-mechanical apparatuses (specialized exercise machines) were employed in the physical therapies used to help rehabilitate the disabled.[125] Exercise was combined with specialized vocational training in order to facilitate people's transition to work life. At the same time as an emerging school of psycho-technics promised to match people with jobs that complemented their specific psychological abilities (e.g., testing people's reaction times to figure out whether they were suited to operate certain kinds of machinery or vehicles), orthopedic military surgeons tried to match men with specific disabilities with prostheses and jobs they could perform after a period of rehabilitative physical exercise and specialized vocational training.[126]

In this line of thinking, restoring the productivity of the non-productive, be they mentally or physically impaired, became a bio-political necessity. The Oskar-Helene-Home for crippled children in Berlin took a leading public role in the campaign to rehabilitate wounded soldiers. Its educational director, Hans Würtz, thought that restoring people's performance capacity provided them with a sense of self-worth and a will to contribute to society. In this view, being physically disabled was not just a physical condition; it was a psychological state that needed to be overcome by fostering people's will to work. One of Würtz's favourite mottos was "work is the source of strength for de-crippling." Work therapy, as well as games, exercise, and sport were considered means to develop such performance-oriented predispositions, which would lead to the "de-crippling" of subjects by making them realize that their physical condition was not an obstacle to performance. The goal of this type of "cripple welfare" was to overcome a "cripple" mentality that was resigned to a life of self-pity, disability, and pension seeking.[127]

The economic assumptions of this rehabilitation discourse are also evident in the work of the national Testing Centre for Prostheses (*Prüfstelle für Ersatzglieder*) in Berlin, which opened in 1916. In collaboration with the director of the Oskar-Helene-Home, the orthopedic surgeon Konrad Biesalski, the *Prüfstelle* developed and tested special prostheses for workers with particular disabilities in order to enable them to operate various types of machinery. Its goal was to "bring the war wounded into the 'work community of humans' as members in full standing."[128] As in the case of the war neurotics, therapy and rehabilitation of the physically disabled did not only aim at the restoration of people's working capacity. It was also meant to save pension expenses.

In the army, work training in specialized workshops and rehabilitative centres was meant to facilitate the rehabilitation of wounded soldiers. As in the case of soldiers with mental problems, therapeutic interventions were aimed at people's will in order to strengthen their desire to overcome their disability and become valuable members of society. Psychological considerations played an important role in the views of those who advocated sport and gymnastics for the rehabilitation of disabled soldiers. Johannes Rissom, the director of the Ettlingen (Baden) rehabilitation centre for soldiers who had lost an arm or a leg, proclaimed that while it was important to improve the "physical nimbleness" of the disabled, the main effect of exercise was psychological. Sport and gymnastics were to restore people's confidence in their own abilities and performance and foster their working capacity:

"All of them should not only become useful ... but if possible fully valuable productive workers."[129] In some cities, gymnastics associations volunteered to organize exercise sessions for soldiers who lost an arm or a leg. These actions were also justified similarly by reference to the positive psychological benefits: "Gymnastics exercises and games are ... suited ... to increase their confidence in the performance ability and adaptation capacity (*Anpassungsvermögen*) of their body and provide them with new courage for life [and] heightened strength of will in their difficult struggle for survival."[130]

The physician Arthur Mallwitz, who was in charge of the rehabilitation program at the army reserve hospital Görden in Brandenburg, also pointed mostly to the psychological benefits of sport. By restoring soldiers' working capacity and their joy in life and work, sport for disabled soldiers was to put an end to "pension-chasing."[131] In Görden, Mallwitz had the support of the corps physician of the III Army Corps, Generaloberarzt Leu, to organize sporting competitions for disabled soldiers. The participants were categorized based on the nature and degree of their impairments. There were track and field, swimming, and weightlifting competitions for the "one-armed" and "one-legged," as well as for people with lighter impairments. Altogether six major competitions were held in the spring, summer, and fall of 1917 and 1918. These events were turned into exhibitions before high-ranking army and government officials and ladies and gentlemen from Berlin and Brandenburg society. The staging of these competitions (in front of a mixed military and civilian upper-class audience) reveals that the organizers intended to raise official and public awareness about the social and economic significance of sport.[132] The army reserve hospital Ettlingen organized similar exhibitions, which were attended by the Grand Duke of Baden, his wife, high-ranking army officers, the minister of the interior, civil servants, and a large number of other invited guests.[133]

Public sport competitions of disabled soldiers were part of a larger phenomenon of public displays of disabled people that conveyed the message that men could overcome almost anything if they trained hard enough. Army physicians presented "model-invalids," who demonstrated remarkable physical feats despite their disabilities. Some like Rudolf Gürtelschmied, also known as the "man without extremities," almost gained celebrity status. Gürtelschmied had become disabled through a work accident before the war, but he was used to demonstrate to disabled soldiers the degree of "perfection [...] which the functions of amputated extremities" could achieve.[134] For historian Sabine Kienitz, rehabilitation was part of a remasculinization process in which disabled soldiers were pushed to leave behind their feminine helplessness and dependence on welfare and become self-sufficient.[135]

Sporting competitions were seen as a particularly effective means to reactivate the disabled. While the wounded showed only limited eagerness for orthopedic exercises, their training for public sporting competitions allegedly led to a "lively enthusiasm, which made every additional stimulus superfluous."[136] By contrast, many remedial orthopedic exercises with exercise machines for resistance training lacked competitive elements and therefore did not stimulate high performances.[137] Reliance on such medico-mechanical machinery was criticized for other reasons as well. H. Kuhr, an army reserve officer and gymnastics teacher at the University of Leipzig, did not deny that these therapies had their uses in the early stages of rehabilitation. Their effectiveness, however, was limited to the improvement of simple physiological functions (e.g., the mobility of injured limbs); they did not have a positive impact on people's emotions, which were considered vital for people's recovery. By contrast, sport and gymnastics furthered people's "joy, optimism, courage of life, [and] the belief in one's own future as well as the [future] of Volk and Fatherland." Because of these positive effects, Kuhr believed that people would for the most part engage voluntarily in sport. Compulsion and "barrack-style tone and drill" were not only regarded as unnecessary but as inappropriate because they compromised the positive psychological effects of what should be a voluntary activity.[138]

In reality, participation in rehabilitative exercise and sport was by no means voluntary.[139] Wounded and disabled soldiers were still soldiers who had to follow orders even though these orders were now often justified by a rhetoric of pastoral care that depicted superiors as "comrade[s] and helping friend[s]" who had the trust of their charges even as they exercised "kind compulsion" (*liebenswürdiger Zwang*).[140] According to Rissom, initial resistance to exercise could be overcome with the guidance of an optimistic and empathetic gymnastics teacher who ensured that "compulsory participation soon turned into joyful joining in."[141] The effectiveness of this discourse of care and compassion depended on mutual trust between people who perceived each other as more or less equal because they participated in the same exercise and sporting activities. This egalitarian ethos was reinforced by a sporting dress without rank insignia that was worn by the exercise leaders (often non-commissioned officers) and the wounded soldiers. Based on his experience in an army field hospital, the army and sport physician Wolfgang Kohlrausch reported that sun bathing and common sporting activities created special bonds between soldiers and physicians who served as officers: "Since all insignia of rank were missing ... I was not anymore the superior but the comrade. This is when the soldiers start to talk, and the increased trust was not rarely valuable to me."[142]

The ethos of care and equality in rehabilitation centres for the physically impaired was in marked contrast to the harsh therapies and rehabilitation procedures that soldiers with war neuroses had to endure.[143] As Paul Lerner has shown, hypnotic and shock therapies for war neuroses were based on the suggestive force of a charismatic healer personality that was reinforced by the physician's officer rank.[144] While such therapies were predicated on a reinforcement of authority and military and social hierarchies between physicians and ordinary soldiers, exercise and sport therapies for physically disabled soldiers tried to downplay such distinctions in order to build trust and self-confidence in people's own abilities. The latter was a strategy that drew its persuasive force from the egalitarian and nurturing aspects of *Kameradschaft*, whose complex meanings have been analysed by Thomas Kühne.[145] The purpose of these contrasting therapeutic strategies and social technologies of power was, however, the same: strengthening the will of the disabled and turning them into useful, productive citizens who did not become a burden on the national economy.

Yet, even in the case of physically disabled soldiers, there were limits to softer forms of encouragement. Communal sporting activities might have emphasized care, mutual support, and comradeship. Military discipline and hierarchies of rank were still emphasized in the workshops where disabled soldiers were instructed in the use of prostheses and underwent retraining for jobs commensurate with their disabilities.[146] In part this disciplinarian thrust was a consequence of an attitude that saw physical disability as a psychological problem that could be overcome through determination and hard work. If people were convinced that they could compensate for their disability through their own efforts, so the argument went, they would not develop the typical "cripple" mentality which only led to pension-seeking. At the beginning of the war, war invalids were still celebrated as heroes for their sacrifices. As casualties mounted, attitudes shifted. The disabled were now expected to demonstrate that they were work and performance-oriented or face denunciation as "drones" and "parasites."[147]

Before 1914, members of the Wilhelmine establishment voiced concerns about the declining productive capacity and military fitness of the German population. The ZA lobbied local and state officials to provide more sporting opportunities for young workers in the cities. The mostly liberal reformers wanted to raise the physical fitness of people, but they also believed that sport and gymnastics had wholesome educational benefits. Sport, they hoped, would transform young workers' attitudes towards society. They would become responsible citizens and performance-oriented subjects who rejected the false promises of socialism. In the final years of the empire, the efforts of the reformers received official support from the state. The Prussian youth care decree sanctioned many of the ideas suggested by the ZA and provided money for organized leisure activities and sport for male working youths. Women remained excluded from state support even though many liberal reformers considered women's fitness important for the economic strength of the nation. The war changed this. Women's productive roles were now acknowledged by state support for women's leisure and sporting activities.

The public significance attributed to sport fueled scientific interest in the physiological possibilities and limits of human endurance and performance. The sport science section at the Dresden Hygiene Exhibition and scientific congresses provided an organizational basis for an emerging sport science. Before the war sport researchers were mostly interested in establishing the dangers and physiological limits of sport performance. During the war supporters of sport science like Carl Diem argued that the war had demonstrated that humans had a far greater performance potential than previously assumed, and sport could be used to develop this potential and utilize it for the rebuilding of the productive capacity of the nation. In 1918 the army announced the emperor's plan to build a military institute for research on sport and gymnastics. Because of the German defeat the creation of such an institute under army auspices was out of the question but the plan demonstrates how accepted ideas about the social utility of sport had become.

During the Weimar period governments at all levels would provide financial and logistical support for an expanding sport movement and for sport-related research. As the next chapter demonstrates, the promotion of sport became a central element of biopolitical strategies to restore the productive capacity of the German population, contain welfare expenses, and foster people's commitment to work.

Chapter Two

Conditioning Bodies and Minds during the Weimar Republic

In 1926, the President of the German Reich Committee for Physical Exercise (DRAL), Theodor Lewald, discussed the significance of sport for the German economy and national health in a presentation to the Berlin Chamber of Industry and Commerce. He deplored the physical state of the German population as a consequence of the lost war. Two million of the physically and mentally strongest German men had been killed, while millions of German men, women, and children were permanently weakened as a result of starvation during the war and the allied hunger blockade after the armistice. To make matters worse, the hygienic benefits of military service that had guaranteed the physical strength and fitness of male youth had been lost. Prior to the war about five hundred thousand men had served in the German army or navy where they had learned regimens of cleanliness, order, and discipline. According to Lewald, by limiting the size of the German army to one hundred thousand men, the victorious allies had not only sought to weaken Germany militarily but they had also tried to paralyse it economically by permanently weakening the "strength of the German people."[1]

In this formulation, Lewald posited a connection between compulsory military service, the physical and psychological fitness of the German population, and the state of the German economy. Citing President Hindenburg's autobiography, Lewald claimed that army service had instilled inner strength and self-confidence in the physical and psychological performance potential of thousands of men. Now, not only the educational benefits of military conscription were lost but also the annual medical inspections of new recruits that had provided the most reliable measures for the state of the nation's health. Even so, the remaining general medical statistics, along with social insurance statistics of the state sickness, accident, and disability insurance system, gave some alarming information about the problems that the lack of fitness of the population posed for the German economy. In this context, the improvement of the overall health and performance level of the German population was seen to be the key to controlling spiraling social insurance costs. This change for the better could best be achieved by promoting sport and other physical activities; to do so, Lewald tried to enlist the support of the Berlin business community.[2]

Conditioning the body for performance was, in Lewald's view, an integral part of Germany's task of biological reconstruction after the lost war. Along with a number of physicians, psychologists, business leaders, and government officials, people such as Lewald promoted performance conditioning through sport as part of a comprehensive program to rebuild and refine human resources. Since they successfully mobilized scientific, financial, and political support for sport and physical education, they turned *Leibesübungen* into an important element of qualitative population policy that intended to restore the productive capacities of the German population.

During the Weimar years all levels of government extended their support for sport. Cities built sport grounds and stadiums and they created offices that administered them and provided help for sport and gymnastics clubs. Counseling centres for sport medicine (*sportärztliche Beratungsstellen*) provided advice for people who wanted to take up a sport or suffered from sport injuries. The largest German state Prussia continued to support mass sport as part of its commitment to government-sponsored youth care. In many German states universities founded institutes for physical exercise to train sport and gymnastics teachers and encourage students to exercise. The Reich government subsidized sport science and sport-teacher education through the *Deutsche Hochschule für Leibesübungen* or DHfL.

These efforts (far more comprehensive than government initiatives during the Empire) should be seen in the context of the expanding Weimar welfare state, which tried to ensure the "physical, mental, and social fitness" of the younger generation.[3] But they were also a reflection of the fact that more and more people joined sport and gymnastics clubs during the period. Club membership more than tripled between 1913/14 and 1931 from more than 2 million to more than 6.5 million.[4] During the 1920s, sport also became mass entertainment, not just in Germany but also in most Western societies. The prominent role of popular, college, and professional sport in the United States particularly impressed German promoters of sport.[5] The rise of mass spectator sport, in particular soccer, cycling, and boxing, as well as the millions of people who took up exercise during the Weimar period, attest to a widespread popular fascination with sport as part of a hedonistic mass culture. The sport literature of the 1920s missed no opportunity to promote exercise as a wholesome source of fun, and there is no reason to believe that popular enthusiasm for sport was not genuine. People's enthusiasm for sport and the promotion of *Leibesübungen* for utilitarian purposes are not contradictions, however. Because it was fun, many people regarded sport as a promising instrument for the creation of fitter, performance-oriented individuals.

The large historiography on Weimar sport has produced many valuable studies on working class and bourgeois sport, conflicts between sport and the gymnastics movement, sport and gender relations, and sport as a form of hedonistic mass culture.[6] Historians have also examined the attempts by the military to utilize sport as a means to rebuild the military fitness and "defensive will" (*Wehrwille*) of Germans, in violation of the treaty of Versailles.[7] By contrast, the substantial efforts by governments, sport officials, politicians, employers, and medical professionals to promote mass sport as a means to increase the *productive* fitness of the population have not received the attention they deserve.[8]

As I argue, the promotion of mass sport was part of a qualitative biopolitics that included both eugenic and environmental approaches.[9] While not trying to improve people's genes directly, such efforts were part of a "care for the hereditary endowment" (*Anlagenpflege*) that tried to make sure that people could realize their full hereditary potential without being stunted by an adverse environment. Along with social welfare, better nutrition, and improved housing, medical professionals, psychologists, and physical educators believed sport mobilized psychological performance potentials that raised people's enthusiasm for physical and mental work, in addition to it overtly strengthening the physical constitution and health of people. During the 1920s, such an emphasis on improving the productivity of the populace paved the way for close collaborations between the work and sport sciences. Their efforts were part of a larger biopolitical discourse about a human economy that fostered the rational development, refinement, and deployment of human resources in the interest of national efficiency.

In this chapter, I will focus on three aspects of performance conditioning through *Leibesübungen* and sport research. In the first part, I will consider proposals by medical scientists and physical educators that sought to condition the bodies of workers and athletes in order to restore the fitness and productivity of the population after the war, and discuss how national, state, and local governments responded to such demands. The second part focuses on the use of sport to transform human subjectivity. Psychological conditioning through sport and physical exercise was a central aspect of Weimar sport discourses. Sport psychologists and physical educators believed that sport was not only important for the physical health of the German national community; they also assumed that sport was important for the building of character. Employers looked to sport as a way to foster performance-orientation and loyalty among their workforce. Sport would raise the productivity of people by instilling in them a performance-oriented habitus based on a strengthening of the will and self-discipline. Some also claimed that physical exercise was an important tool to enhance the mental performance level of students as well as adults. The last section will examine shifting emphases of sport discourses during the final crisis years of the republic when the military and conservatives looked to sport to raise the military fitness and "defensive will" of the population and foster discipline, order, and patriotism among unemployed youth.

I. Conditioning the Body for Physical Performance

In 1920, the DRAL celebrated the founding of the *Deutsche Hochschule für Leibesübungen.*[10] During the opening ceremony, Lewald emphasized the central role the DHfL was to play in the reconstruction of Germany. "Physical healing" through physical exercise should provide the "strength for mental and moral renewal." The school was not to breed "brainless athletes" but the "harmoniously developed human leader (*Führermensch*) of the future who, based on healthy physical strength, full of courage and the will to act (*Tatwillen*), mentally trained with the entire armory of science, with sober judgment and self-confident patriotic feeling should show his people the path to new heights." Lewald pointed here to one of the main purposes of the new institution: the education of academically and practically trained sport and physical education teachers who should become the backbone of a broad-based physical education offensive in schools and private sport associations.[11]

Like Lewald, Carl Diem, the designated acting director of the DHfL and General Secretary of the DRAL, explained the founding of the institution as a response to the human losses of the war. Since the leadership of German gymnastics and sport associations had been decimated by the war, the DHfL had to replace them. As before the war, Diem, probably best known for his role as chief organizer of the 1936 Olympics, was a tireless promoter of popular fitness through mass sport.[12] In his view, it was necessary to raise the "health of the people" and their "strength of will." Only gymnastics and sport were suited to develop human beings with firm and balanced characters who were filled with a joy of life and, most importantly, the "will to work." In other words, sport was to create a performance-oriented individual physically "accustomed to the strains of life" in postwar Germany.[13] A brochure by the supporters of the new institution pointed out that the promotion of physical exercise was crucial to the survival of the German nation, because the "strength and health of the people" were "our most precious and noble capital" and these had to be increased through physical exercise.[14]

The DHfL was conceived as a private institution of higher education run by the DRAL, the umbrella organization of so-called "bourgeois" (*bürgerliche*) sport and gymnastics federations. The DRAL was by far the largest sport federation in Weimar Germany.[15] Despite the private character of the institution, the interest of the Reich government in the DHfL was considerable. Reich President Ebert and other high-ranking government officials attended the opening ceremony and in the late 1920s almost half of the budget for the institution came from the Reich Ministry of the Interior.[16] (Ebert seems to have taken a keen interest in the new institution because he attended lectures at the Hochschule on other occasions, see figure 2.1.)

The Reich's interest in the DHfL should be seen in the context of the greater financial and political support that was being lent to sport and *Leibesübungen*. During the 1920s, subsidies for sport increased at all levels of government, because officials believed that physical exercise was essential for the recovery of the German population. In 1921, a sport fund was created by the Ministry of the Interior to support sport-related activities and institutions such as the DHfL, which were to serve as a national model for sport and sport-teacher education. In 1928, the fund distributed 1.5 million RM and smaller funds were available in other Reich ministries.[17]

The states also used public funds for this purpose. Until 1931, Prussia provided about 1 million RM per year for sport and sport medicine and a considerable part of the funds for youth care (3 million RM) was

2.1 Reich President Friedrich Ebert (front row centre) together with Theodor Lewald attending a lecture at the DHfL. Carl Diem, *Die Deutsche Hochschule für Leibesübungen* (Berlin: DHfL, 1924), 7. Private Collection.

also earmarked for sport-related activities.[18] The Prussian gymnastics teacher seminary in Berlin-Spandau was turned into the Prussian College for Physical Exercise (*Preussische Hochschule für Leibesübungen*, or PHfL), which the state government tried to build up in competition to the DHfL. In addition to this, the states founded University Institutes for Physical Exercise (*Hochschulinstitute für Leibesübungen*) at universities, which promoted physical exercise in order to increase the fitness of university students.[19] To be sure, the combined state and federal support for sport was probably still rather modest, especially if one believes sport physicians and officials who always complained about insufficient financial support; however, there is evidence that municipalities and local governments poured considerable resources into sport. Part of the money went to building sporting venues, such as the major stadiums in the cities of Munich, Nuremberg, Frankfurt, and Cologne.[20]

In 1929 there were 86 counseling centres for sport medicine in 74 Prussian cities. They were staffed by 131 sport physicians who advised people who wanted to take up a sport or suffered from sport injuries. By October 1931 the number of counseling centres had increased to 146.[21] The sport physician Herbert Herxheimer, whose research was on physiological aspects of sport performance, directed the *sportärztliche Beratungsstelle* of the second medical clinic of the Charité, the large teaching hospital affiliated with Berlin's Friedrich-Wilhelm University. The counseling centre was financed by the city of Berlin, with support from the Prussian state, and was open to the employees and students of the Berlin universities, school students, members of Berlin gymnastics and sport clubs, and all Berliners who were interested in taking up a sport. It also provided advice to physicians and expert opinions on difficult medical cases.[22]

The 1920s also witnessed a founding wave of City Offices for Physical Exercise (*Stadtämter für Leibesübungen*). These administrative bodies served as a liaison between local government and private sporting associations. They organized the provision of sport fields for schools and sport clubs and promoted physical exercise among the population at large. According to a 1927 survey by the DRAL, there were twenty cities with more that two hundred thousand inhabitants that had founded *Stadtämter* after the war, and there were many smaller cities who had designated other offices to administer sport fields and/or promote sport or activities related to physical education.[23]

City officials such as Dr. Otto Wagner, the mayor (*Oberbürgermeister*) of the Silesian city of Breslau, made clear their belief that physical exercise countered the population's moral waywardness and degeneration. Wagner argued that it was "shocking to see how many funds a city such as Breslau has to raise for all those who were physical and moral failures."[24] He saw in physical conditioning a means to create productive citizens. The spectre of rising welfare expenses, attributed to a decline of the moral fibre and physical fitness of the population at large, was thus one of the reasons that Weimar municipalities promoted *Leibesübungen*. According to Diem, the *Stadtämter für Leibesübungen* had to ensure that schools, sport associations, and the government promoted physical activities that strengthened all those who were physically weak, kept the healthy fit and well, and enabled the physically talented to become champions. In his vision, these offices were an integral part of a physical education offensive for the population in general.[25]

The claim that regular exercise prevented illness and social dependency by making people socially and economically self-sufficient was made frequently. Citing memoranda by labour minister Heinrich Brauns (of the Catholic Centre (*Zentrum*) Party) and the statistical office of the Reich, Lewald painted a devastating picture of German national health that imposed a grave burden on the German economy.

He claimed that the expenses of health insurance funds had risen by 37 per cent from 1924 to 1925, which was in part due to the rise in sick days from 187.5 million to 229 million. Early invalidity was on the rise at a time when, as a consequence of the war, there were fewer people of working age than in previous generations. In order to preserve the working capacity of people as long as possible, he insisted that the entire population be required to exercise from an early age.[26] The DRAL had no trouble enlisting the support of renowned members of the medical profession for mass sport, since many shared the assumption that exercise and sport promoted health and social fitness and contributed to lower social and health insurance costs. They justified their support for *Leibesübungen* in economic terms: it was an investment in Germany's productive future that would help prevent illness and invalidity.[27] In Lewald's view, physical exercise would also significantly lower the costs of accident insurance, because more than half of all accidents were caused by a lack of physical dexterity.[28]

The mayor of Berlin, Gustav Böß, maintained that sport-educated people were "competent in life" and he was glad to see that the national business community (*Volkswirtschaft*) recognized in sport the "unrecovered treasures" necessary for the "struggle for survival." Experience showed that the strength of the *Volk* grew on the sport field where the "physical devaluation" (*physische Entwertung*) of people could be reversed. By using the term *Entwertung*, an allusion to the hyperinflation of 1923, Böß tried to make a connection between the economic chaos of the German postwar crisis and the physical state of the German population. The implication was that human bodies were precious economic capital whose value had to be carefully preserved.[29] In Böß's view, it was urgent "to care for and develop the forces of the people that we still have" because medical surveys had shown that one fourth to one third of all school-leavers in big cities lacked the physical strength to undertake gainful employment.[30] Böß was one of the most vocal advocates of *Leibesübungen* in Weimar Germany. As mayor of the largest city in Germany, he used his influence to successfully lobby members of the Prussian Landtag to provide youth welfare funds for sport. He also convinced leading businessmen to create a private foundation, which, according to a report of the Berlin *Stadtamt für Leibesübungen*, provided considerable sums for the financial support of public sporting facilities.[31]

That sport and gymnastics were widely regarded as a means for the physiological reconstruction of the German nation is also evident in the prominent role given to physical exercise during the large hygiene exhibition Ge-So-Lei in Düsseldorf. The acronym Ge-So-Lei stood for Health Care, Social Welfare, and Physical Exercise (*Gesundheitspflege, Soziale Fürsorge und Leibesübungen*). The exhibition advocated preventive hygiene and exercise as the means to rebuild national health. It took place over a period of several months in 1926 and attracted more than seven million visitors. For Ernst Poensgen, a major industrialist, promoter of sport, and co-organizer of the event, the Ge-So-Lei had great economic importance because it pointed to the value of a rational human economy (*rationelle Menschenwirtschaft*) by demonstrating how human beings could preserve their health and working capacity, prevent impairments, and remedy damage to their health. Poensgen's goal was to rebuild the working capacity of people so that they could deliver work performances of the highest level with great endurance.[32] The emphasis of the Ge-So-Lei sporting exhibitions, therefore, was on exercise for the mass of the population. Gymnastics associations and sport clubs demonstrated the athletic skills and fitness of their mostly male members. Athletes introduced different sports, ranging from gymnastics and track and field disciplines to soccer and handball competitions, to encourage visitors to take up physical exercise "in order to boost their physical abilities."[33]

The idea that sport and sport-related activities were a means to create reliable and productive workers ensured considerable support for sport from private industry. In 1920, German industry supported the DRAL with several million RM, hoping that sport would help ease tensions in industrial relations. The electrical giant Siemens and a couple of Berlin banks also helped to finance the construction of sport fields in the capital. Throughout the 1920s, sport was credited with raising the productivity of the workforce. In 1927, the Siemens company newspaper, for example, praised exercise as a means to compensate for the unavoidable one-sided physical burden that industrial labour imposed on workers. Sport would also "increase our economic performance through exercise and training of physical and mental traits" that were important for job performances.[34]

During the 1920s, the DHfL in Berlin would become one of the most important German institutions for training sport coaches and physical education teachers as well as an internationally recognized institution for research into various aspects of work and sport performance. High expectations about the DHfL were closely linked to expectations about the rational manageability of physical performance in fields such as work physiology.[35] In the 1920s, the Hochschule established a close collaboration with the Kaiser Wilhelm Institute for Work Physiology (*Kaiser Wilhelm Institut für Arbeitsphysiologie*, or KWIA) that lasted from 1921 to 1929. The director of the physiological-experimental department of the KWIA, Edgar Atzler, was also the director of the physiological institute of the DHfL. Atzler and his assistants worked on issues that were relevant for work and sport physiology, but his work was determined by his own research interests since his contract with the DHfL specified that there was to be no interference from officials of the Hochschule.[36] The close collaboration between the two institutions emerged because work and sport physiology promised to provide basic knowledge on the "optimization" of processes of physical labour in sport and work. According to this view, sport was a special form of physical labour. The understanding of athletic performances therefore had implications for the rationalization of physical labour in industry and vice versa.[37]

The KWIA's journal *Arbeitsphysiologie*, one of the leading international journals on work physiology, was devoted to research on the "physiology of man at work and during sport."[38] German research on work and sport physiology focused on increasing the overall efficiency of physical labour. Time and motion studies sought to gain insights into the nature of sport performance by breaking down complex movements into their basic components. The Frankfurt sport physician Otto Schmith, for example, analysed films of elite hurdlers in this way.[39] Wilhelm Knoll from the Institute for Physical Exercise of the University of Hamburg used film in order to establish the most efficient motions for coaches and athletes. Such beliefs in the rationalization of physical exercise had a wider currency in Weimar culture. As Michael Mackenzie has pointed out, artists like George Grosz and Willi Baumeister represented athletes as mechanized bodies that could be rationally managed and disciplined.[40]

Research in work physiology was based on the assumption that all forms of labour in sport and work could be divided into fundamental components of movements, for each of which the optimum energy efficiency was experimentally determined in respiration studies. The hope was to provide scientific knowledge for the design of machinery, sport equipment, and the organization of work processes. Time and motion studies would provide a scientific basis for determining the lengths of working periods and the spacing and durations of work breaks in order to assure the most efficient use of physical labour and prevent the exhaustion of the workforce.[41]

Initially, sport physiologists and physical educators thought that it was possible to dissect human movements in order to establish degrees of efficiency for work processes and sport movements.[42] Atzler thought that there were about thirty to forty basic movement components that, in various combinations, could account for all physical movements in human beings. By disassembling and joining these elementary movements one could create the most complicated movement forms in human beings, similar to the way in which the vocabulary of a language could be created from the letters of the alphabet. By determining the energy used for each of the elementary movements, Atzler hoped to develop strategies for optimizing movement complexes. By 1925, his research program had managed to determine the energy efficiency of five elementary movements (such as weight lifting and turning a crank under different working conditions; see figure 2.2) and he hoped that in coming years he would be able to examine the rest of them.[43]

From a practical point of view, however, an analytical approach such as Atzler's proved to be unsatisfactory because it promised few immediate practical applications.[44] Atzler himself estimated that it would take his laboratory about a year to assess the conditions for the optimal efficiency of a single work or movement component.[45] The emphasis of physical educators shifted, therefore, towards a more holistic assessment of movement complexes that relied a great deal on the experience of coaches and athletes and therefore promised greater practicability.[46] In the mid-1920s, research by work and sport physiologists was based on the assumption that the physiological processes were the same for work and sport performances. Scientific knowledge based on one type of performance was therefore considered directly applicable to the other. Sport research could produce knowledge about the nature of physical performances in general and thus provide insights for the rationalization of physical labour. The KWIA, for example, promoted research about the ways in which physical activities during work breaks might counter fatigue and restore the overall performance level of workers.[47] The goal was to find out how to optimize the output of physical labour without compromising the long-term health and performance levels of workers. In an Universum Film AG (UFA) movie with the title Working Powers and their Protection (*Arbeitskräfte und ihre Schonung*), work physiologists promoted rationalization as a kind of sustainable performance management that guaranteed higher workplace productivity by allowing for recovery periods to restore the working capacity of employees.[48]

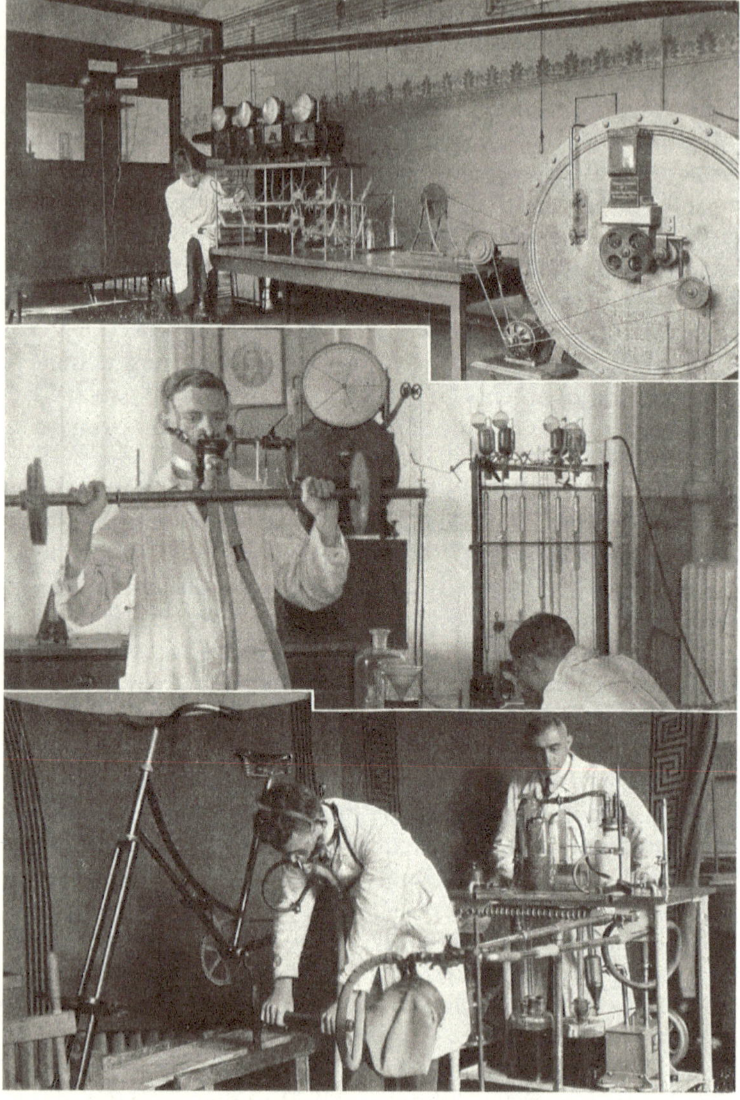

Bild 23. Der Pettenkofersche Respirationsapparat im Physiologischen Institut der Universität, mit dem Stoffwechseluntersuchungen bei sportlicher Arbeit vorgenommen werden. — Bild 24. Dr. Herbst untersucht seine Ausatmungsluft beim Gewichtheben. — Bild 25. Dr. Lehmann das gleiche beim Drehen einer Rolle. Am Untersuchungstisch Dr. Full.

Beschreibung des Pettenkoferschen Respirations-Apparates auf Seite 22, unten. *Tafel 9*

2.2 Determining the energy efficiency of movements: (top) Pettenkofer respiration apparatus for analysis of metabolic exchange; (centre) Dr Herbst has his expiration analysed during weight exercises; (bottom) Dr Lehmann the same turning a crank. Diem, *Hochschule*, 23. Private Collection.

Sport fulfilled an important rationale in this "human economy." Physiologists emphasized the importance of regular exercise for the improvement of the physical performance level of individuals. Physical exercise promoted the functional adaptation of specific muscle groups for specific types of physical labour. According to the work and sport physiologist Robert Herbst, who worked in the physiological laboratory of the DHfL as well as in the KWIA, physical exercise steeled the body and enabled it to resist the effect of economic deprivation. Proponents of sport also pointed to the remedial aspects of exercise. Exercise could compensate for health damage caused by one-sided physical labour that compromised workers' health and posture. It increased the performance level and diminished the predisposition to a range of diseases. From the perspective of many physicians, sport had definitive hygienic benefits. Herbst, however, warned that exaggerated sport training could also lead to fatigue and have negative consequences for people's performance level at work.[49]

Weimar physiologists wanted to optimize the long-term performance potential of workers and athletes. They were not interested in maximizing short-term performances since they believed that this compromised long-term health and productivity. They counseled against exaggerated exercise and performance enhancement because they considered the human body a most valuable resource for a rationally organized modern economy.[50] German physiologists thus rejected Frederick Winslow Taylor's system of scientific management. The Taylor system, they claimed, aimed at maximizing performance through the intensification of labour. In Atzler's view, such an approach to productivity enhancement might be possible in an immigrant society, such as the United States, where labour was easily replaceable. A country with limited human resources, such as Germany, had to husband them more carefully. In addition, the Taylor system was based on the utilization of healthy people whose ability to perform was not diminished through war and hunger. By contrast, Germany had to integrate impaired and weakened workers into the work process without overtaxing them. Weimar's human economy, therefore, had to be based on an understanding of the physiological implications of rationalization.[51] This tempered approach to performance enhancement fit in well with the pluralistic political landscape of the republic. Advocating performance enhancement at the expense of workers' welfare would have been problematic considering the Social Democrats still wielded abundant political influence in national politics and at the state level. Between

1928 and 1930 there was an SPD-led national government and Prussia, the largest state, was governed by a coalition of the SPD and the Catholic Centre Party until 1932. Atzler acknowledged the influence of Socialists and labour unions when he explained his ideas in the labour union journal *Die Arbeit*.[52]

At the core of the debate about human performance enhancement through sport were questions about the malleability of the human constitution. Was human performance potential determined by heredity, and if so, could it nonetheless be enhanced? Sport physicians considered it important to diagnose hereditary performance potential. In particular they hoped to diagnose specific genetic aptitudes for particular sport disciplines. While most Weimar physicians considered eugenics an important element of biopolitical population management, many of them did not adhere to a strict hereditarian determinism.[53] Herbst, for example, argued: "Certainly there is much in the genotype that cannot be changed, [but] at the same time there are things that can be changed through the conditioning influences of the environment."[54] Herbst believed that the degree of malleability of the human body was determined by heredity. But he also thought that it was worth investigating whether genetic "minus-variants" could be changed by physical exercise.

Disentangling the complex relationship between heredity, environmental influences, and physical conditioning was an important if somewhat elusive goal of sport physicians. The director of the anthropometric department at the DHfL, Wolfgang Kohlrausch, developed a research program on "sport types research" (*Sporttypenforschung*) based on anthropometric measurements.[55] All students who entered the DHfL underwent such physical measurements, and their physical development was monitored regularly. Kohlrausch tried to relate his findings to the constitutional typology developed by the psychiatrist Ernst Kretschmer. The asthenic (weak) or leptosome body type, Kohlrausch claimed, could be found especially among long- and middle-distance runners because this body type was best suited for sport disciplines that required endurance.[56] Behind these classification attempts (see figure 2.3) was the assumption that it would eventually be possible to determine the specific hereditary aptitude of athletes (and by implication workers) based on their "constitutional type."[57]

The anthropometric surveys conducted by sport physicians have to be seen in the context of a whole range of surveys into the health of the German people during the Weimar Republic. These studies tried to assess

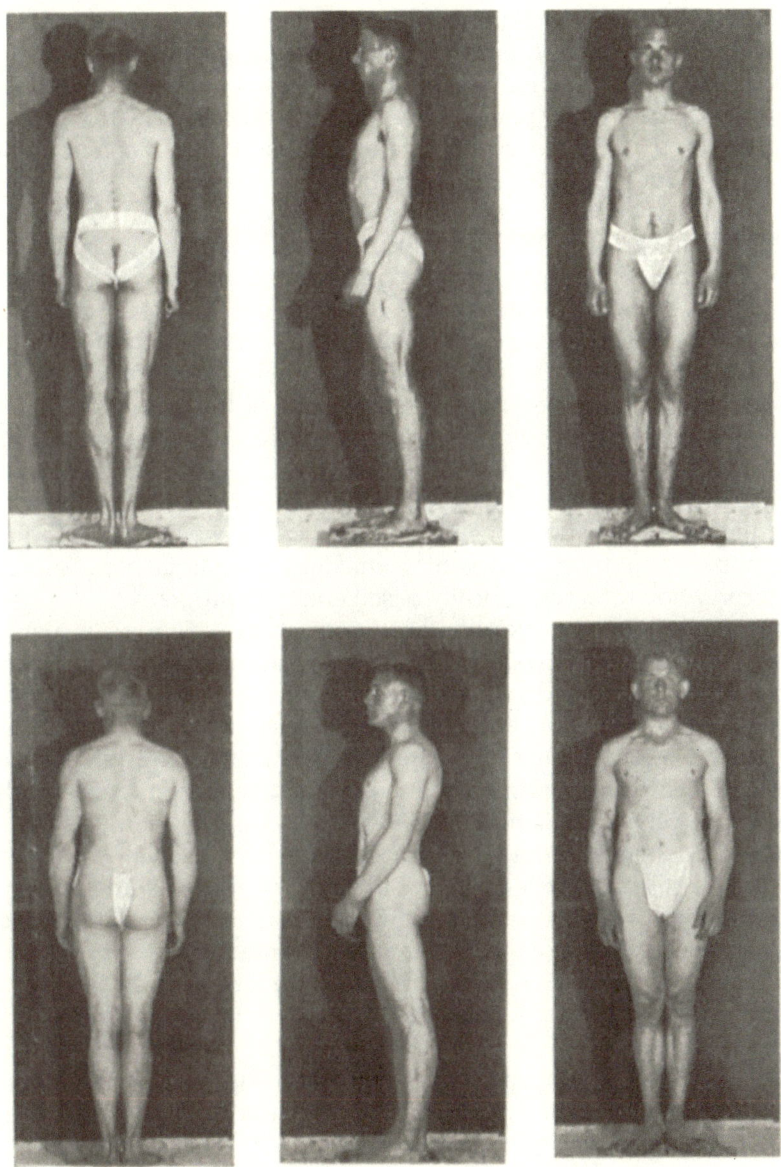

Bild 21. Peltzer (Deutscher Meister im Mittelstreckenlauf).
Bild 22. Breitensträter (Deutscher Meister im Berufsboxen).

Tafel 8

2.3 Sport types: (top) Peltzer, German middle distance running champion; (bottom) Breitensträter, German professional boxing champion. Diem, *Hochschule*, 19. Private Collection.

the physical and psychological state of the population in order to formulate policy suggestions for rational population management. The deficits of the German population were to be diagnosed, and scientific experts would propose various remedies for them as part of an all-encompassing human resource development. One emphasis of the Emergency Community of German Science (*Notgemeinschaft der deutschen Wissenschaft*), the most important funding body of German science, was anthropological research on the state of the German population, which was complemented by funding from the Rockefeller Foundation. During the interwar years, the foundation funded biomedical research in many western and central European countries. In Germany, Rockefeller funding focused on research in human biology with an emphasis on psychiatry and anthropology. Perceived as state-of-the-art research at the time, these approaches promised long-term solutions to serious social and medical problems.[58] The anthropological research aimed to assess the hereditary quality of the German population by determining mental and physical predispositions of large groups of people. A goal was to diagnose hereditary psychopathic characteristics in large populations as a precondition for a scientifically based eugenics program.[59]

There were other surveys without such an explicit eugenic agenda, however. The sport physicians Herrmann Rautmann and Fritz Duras, for example, developed a survey for the health assessment of students at the University of Freiburg. The surveys were conducted from 1923, and the participation of male and female students was compulsory. Before 1933, about thirteen thousand Freiburg University students underwent such physical examinations. The goals were to identify diseases at an early stage and diagnose physical deficiencies. The assessments included anthropometric as well as physiological examinations such as a cardiographic test of heart functions. Investigators passed judgment on the general health of the students and pointed out specific deficiencies such as weak muscle development, deformations of the thorax, and problems with posture. As a remedy, the physicians suggested specific gymnastic exercises.[60]

The main aim of this type of survey was not eugenic selection, at least not during the Weimar years.[61] There was a strong element of therapy and social care (*Fürsorge*). Physicians, who advocated remedial exercises for apprentices, young workers, and students, were often sensitive to issues of poverty and social exclusion and they believed that their exercise programs could address these issues. Duras, for example, wanted to help weak students, who were "laughed at because of their lack of performance" and therefore lost interest in exercise. These students, he believed, were deprived of an opportunity to remedy their weaknesses. By introducing special programs for them the sport physician could do much good. Students would find "new courage and once convinced of their performance capacity their sense of achievement (*Leistungsgefühl*)" would help them get healthy.[62]

Apart from diagnosing infectious diseases among the student population, the Freiburg surveys tried to identify students who had performance deficits because of "physical inferiority, constitutional weakness, or a lack of exercise."[63] These students received the opportunity to exercise under medical supervision in special exercise groups (*Förderriegen*). According to Duras, it was especially important for the physically less developed to exercise and improve their health and physical strength.[64] The rationale of the Freiburg health survey was, therefore, educational and rehabilitative. Physicians hoped to help people fully develop their physical potential through exercise that was tailored to their specific needs. This idea was in line with Diem's thinking that people should do remedial exercises to rid themselves of partial physical "inferiorities." Such "compensatory work" (*Ausgleichsarbeit*) was, in Diem's view, one of the most important ways in which sport could contribute to the "health of the people."[65]

Similar assumptions informed the health surveys that the sport physician Hans Hoske conducted on young apprentices for the German National Union of Commercial Employees (*Deutschnationaler Handlungsgehilfenverband*, or DnHV), a right-wing union for lower-level employees in commerce and industry that was concerned about the impact of the war on the physical health and performance capacity of young apprentices. Hoske had been a student at the DHfL and worked there as a teacher and scientific assistant until 1926 and as a sport physician from 1926 to 1929. In 1925, Hoske also served as a medical intern at the KWIA. In 1929, he became director of the section for preventive health care of the DnHV health insurance. In this capacity, he was concerned about the social burdens imposed by the deplorable physical conditions of young people.[66]

In 1931, 4,200 DnHV male apprentices in 174 cities were examined during the second year of their apprenticeship to determine their physical fitness. Hoske's survey gathered data on their age, height, weight, chest circumference, lung capacity, pulse, and blood pressure. The apprentices were also asked whether they exercised regularly. The survey confirmed contemporary suspicions about the bad state of health of German youth. The typical commercial apprentice was tall but underweight with a narrow chest. Weakness and inhibited physical development, bad posture, bad teeth, flat feet, weak circulation (*Kreislaufschwäche*), and neurasthenia were also frequently diagnosed. Hoske did not attribute these deficits to bad heredity. Instead he blamed poor environmental and working conditions that inhibited the development of young people and prevented them from reaching their hereditary potential. According to Hoske, the physical neglect among young employees could only be remedied through more leisure time for sedentary workers. He shared the views of life reformers and physicians advocating social hygiene and argued that physical exercise, sun, and fresh air were important aspects of healthy living and contributed to the creation of a healthy and productive populace.[67]

The physical deterioration of apprentices was also the subject of the work of the surgeon Karl Gebhardt. While Gebhardt is best known as one of the most notorious medical criminals of the Third Reich and personal physician of SS leader Heinrich Himmler, during the Weimar years he developed a keen interest in exercise therapies that fortified young people through sport, an interest that he would develop further during the Nazi period (see also chapter 3).[68] Influenced by Hoske's work at the DHfL, between 1926 and 1933 Gebhardt organized annual exercise boot camps for weak and injured apprentices and students near the Bavarian town Hohenaschau. Each year between eighty and one hundred apprentices were selected for the camp in consultation with parents, schools, and employers.[69] Apart from medical and vocational criteria, participants were chosen according to the "value of their personality" (*Persönlichkeitswert*), which Gebhardt defined in terms of "good conduct" and "orderly work performance," attributes that were important for employers. The potential for social usefulness was thus a precondition for being included in the program. From a physiological point of view, the purpose of the camp was the preservation and increase of people's working power so that they could cope with the physical demands of their workplace. Participants spent four weeks in Hohenaschau during August. Divided into four groups based on their needs, the apprentices were subjected to different regimes of physical exercise depending on whether they were categorized as vulnerable to colds, congenitally weakened by tuberculosis or other infectious diseases, had a nervous predisposition, or suffered from orthopedic or various other kinds of debilitating disorders.[70] In Gebhardt's view, sport could raise people's "performance value" (*Leistungswert*), which was determined by heredity, sex, and environmental conditions. Since people could be categorized according to "performance types" (*Leistungstypen*), it was possible for physicians to develop individualized exercise regimes that stimulated their individual performance potential.[71] The goal of the exercise program was to enable young workers to reach "a uniform average performance ... corresponding approximately to *the exertion of the eight hour day*." In other words, "inferior" workers were to be remade into fully valuable members of the productive community (emphasis in the original).[72]

Workers' bodies were of great concern in Weimar biopolitical debates. Atzler, for example, thought that the declining birthrate of the war years would result in a significant worker shortage by the mid-1930s. Therefore one had to keep the existing human resources as fit as possible for as long as possible to avoid their premature physical deterioration.[73] The first International Workers Olympics held in 1925 in Frankfurt am Main offered a unique opportunity to assess the physical condition of working-class athletes and thus gain some insight into the physical condition of healthy workers. A group of physicians and anthropologists received permission from the organizers to systematically assess a large number of athletes. According to Alfons Gersbach, the director of the Frankfurt Physicians' Association, the *Arbeiterolympiade* would provide new insights into the influence of different sports on the performance capacity of workers in different occupations. The worker athletes seem to have participated enthusiastically in the Frankfurt survey.[74] One of the participating physicians considered it to be in the interest of all the competitors to "subject themselves to continuous medical control" throughout their lives as a preventive measure.[75]

Of particular concern to the investigators were athletes with one-sided physical development. The physical anthropologist Ernst Schwartz, who conducted the anthropometric measurements at the event, was concerned that too many workers neglected the remedial effects of physical exercise. Instead of choosing sports that compensated for the deleterious impact that their working conditions had on their physical conditions, some workers chose sports that reinforced the negative impacts of their work. "Heavy athletes" such as weight lifters, who tended to work in physically demanding occupations such as locksmithing and woodcutting, often reinforced their occupationally acquired dispositions through the sport they chose. While these predispositions enabled them to do well in their sport, they frequently damaged their health and productivity.[76]

The anthropological survey of the Frankfurt Workers' Olympics examined the relationships between sport, health, and the working capacity of women as well as men. At the time, medical concerns centred not only on the impact of sport on women's reproductivity, a topic that has found extensive treatment in the historiography on women's sports and sport medicine,[77] but also on worries about women's productivity as workers and employees. While conservative physicians, such as the gynecologist Hugo Sellheim, continued to warn about the adverse effects of competitive sports on women's reproductive systems, male and female physicians working at the DHfL rejected, for example, claims that sport had a negative impact on women's menstruation.[78] Instead, physicians and physical educators saw exercise and competitive sports as increasingly important for women's general health and physical performance.[79] Feminist sport teachers claimed that sport was the best way to prepare women for the competitiveness of modern life.[80] Others thought that physical fitness made it possible for women to cope with the double burden of their jobs and housework. Toughening up women's bodies was important for the health and productive strength of the nation. While the physician Fritz Kirchberg expressed concern about the negative impact of the declining birthrate on the biological viability of the German people, he thought that not much could be done about declining reproductivity, and he advocated instead increasing the working power of men and women. In his view, a new type of female sport teacher emerging from the DHfL had demonstrated that the most strenuous kind of physical labour had no adverse effects on women's health. In keeping with traditional notions of femininity, he still demanded that female sport teachers learn how to cook in order to prepare meals in accordance with the nutritional requirements of modern exercise science, but like other advocates of physical exercise, among them the outspoken mayor of Berlin Böß, he had abandoned notions of a deficient female physiology that needed special protection from physical exertions.[81]

Some employers recognized the importance of sport for women's health and well-being and promoted exercise programs in order to keep their female workforce happy and productive. The Berlin-based shoe store chain Leiser, for example, urged its female sales force to participate in gymnastics exercises during breaks as compensation for long hours of standing and unnatural postures. Physicians and physical educators also maintained that sport had a positive effect on the intellectual performance and character of women.[82] This was in line with their thinking more generally: they thought that exercise could improve the intellectual performance of men, women, and schoolchildren and turn them into performance-oriented subjects. The shaping of the body thus had important psychological components, which I discuss next.

II. Psychological Conditioning through Sport

Research on the physical performance potential of different body types found its counterpart in the attempts of psychologists to identify "the right man for the right job" through psychological testing. In the early Weimar years, industrial psycho-technics sought to pinpoint specific elementary abilities such as reaction times, visual and aural perspicacity, and manual dexterity in order to assess the suitability of job candidates. From the mid-1920s onward, psychologists shifted their assessment criteria to less tangible character traits of the worker personality as a whole, such as reliability, diligence, and conscientiousness.[83]

There are interesting parallels to be drawn between the research programs of sport and work psychologists that illuminate how they perceived the relationship between sport and work performances during the Weimar years. The DHfL took research and teaching on the psychological aspects of sport very seriously. Psychological discourses informed the practice of sport-teacher education in the Hochschule and a sport psychology laboratory pursued basic research on psychological aspects of sport.[84] As in the case of sport physiology, sport psychology was initially based on the premise that sport was a type of work (*sportliche Arbeit*). The first director of the DHfL's sport psychology laboratory, Robert Schulte, promoted a view of sport psychology as a form of aptitude psychology based on psycho-technical tests. Schulte was a former student of Wilhelm Wundt, the influential Leipzig psychologist who, from the 1870s onward, had devised a number of tests to measure basic psychological traits and abilities such as sensations, reaction times, and attention spans.[85]

Schulte believed that the theory and methodology of work psychology applied to sport psychology and that sport and physical exercise should play a vital role in a human economy, which aimed at the most efficient use of human resources.[86] Sport science was not a "luxury science." It was a practical science that promoted education through physical exercise and contributed to the strength of the people. The goal was to improve the mental and physical performances of individuals in the "interest of job performance and the national economy."[87] Sport was a means to lift the "efficiency (*Wirkungsgrad*) of the nation." It improved national "economic fitness" at a time when economic competition replaced war as a means of politics between nations. Schulte demanded that physicians, psychologists, and national economists quantify how physical exercise increased job performance.[88]

At the DHfL Schulte examined the abilities of elite athletes to determine the psychological traits that made them exceptional performers, but he also wished to apply the findings of this research to the physical education of the "broad mass of our people" in universities, schools, and sport associations. Sport was to help people reach their optimal physical and mental performance. Mental and physical inferiorities of individuals had to be diagnosed and corrected through sport therapy based on a close monitoring of their physical and mental development.[89]

As in the case of work psychology, Schulte designed tests that measured elementary abilities such as reaction times, dexterity, and visual abilities as well as attention spans and the ability to concentrate (see figure 2.4).[90] He devised psycho-technical experiments and tests to diagnose with some precision the aptitude of individuals for specific sports or jobs. This procedure again shows that he assumed that the psychological processes in work and sport were quite similar and that psychotechnical tests could identify the right person for an athletic discipline or work. The acuity of eyesight, the ability to measure distances, the accuracy of the fencer, the "beat and rhythm feeling" of rowers, attention, and concentration were all subject to physiological and psychotechnical measurements advocated by Schulte.[91] He maintained, for example, that relatively simple reaction trials could provide valuable insights into the relationship between physical and mental processes. The mental expressions (*seelische Ausdruckserscheinungen*) of physical impressions should therefore be subjected to exact psychophysical measurements. Schulte was quite aware of the shortcomings of the experimental measurements of elemental abilities in psycho-technics. Such simple measurements could not, for example, account for motivation and complex cognitive processes such as "the higher and more complex activities of the human will." Schulte insisted, however, that scientific laboratory experiments were fundamental to both work and sport psychology.[92]

In 1925, Schulte resigned from the DHfL. His successor, Hanns Sippel, was a psychologist who had made a name for himself with a dissertation on the impact of sport on the performance level of schoolchildren.

2.4 Sport psychologist Robert Schulte (centre) measuring reaction times during sprint start. Diem, *Hochschule*, 15. Private Collection.

As we shall see, the appointment of Sippel was more than just a change in personnel. It reflected a theoretical and methodological shift in the practice of sport psychology and physiology. The shift from the dissection of movements to the examination of entire movement complexes in sport physiology was accompanied by a similar shift to a more holistic and synthetic sport psychology with less emphasis on the diagnosis of elemental abilities through laboratory experiments. In a letter to Diem, Schulte regretted that after his departure from the DHfL scientific methods of performance testing based on laboratory experiments were neglected.[93] Diem did not share this regret. In his view, the DHfL had become an ideal place for a new "synthetic science" that integrated physiological and psychological approaches in sport research. Psychological research had demonstrated that the Italian physiologist Angelo Mosso's position that sport inevitably led to mental fatigue was wrong because sport could counter mental tiredness and increase the intellectual performance of individuals.[94] This conclusion meant that sport was no longer considered just another form of physical labour. It was seen as a form of work that took place under more favourable psychological circumstances; in other words, "sport labour" was motivated by considerable enthusiasm.[95]

The German sport and gymnastics movement had long claimed that physical activity during the school day could enhance the mental performance level of schoolchildren and so had campaigned for a daily hour of gymnastics.[96] Sippel provided the scientific rationale for this demand with his work on the relationship between physical exercise and mental performance.[97] With his study of the impact of physical exercise on schoolchildren, Sippel pursued two goals. First, he wanted to reject the prejudice that good physical development and high mental performance levels were mutually exclusive. Good gymnasts and good athletes, he argued, were more successful in school than those without sporting ability. He backed this up with statistical evidence from a 1915 study published in the *Journal for Applied Psychology* that showed that the best gymnasts earned better grades. Compared to students with lesser physical abilities they also had lower failure rates.[98] The second of Sippel's goals was to demonstrate that sporting activity did not diminish people's mental performance as Mosso and others had argued.[99] Instead, he claimed, physical exercise during school breaks could enhance students' mental performances and enable them to achieve their full performance potential. To demonstrate the validity of this claim, Sippel tested the mental performance of students before and after physical exercise. One of his tests asked students to add as many numbers as they could in a short period of time. The result was represented in the form of performance curves for individual students and as aggregate results for entire classes. He concluded that the results showed considerable improvement in students' mental performances after periods of physical exercise in terms of both quantity (the quantity of numbers students managed to add) and quality (the accuracy of students' calculations). Memory tests that evaluated students' ability to memorize words, pairs of words, or foreign language vocabulary provided additional evidence for Sippel's hypothesis that physical exercise served to improve the mental performance of students.[100]

Sippel moved away from a sport psychology based on the principles of psycho-technical work physiology. Instead of diagnosing elementary psychological characteristics that could be taken as an indicator of sporting or working ability, he claimed that his work demonstrated the "psychological depth structure" (*psychologische Tiefenstruktur*) of individuals and he tried to determine the ways in which the development of this structure in children and youths was influenced by physical exercise.[101] Sippel maintained that sport profoundly shaped the character of individuals by strengthening their will, self-confidence, and determination. He believed the physical labour in sport was different from other kinds of physical labour. Sport was not so much work; it was play that appealed to the natural drives of children and adults to move and therefore had a liberating and rejuvenating effect. Sport increased performance not because it reversed *physiological* fatigue but rather because it mobilized people's enthusiasm and helped them overcome *psychological* fatigue.[102] Children who were inattentive and unenthusiastic about schoolwork had to be given the opportunity to indulge their "natural" urges to move about. Then they would abandon their psychological inhibitions against mental work and their school performance would improve.[103] In that way sport helped to improve physical and mental performance levels. This thinking was in alignment with Diem's emphasis on the transformation of individual subjectivities as a precondition for a healthy and productive nation: sport formed firm and balanced characters who were not only full of joy but also endowed with a "will to work."[104]

Similar notions about psychological performance conditioning through sport informed contemporary debates about the psychological conditioning of young workers. The German Institute for Technical Work Schooling (*Deutsches Institut für Technische Arbeitsschulung*, DINTA) promoted sport and physical exercise for young workers and apprentices. Founded in 1925 and supported by heavy industry in Germany's west, the institute was led by Karl Arnhold who tried to develop new models for industrial leadership. He envisioned a new type of leadership that encouraged and educated workers to voluntarily submit to the hierarchies of the industrial workplace. DINTA-trained work engineers established training and educational programs for apprentices in many iron and steel and machine-building firms. Their pedagogy encouraged workers to develop a sense of individual responsibility and commitment to quality work and productivity. The programs tried to instil performance-oriented attitudes in workers by fostering a competitive spirit. The goal was to educate "skilled and flexible workers" (*wendige Arbeiter*) who were motivated to work enthusiastically for the benefit of the "company community" (*Werksgemeinschaft*). The DINTA concept was based on an assumption that a complex modern economy required certain subjective predispositions on the part of workers. Workers had to be able to work independently and make their own decisions, motivated by the will to contribute productively to the corporate community.[105] The institute tried to foster this will by "educating the worker for work." DINTA education, therefore, envisioned rationalizing the human factor in production by overcoming the worker's "inner resistance" against work.[106]

DINTA promoted sport for young apprentices to instil in them the "love of orderliness and cleanliness."[107] As part of an economic program for the rational utilization of human resources, Arnhold saw in sport and physical education a means to form reliable and performance-oriented worker characters. Competitive sports incited rivalries between different apprentice groups and raised their "will to perform." Arnhold shared Lewald and Diem's concern that the end of military conscription deprived German males of the character-forming benefits of military service. As compensation he advocated sport to create a new worker type who was accustomed to hard physical labour. The new worker would transfer his competitive attitude from the sport field to his work, and would be prepared to sacrifice his own interests for the benefit of the company community.[108] According to the DINTA engineer Hans Riedel, sport was a promising tool in the training of apprentices because education had to be linked with the experience of the young worker. (Such reasoning would later inform the rationale behind Nazi efforts to turn work into sport through the so-called Reich Vocational Competitions of the 1930s in which apprentices competed against each other in demonstrations of their vocational skills, see chapter 4.) Since apprentices had little work experience, Riedel maintained that vocational training had to appeal to experiences with which they were familiar. If workers understood their work training as analogous to sport training, they would be more prepared to work in a disciplined manner and accept unavoidable sacrifices. This value was in addition to the other benefits of sport, which included improving the physical fitness of young workers, making them more dexterous and skilful in their work, and turning them into tenacious and energetic human beings with a strong will.[109]

To the same end, at Hohenaschau, Karl Gebhardt tried to achieve a similar synthesis between sport and work training. While his exercise camps expended a great deal of effort in seeking to restore the physical working capacity of young workers, the main benefits of exercise therapy, according to Gebhardt, were psychological. Sport had a positive effect on people's entire nervous system. The "entire personality, mood, and character" would be "carried away," demonstrating that "physical exercise ... serves the intellectual and moral education of the people."[110] The first of Gebhardt's exercise camps in 1926 mirrored the hierarchical structures of industrial workplaces. He was leader, his deputy was an engineer, and various sub-leaders had different administrative functions. Others were skilled foremen in various vocational training roles. Exercise was meant to improve people's dexterity and lead into early "vocational training" (*Berufsvorschule*), which was supposed to be relevant for people's work.[111] This organization should not be seen as the idea of an idiosyncratic sport physician who had little experience of industrial work processes. It was in line with suggestions by employers to use sport movements for the rehearsal of "work movements" (*Arbeitsgriffe*). Friedrich Wilhelm von der Linde of the Union of German Employer Associations (*Vereinigung der deutschen Arbeitgeberverbände*), for example, suggested that sport could be used to train workers to balance and carry heavy loads.[112]

Similar to DINTA pedagogy, sport in combination with prevocational training was to form skilled, dexterous, and flexible workers who were well adjusted to the demands of a hierarchical, industrial workplace. Overt political indoctrination and military exercises were to be avoided during the camps but the apprentices were subjected to permanent control and military-style discipline to shape their character. They had to wear uniforms; follow strict rules; and keep themselves, their beds, and their workplace meticulously clean. The disciplinary regime at Hohenaschau was to foster a spirit of comradeship and community as a substitute for the military discipline that had supposedly underwritten work discipline before the war.[113]

The experience of the 1926 camp showed that the concept of prevocational education proved to be problematic. Attempts to develop specific physical exercises to improve dexterity for distinct work processes failed, because the movements for different work processes were too varied and complicated. Not unlike Sippel and Diem, Gebhardt realized that sport and exercise were not just another form of work. Lessons learned in sport could not simply be transferred to the workplace nor was it easy to adapt sport and exercise to needs of the industrial workplace.[114] In response to this realization, Gebhardt put even greater emphasis on the psychological benefits of play and sport. Similar to disability sport, Gebhardt's exercise therapy tried to instil self-confidence in his charges in order to counter feelings of inferiority. If weaklings could be brought to believe in the benefits of remedial exercise, they would develop "*joy* and [the] *will for performance*," which would have a positive effect on their working attitudes (emphasis in the original).[115] These performance-oriented attitudes were to be reinforced through the social settings at the camps. The apprentices were encouraged to take personal responsibility for their own health and for the running of the camp. In this respect sport served as an enabler for limited "self-governance by youth" within the boundaries and goals set by the camp's organizers. Young workers would thus become performance-oriented characters who wanted to do what they were expected to do because, as Gebhardt put it, they developed "self confidence and joy in their work obligation."[116]

During the Weimar years many employers promoted sport or physical exercise among their employees. According to an incomplete list by Friedrich Wilhelm von der Linde, there were more than one hundred plants of major corporations or mid-sized firms that supported sporting facilities or company sport clubs. Among the large corporations, there were Siemens, the United Steel Works, and IG Farben. Many of them introduced regular gymnastics and sport training for their apprentices.[117] In Linde's view, "a *good sportsman* is also a *good worker*" and "the educational effects of sport on the *character* of man are useful and significant for the office and factory" (emphasis in the original). Team sports were particularly valuable because they promoted "community feeling" and a "sense of personal responsibility" (*Selbstverantwortungsgefühl*) that fostered "leadership performance" and the will to act responsibly. At the same time, sport furthered discipline and the will to subordinate oneself and sacrifice "in the interest of a common ... goal." As a result, workers would have a positive attitude towards their work and would interpret the "fulfillment of their duties" in terms of a "sport performance."[118] In other words, sport fostered a performance-oriented human being willing to work and take initiative within the parameters set by the employer. Such ideas informed the practices of many employers who made regular participation in sport compulsory for their apprentices.[119] In Berlin, the electrical giant Siemens took this commitment so seriously that it monitored the sport performances of its apprentices in a special sport file.[120]

Employer support for sport was tied to the promotion of a company-community ideal that aimed to foster a sense of loyalty among their employees. In 1928, the Society for German Economic and Social Policy (*Gesellschaft für deutsche Wirtschafts- und Sozialpolitik*, or GWS), a right-wing employer-friendly lobbying organization supported by a number of major German banks (including the *Deutsche Bank* and the *Darmstädter und Nationalbank*), organized a workshop on gymnastics and sport in industry that was held during the Berlin Gymnastics and Sport Week. It included presentations by DRAL president Lewald and members of the GWS and served to promote the hygienic and economic benefits of company sport. During the afternoon, gymnastics and exercise presentations by workers of major Berlin employers (*Deutsche Bank, AEG,* and *BEWAG*) advertised their companies' sport programs in what was, as a critical observer noted, a promotion of the "company-community idea" in which sport and gymnastics served the "yellow" cause (a reference to employer-friendly pseudo-unions).[121]

The GWS argued that the German economy had no choice but to increase its profitability through technological rationalization and "greater and more intense performance" by workers. Sport and gymnastics were to compensate for the adverse health effects of intensive work and ensure the long-term viability of increases in performance.[122] The main advocate of such ideas in the GWS was Friedrich Bartels, later a promoter of Nazi performance medicine in his function as Deputy Reich Health Leader.[123] In Bartels' view, sport was a means for the "education of the performance-capable, performance-merry (*leistungsfroh*) and morally firm human," a notion that anticipated the concept of the performance-oriented people's comrade of the Nazi period (see chapter 3).[124] In combination with positive incentives for workers, such as performance-based wages, the GWS, like DINTA, used sport to promote the idea of a company community of employers and employees with a common interest in the economic success of the enterprise. In order to further these goals, the GWS offered financial support to the German umbrella organization for company sport, the *Reichsarbeitsgemeinschaft der Behörden- und Firmensportverbände,* or RAG, an organization that attempted to incorporate company sport clubs all over Germany.[125]

Not surprisingly, socialist and communist advocates of worker's sport were for the most part hostile to the company-community idea and company sport clubs controlled or fostered by employers. For them the principle of using sport to increase work performance was a particularly devious means to exercise control over the workforce and undermine working-class solidarity.[126] The ways in which some employers imposed sport on their workers must have exacerbated their concerns. Some companies forced their workers to exercise during breaks to compensate for sedentary or one-sided work. Workers and unions resented this demand because it deprived workers of self-determination during their work breaks.[127] Sippel also criticized this type of physical exercise as counterproductive, because it turned sport into an aspect of work instead of mobilizing the enthusiasm generated by voluntary physical activities for better work performance.[128]

Consequently, the DINTA and many employers supported the voluntary engagement of young workers in popular sports during their leisure time. Soccer teams were promoted because team sports encouraged comradeship and sacrifice for the good of the team. Gymnastics promoted vigour and dexterity, while track and field disciplines and boxing pitted "man against man" and rewarded strong and assertive characters. In this way sport promoted "working skills, the will to perform, the ability to subordinate oneself, and the joy of fighting," which, according to DINTA pedagogy, were all important character traits of productive and happy workers.[129]

Psychological discourses on performance enhancement and character formation promoted sport as an important educational tool. They played a central role in the spread of sport in schools, private industry, and public services such as the German railroad or the German postal service. Transforming the subjective attitudes of workers and citizens was as important to Weimar sport scientists, educators, government officials, and employers as was the preservation and enhancement of their physical health and performance potential.

III. Sport, Qualitative Population Policies, and *Wehrhaftmachung* between Weimar and Nazism

During the 1920s, physicians, psychologists, physical educators, business leaders, and government officials thought that sport would have to play a central role in the recovery of the German nation. In survey after survey, physicians diagnosed the deficient fitness of the population and warned of dire consequences for the health, performance levels, and productivity of people. Sport was to be a therapy of the national body or, as the mayor (*Oberbürgermeister*) of Cologne and the future chancellor of the Federal Republic Konrad Adenauer put it in 1927: "Sport is the practical physician at the sick bed of the German Volk."[130] Sport figured prominently in discussions about human resources, their utilization, and their refinement. As a performance enhancement tool, the promotion of sport held promises similar to the rehabilitative, therapeutic, and preventive trends in social welfare, medicine, and psychiatry: the production of healthy and willingly productive citizens.[131]

There were similarities as well as differences between German promotions of mass sport and what happened in other countries. Some American and French employers, for example, also hoped that company sport would lead to a greater identification of workers with their companies and make workers more productive and contented.[132] In France and in Britain there was also a broad public discourse about national regeneration through physical education and sport, which linked anxieties about declining virility with concerns about productivity and the military fitness of recruits.[133] But while Weimar governments at all levels turned to the promotion of sport in order to cope with the human costs and social dislocations caused by the First World War, at least in the 1920s such government interventions did not have a counterpart in most Western countries.[134] There were, however, similarities with the situation in the early Soviet Union where the government looked to mass sport as a means to raise the quality of the population. After the massive human losses caused by epidemics, civil war, and the famines of 1921/22, the Soviet promotion of *Fizkult'ura* addressed hygiene and public health concerns.[135] As one of the first steps in restoring the health of the population, the Higher Soviet for Physical Education (founded in 1922) declared physical culture a compulsory subject for all schoolchildren in 1923. As in Weimar Germany, mass sport was promoted to improve the quality of the labour force and the productivity of men and women. Factory-based sporting activities were supposed to develop useful physical skills, reduce workplace injuries, and improve the psychological and physical performance levels of workers. From the early 1930s, sport also served to foster competitive values among workers in a system of socialist competition that promoted ever-increasing productivity.[136] While there were efforts in both countries to harness sport in the service of productivity, the impoverished Soviet Union could not pour as many resources into the mass promotion of fitness as the Weimar state or later the Nazi regime.[137]

In Germany psychological and medical debates about human performance management were informed by similar economic assumptions as the discourse on hereditary health and eugenics. Both demands for eugenics or *Rassenhygiene* and discussions about performance conditioning of body and mind were complementary aspects of Weimar biopolitics. Propagators of sport and eugenics argued that it was necessary to improve the quality of the population because the war had done great damage to the health of the workforce and limited the nation's human performance potential at a time when it was urgently needed for the economic recovery after the war. Therefore, they proposed countermeasures to raise the fitness of the population, which they defined in terms of people's ability to contribute socially and economically to German society. Eugenics and performance enhancement through sport were both based on a rationale of preventive social hygienic engineering. Eugenics or racial hygiene aimed at preventing hereditarily diseased offspring, while the promotion of sport was based on a notion of "preventive care" (*vorsorgende Fürsorge*). Because they promised to create productive citizens, both strategies were seen as recipes for controlling spiralling health and social insurance costs. The complementarity of these approaches is sometimes apparent in the work of the same person. A good example is the psychiatrist Ewald Stier, an important figure in the Weimar debate on pension neurosis and its cost to the German state. While Stier favoured the compulsory sterilization of "degenerative psychopaths," he also advocated sport and rational body care to promote the productivity of the workforce.[138]

Eugenicists intended to improve the hereditary performance potential of future generations; propagators of performance enhancement through sport claimed that physical exercise helped people fully mobilize their hereditary potential. While these strategies were complementary and promised to improve the efficiency, performance, and competitiveness of the German population in the future, their relative importance varied depending on the circumstances. Between 1924 and 1929/30, the years of stability of the Weimar Republic, sport and physical exercise received comparatively generous financial and organizational support from national, state, and municipal governments. This would change during the Great Depression. With the transition from the "regenerative" to the "degenerative" welfare state, to use the terms coined by Greg Eghigian, there was less emphasis on "preventive welfare" through physical exercise.[139] Because of the crisis of the Weimar welfare state, the emphasis on the prevention of hereditarily diseased offspring received greater credence with political authorities towards the end of the republic, in part because it promised to curb welfare expenses in the long run. Public support for sport would dwindle, as would other programs of the Weimar welfare state. Reich support for gymnastics and exercise was halved between 1928 and 1931, troubling both the DRAL and the army, which looked for new strategies to ensure the physical fitness and defensive preparedness (*Wehrhaftmachung*) of the entire population.[140]

During the 1920s, support for sport was an important element of social rationalization in private companies. But this backing could not be sustained after 1930. During the Depression, many employers had to scale back their support for company welfare and sport. Still, there is evidence to suggest that some large employers rated the disciplinary and educational aspects of sport so highly that they continued to fund sport-related activities.[141] In 1931, for example, employers in the port cities of Bremen and Hamburg (among them the Darmstädter, National-Bank, and two major oil firms) formed a sponsorship committee for the Reich League of Company Sport Clubs to promote company sport more effectively.[142]

While state and private support for sport came under intensifying pressure during the Depression, mass sport found an increasingly influential advocate in the *Reichswehr*. With the demise of the last parliamentary government under Reich Chancellor Hermann Müller in March 1930, the army took the chance to push for greater state support for enhancing the military fitness of the broad mass of the German population. *Reichswehrminister* Wilhelm Groener's plans for "youth fortification" (*Jugendertüchtigung*) were part of his concept of a militia designed to support the professional core of the *Reichswehr*. In his view, mass sport promoted both physical and psychological fitness and strengthened the defensive will of the population, which had suffered since the end of conscription.[143]

Earlier attempts by the army to support mass sport training in so-called *Volkssportschulen* had to be abandoned in 1926 after protests by the Inter-allied Control Commission, which saw in such efforts a violation of the Treaty of Versailles.[144] While Versailles explicitly prohibited connections between the military and private associations including sport clubs, Groener argued that this did not preclude state support for physical education of male youth "in the interest of the defence of the country." He demanded that the state push the envelope and support "the physical education of its youth to the boundaries where the specific 'military' training according to the wording of the Treaty of Versailles begins." He also demanded a shift in the priorities of sport funding according to the needs of the army. He questioned, for example, the need to provide funds for special interests such as the Mary Wigmann School for dance or youth hostels.[145] With reference to the 1930 September Reichstag elections, in which the Nazi Party had for the first time received mass electoral support on the national level, he declared that "the state with its passivity and partial intolerance of [popular] ... striving for *Wehrhaftigkeit* has provided the ground for radical agitation." According to Groener, state support for premilitary physical training would thus help to curb the rise of the radical right and serve the interests of the *Reichswehr* and the republic at the same time.[146]

In pushing for greater state support for premilitary training, the army leadership insisted on a distinction between the promotion of general fitness that benefited the military and specialized military training, claiming that "'*Wehrhaftmachung*' is not 'military training.'"[147] It supported the long-standing DRAL demand for one hour of gymnastics and sport per day for schoolchildren and endorsed the DRAL's request for more Reich funding for physical exercise. The DRAL demands for 3 to 5 million RM per year would not only have reversed the funding cuts after 1929 but more than doubled the annual funding compared to 1928. (Reich funding projected for 1931 was only 750,000 RM.)[148]

As the Depression worsened and violent political confrontations on the streets between the left and the right became more frequent, considerations of social cohesion gained importance for the military leadership, who advocated physical exercise for unemployed youth as "education for self discipline and order" (*Erziehung zu Zucht und Ordnung*).[149] Under the new Reichswehrminister, Kurt von Schleicher, plans to create an institutional basis for the physical training of youth finally materialized. In September 1932, the army's efforts culminated in the establishment of the Reich Board for the Fortification of Youth (*Reichskuratorium für Jugendertüchtigung* or RK) by Reich President Hindenburg. The new institution was jointly administered by the Ministry of the Interior and the Reichswehr but its acting president was the retired infantry general Edwin von Stülpnagel. The RK supported field sport (*Geländesport*) as preparation for military training. Similar to the Prussian youth care decree two decades earlier, the new initiative tried to change the attitude of young men towards an authoritarian state. Apart from the "steeling of the body," this militarized version of sport aimed at fostering conservative attitudes, including "self discipline, love of order, [military] comradeship, preparedness to sacrifice for the whole," and "love of the common fatherland and the soil of the *Heimat*."[150] The authoritarian thrust of the new decree was most succinctly expressed by the famous surgeon and new director (*Rektor*) of the DHfL, Ferdinand Sauerbruch: young people had "to learn to obey, shut up, accept authority and dispense with their individuality (*Eigenart der Person*)."[151]

The RK was dominated by the Reichswehr, which tried to get bourgeois sport and youth organizations as well as right-wing paramilitaries, including the Nazi SA and the Stahlhelm, interested in the idea. By November 1932, there were sixteen schools, which offered three weeks of training in *Geländesport*.[152] The impact of the new institution was short-lived. It became superfluous after the Nazi takeover because the new regime used its mass organizations (in particular the SA, the Hitler Youth, the Labour Front, and the Reich Labour Service) to promote the physical training and toughening up of German youth.[153] The short history of the RK, however, demonstrates the degree to which the idea to utilize sport as a means to build social cohesion had been accepted. While right-wing paramilitary organizations and bourgeois youth clubs dominated the RK's membership, in the beginning even the paramilitary organization *Reichsbanner Schwarz-Rot-Gold*, which was close to the Social Democratic Party and supported the republic, considered seeking representation at the RK. This did not happen, however, because of pressure from the SPD.[154]

In the 1920s, most promoters of sport thought in terms of strengthening Germany's *Volkskraft* as a way to raise the health and productivity of the population. They also emphasized the psychological benefits of physical exercise. Sport, they believed, would shape firm and reliable characters that were willing to subordinate their own interests to the interests of the productive community. Demands to foster military fitness only moved centre stage during the final crisis period of the republic. It was the Nazi regime that created a new biopolitical synthesis that connected civilian and military fitness. The Nazis embarked on a ruthless campaign of racial hygienic elimination as they also tried to mobilize millions of Germans in sporting competitions in order to advance the project of a German performance community (*Leistungsgemeinschaft*) ready to work hard and go to war.

Chapter Three

Conditioning People's Comrades

"The fight against the inferior is a self-evident precondition ... for a ... farsighted population policy. Apart from the number of people the quality of the population plays a decisive role for the continued existence of the state. With the elimination of bad hereditary lines only the minimum has been achieved; what matters is to unburden the good existing hereditary predispositions from disruptive inhibitions and do everything on the part of the state to further these predispositions ... toward the best performance."[1]

In 1934 sport physician Hans Hoske wrote these words, which encapsulated the most important goals of Nazi population policies. On the one hand, the quality of the population was to be guaranteed through racial hygienic selection that aimed to exclude the "inferior" from procreation. On the other hand, the state had to make sure that people with "valuable" hereditary traits could develop their individual performance potential to the fullest for the benefit of the state. Racial hygienic measures had been discussed in Germany for a long time. What was new after 1933 in terms of population policies was the political will and the capacity of the state to enforce negative population measures, such as forced sterilization, through the Law for the Prevention of Hereditarily Ill Offspring of July 1933. Nazism radicalized eugenic trends in German biopolitics by promoting a radical biological selectionism that culminated in Nazi sterilization and extermination programs.

Yet, despite the Nazi obsession with heredity, one should not overlook continuities with other aspects of German biopolitics. While improving the heredity of people was crucial in the Nazi world view, it was equally important to make sure that all healthy "Aryan" Germans realized their full hereditary potential. Since *Leibesübungen* were to create healthy and productive people with performance-oriented characters, the promotion of sport for the masses promised to turn the racial *Volksgemeinschaft* into a *Leistungsgemeinschaft* of productive citizens. This other side of qualitative biopolitics – the elimination of social and environmental factors inhibiting people's performance potential – had always been a non-controversial aspect of Weimar biopolitics. In this respect physicians such as Hans Hoske and Karl Gebhardt could simply continue with what they had promoted since the 1920s: healthy living including systematic physical exercise and sport as a way to enhance the physical performance and the self-confidence of children, youths, and adults. Hoske and Gebhardt had successful careers during the Nazi period. While sport physicians with Jewish ancestry, like Fritz Duras and Herbert Herxheimer, lost their university positions in Freiburg and Berlin, Hoske became an official in the Nazi Party's Main Office for People's Health (*Hauptamt für Volksgesundheit*), while Gebhardt became one of the leading sport physicians of the Third Reich and one of the most senior physicians of the SS with close links to Heinrich Himmler.[2] They both exemplify a strand in Nazi biopolitics that tried to exploit the full hereditary potential of Germans in the service of higher productivity and military preparedness.[3]

This chapter first looks at the changing political and institutional landscape for the promotion of mass sport. It examines the final years of the DHfL briefly and discusses how the establishment of the Reich Academy for Physical Exercise (*Reichsakademie für Leibesübungen* or RAL) reflected political changes in the utilization of sport as a means to enhance the fitness and psychological mobilization of the nation. Exercise as a form of "political physical education" (*politische Leibeserziehung*) in a dictatorship merged pre-1933 utilitarian approaches of the use of sport in the service of higher productivity with political indoctrination. Sport teachers trained at the RAL were to instil in students soldierly virtues, courage, and the mental and physical toughness required of the ideal people's comrade, one who was expected to make great sacrifices in the service of the national community.

The second section examines physicians' attempts to promote sport in order to improve people's fitness. While Nazi sport physicians were also concerned about the health of German top athletes – the physicians of the RAL, for example, were responsible for the examination of Germany's Olympic athletes[4] – their main focus was on increasing the fitness and productivity of the broad mass of people. Making people productive, the "*Produktivierung des Menschen*" as Susanne Heim called it, was central to Nazi performance medicine and biopolitics and sport was to play a crucial role in this project.[5] Physicians and other promoters of sport worked within the political frameworks of the regime's hereditary health and racial policies, but they also emphasized the importance of environmental factors for national health. In their view, there were many hereditarily healthy and racially acceptable people's comrades who, for reasons of personal irresponsibility or social disadvantage, were physically weak and thus unable to cope with the physical demands of their jobs. Fitness campaigns and sport therapies could remedy this state by turning underperforming but hereditarily valuable people's comrades into valuable productive members of the racial community.

The final sections discuss attempts to promote mass sport through Nazi mass organizations and the workplace. A "people in physical exercise" (*Volk in Leibesübungen*) was the professed goal of Nazi sport officials who thought that mass sport had a unifying effect on the German population and would increase people's willingness to work and be productive. Nazi mass organizations, such as the Hitler Youth, the SA, and the German Labour Front leisure organization "Strength through Joy," promoted *Leibesübungen* for their alleged pedagogical and ideological benefits. In addition, the Nazi period witnessed the widespread use of physical performance tests and surveys, which not only gave indications about the state of fitness of the population but also served to encourage people to work on their own fitness. The SA sport medal, for example, was awarded to three million Germans who had demonstrated their fitness in a series of fitness tests and sporting competitions. People who were considered racially and hereditarily inferior were excluded from these assessments, while healthy Germans were encouraged to exercise and demonstrate at regular intervals that they were valuable members of the racial community.[6] Members of the Hitler Youth were subjected to regular health examinations as well as encouraged to train for the HJ "Performance Medal" (*Leistungsabzeichen*), for which they had to demonstrate basic capacities in sport, paramilitary, and shooting exercises.[7]

Going back to the Weimar period, there was the hope that competitive attitudes in the sport arena would translate into improved workplace productivity. In this respect, *Leibesübungen* were not only a means to improve people's health and physical performance levels; rather, the excitement and joy generated by sport were instruments for the psychological moulding of performance-oriented subjects. Ideally, increased productivity was not the result of coercion but the pedagogical outcome of a competitive, performance-oriented habitus that shaped people's understandings of themselves and the society they lived in. The German Labour Front, through its "Strength through Joy" leisure organization, offered sport courses and activities after work. It promoted company sport events to break down social barriers between different categories of employees and, to a lesser extent, between employers and employees. Sport and physical education sought to train performance-oriented, combative individuals who were prepared to voluntarily make sacrifices for the good of the national community at work and ultimately at war as well. Claims to community membership, citizenship rights, and social rewards were thus based on an individual's fitness and productivity as well as his or her commitment to the political ideals of Nazi Weltanschauung.

I. Sport Science, Sport Pedagogy, and Politics: From the DHfL to the Reich Academy for Physical Exercise

In the years 1933 and 1934, the DHfL, the only national sport science and training institution in Germany, experienced a slow but steady decline. In some ways this can be interpreted as a continuation of the problems that the institution had faced since 1929. Even before the onset of the Depression, the DHfL was forced to end its promising collaboration with the Kaiser Wilhelm Institute for Work Physiology. The KWIA was moved to Dortmund to be closer to the expected funding opportunities provided by West German industry.[8] The funding shortages caused by the Great Depression worsened the situation. The DHfL had to cut staff and for financial reasons was forced into a close working relationship with its Prussian competitor, the PHfL, as well as the Institutes for Physical Exercise at Friedrich Wilhelm University and the Technical University in Berlin-Charlottenburg. The goal of this organizational change was to streamline the education of sport teachers.[9] Given the financial constraints, sport science research came to a virtual halt during the final years of the DHfL. The de facto director of its three medical laboratories (anthropometric, x-ray, and physiological laboratory) was a single physician, Frohwalt Heiss, who from 1931 gave lectures in sport medicine and was responsible for the medical education of the students. Since he worked only part-time at the DHfL, the medical sport research that was conducted there must have been rather limited.[10] The DHfL did not fare as badly as the PHfL, which was closed in 1932, but it never regained its former status as a nationally significant institution that combined state of the art sport research with sport-teacher training.

The Nazi rise to power not surprisingly brought about changes in the leadership and structure of German sport institutions. Carl Diem, acting director of the DHfL and general secretary of the DRAL, lost both his positions, even though he tried to adapt to the new political circumstances. He made suggestions for the coordination of German sport associations and advocated the introduction of the Führer principle to the administration of sport with the aim of recommending himself as Reich commissioner for German sport. These moves turned out to be in vain when in April 1933 the SA Gruppenführer Hans von Tschammer und Osten was appointed to the leadership position. As *Reichssportführer*, Tschammer became the leader of the Reich League for Physical Exercise (*Reichsbund für Leibesübungen*, or RBL), which was founded in January 1934. The Reichsbund (from 1938 called NS-RBL) replaced the DRAL as the national organization for sport and gymnastics associations. But, in contrast to the DRAL, the RBL was not a free association of sport clubs. It operated strictly according to the *Führerprinzip*. Within the Reichsbund, the bourgeois sport clubs continued to exist, but in the course of Nazification (*Gleichschaltung*) politically unreliable leaders were purged and Jews were expelled from both the leadership and membership.[11] Almost all sport and gymnastics clubs associated with the Socialist and Communist labour movements were dissolved. The former members were scrutinized to ensure that they did not oppose the new regime before they were allowed to join bourgeois clubs.[12]

Despite being removed from his most important positions, Diem remained as chief organizer of the 1936 Olympic games. The president of the organizing committee was Lewald, who was also a member of the International Olympic Committee (IOC) from 1924 to 1936. Lewald's position was also rather tenuous because he was considered partially Jewish, but the Nazi regime drew on the international connections and reputations of Lewald and Diem in order to deflect criticism of Nazi racial policies in the lead-up to the games. After 1936, Lewald was forced to retire and resign his post as an IOC member, while Diem had to content himself with relatively minor positions in the Nazi sport administration.[13]

The *Rektor* of the DHfL, the famous surgeon Ferdinand Sauerbruch, who had been Karl Gebhardt's teacher at the University of Munich in the 1920s and who had taken over the formal leadership of the DHfL from his colleague the surgeon August Bier in 1931, was also regarded with suspicion by representatives of the new regime because of his prominent role during the Weimar Republic. He had to resign because of doubts about his political reliability. According to Gebhardt, the professor of surgery at the University of Munich, Erich Lexer, had passed on incriminating information about Sauerbruch to Reich Physician Leader Gerhard Wagner who used this information to press for Sauerbruch's removal. In 1930 and 1931, Sauerbruch had voiced doubts about the Nazi movement to a leading member of the NS Physicians' League and denounced the anti-Semitism of the movement. Sauerbruch had claimed that a true physician could not be a Nazi: "A physician cannot be anti-Semite, otherwise he is not a physician. But you must be anti-Semite if you are a National Socialist."[14] To make matters worse, it was well known among physicians that Sauerbruch had (unsuccessfully) supported his Jewish assistants when they were threatened by dismissal through the Law for the Restoration of the Civil Service and, in 1933, he had been the only surgeon to oppose the decision by the committee of the German National Congress of Surgeons not to allow presentations by Jewish surgeons. He was accused of speaking out "openly and unambiguously against one of the main goals of National Socialism, namely the purging of the German intelligentsia and science from racially alien spirit (*artfremden Geist*) and racially alien leadership." While Sauerbruch was forced from the DHfL, his public and scientific reputation ensured that he retained his professorship and remained one of the most influential German medical professors. Nonetheless, he stood in the way of the political transformation of the DHfL, which in Reich Physician Leader Wagner's vision was to become one of the main educational institutions for the leadership of German youth.[15]

Coinciding with the Berlin Olympic games, the DHfL was replaced by the *Reichsakademie für Leibesübungen*. The reasons for the closure of the DHfL are not fully clear. A key factor in its further decline and eventual replacement by the *Reichsakademie* were the rivalries between two competing ministerial bureaucracies. Both the physical education official Carl Krümmel in the newly founded Reich Education Ministry and the *Reichssportführer* von Tschammer und Osten in the Reich Ministry of the Interior tried to obtain control of the DHfL. As a result it was caught in limbo. As Tschammer explained to Diem in March 1934, he did not intend to invest in the DHfL at that point because he feared he might lose control of the institution.[16] Eventually the founding of the RAL would solve this situation with a compromise: as a result of Hitler's decision, the Reich Ministry of the Interior and the Reich Education Ministry would jointly administer the new institution. In a solution that saved his face as Reich Sport Leader, Tschammer became president – purely a figurehead of the new institution – while Krümmel became its acting director responsible for running the academy.[17]

The opening of the *Reichsakademie* did not mean a complete break with the DHfL. Many sport teachers at the DHfL continued to give courses in sport-teacher training and Frohwalt Heiss remained the senior resident physician at the institution under the new director of its medical institute, Karl Gebhardt. Yet, while there was significant continuity between the two institutions in terms of personnel, the RAL was in many ways quite different from its predecessor. In contrast to the DHfL, which during the Weimar years had been a private organization owned by the *Deutscher Reichsausschuss für Leibesübungen* and also had received some state support, the *Reichsakademie* was a state-run institution. As such it was a vehicle for the practice-oriented educational agenda of the regime. Its main task was to provide uniform leadership training for sport teachers in schools and exercise leaders who taught sport in the growing sector of NS mass organizations, though it also offered additional qualifications for physicians who wanted to practice as sport physicians. Furthermore, the *Reichsakademie* was primarily a teaching college. Unlike the DHfL in the 1920s, it did not have departments for basic research on the physiological and psychological aspects of sport science.[18] In this respect it was similar to the fascist sport academies for men and women in Italy that opened in Rome and Orvieto in 1928 and 1932 respectively, places where sport instructors were trained for the fascist militia and youth and mass organizations.[19]

Sport teachers and exercise leaders were highly sought after commodities during the Third Reich due to the promotion of physical fitness in Nazi mass organizations. The Reich League for Physical Exercise came under increasing pressure from the Hitler Youth, which claimed sole responsibility for the physical education of children and young people and eventually forced the RBL clubs to focus on competitive sports for adults. Along with the HJ, the SS, SA, and the German Labour Front organization *Kraft durch Freude* (KdF) also recruited exercise leaders. The Labour Front saw in popular sport a means to enhance the productivity of workers and shape their attitudes towards the regime. Demand from the KdF was so high that it caused major tensions between itself and the RBL whose leaders accused the KdF of luring coaches and exercise teachers away from sport clubs.[20]

While the *Reichsakademie* was not the only institution in Nazi Germany that trained sport teachers and exercise leaders, its one-year courses were to provide a political model for other courses elsewhere. Schoolteachers trained at the academy were encouraged to engage themselves professionally and politically in Nazi mass organizations and sport clubs. Demonstrated political engagement was already a precondition for admission to the course.[21] Apart from university graduates who tried to qualify as sport teachers, the academy also admitted skilled workers after they had finished their vocational training. "A typesetter, a fitter, a carpenter who has excelled in sport and ... proven himself in competitions can become a sport teacher here," the *Reichssportblatt* declared. This principle underscored the regime's claims that Nazi society was open to talents from all walks of life, provided they met racial selection criteria and demonstrated an appropriate level of political engagement.[22]

The *Reichsakademie* had three departments: a sport training institute (*Sportpraktisches Institut*), which conducted sport teacher training; a biological institute, which focused on racial political indoctrination; and a medical institute, which specialized in sport and work injuries. Responsible for the practical training of sport teachers at the RAL was the director of the training institute, Otto Nerz, former national coach of the German soccer team.[23] Nerz was a graduate of the DHfL and worked there as a lecturer between 1924 and 1935. In 1936 he received a doctorate in medicine from the University of Berlin. His medical dissertation, "Late Injuries of Knee Joints after Accidents at Work and at Sport," was a topic that fitted in well with his qualification as a soccer coach and the rehabilitative medical emphasis of the academy's medical department under Gebhardt. He was appointed extraordinary professor at the University of Berlin for the pedagogy of physical exercise even though he did not have a habilitation (the formal academic requirement to become a professor at a German university). The professorship was an irregular arrangement that was financed by the Reich and only nominally located at the university. Nerz had no teaching obligations there; he only taught at the *Reichsakademie*.[24] From the point of view of the NS University Teachers League (*NS-Dozentenbund*), Nerz had a tainted past because he had been a member of the Social Democratic Party during the Weimar Republic. In January 1939, the district leader of the league, Willi Willing, denounced Nerz's attitude as opportunistic. He considered his appointment a great mistake, only made possible by the negligence of the Reich Education

Ministry. Since it was impossible to get Nerz fired, the NS University Teachers League wanted to at least make sure that he was never appointed as a full professor.[25]

The concerns about Nerz's political reliability proved to be unfounded. After 1933, the former Social Democrat more than made up for his allegedly problematic past with tirades about threats of "Jewification" (*Verjudung*) of soccer during the republic.[26] Nerz's anti-Semitic attitudes made him perfect for an institution that regarded political commitment to Nazism as a sine qua non for sport teachers. This pattern also holds true for the racial scientist Bruno K. Schultz, the director of the biological institute of the *Reichsakademie*. Schultz's qualification was in racial anthropology. His habilitation thesis examined the racial make-up of populations in the border regions of Bavaria and Austria. As an expert in racial science, he continued his career in the NS state as an SS officer in the Race and Settlement Main Office of the SS and finally as a professor for racial biology at the University of Prague.[27]

Schultz used the occasion of the 1936 Olympics to develop his racial ideas further. In his view, the games provided a unique opportunity to investigate the relationship between race and performance. But, because of international suspicion of the regime's racial-political intentions, which he attributed to "Jewish rabble-rousing" (*jüdische Hetze*) abroad, he could not take full advantage of this "opportunity." A thorough physical examination of athletes from different countries, as Wolfgang Kohlrausch had done during the 1928 Amsterdam Olympics, was therefore not possible. Schultz had to make do with impressionistic observations about the racial composition of the different Olympic teams. He was, for example, impressed by the "positive racial image" of the Finnish, Belgian, and Hungarian teams and disturbed by the racial composition of the American team.[28]

For Schultz, competitive and combative attitudes were typical of Nordic racial types as evidenced by Germany's athletes. Top sport performances were important for the racial community because good competitors inspired the community by providing a "performance ideal" or *Leistungsvorbild* (see figures 3.1 and 3.2). They also facilitated racial selection by matching men and women of good physical development, an argument that already had great currency among some promoters of physical culture at the turn of the century.[29] The strong emphasis on racial science further reveals how the *Reichsakademie* was quite different from the DHfL before 1933. It was an institution with an explicit political mission in the service of National Socialism. In addition to

3.1 Nordic Performance Ideal: 1932 Olympic Weightlifting Champion Rudolf Ismayer. Bruno K. Schultz, "Die rassenbiologische Bedeutung der Leibesübungen," in *Volk und Rasse* (1936), 342. Printed with permission from Universitätsbibliothek Tübingen.

3.2 Nordic Performance Ideal: 1936 Olympic Discus Throwing Champion Gisela Mauermeyer during the Shot Put. Schultz, "rassenbiologische Bedeutung," 344. Printed with permission from Universitätsbibliothek Tübingen.

providing technical training for sport instructors, it also indoctrinated them with the racial-biological principles of Nazism.

Claims about a racial basis for sport performance were common during the Nazi period. These were not just tied to older anti-Semitic assertions about an innate Jewish inaptitude for sport and military service.[30] In the wake of the 1936 Olympics, these notions were also used to argue for an innate German or Nordic superiority on the sport field more generally. Walther Jaensch, an expert in constitutional medicine who had given psychology lectures at the DHfL during its final years, and Auguste Hoffmann, an Olympic physician and former colleague of Jaensch at the DHfL, argued that race was an important factor in top sport performances. Winners in the track and field and gymnastics disciplines, they claimed, usually exhibited pronounced Nordic racial traits. This conclusion was not disturbed by the fact, discussed extensively by the authors, that African-American athletes like Jesse Owens dominated most track and field disciplines during the Berlin Olympics. The authors even published a surprisingly intimate image that showed "the primarily Nordic" German Lutz Long, the runner-up in the long jump, together with the "mixed-blood" Olympic champion Owens. According to Jaensch and Hoffmann, the psychological racial type of Nordics was particularly suited to sporting competitions, "because performance is the dominant value in the order of values" of Nordics. In the Nordic man (and Nordic woman) "physical form, character, and race" reinforced each other with the effect "that he seemed particularly suited for the highest Olympic performances." In this view, the "German Olympic champions represented a selection of the best Nordic race."[31]

However, while the highest performances among German elite athletes were welcomed by the Nazi regime as evidence of racial superiority, Nazi biopolitics was organized around improving the fitness of all Germans, including "weaklings" who posed a burden to society because they were underperforming.

II. Sport, Productivity, and the Regeneration of the *Schwächling*

The medical institute of the *Reichsakademie* was committed to the principles of Nazi "performance medicine," which was concerned with enhancing or restoring the physical and psychological performance capacities of people. In doing so, the academy's medical director Karl Gebhardt further developed what he called "exercise therapy"

(*Übungsbehandlung*), carefully administered doses of exercise that zeroed in on the rehabilitation of people who had suffered from serious sport and work injuries. Gebhardt had obtained his position at the *Reichsakademie* in part by denouncing Wolfgang Kohlrausch, the former director of the anthropometric laboratory at the DHfL, as a "typical representative of a liberalistic, unrealistic ... individual attitude." Kohlrausch had built a school for physiotherapy in the surgical clinic of the University of Berlin and was thus one of Gebhardt's main competitors in the field of exercise therapy.[32] Rehabilitating injured people was only one aspect of Gebhardt's exercise therapy. Equally important were social-political applications that promoted the health and fitness of socially disadvantaged, underperforming youths. Building on his work with apprentices during the Weimar years (see chapter 2), Gebhardt wanted to turn "weaklings" (*Schwächlinge*) into worthy, productive members of the racial people's community in exercise camps that provided them with good nutrition, wholesome outdoor activities, and exercise.

It is possible to describe changes between Weimar and Nazi social hygiene and welfare in terms of a shift from need-based social care to community-oriented social prevention. While in the 1920s progressive social welfare advocates tended to emphasize individual social needs, the years after 1930 saw a pronounced shift towards preventive welfare in which measures were increasingly justified in terms of racial hygienic prevention. Nazi welfare rejected help for the inferior (*Minderwertigenfürsorge*) aiming instead to prevent future harm to – and financial burdens on – the national community through racial hygienic intervention.[33] After the Nazi seizure of power, the principle of "racial general prevention" tried to nip biological threats to the people's community in the bud either through negative eugenics or repression against people who were either unwilling or unable to be productive.[34] There is a lot of truth in this account but it can also be misleading if cast in terms of a linear development. As we have seen in the chapters on the Weimar period, the propaganda for mass sport certainly addressed issues of individual needs and social care (*Fürsorge*) by promoting the fitness of apprentices, young workers, and university students. But the encouragement of mass exercise also had a deep utilitarian, preventive thrust: sport officials, employers, and government bureaucrats promoted sport in order to increase people's ability and willingness to work. Sport would promote health, productivity, and the will to work and thus limit the costs to the social insurance and welfare systems. Mass sport, fitness campaigns, and exercise camps aimed at long-term sustainable performance enhancement and, from the beginning, there was an emphasis on social and hygienic prevention.

After 1933, the emphasis on prevention undoubtedly became much stronger. The Nazi regime subordinated social welfare to utilitarian goals concerning the productivity of the community. Nazi performance medicine had a strong eliminationist and ultimately murderous element. People who were deemed to lack the capacity to contribute to the productivity of the nation were ostracized, persecuted, and eventually even killed. Yet Nazi physicians and promoters of sport emphasized racial inclusion as much as exclusion. Biopolitical prevention through negative racial hygiene did not entirely eclipse the social welfare aspects of Nazi population policies. Many health professionals recognized that productive underachievement could be caused by social disadvantage as well as bad heredity, and they were prepared to address these obstacles to people's productivity. Young people who were sick and weak because of poverty and social disadvantage received special attention in order to bring them up to an acceptable standard of performance.

Such approaches are all evident in Gebhardt's work, which started in the 1920s with his exercise camps for "valuable" but performance-inhibited young people.[35] While Gebhardt had argued even at that time that it would be unreasonable to spend resources on the "absolutely useless," he still favoured a need-based concept of welfare that interpreted "physical inferiority" and weakness as a result of social disadvantage and poverty, and he believed these could be alleviated through better nutrition, relaxation, and physical exercise. Still, as with most other Weimar fitness promoters, Gebhardt's commitment to *Fürsorge* was also clearly driven by the utilitarian concerns of human economy. He was worried about "those valuable forces in the great army of the physically retarded" who could be turned into productive citizens with the help of social care and exercise.[36]

By 1933, Gebhardt's language had hardened. He now propagated his exercise camps as a form of mobilizing welfare that fostered physical recovery and discipline through remedial exercise and compulsory work for those who were weak. "The National Socialist welfare physician has to reject the notion that only the fit can be burdened with obligatory labour service," a measure the regime had just introduced. Since, according to Gebhardt's estimates, only between 25 and 30 per cent of young people in big cities were fully fit (compared to 50–60 per cent of youths in normal peacetime conditions), it was important to focus attention on the great group of weaklings that existed between the fully capable and the inferior and sick. These people had to be trained to become fully productive.[37] The work of the NS physician was crucial for saving health and social insurance costs in the long run but this meant that he had to make unsentimental choices: the appropriate "schooling of the weaklings separates ... the valuable from the worthless [and] prepares [them] step by step for the best performance and supplies the public with fully valuable workers, *people who are eager to work and self-confident*" (emphasis in the original).[38] Gebhardt advocated a systematic process of human resource selection among the weak and injured that he equated to a filter. Those who were impaired but hereditarily healthy were prepared for work in transitional exercise camps. After experiencing "the toughness of team schooling" (*Härte der Mannschaftsschule*), people were assessed and then either moved to the "work front" or, in exceptional circumstances, referred to further training. Exercise therapy was more than physical rehabilitation; it was education for work. The impaired had to collaborate in their recovery. They had to work on themselves and prepare themselves psychologically for their return to work in a supervised communal setting. Otherwise they would succumb to the ever-present danger of pension seeking.[39] Only the racially valuable and hereditarily healthy were entitled to such treatment. Before the process of "up-schooling," as Gebhardt put it, could begin, an assessment of the human resources according to the criteria of racial hygiene was necessary. Such "hereditary-biological stock taking" was the foundation of Nazi biopolitical practices of selection more generally.[40]

Like other sport physicians, Gebhardt emphasized environmental factors in "racial care," but, even after 1933, environmental approaches were not confined to sport medicine. The senior physician in the Berlin school administration (*Stadtoberschularzt*), Wilfried Zeller, praised Gebhardt's approach as a way to foster the development of socially disadvantaged young people.[41] As Richard Wetzell has shown for criminological research in the German Psychiatric Research Institute, criminologists like Johannes Lange thought that in many cases crime could not be attributed to bad heredity alone. There were a large number of young people who became criminals because they were socially disadvantaged. While there were some hopeless degenerates with criminal proclivities, there were others who could be reformed.[42] Some Nazi experts on homosexuality held similar assumptions about the interplay between hereditary and environmental factors. In 1937, the SS paper *Das*

Schwarze Korps, for example, claimed that 98 per cent of accused homosexuals were simply seduced fellow travellers who could be cured. The other remaining 2 per cent would have to be eliminated. As in the case of Gebhardt's weaklings, the diagnosis of hereditary homosexuality required some hereditary-biological stocktaking before deciding whom to eliminate. At the Göring Institute for psychological research and psychotherapy (which was run by Hermann Göring's brother Matthias), the psychotherapist Johannes Schultz ordered accused homosexuals to have supervised sex with a female prostitute. Those who revealed their incurability by failing to perform were sent to concentration camps.[43] Walther Jaensch, also a promoter of sport as a means to enhance people's social fitness, similarly stressed the significance of environmental factors in human development. As director of the Institute for Constitutional Medicine at the Charité in Berlin, he developed methods to diagnose retarded children and youths with developmental inhibitions despite their good heredity. His interventions tried to "disinhibit healthy hereditary mass" in order to turn people into socially useful, productive citizens.[44]

Such environmental assumptions were controversial at the time because they could be interpreted as a threat to the hereditarian racial hygienic assumptions of Nazi medicine. Despite such concerns, some sport physicians assumed a greater plasticity of the human constitution based on environmental factors. According to the sport physician Arno Arnold, anthropometric work with athletes at the DHfL and other institutions had shown that the physical types of students who had arrived with quite different body types – leptosome/asthenic, pyknic, and athletic types in the typology of psychiatrist Ernst Kretschmer – had converged under the influence of sustained exercise. He even speculated whether exercise could improve the hereditary fitness of the race.[45] In a similar vein, the sport physician Martin Brustmann argued that sport could have positive cumulative long-term effects on hereditary health: "I believe that ... rational, quiet and patient work on one's own body and character has a permanent effect, preserves and enhances performance and health ... and benefits the hereditary mass."[46] From the point of view of the dominant racial hygienic paradigm of hard heredity (the notion that acquired characteristics had no impact on people's genes) these Lamarckian assumptions were unacceptable. But Brustmann's conviction did not disqualify him from a career in Nazi medicine and the SS. He became Berlin district leader of the German Sport Physician League, sport medical consultant in the SD main office, and SS Standartenführer (Colonel) in the SS Reich Security Main Office. He was also the personal physician of his boss Reinhard Heydrich and treated the families of several high-ranking SS leaders including Himmler's.[47] This was certainly in line with his expertise, which he described as "nutrition, lifestyle, [and] marriage conduct of high performance humans (*Hochleistungsmenschen*)."[48]

To be sure, most Nazi physicians rejected neo-Lamarckian assumptions about the heredity of acquired characteristics, which is why they enthusiastically promoted the repressive racial hygienic measures of the regime. Leonardo Conti, a high-ranking health official in the Interior Ministry who would become Reich Physician Leader in 1939, rejected the possibility that sport could improve people's heredity but he nevertheless envisaged an important role for sport in Nazi biopolitics. According to his orthodox view, heredity circumscribed individual developmental possibilities but sport and welfare measures could play a role in determining the extent to which a person could achieve the maximum of his or her performance potential. In addition, he believed that sport had a wholesome effect on the process of natural selection. A people that placed a high value on "courage, decisiveness, strength and health" would create "selective conditions" (*Ausleseverhältnisse*) that favoured those characteristics – like athletes who embodied such qualities. "Therefore, we promote ... through physical education, the heroic man, the courageous, the athletic fighter ... as an ideal," which would have a positive impact on processes of hereditary selection.[49] In general, Nazi sport physicians emphasized the importance of environmental factors for the health of racially acceptable people but they were happy to participate in the ill treatment and persecution of those who did not fall into this category. The best example of this is Gebhardt, who was sentenced to death in the Nuremberg Doctors' Trial for his role in medical experiments involving concentration camp inmates.[50]

Sport physicians such as Gebhardt situated their expertise at the intersection between sport and work medicine. An official introduction to the role of sport physicians in the Third Reich maintained that sport physicians were particularly suited for the medical supervision of physical labour in the Reich Labour Service because sport physiology and work physiology were inextricably linked.[51] From May 1933, Gebhardt was ordered by Reich Physician Leader Gerhard Wagner to work as a consultant for the Reich Interior Ministry and the Reich Labour Ministry on medical issues regarding the Reich Labour Service and sport more generally.[52] At the same time, he worked as a consultant for Reich Sport Leader von Tschammer und Osten and organized medically supervised recovery camps (*Erholungslager*) for injured athletes in this capacity.[53] Gebhardt was, however, not a physiologist like the physicians who had worked under Edgar Atzler in the sport science laboratory at the DHfL until 1929. As a surgeon, Gebhardt expressed scepticism about the usefulness of physiological parameters for the assessment of fitness. In his view, blood pressure, pulse, and lung capacity were at best indirect indicators of a person's fitness. Nor was high performance in particular sport disciplines a good indicator of general physical fitness, as demonstrated by the case of a young apprentice with a goiter who was a good runner but lacked the quiet steadiness required for his work.[54]

Gebhardt seems to have preferred a more phenomenological approach in assessing people's fitness. The weak and sick had to be "upschooled" for their best possible performance based on an assessment that relied on the empirical, experiential knowledge of a physician who knew about the effectiveness of specific exercises and administered them in well-considered doses. This method was far less ambitious than Atzler's attempt to determine the physiological alphabet of movement components (see chapter 2). Consequently, Gebhardt's program was probably better suited for the practical purpose of training sport physicians and sport teachers for schools and Nazi mass organizations.[55]

In his capacity as medical director of the *Reichsakademie*, Gebhardt taught courses for physicians, medical students, and physical therapists on sport injuries and rehabilitative medicine, but in 1937 he was also appointed full professor of surgery at the University of Berlin. Gebhardt's specialty was "restorative surgery" (*Wiederherstellungschirurgie*) for people who had suffered physical trauma as a result of injury.[56] The skills involved in this practice were not just relevant for work and sport injuries, they were also important for the treatment of war casualties. The latter would become critical during the war when Gebhardt served as consulting surgeon of the Waffen SS.[57]

Gebhardt rarely taught at the university or at the location of the *Reichsakademie* in Berlin. The reasons he gave for this were his commitments in Hohenlychen where he had been appointed as chief physician of the tuberculosis sanatorium in November 1933. He greatly expanded the institution to make it into a centre for sport and work therapy.[58] Hohenlychen specialized in reconstructive surgery and rehabilitative treatment for people with serious joint and bone injuries. Exercise grounds and the state of the art indoor bathing facilities with a movable glass roof served rehabilitative purposes, as did the workshops for work therapies to facilitate patients' readjustment to work.[59] Gebhardt also conducted special courses for physicians on the order of Reich Physician Leader Gerhard Wagner. There were about four hundred physicians who visited Hohenlychen each year, many of whom took extended courses on the principles of exercise therapy.[60]

As during the Weimar Republic, sport was meant to make people fit for work but, compared to the earlier period, Nazi fitness and productivity drives were willing to accept more casualties. In other words, there was a more reckless approach to the human material, which served educational purposes. Physical exercise was not only important in Nazi educational projects because it contributed to people's physical health and productivity but, in the Nazi view, sport had a fighting element that instilled martial values such as determination, willpower, endurance, ruthlessness, and courage. Sport education was to foster toughness. Men and women had to be trained to overcome their fear and "inner resistance" (*innerer Schweinehund*) against difficult, exhausting, and sometimes dangerous tasks.[61] According to such views, courage could only be acquired if sport entailed a certain element of risk, as in boxing, a sport that was a particular favourite among Nazi educators (see figure 3.3).[62] Ruthlessness was also a desired outcome. A school teacher appreciated the "beaten red faces and bloody noses" of his students because this "demonstrated a certain toughness in taking and receiving," but he was concerned that his students still had inhibitions to "finish off" a tattered opponent who could only put up weak resistance.[63]

While Weimar physical educators and sport physicians had been keen to avoid injury risks because they might compromise people's long-term health and productivity, during the Nazi period such people deliberately cultivated injury risks in their educational practice. In apparatus gymnastics previous training practices had emphasized the slow building up of skills to avoid injuries. Now Nazi educators preferred to build up skills despite the risk of physical danger to the athlete. Timid step-by-step adjustments to the slowly growing skill level of athletes would negate wholesome influences on the character. "For us the courageous risk is more important than an easily completed task."[64] Whether a young student could complete an exercise correctly was less important than the "fighting performance." It did not matter how often the student got his feet in a tangle and fell.[65]

This reckless approach was not only adopted for male students. Girls were to be toughened up as well: "'To be tough as leather and hard like

Abb. 3 Pfui dem Mann, der sich nicht wehren kann! Aufnahme E. Solterts

Schüler einer nationalsozialistischen Erziehungsanstalt üben sich im Faustkampf. Nicht nur Kraft und Geschicklichkeit, sondern auch Mut, Ausdauer und scharfe Beobachtung des Gegners erfordert diese Leibesübung

3.3 Education for toughness: "Shame on the Man who cannot defend himself!" From: Schultz, "rassenbiologische Bedeutung," 343. Printed with permission from Universitätsbibliothek Tübingen.

Krupp-steel' – developing these traits in girls through physical exercise is a national duty of the school," declared a sport teacher, Margarete Knipper. "Each woman needs those [traits] regardless whether she goes through life as mother, educator of children or a working woman," she also argued.[66] As will be shown in the following chapter, preparing women for the double burdens of motherhood and paid work was a key emphasis of the regime's work productivity campaigns.

Some physicians had difficulties with the ruthless toughening up of children and youths. The above-mentioned Auguste Hoffmann, who in 1933 held a post as physician with the Nazi League of German Girls (BDM), was concerned about the lack of consideration for girls' health. Hoffmann was an accomplished sport physicians who, from 1930, had taught classes on the influence of exercise on women and children at the DHfL. During the Olympics she was responsible for the health of the non-German female athletes. Between May 1933 and December 1936, she also served as senior district physician (*Obergauärztin*) in the upper BDM district (*Obergau*) of Berlin and as medical consultant for the Reich Youth Leadership until June 1935.[67] However, when Hoffmann complained about the ruthless mobilization drives by inexperienced Hitler youth leaders, who sent their young charges on forced marches or supervised sport events that led to life-threatening overexertions, she came into increasing conflict with the Hitler Youth medical establishment.[68] This conflict escalated in 1935 when Karl-Walter Kondeyne, the Reich Physician of the Hitler Youth and director of its health office, banned her from practicing for the BDM on the grounds that she had ignored the rules and regulations issued by the health office, the Reich Youth Leadership, and the Reich Physician Leader.[69]

The Hoffmann affair indicated wider problems with the treatment of youths. At one point Goebbels confronted the youth leader Artur Axmann with reports about bad living conditions and physical abuse in HJ camps; he worried that such circumstances undermined the loyalty of young people.[70] In 1936 complaints about the mental and physical dangers of the "toughening up" regimes in the Hitler Youth moved Reich Youth Leader Baldur von Schirach to reassure parents that there was no danger to their children's health. But, according to government health reports, such abuse continued throughout the 1930s.[71]

A reckless approach to performance enhancement characterized Nazi fitness campaigns in general. Martin Brustmann, for example, criticized the assessments for the SA sport medal, which in his view had led to almost four hundred unnecessary deaths between 1935 and 1939.[72]

Other sport physicians had no such qualms about the health of their charges. Gebhardt, for example, conceded that the *Volk in Leibesübungen* inevitably suffered losses and injuries but he argued that "from an educational point of view it would ... be erroneous to dispense sport in small doses in order to avoid dangers." The risk, danger, and "toughness of sport" were an important educational factor to prepare people for manly action at work and at war and casualties were a necessary price that had to be paid. However, work and military preparedness also demanded people's "enduring usability" and this reality made early detection of physical damages and injuries a top priority. During rehabilitation, work, exercise, and rest under medical supervision were to secure people's physical and mental "preparedness" (*Bereitschaft*), a term with a military association that indicates the degree of militarization of German society by the mid-1930s.[73]

The Nazi leadership publicly demonstrated the necessity to accept sport casualties through the creation of the foundation German Sport Thanks (*Deutscher Sportdank*). Launched on the occasion of the German Gymnastics and Sport Festival in Breslau in 1938 by Reich Interior Minister Wilhelm Frick (the superior of the Reich Sport Leader), the foundation recognized that "sport is fighting, and where there is fighting there are injuries." Sportdank provided 100,000 RM per year for the support of those who suffered permanent injuries through sport, and was hailed as the first institution in the world that cared for the "heavily sport-impaired" (*Sportschwergeschädigten*).[74] In fact, only a small amount of money was provided for those who suffered permanent impairments through sport. The importance of the foundation was largely symbolic. If casualties were an unavoidable consequence of the struggles of civilian life, casualties in military conflicts of the future would have to be accepted as a matter of course.

The former DHfL physician Hans Hoske also rejected what he considered the excessive "sparing and protective caring" of people in the social hygiene of the past.[75] He promoted a "biological politics" that combined concerns about military fitness and work productivity. In commenting on Hoske's habilitation thesis at the University of Berlin, the director of the hygiene institute, Heinz Zeiss, argued that NS health leadership had its source in military hygiene, with its procedures for determining different fitness categories, disabilities caused by military service, and invalidity. Furthermore, Zeiss claimed that this kind of medicine had been neglected during the Weimar period and as a result the military and vocational fitness of youths had been undermined.

According to Zeiss, Hoske's work for the German National Clerical Employees Union and later for the German Labour Front had helped to reverse this trend by promoting performance enhancement in people through sport, physical exercise, leisure, and nutritional reform. By "restoring the performance in hereditarily healthy people who had suffered environmental damage," he made people "more valuable" for the nation and the state.[76]

Physical exercise was a means to physical and psychological regeneration. Hoske's exercise and rehabilitation camps for young apprentices at Lobeda, Gebhardt's rehabilitative initiatives with apprentices in Hohenaschau and with injured workers and athletes at Hohenlychen, and similar efforts by other physicians provided models for successful exercise-based "stimulus therapy" (*Reiztherapie*).[77] People who had suffered injuries in the course of their work or sport training were to be rehabilitated through medically supervised exercise and slowly inducted back into the work process. Gebhardt was adamant that physical rehabilitation should remain in the hands of trained physicians. Lay people, be they other athletes or sport trainers, were ill-suited for this task because of their lack of medical training. They often forced the pace of rehabilitative exercise and posed a danger to patients, which is why he denounced their practices as "quackery with physical exercise."[78] If physicians carefully monitored the reinduction of the injured into jobs, people's working capacity could slowly be enhanced and even those who were partially incapacitated could be reintegrated into the work process for the benefit of an economy that suffered increasing labour shortages from the mid-1930s onwards.

Even though the physical health benefits of exercise therapies were thought to be substantial, the psychological benefits were considered even more significant. Hoske believed that the "work on the self" in the course of such therapies transformed people's understanding of themselves and their responsibilities in the Nazi performance community. Graded assessment of people's performance capacity made it possible to integrate them into the work process early on and raise their performance levels step by step through combined efforts of schools, the labour service, the army, the German Labour Front, and sport clubs. In this way the financial burdens on the social insurance system could be reduced. Caring only for the fully fit had adverse effects on the *Volksgemeinschaft* because such an approach fostered "feelings of inferiority" among people who were partially fit. Because of this the "weakling has no interest to compensate for his deficits through work on himself."

Instead he "cultivates" his deficits and an attitude that has a "corrosive" (*zersetzend*) effect on the people's community.[79]

This approach was contrary to the interests of the total state, which had to rely on the voluntary and enthusiastic commitment of all of its citizens. In Hoske's view, Weimar social welfare had made people into passive recipients of social benefits who were more concerned about disability pensions than about contributing to the community.[80] "Pension neurosis," the pathological desire to obtain a pension in order to avoid work, had been a long-standing concern in sectors of the German medical community who feared the abuse of social benefits by soldiers who had experienced shell shock or by workers who filed work-related disability claims.[81] The spread of "personal social responsibility" (*Selbstverantwortung*) among people's comrades was crucial for the health and performance capacity of individuals and future generations.[82] Since the willingness to become healthy and performance-oriented could not be created by orders and force, activating therapies involving exercise were meant to overcome antisocial attitudes among underperforming people's comrades. To mobilize people's will to perform, performance was defined as an inner attitude. Actual weaknesses and disabilities were less important than performance-orientation. What counted was not

> the absolute degrees of weakness and frailty, but the attitude which its bearer takes up in relation to them. The will to perform alone determines the social value of the human being ... The performance as the governing thought in all areas of life can only be the expression of a special mental disposition, which cannot be achieved through laws and therefore cannot be the task of the state and its organs. [It is] purely based on the [Nazi] world view and [its promotion is] thus one of the most responsible tasks of the national socialist movement.[83]

According to Hoske, the agency best suited for this was the Main Office for People's Health of the Nazi Party, the place at which he worked.

Emphasizing the pedagogical benefits of physical exercise was quite common among Nazi physicians and promoters of sport. "The main value of all physical exercise lies in its influence on the psyche," claimed Gebhardt. The physical exertion, relaxation, and endurance training of exercise therapy had to be combined with meaningful work that strengthened the will of participants. The therapy was designed as a community experience with a competitive edge that raised people's enthusiasm: "Joint rousing performance turns into deeply felt

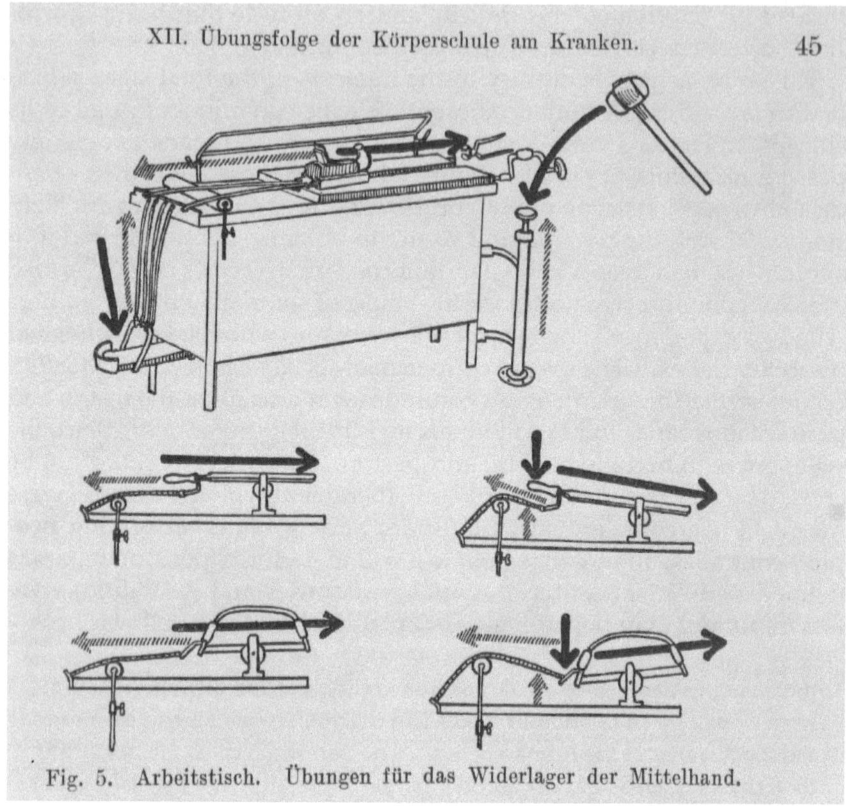
XII. Übungsfolge der Körperschule am Kranken. 45

Fig. 5. Arbeitstisch. Übungen für das Widerlager der Mittelhand.

3.4 The workbench as gym: Karl Gebhardt's exercise therapy. Karl Gebhardt, *Übungsbehandlung* (Jena: Gustav Fischer, 1934), 45. Printed with permission from Württembergische Landesbibliothek Stuttgart.

experience" while play and rambling provided relaxation for the soul.[84] Exercise therapy deliberately used the joy generated by sport and play for work education. Training people's dexterity and agility was meant to build self-confidence in their physical abilities. The utilitarian assumptions behind the cures are most evident in the design of exercise equipment that mimicked workbenches. Versatile worktables were used for practicing elementary work movements using planes, saws, screwdrivers, hammers, and foot pedals. Gebhardt's Hohenlychen merged gym equipment with the workbench, turning exercise into a tool for the "*Produktivierung*" and "*Re-produktivierung*" of injured athletes, workers and, ultimately, soldiers (see figure 3.4).

III. *"Ein Volk in Leibesübungen": Mannschaft* Spirit and the National Community

"A People in Physical Exercise" was the slogan used by the Reich sport leadership for the promotion of mass sport. According to this vision, sport was to turn every racially valuable people's comrade into a valuable and productive citizen or soldier who willingly sacrificed himself for the good of the *Volksgemeinschaft*. According to Heinrich Meusel, a sport teacher at the DHfL and the *Reichsakademie*, every German citizen was obliged to train his body and character for the good of the community: "Unfolding the innate physical aptitude in each human being is today not only a precondition for sport performance but has become a general educational duty (*allgemeine Bildungspflicht*) for every new German man. Every German citizen growing up has the holy obligation to the fatherland to extract every health and performance value (*Gesundheits- und Leistungsgut*) that can be extracted through correctly applied physical exercise."[85] Meusel's task at the *Reichsakademie* was to train sport teachers and coaches for the extraction of *Leistungsgut*. He was also director of the educational department of the RBL, the NS umbrella organization for sport clubs led by the Reich Sport Leader. In 1938, he edited a practical guidebook on basic physical education for sport teachers working in NS mass organizations. The popularization of sport was supposed to reach those "half-healthy" individuals of all age groups who had not been reached by traditional sport clubs. Popular sport, Meusel hoped, would unleash people's "fighting dispositions" and give them psychological energy and vigour to cope with the strains of work.[86]

Sport was to prepare everyone for better performances whether it was ordinary citizens or the self-styled elite of the Nazi movement. The *Reichsführer* SS, Heinrich Himmler, demanded that all SS men and officers regularly submit to the performance tests for the SA sport medal and the more rigorous assessments for the Reich sport badge (*Reichssportabzeichen*), which was only awarded to more accomplished athletes. From 1937, SS men who had not gained such recognition could be refused promotion or permission to marry. Himmler believed that good sport performances demonstrated soldierly qualities such as courage, character, and toughness and should be used as criteria for leadership selection. In addition, the success of SS athletes in national and international sporting competitions was meant to underscore the elite status and fighting determination of the organization.[87]

Champions of the 1936 Olympics were held up in the press as embodiments of the Nazi performance ideal. A German Olympic champion was not to be a sport star who only achieved fame, glory, and financial rewards for himself. These notions were rejected as the false individualistic ideals of a bygone liberal era. NS performance discourse condemned the idolatry of sport stars – "cannons" as they were called at the time – and emphasized the selfless community-orientation of prominent athletes. "The task of our national sport education must be ... [to make] these people [the German Olympic champions] central to our national life and not allow them to become outsiders."[88] In other words, elite sport had to fulfil a political purpose by encouraging mass sport.

According to the Nazi philosopher Alfred Baeumler, the director of the Institute for Political Pedagogy at the University of Berlin, there was a distinction to be made between pure competitive teams that coordinated and enhanced individual performances for the sake of a better sport performance and the "real men's squad" (*echte Mannschaft*), a team of men that fulfilled a higher mission for the political community. A high-performance team could only be a *Mannschaft* if its performance had a transcendent political significance, which a conventional sport team lacked.[89]

The Reich sport leadership supported elite high performance sports and professional sports if they promoted the values of the people's community. When the German amateur cycling world champion Toni Merkens defeated the Dutch cyclist Arie van Vliet and won a gold medal at the Berlin Olympics, the Nazi press turned him into a poster boy for a pedagogical lesson on sacrifice and community-orientation; after his victory, twelve thousand spectators in the Berlin velodrome sang the national anthem and the Horst Wessel song about a Nazi martyr who had been killed by a communist in 1930. According to the Nazi press, Merkens had achieved his success as a result of discipline and sacrifice, because he had "worked for years in a goal-oriented manner towards this day." The joyful masses thanked him after the race: Their gratefulness was not only a response to "his performance in the fight, it [recognized] the entire life of the sportsman, the force of will of this youngster, and his serious understanding of his duties as the best of his sport. First he thought of his country, then he thought about himself, and this is what we all want to remember."[90]

Merkens had not only sacrificed time and energy for his sport and nation but, as a true amateur sportsman, he had also made serious financial sacrifices:

> His personal interests took a back seat when the young man from Cologne prepared for this day as almost no other of his German sport

> comrades. When he became world champion of the amateur sprinters (*Amateurflieger*), the biggest cycling sport centres of Europe inundated him with the most alluring offers. Toni Merkens remained firm. He would become a professional rider – later. He had once promised to break the curse that seemed to bedevil Germany's cyclists in Olympic competitions, he wanted to conquer the first gold medal for the German cycling sport! Now he has kept his word – a shining example for our Youth![91]

The lesson for German youth in the Merkens story was that the community always came first while personal interests came second. Merkens was not a sport star who gained glory for himself; he was part of an Olympic "*Mannschaft*" that fought for the greater good of Germany. Athletes like Merkens demonstrated "*Einsatz*," which is best translated in this context as "combative commitment" to the racial people's community. Preparedness to demonstrate such an aggressive commitment (*Einsatzbereitschaft*) in sport, at work, and at war was a core value in Nazi discourse and it was demanded from every good people's comrade. The Merkens story is thus a parable for Nazi values that emphasized *Einsatz* and material sacrifice for the common good over self-interest. In the workplace, this hierarchy of values was promoted through the Olympics of Labour, the Reich Vocational Competitions that invoked amateur sporting ideals in the service of personal sacrifice and higher labour productivity (see chapter 4).

Outstanding amateur athletes such as Merkens were not the only ones celebrated in the Nazi press as role models. Professional athletes were sometimes used to convey the same lesson. The former professional world champion heavyweight boxer Max Schmeling was presented as an example of white Aryan virtues, in stark contrast to the "Jewish" materialism of American capitalism. After Schmeling defeated the African American heavyweight Joe Louis in their first fight in 1936, the German press rejected the notion that he was a prizefighter who was primarily interested in money. Instead he was hailed as a noble sportsman, a professional with an amateur spirit who had fought for a higher cause while embodying the superior strength, character, and "will power of the resurrected nation."[92] When Schmeling lost his second fight against Louis in 1938, official accounts attributed his embarrassing defeat at the hands of a black fighter to Louis' savage nature, which conquered the superior mental ability of the German. Even in defeat, Schmeling represented Aryan values of disinterested idealism and strength of character. Unlike other boxers, he "did not let himself be blinded by money, did not succumb to the petty cravings of life."[93] What was important was *not* glory, fame, or material rewards for the individual but his willingness to make sacrifices for the greater good. This also held true for the average people's comrade who was constantly reminded by the Labour Front and its leader Robert Ley that personal sacrifice and "social honour" were more important than material rewards.[94]

Using elite athletes as role models for sacrifice, asceticism, and performance-orientation did not automatically translate into greater sport participation by the mass of people. Critics of elite sports clearly recognized this. The chief of staff of the SA Viktor Lutze, for example, conceded that great performances provided valuable incentives for the masses ("each champion is a pacemaker for countless others, who are inspired ... through his skill") but he worried about the passive consumerism that was engendered by spectator sport. "His majesty the spectator must be dethroned" because it was unacceptable that 100,000 spectators were watching 22 men on a soccer field without ever entering a sport field themselves. A group of forty-year-olds who ran 100 metres in 12.5 seconds was, in his view, much more valuable for the defensive strength of the people's community than a single man who ran 10.3 seconds.[95]

After the 1936 Olympics, regime officials emphasized the importance of community-orientation and *Mannschaft* even more. This was most evident in the sporting competitions that selected athletes for the NS-Fighting Games (*NS-Kampfspiele*), the annual sporting competitions that were announced by Hitler during the 1936 Party Rally of Honour and that took place during the Nuremberg rallies in 1937 and 1938. The *Kampfspiele* were organized by the SA and participants were selected in the course of national sporting competitions of the SA, SS, HJ, and other Nazi organizations. Ultimately these Nazi Olympics were supposed to dwarf the scale of the 1936 international Olympics. Architectural planning for them was typical of Nazi projects. At the core of the plans was a gigantic stadium that could hold more than four hundred thousand people, four times as large as the Olympic stadium in Berlin.[96]

Competitions at the NS games emphasized militarized forms of team sports involving 20 kilometre marches with heavy baggage, hand grenade throwing, and shooting. "This is how through the *Mannschaft* the community idea is brought to its highest blossom. Beside the pure physical performance of the individual man, devotion for the whole is demanded which is the highest expression of the national socialist world view."[97] This type of "defense competition" (*Wehrkampf*) was not conceived as a form of "premilitary training" for the Wehrmacht.[98] Such sports sought to promote disciplinary values more broadly. In a society that promoted military values in most areas of life, "*Einsatzbereitschaft*," "*Leistungsfähigkeit*," and "*Kameradschaft*" were also relevant for those "unknown fighters of the SA who worked during the day on the blast furnace, the anvil, behind the plough, and on the desk."[99]

The Reich Sport Competitions (*Reichssportwettkämpfe*) of the Hitler Youth supposedly involved between six and seven million members of both sexes in 1937 and 1938. The NS propaganda called them the "largest sport celebration in the world." Like the SA competitions, they were introduced in 1937 and selected competitors for the NS-Kampfspiele. The chief of the Hitler Youth Office for Physical Exercise, Dr Ernst Schlünder, emphasized the difference between the Hitler Youth competitions and the Reich Youth Competitions of the Weimar years. The latter were mainly competitions between school children that emphasized individual performances, whereas the Hitler Youth competitions focused on team performance: "Every Hitler Youth member should be able to run, jump, and throw and in these sport disciplines ... every single one should bring out his personal best performance. The performance, however, serves the community, in which everyone stands. The ideal of the *Mannschaft* ... finds in the Reich Sport Competition its best expression." The assessment at the competition included 100 (or for younger competitors 60) metre sprints, long jump, and the throwing of balls and clubs. The performances of the ten best performers in each unit were then counted as "*Mannschaftsleistung*." The best teams would try to fight their way to the national Hitler Youth competitions, which determined who was sent to the *NS-Kampfspiele*, where "before the eyes of the Führer a grand performance picture of the entire German youth" emerged. "As in the vocational competitions of all working Germans ... the strength of a people is expressed which sees its highest calling in the eternal perfection of its performances."[100]

IV. Company Sport and Social Cohesion

After the Nazi takeover of power, employers and regime officials amplified the Weimar legacy of company sport and promoted physical education as a way of moulding performance-oriented subjects. With the destruction of unions and Marxist working-class parties, there was no opposition left against the instrumentalization of sport in the service of greater industrial efficiency. In late 1933, the National Productivity Board (*Reichskuratorium für Wirtschaftlichkeit* or RKW), a semipublic institution supported by the Reich and industry, presented a report on the human factor in rationalization that explained why sport should be a tool for the "performance enhancement" (*Leistungssteigerung*) in workers. Industrial pedagogy should foster sport as a means of improving the physical quality of workers by providing compensation for physically one-sided industrial labour. Equally important were the psychological benefits of physical exercise, because sport during or after work strengthened "goal orientation and comradeship within the work community." The report pushed for industrial training programs for apprentices and workers that appealed to the "spirit of sport" (*Sportsgeist*) in employees. This spirit would produce a "healthy ambition" in workers, which made them into "permanent bearer[s] of high quality work."[101] Such reasoning was an extension of the Weimar-era discourse about the company community that united employers, white-collar employees, and blue-collar workers. But as the Nazis consolidated their power there was, however, a significant semantic shift in this discourse. While the Labour Front, the Nazi mass organization that included most workers and employers, heavily promoted worker sport, it did so to foster loyalty to Nazism and its racial ideas. Membership in the performance community was now defined in racial terms and excluded Jews and all those people who were denounced as racial inferiors.

The DAF promoted mass sport in the workplace through its leisure organization *Kraft durch Freude* or KdF. As one of the most influential institutional players in labour relations in Nazi Germany, it intended to integrate sceptical workers into the racial *Volksgemeinschaft* as useful and performance-oriented members through promises of respectability, social upward mobility, welfare, and leisure activities. Since the Labour Front promised to do away with class conflict, its membership included employers – now called "company leaders" (*Betriebsführer*) – and workers and salaried employees who were now referred to as "retinue" (*Gefolgschaft*). The DAF was the largest and wealthiest NS mass organization. By the spring of 1934 it already had more than ten million dues-paying members, in 1939 there were twenty-two million, and in 1940 twenty-five million, almost all of them waged workers or salaried employees. The Labour Front was not a union, even though it sometimes put pressure on employers to provide social benefits for their employees. It was excluded from negotiating or setting wages and working conditions since these areas were the preserve of the labour ministry's "trustees of labour." Its official mission was political education, and the promotion of mass sport through KdF was part of this educational mission.[102]

Before the war, Reich Sport Leader Tschammer was also leader of the sport office of the KdF, which promoted sport in order to bring about the "true Volk and performance community."[103] According to the deputy leader of the office, Karl Lorch, KdF sport was to provide elementary training for those people's comrades who were not interested in sport: the so-called "sporting analphabets." These people had to be induced to overcome their "lethargy" and their fear that they looked inadequate or even ridiculous if they were overweight or lacked agility. In the beginning, KdF, therefore, offered sport courses that emphasized play and joy.[104] People could choose between "open" courses that they could visit whenever they felt like it and "closed" courses if they wanted to commit to a training program that developed skills in a systematic way.[105]

From 1937, there was a marked shift in the KdF sport program. It now tried to mobilize as many people as possible in so-called "company sport communities" (*Betriebssportgemeinschaften* or BSG), which were either newly founded or replaced pre-existing company sport clubs.[106] The buildup of the BSG system coincided with a more aggressive social and economic mobilization of society after the proclamation of the economic four-year plan in 1936. As one company paper explained the need for company sport, "the *four-year plan* in connection with the *lack of skilled workers*, the *declining birth rate* and the *increasing ageing* of our people make necessary the strongest measures for the raising of the performance age and the performance capacity" (emphases in the original).[107]

The four-year plan was a productivity drive that aimed at making Germany ready for war by 1940. It gave a renewed impetus to productivity campaigns like the Reich Vocational Competitions and the fitness drives in NS mass organizations. In this context, KdF sport was heralded as "a gigantic contribution to the performance enhancement of the German people." It was meant to educate people for "community, health, and company unity."[108] Control mechanisms were designed to ensure that people participated in sport. The so-called KdF sport card was a thirty-two-page booklet that recorded the fitness and sporting activities of each KdF sport participant. It provided employers with information about a retinue member's health and physical performance level, and his or her *Einsatzbereitschaft* for the community. People's size, weight, and chest circumference could also be recorded. Like the workbook that detailed an employee's employment history, the DAF membership booklet, and the military service record, the KdF sport card was a "performance document" (*Leistungsnachweis*) for workers who wanted to demonstrate their commitment to the performance ideal.[109]

The KdF tried to get workers of all ages to exercise. When the Labour Front leader Robert Ley announced the founding of the KdF sport office, he reminded people that it was especially important to encourage the middle-aged to become physically active and fit. "Sport and physical movement are more necessary for the 40 and 50-year old than for youth. We must get rid of the superfluous fat in our people so that the body regains the necessary vigour."[110] Mass competitions should aim to enhance average performance levels of all people so that they could preserve their health and physical performance capacity into old age. In this way sport was used to prevent the so-called *"Arbeitsknick,"* the abrupt downturn of the physical performance curve after age forty, which the advocates of Nazi performance medicine tried to postpone until people reached their 60s.[111]

To encourage sport participation among its older employees, the Kalle chemical firm in Wiesbaden, a subsidiary of IG Farben, divided its employees into separate "blocks" of about forty members each, forming "competition communities" (*Wettkampfgemeinschaften*). Each member received individual points for participating in a sporting activity and the blocks competed against each other by gathering as many points as possible. The points collected by people above thirty-five counted one and a half times as much as those collected by younger people, while people over forty-five received double credit to encourage and reward their participation. Workers who worked closely together and knew each other well were put into the same blocks. This practice ensured mutual supervision and transferred the *Mannschaft* principle to the workplace. In this way, co-workers were supposed to be merged into a "fighting community" of all ages for the benefit of collective fitness and increased productivity.[112]

There is some uncertainty among historians about the extent to which the regime actually achieved its goal of mobilizing people for company sport. Numbers of participants are not easy to come by and are often based on official proclamations trumpeting unrealistic achievements, as historian Hajo Bernett has noted. Official numbers for 1936 proclaimed up to 6.3 million participants, 9.5 million in 1937, and 22.5 million in 1938.[113] If one believes official numbers in the Nazi press, the *"Volk in Leibesübungen"* was becoming a reality. In April 1938, a headline in the

Völkischer Beobachter claimed "Until now 21 Million Participants in KdF Sport."[114] These growth rates are implausible. If for the Weimar Republic the wider popularity of sport can be attributed in part to the introduction of the eight-hour day and longer leisure time for workers and employees, it is hard to believe that, given the intensification of work and longer work hours (as a result of the rearmament drives), there was an even larger surge in sporting activities in the 1930s.

There is indeed evidence that the large participation numbers were the result of creative statistical representation. For one, the numbers for sport participants after 1937 were based on the numbers reported by employers who had an interest in demonstrating that they were committed to the regime's policies of performance enhancement and social welfare.[115] By establishing BSGs, employers could demonstrate their concern for the welfare of their retinue and their support for the social policies of the Labour Front. Like many other firms, the Swabian textile firm J.F. Adolff in Backnang presented performance reports to highlight its social political achievements for the Performance Competition of German Companies (*Leistungskampf der deutschen Betriebe*) in which firms competed for various performance diplomas and the coveted designation "NS-Model Company" (*NS-Musterbetrieb*). Well-run company sport organizations and other forms of social welfare measures (such as campaigns to promote beauty in the workplace) were criteria in these national competitions, which were conducted annually from 1937.[116] The J.F. Adolff A. G. emphasized in its reports its commitment to company sport, which included a large investment in a company sport ground from 1938 onwards.[117] Employers who were keen to obtain the Performance Award for People's Health (*Leistungsabzeichen für Volksgesundheit*) also had to demonstrate support for company sport. Therefore, firms clearly had an interest in reporting inflated numbers of participants.[118]

There is also tangible evidence that the DAF itself regularly overrepresented participation. A report from the immediate postwar era for the KdF district of Bremen found that the 85,000 in official reports were the result of counting frequent participants repeatedly. In reality only about 4,000 to 5,000 different people participated in KdF sponsored sporting events.[119] A 1941 report on the activities of the Leverkusen BSG of the IG Farben points to similar accounting practices. The internal document puts the number of BSG members at 1,800, of which more than half (955) served in the Wehrmacht. This meant that only about a tenth of the Leverkusen workers participated in the BSG. At the same time, the report counted each individual visit to an exercise or sporting session separately to claim participation of 44,921 members, about four times the workforce of the entire branch! In reality, attempts to mobilize the voluntary performance commitment of the work community through regular participation in sport met with rather limited success, especially since not everyone participated voluntarily. Almost half of the participation numbers (20,950 visits) were due to "compulsory sport" (*Pflichtsport*) for youths.[120]

Representing inflated numbers was the rule rather than the exception. This practice is evident in a report on the activities of the KdF sport office from August 1939. The report, written by the Work Science Institute (*Arbeitswissenschaftliches Institut* or AWI) of the Labour Front, summarized the sport office's activities for the year 1938. Like many newspaper headlines in the Nazi press, the report is exuberant about the fantastic growth numbers of KdF sport: the number of participants in KdF organized exercise sessions nearly doubled, from 10,985,807 to 20,656,508, while the number of company sport communities did much the same, growing from 5,516 to over 10,421 during the same period. The growth rate for (often compulsory) participation by apprentices was even more impressive. It grew tenfold from 312,884 to 3,662,114. The precision of the data was clearly intended to suggest accuracy but a close reading of the report reveals that participation in company sport was not quite as impressive as these numbers suggest.

The report attributed the rise in participants primarily to the growing number of BSG members. In 1938 the 10,241 company sport communities had, however, only slightly more than 500,000 confirmed members who, on average, went to twenty exercise sessions per year; 21 per cent of these were women. These numbers amounted to more than 10 million individual visits to exercise sessions by BSG members, not to 10 million different participants, as the headlines in the Nazi press seemed to suggest. In any case, about 500,000 people's comrades who exercised on average less than once every two weeks hardly constituted an entire "*Volk in Leibesübungen*."[121] The AWI report also conceded that only a third of all BSG members participated in each session and that smaller BSGs had a higher participation rate than larger ones. These findings indicate that sporting participation might have been a function of social control and that even many BSG members showed sometimes little enthusiasm for sport.[122] Given the longer work days in many industries, it is hardly surprising that many people were reluctant to spend their remaining leisure time in the regimented environment of their BSGs. Circumstantial evidence from company archives further confirm their limited appeal. In the case of the J. F. Adolff A. G., which in 1941 employed almost 1,700 people (almost 1,200 of them women), only between 140 and 150 people joined up, despite the company's considerable investment in sporting facilities.[123]

To compensate for or to supplement the modest success of its BSG campaign, the Labour Front came up with a number of special fitness campaigns that tried to get everyone involved, not just participants in KdF sport courses and members of the BSGs. In 1938, it launched an annual "company sport roll call" (*Sportappell der Betriebe*) in which all male blue- and white-collar workers were supposed to participate. Women were included during the following years. The *Sportappell* was designed to be a "performance show which would not only activate the masses but also convey an annual picture of the development of the physical state of the working people."[124] During the 1938 roll call, all male employees of a company who were capable of participating in sport had to compete. It was meant as a competition between all able-bodied retinue members of different firms and it consisted of three parts. In the "competition of good will," individual employees participated in simple throwing, jumping, and running exercises. A second set of competitions took place between teams of more accomplished sportsmen. In a third round of assessments, companies received points for the percentage of their members in BSGs. The score was made up of the sum of the scores of the individual and team competitions plus bonus percentages for the size of BSGs.[125]

While the sport roll call was a DAF initiative, employers often took great care to present a favourable image of their company's participation. Participation numbers and results were emphasized in a company's performance reports.[126] The J. F. Adolff A. G. reported that 500 workers – almost all of its eligible male workers – had signed up for the 1938 event, evidently hoping that the high participation rate would boost its chances in the performance competition for companies.[127] In the large Leverkusen branch of IG Farben, participation was practically compulsory for employees at least from 1939 onwards. In 1938, the Leverkusen branch had achieved a *Sportappell* victory at the Gau level, allegedly based on the participation of 9000 male retinue members.[128] Its director, Hans Kühne, was determined to improve on this success in the following year. In accordance with Labour Front participation criteria, all male retinue members between 18 and 55 and all female retinue members between 21 and 30 were asked to participate. To prevent any malingering during the event, Kühne emphasized that "minor ailments or injuries for example injuries of the finger do not preclude the capacity to participate." Refusal to participate was damaging to the company community, because it "earned our company minus points … [and] questioned our prospect of victory."[129] In a report to the DAF, the Leverkusen branch anticipated that 1,037 female and 8,228 male retinue members could participate in the event.[130] Because of the large number of participants, the competitions had to be stretched over a two-week period in July. For those who could not participate, an alternative date was set in late August,[131] and the Labour Front kept a list of those who did not participate in July and sent it to plant managers to make sure that all of them "complied with their participation requirement."[132] It seems that neither the Labour Front nor management trusted the voluntary sporting spirit of their retinue. Nazi fitness campaigns were mobilization drives, social technologies of power that aimed to create performance-oriented subjects. Given the above evidence, however, the DAF far from achieved its totalitarian goal of fostering a new performance mentality among workers.

During the early years of the war, fitness campaigns supported the psychological mobilization for the domestic front. In May 1940, the Reich Sport Leader announced a Pentecost Day of German Exercise.[133] There was a winter sport day, a company sport group competition, a company cross-country run, and a national company summer sport day. The main event of the last of these was a performance test of the company retinue. Whether millions of men and women welcomed such campaigns "despite shift work and overtime," as the new director of the sport office Karl Lorch claimed in 1940, remains doubtful.[134] In spring 1940, for example, the director of the *Württembergische Metallwarenfabrik* (WMF), a firm that produced cutlery and other metal goods, worried that the number of workers who had signed up for the company cross-country run was inadequate for a firm of its size, and he demanded greater participation of male and female working comrades: "The only precondition of participation in the roll call is good will, top sporting performances are not required."[135]

The Labour Front looked to company sport as a means to promote social cohesion between company leaders, white-collar employees, and blue-collar workers. Sport was important for the promotion of a *Volks- und Leistungsgemeinschaft* in which social rewards and social recognition were allegedly based not on undeserved privileges but instead on performance.[136] In Nazi Germany, *Volksgemeinschaft* referred to the ideal utopian society in which pre-1933 class differences ceased to be important because each racially acceptable people's comrade had a respected place in German society, a position that was based on his or her own work and achievements (see also chapter 4). Class differences in terms of income, professional status, and career opportunities continued to exist in Nazi Germany but Nazi performance discourse tried to negate this fact by promoting leisure activities as social arenas in which traditional status distinctions were unimportant. Mass sport meant to provide a sphere in which social distinctions between employers and employees – as well as between different categories of employees – did not seem to matter anymore, at least during leisure time. The *Sportappell* was one arena for ritualistic claims of equality in which "*all retinue members* participate. Nobody excuses himself. In sporting comradeship the plant manager lines up with his subordinates [and] the director, with the simple work comrade. Company leader party comrade *Dr. Kühne* is also there" (emphasis in the original).[137]

An annual sporting ritual did little to bridge the vast social gap between a branch director of IG Farben and a simple worker. But did company sport in general contribute to a more egalitarian ethos within companies because in sport only performance counted? As sport historian Andreas Luh has pointed out for the late Weimar Republic, white and blue-collar workers rarely mingled during their leisure time. At the chemical firm Henkel, company sport remained informally segregated between white-collar employees and common workers. While the former played tennis and joined the hiking club, soccer, boxing, and handball had become the domain of workers. In the lady gymnastics department all the clerical employees quit when women workers joined while some male employees refused to do sport with manual workers for "hygienic reasons."[138]

In Nazi Germany, the Labour Front decried such white-collar snobbery because it undermined the people's community. A cartoon in a construction workers' paper, for example, denounced "*Schnösel Schmidt*," an arrogant white-collar upstart who refused to greet and sit with common construction workers, for his rejection of the *Volksgemeinschaft*. Due to his arrogance, Schnösel Schmidt lost the respect of the common people and landed in the mud when the workers got up and unbalanced his seat (see figure 3.5).[139] The ubiquitous DAF rhetoric about *Volksgemeinschaft* and the honour of labour might have discouraged openly disparaging remarks about manual workers but it is difficult to say how this impacted on people's actual attitudes. The KdF

3.5 *Schnösel* knew no People's Community. Printed with permission from Bundesarchiv Berlin-Lichterfelde, NS 5 VI, Nr. 18793.

organization promised that activities that were once only accessible to the privileged few would sooner or later be open to all racially acceptable people's comrades. At least in the sphere of leisure the spirit of class conflict was to be eliminated by promising people that they would be able to participate in activities that had been previously denied to them. Still, despite official criticisms of class arrogance and status privileges, established status distinctions were hard to eliminate and there is enough evidence to suggest that the Labour Front's rhetoric was not matched by reality. As historians have pointed out in respect to the leisure and travel programs of the DAF, class-based patterns of consumption persisted. As a rule, cruises with KdF cruise ships or other expensive holidays remained middle-class privileges even though some employers occasionally subsidized these trips for some of their "deserving" workers.[140]

KdF publications claimed that Nazism did away with the prejudice that "feudal sports" were out of the question for the broad mass of people. These included sports like horseback riding, skiing, tennis, hockey, and golf, which all had a reputation as upper class sports. "And now the *golf sport*! This was only a thing for millionaires. A normal mortal could absolutely not participate in it! This legend ... has also been destroyed, and great golf clubs make the effort to make golf as popular as it has been in America and in Anglo-Saxon countries for a long time," an article in the *Westdeutscher Beobachter* claimed (emphasis in the original). What counted in sport was not a person's social background or profession but one's "quality as sporting comrade" based on performance. In the new Germany, social segregation on sport fields was allegedly a thing of the past. Social differences only existed in the "heads of people who apparently have not yet fully understood our time."[141]

In reality, class-based patterns of sporting sociability often persisted. It was one thing to bring all the managers, employees, and manual workers together in an annual mobilization ritual such as the *Sportappell*. It was quite another to dissolve class-based patterns of sociability in regular sporting activities. In part this hierarchy was due to the ways in which company sport was organized in big firms. In the Leverkusen IG Farben works, for example, the exercise units of the BSG were based on people's workplaces.[142] This setup had practical, organizational reasons. In a large BSG, people had to be split into separate groups based on proximity and work requirements. But in practice division meant that people working in administrative clerical jobs would not be able to or not have to exercise with manual workers. The Kalle chemical firm in Wiesbaden divided its 5,800 blue-collar workers and white-collar employees into "competition communities" (*Wettkampfgemeinschaften*) based on their workplaces. Instead of bridging the social differences within the firm through leisure activities, this kind of organization emphasized them.[143] The price of different sporting activities was also a factor in determining who pursued which sport at Kalle. While most of the sporting activities were free or required a small fee (5 Pfennig [Pf] for swimming), an hour of tennis cost 30 Pf and horseback riding, which was socially even more prestigious, cost 50.[144]

While the Labour Front liked to trumpet the end of class and social distinctions in sport and other leisure activities, the effects of such proclamations were limited. DAF claims about the end of social privileges tell us a lot about how the regime wanted people to think about themselves and their positions in society: not as members of a social class but as respected members of a community in which they could achieve distinction based on their performance. This philosophy implied that access to leisure activities, social status, and privileges was in theory open to everyone if they demonstrated their worth to the racial performance community.[145]

Nazi efforts to foster national consciousness at the expense of class allegiances were in part inspired by the *Opera Nazionale Dopolavoro* or OND, the fascist "after-work" organization that offered supervised leisure activities for many Italian workers from the 1920s. As the KdF, the OND attempted to harness leisure and sport in the service of greater efficiency, productivity, and social cohesion. Its activities were intended "to break the ties that had previously bound worker sociability to socialist and democratic politics" and build "a new 'Italian' identity," as Victoria de Grazia has argued.[146] Sport, whether organized by large companies such as Fiat or by local Dopolavoro sections, played a significant part in this agenda.[147]

But fascist regimes were not the only ones that tried to mobilize the sporting spirit for productivity and community building in the 1920s and 1930s. Soviet authorities built sport associations affiliated with unions, the armed forces, or the security services. People who met certain performance standards in a number of sports were presented with so-called GTO (*Gotov k trudu i oborone*) sport badges as recognition that they were "ready for labour and defence." Similar to the SA sport medal, the GTO badge was meant to encourage mass participation in sport. The regime saw in physical culture a means to educate the "New Soviet Man and Woman" who was fit, disciplined, productive, and dedicated to the creation and defence of a new socialist society.[148] But even though sporting advocates in both the Nazi and Soviet regime emphasized the transformative utopian potential of physical culture and sport, the political goals of both dictatorships were quite different. While Nazism aimed to create a racially defined people's community as the basis for a genocidal racial war, Soviet ideology envisioned a "more universalist project of creating a classless, socialist society to serve as the model for the emancipation of humanity as a whole."[149]

At the time, the promotion of sport for purposes of political mobilization was not confined to totalitarian regimes. As Joan Tumblety has shown for France, sport and physical culture was propagated by movements ranging from the radical communist left to the extreme right of the *Faisceau* and *Jeunesses Patriotes* to prepare their supporters for the violent street fighting of the period.[150] The sport and physical education society of the extreme right, *Croix de Feu/Parti Social Français*, also promoted physical exercise to reverse what it considered the biological degeneration of the French nation.[151] French cities established *colonies de vacances* – summer camps for children of the working poor – in which physical education was meant to reverse the debilitating effects of urban life, evoking the recovery camps organized by German physicians like Gebhardt and Hoske. But it was the Popular Front government from 1936 to 1938 that created a new government portfolio for sport and leisure under the Socialist under secretary Léon Legrange. The leftist government provided subsidies for the construction of sport grounds and introduced an optional sport certificate. About four hundred thousand children acquired the *brevet sportif populaire* by 1937. Not unlike the KdF, the Popular Front promised to open socially elitist sports such as aviation, tennis, and skiing for a wider public. The sport policies of the Popular Front also had a social hygienic aspect. The government experimented with increasing the time for sport in primary schools and devoting half a day per week to outdoor activities; it also tracked the physical and psychological development of some of the children.[152] The French defeat of 1940 greatly exacerbated concerns about the physical and mental fitness of the nation. The authoritarian Vichy regime, which until late 1942 had a semi-autonomous status under the control of the Germans, expanded popular front initiatives in the realm of physical education by increasing public expenditures on sport to an unprecedented level from 1940 to 1944.[153]

In Britain, the government turned to the promotion of sport in the interest of national efficiency only in the late 1930s. Before that, government policies in support of sport were limited to the physical education of schoolchildren. The disappointing results of the British team at the Berlin Olympics (tenth place in the medal count) contributed to a change in government attitudes and policies. A British Board of Education delegation to Germany expressed admiration for Nazi achievements in popular physical education even though it had some reservations about the compulsory aspects of Nazi physical education. The British responded by launching a National Fitness Campaign through Prime Minister Neville Chamberlain in September 1937. The Physical Training and Recreation Act provided capital grants to local authorities and voluntary organizations for improved recreational facilities and funding for the training of instructors. The fitness campaign was aimed at the "man in the street" who was admonished to contribute to the national well-being by keeping fit.[154] While the impact of these efforts is difficult to assess, this belated campaign did not come close to the sustained promotion of sport and physical fitness in mass organizations, the workplace, and educational institutions in Nazi Germany during the same period.

In Nazi Germany, sport in mass organizations and at the workplace did not just promote health and physical fitness, even though these were considered important. Their main effect was to be psychological in that they encouraged a sense of "higher responsibility ... towards the community" and a firm performance-oriented character.[155] "Through the body the superiority of the psyche is formed," a company paper from Thuringia declared, denouncing at the same time underperforming workers who could not keep up with the productivity demands of the four-year plan. "In the future we cannot drag along mediocre workers. From every work comrade the highest performances in every area of work will be demanded."[156] The people's comrade's performance in sport and at work was supposed to be the basis of his or her social esteem and the failure to fulfil minimum requirements in one or both of these areas led to social censure. "Only performance counts" was one of the mottos of the most ambitious harnessing of the sporting principle in the service of labour productivity, the Reich Vocational Competitions, which were also known as the "Olympics of Labour," the subject of the next chapter.

Chapter Four

The Olympics of Labour: The Reich Vocational Competitions, 1934–1939

In April 1938, the Labour Front leader Robert Ley revealed one of his visionary plans for the National Socialist future. The occasion was the proclamation of the national winners of the annual Reich Vocational Competitions (*Reichsberufswettkampf* or RBWK) in front of thirty thousand spectators in the Hanseatic Hall in Hamburg:

> From every last village we will bring in the boy and the girl, who are achievers, and send them to the city to vocational school and, if necessary to universities. Significant resources are committed to support the winners in the Reich Vocational Competition. It is the first time in Germany and also the first time in the world there will be such generous support for the talented. Not the purse is decisive any more, but solely performances. Now we will move to build a *competition site*, a *Stadium for the Reich Vocational Competition*. No other location is better suited [for this project] than the site where the *Volkswagen* will be produced. In this *new city*, which will be built according to the will of the Führer, there will [also] be work shops and accommodation for the participants ... [in this] Kampf.[1] (emphases in the original)

The city Ley talked about was the "City of the KdF-Car" near Fallersleben in Lower Saxony, which today is called Wolfsburg. The KdF-Car or "People's Car" (*Volkswagen*) was one of the most potent symbols for the Labour Front's promise of a future mass consumer society that would benefit ordinary Germans. Because of the war, not much came of Ley's plans for a stadium for the Olympics of Labour, as the Reich Vocational Competitions were also called (see figure 4.1).[2] Like the promise of the *Volkswagen* that every racially "valuable" *Volksgenosse*

4.1 Olympics of Labour. Cover image from Artur Axmann, *Olympia der Arbeit. Arbeiterjugend im Reichsberufswettkampf* (Berlin: Junker und Dünnhaupt, 1937). Private collection.

could aspire to own, the many leisure activities offered by the Labour Front organization Strength through Joy, or its gigantic (never finished) holiday resort Prora on the island of Rügen, the RBWK was part of the DAF's vision for a racial "performance community" (*Leistungsgemeinschaft*) in which each Aryan German would receive the income, social rewards, and position in society that he or she deserved, based on his or her performance and achievement.[3] While Nazism certainly promoted a collectivist ethic that put the interests of the racial community before individual and human rights, historian Moritz Föllmer has pointed out that the regime also fostered individualistic aspirations and value orientations to further its ideological and political goals.[4]

The RBWK was an annual mass ritual in which apprentices and, from 1938 on, other workers were called upon to demonstrate their vocational and professional skills along with their physical fitness and their political commitment. The idea was proposed by the Hitler Youth official Artur Axmann, who was probably inspired by similar but much smaller competitions between commercial employees during the Weimar Republic.[5] The national competition was a joint endeavour of the Hitler Youth, which had 8.7 million members by the end of 1938, and the Labour Front. They enlisted the support of industry organizations, which encouraged their member firms to provide workshops, machines, raw materials, rooms, and technical personnel for organization and assessment procedures.[6] The Olympics of Labour promoted the idea of a society in which resources and opportunities for social advancement would be distributed according to people's productive contribution to the community. Opened every year by Ley and Reich Youth Leader Baldur von Schirach, it mobilized millions of young people and became one of the most important public events in the ritual calendar of Nazi Germany. Each year Hitler personally received many of the winners of the national competitions on the first of May, the Day of National Labour (see figures 4.2, 4.3, and 4.4).

The RBWK tried to turn work into a kind of sport. The competitive sport logic that shaped the contest was meant to generate enthusiasm for performance among apprentices and young workers in order to increase productivity and foster social cohesion. An analysis of the sporting discourses and meanings that informed the contest can offer valuable insights into the significance of meritocratic ideas in Nazi culture. Meritocracy in this context refers to the belief that social or economic rewards should be based on an individual's performance or *Leistung*, a notion that served complex ideological functions. In promoting *Leistung*

der Reichsorganisationsleiter das Zeichen zur Eröffnung und

4.2 Labour Front leader Robert Ley addresses opening ceremony for the RBWK. Axmann, *Olympia der Arbeit*, 50. Private collection.

der Reichsjugendführer den Befehl: „Deutsche Jugend, fange an!"

4.3 "German youth, begin!" RBWK opening speech by Reich Youth Leader Baldur von Schirach. Axmann, *Olympia der Arbeit*, 51. Private collection.

4.4 "The highest honour for the victor: the handshake of the *Führer*." Hitler receives the *Reichssieger*. In the middle, Robert Ley. Axmann, *Olympia der Arbeit*, 83. Private collection.

as a social ideal, Labour Front and Hitler Youth officials attempted to negotiate what they considered to be some of the pre-eminent tensions in German society. By promising people new opportunities for upward social mobility based on good performance at work, they tried to reconcile popular expectations of a better life with the demands for increased productivity in an economy being geared for a future war.[7] In doing so, Nazism appealed to popular notions of fairness and merit in order to mobilize support for the regime's policies.

The RBWK organizers performed what Mary Poovey has called ideological work.[8] Ideology as understood here includes practices as well as discourses that mediate between different and often contradictory understandings of power, social relations, and merit. In Nazi Germany, this type of ideological work, seen by some as a cultural revolution, did not simply naturalize existing hierarchies of class and gender.[9] More important it suggested new social hierarchies based on race and merit. It naturalized utopian ideals of fairer and more "natural" political and social hierarchies while at the same time defusing fears associated with social and political change. Ideological work also refers to the propagation and manipulation of ideas that aimed at changing people's subjectivities and their sense of place in the social order. In this case it included social and political processes and institutions that sustained and shaped ideological assumptions about the social world as well as rituals and symbolic practices, such as the RBWK, that aimed to change such subjective understandings.[10] This chapter analyses the RBWK and the sport logic that informed it in order to understand the complex ideological dimensions of technologies of subjectivation in Nazi Germany.

The first section will discuss how the organizers of the RBWK tried to harness the competitive performance principle associated with sport in order to foster performance-oriented attitudes among workers and white-collar employees. That the RBWK was often referred to as Olympics of Labour was no accident. The RBWK organizers hoped that the competitions would change workers' attitudes towards their work by turning work into a form of sport that would unleash work enthusiasm and competitive spirit among Germans and entice them to make sacrifices for the common good. The second section will discuss different understandings of the concept of *Leistung* and examine how these notions reflected contradictory expectations and possibly tensions between employers, regime officials, and workers. It will also look at the intersection of performance discourse and racial ideology. The third section will analyse promises of social fairness and upward mobility in the RBWK and discuss the implications of such meritocratic discourse for building popular legitimacy for the regime.

I. Work as Sport: The RBWK as "Olympics of Labour"

In the RBWK apprentices and young workers were asked to demonstrate their vocational skills and their political commitment to the regime.[11] Similar to the six-month long compulsory labour service, which young men had to undergo before they joined the military, the contest also attempted to foster an ethos that merged a commitment to work with combative and soldierly attitudes.[12] Participants competed in one of twenty competition groups (*Wettkampfgruppen*) that were divided according to industrial sectors. (From 1936 there was also a separate competition for university students.)[13] The *Wettkampfgruppe Eisen und Metall*, for example, was responsible for occupations in the metal and machine building industries. Other groups were responsible for the leather, textile, or mining industries.[14] Each competition group was further divided into departments for specific occupations (*Fachschaften*). The iron and metal group, for example, had a *Fachschaft* for the machine building industry, which was responsible for organizing the competitions for fitters, mechanics, toolmakers, and turners.

Participants were further split into different performance classes (*Leistungsklassen*) based on their level of training and experience. In 1938 there were ten classes: The first four were for apprentices in each year of their four-year apprenticeships, the fifth for skilled workers and journeymen with up to five years professional experience, and the sixth for those with more than that. The other performance classes were for the semi-skilled and unskilled. The unskilled and semi-skilled classes consisted of youth with a minimum age of fifteen and three months work experience, those with a minimum age of sixteen and at least one year work experience, semi-skilled adults, and the unskilled.[15]

For each performance class different assessment tasks and criteria had to be developed that required the participation of industrial foremen and other training personnel from private industry. The competition had three main parts. For men and women there was a practical task (*berufspraktische Aufgabe*), a theoretical assessment (*berufstheoretische Aufgabe*), and an ideological (*weltanschaulicher*) test. Women were also tested on their domestic skills (*hauswirtschaftliche Aufgabe*). A saddler apprentice in the third year of his apprenticeship, for example, could be asked to make a simple briefcase or military belt to show his practical skills. The theoretical part often involved work-related calculations (e.g., the amount of leather needed for a product with certain specifications). The ideological test asked questions about contemporary politics (e.g., Nazi population policies, the role of Jews as the Bolshevik rulers of Russia) or economics (e.g., the importance of foreign exchange for the German economy).[16] The practical and theoretical tests for girls and women were shorter to free up some time for the assessment of their domestic skills.[17] Both sexes also had to demonstrate their physical fitness in sport.

Participants demonstrated their skills in competitions on the local, district (Gau), and Reich levels. The winners in local competitions would compete at a district level and the winners there provided the pool for participants in the national contest. A selection of the national winners (*Reichssieger*) was invited to the Reich Chancellery each year to shake hands with Hitler. The competitions usually took place between February and late April each year. Beginning with 500,000 participants in 1934, there were 750,000 in 1935, 1,036,000 in 1936, 1,800,000 in 1937, and more than 2,800,000 in 1938. From 1938 adults were also encouraged to participate in what was now called the "RBWK of all working Germans" (*Reichsberufswettkampf aller schaffenden Deutschen*).[18] In 1939, there were 3.3 to 3.5 million competitors, which included participants from occupied Austria and the Sudetenland. The "*Reichsendausscheid*" or national finals took place every year in a different city: 1934 in Berlin, 1935 in Saarbrücken (to celebrate the reclaiming of the Saar), 1936 in Königsberg, 1937 in Munich, 1938 in Hamburg, and 1939 in Cologne.[19]

After the beginning of the Second World War, the competitions were suspended, but Nazi leaders were so convinced of their success in mobilizing people that Hitler personally ordered a resurrection of the event as *Kriegsberufswettkampf* or KBWK in 1943.[20] The KBWK still activated 2.5 million participants under very difficult war conditions between November 1943 and April 1944. It was a desperate and somewhat bizarre attempt to engender enthusiasm for war among German youths who were not drafted into the army and manifested severe disciplinary problems in the face of the intensification of work in industry (see chapter 5).[21]

While the RBWK was an initiative of the DAF and Hitler Youth, some employers lent considerable logistical support as well as put pressure on their employees to participate. At the IG Farben branch in Leverkusen, the Labour Front plant leader *Betriebsobmann* Schwarz and the IG branch manager Hans Kühne called on plant and departmental managers to make sure that everyone who was eligible participated: "We see in the participation of all working comrades ... an immeasurable educational effect, because only striving combative people face up to the fight (*stellen sich zum Kampf*) ... we must draft the last man from his comfort zone for the front because only in this way can we educate the performance men (*Leistungsmenschen*) who measure up to the demands of the future and who can compensate for the shortness of suitable manpower through increased performance."[22] A combative community of racially acceptable Germans who demonstrated their commitment to work and productivity under the leadership of the Labour Front, was a favourite vision of DAF officials, which was also reflected in their propaganda for the National Day of Labour on 1 May (see figure 4.5).[23]

But the joint appeal by Schwarz and Kühne also points to a convergence of interests between employers and the Labour Front, both of which were concerned about increasing productivity and preventing tensions in the workplace. Kühne was, according to his own admission at least, initially attracted by the regime's promise to foster "a sound relationship between employers and workers."[24] In fact he was among the supporters of the RBWK at a time when the significance of the event could not have been foreseen.[25]

In a letter to its member firms, the corporate representation of the German chemical industry (*Wirtschaftsgruppe Chemische Industrie* or WCI) maintained that company leaders "have recognized the value and significance ... of the *Reichsberufswettkämpfe* ... leaving no doubt that the ... [RBWK] as expression of the performance will and commitment of working people evokes the same sympathies among industrial enterprises."[26] Whether the support was always as enthusiastic as this sentence suggests is doubtful. The RBWK was a massive endeavour requiring significant logistical and material support from managers and employers who were not always happy about the disruptions and increased workloads caused by the event. The WCI pointed to such sources of conflict between employers and the Labour Front when it promised that the 1938 contest would try to keep the burden on organizers and the disturbances of official qualifying exams for skilled workers (*Facharbeiter- und Gehilfenprüfungen*) to a minimum.[27]

In order to ensure widespread participation among employees, employers were encouraged to compensate participating youths for their loss of earnings during the contest. Many employers seemed to have done that.[28] As was the case with company sport, employers

4.5 Prepared for work and performance: IG Farben company community, Leverkusen branch. *Von Werk zu Werk. Monatsschrift der Werksgemeinschaft I. G. Farbenindustrie Aktiengesellschaft*. Leverkusen edition, May 1938. Printed with the permission of Bayer Corporate Archive, Leverkusen.

could demonstrate loyalty to the regime by supporting the RBWK and its participants. Firms that, in the view of some Labour Front officials, refused to lend adequate support were sometimes singled out and publicly denounced. Along with another company, the Swabian shoe manufacturer Salamander was accused of "provid[ing] a bad example of unsocial attitude" by the regional DAF commissioner of the RBWK in front of eight hundred competition organizers (*Wettkampfleiter*). The company did not want to pay its employees while they participated in the contest because it had already reduced their hours due to economic difficulties and the competition took place during their day off.[29] But the public reprimand was enough to convince the firm to make at least some payments to its employees.[30]

The Olympics of Labour were a cornerstone of Labour Front productivity drives. As Ley put it, the RBWK was to carry the "sporting spirit" (*sportlichen Geist*) into workplaces to raise workers' enthusiasm for work.[31] In doing so, the organizers drew on discourses and experiences from the Weimar Republic where the health and productivity of the working population had become a central concern of biopolitical initiatives such as eugenics, the work sciences, social welfare, popular health, and fitness campaigns. In the view of many, sport was not only a way of increasing the physical fitness of people but it also promoted workers' willingness to work, which allegedly had suffered in the course of the First World War, the revolution, and the social dislocations of the immediate postwar years.

The German Institute for Technical Work Schooling or DINTA (the employer-sponsored organization that promoted innovations to vocational education, discussed in chapter 2) advocated company sport for white-collar employees and manual workers in order to increase community orientation, workplace competitiveness, and productivity.[32] Before 1933, the director of the DINTA was Karl Arnhold, whose program to "educate workers for work" looked to sport as a way to create performance-oriented workers. During the Third Reich he became the director of the Office for Vocational Education and Company Leadership (*Amt für Berufserziehung und Betriebsführung*) of the Labour Front, a department that played an important organizational role in the RBWK.[33] Arnhold always emphasized the need to shape workers' subjective predispositions. He rejected American approaches in economic rationalization because, in his view, people like Taylor neglected the role that psychological factors played in motivating people. By contrast, with "German rationalization the enlivened (*beseelte*) working man is at the center of the company ... He is the animated motor of all the operations *(Betriebsgeschehens)* and directs with his will and creative forces the organism as a whole." Because they treated humans as soulless machines, neither the American "performance whip" (*Leistungspeitsche*) nor the Russian "hurrier system" (*Antreibesystem*) could foster people's enthusiasm for work. For an "optimum of technical and economic performance," it was necessary to "raise men with high performance skills, with strong performance will who were psychologically prepared for total dedication" to their work.[34]

The ideal worker was committed to performance. He worked willingly and responsibly for the benefit of the company community and the racial people's community, and needed little supervision because his superiors could rely on him.[35] In the RBWK, the competitive logic inherent in sport was to transform young workers into willing, self-directed, and responsible workers. By turning work into a sport, it tried to harness young workers' enthusiasm for competitive sports in the interest of increased labour productivity and a changed attitude towards work.

Sport was important for the RBWK in several ways. The organizers shared widely held assumptions about the character-building qualities of sport and physical exercise, which is why they made the demonstration of physical fitness and sporting ability part of the assessment in the district and national competitions (see figure 4.6). Competitors had to fulfil minimum requirements in simple track and field disciplines. The requirements were not onerous; it was presumed that everyone with basic fitness would be able to meet them. In this way, sport would help to eliminate "careerists and strivers" (*Berufsstreber*) from the competition. These were people who were good in their profession but whose absence of physical fitness testified to their lack of character and commitment to the ideals of National Socialism.[36]

On a more fundamental level, the RBWK drew on the code of honour of amateur sport in seeking to turn work into a form of sport. Winners at all levels should be content with the honour that went along with public social recognition and not expect more tangible material rewards. In this respect the competitions were part of the Labour Front's promise to restore the "social honour" of manual labour in particular. Compared with the dignity bestowed on participants in the RBWK, the "wage question" was presented as secondary and demands for pay rises were denounced as the concerns of a bygone materialistic age.[37]

körperlich und geistig geschult, zur Leistung bereit ist.

4.6 The ideal competitor: "mentally and physically trained, ready to perform." Axmann, *Olympia der Arbeit*, 46. (Private collection)

Like amateur athletes, competitors were encouraged to give their best in what was presented as a noble struggle. Indeed, it is tempting to see the RBWK as an extension of the Social Darwinist struggle for survival invoked regularly by Nazi leaders. Yet, while there were certainly resonances with the Nazi valorization of the struggle for survival, officials were keen to point out that participants were expected to follow an ethical codex that respected their opponents. They were competitors – not rivals who aimed at humiliating their competitors. According to the Nazi press, German people's comrades were engaged in a *Wettkampf* for honour, while professional athletes and racial aliens tried to vanquish their enemies in the pursuit of material gain. The professional athlete driven by egoism (*Eigennutz*) was quite different from the competitor in the RBWK who supposedly saw himself and his competitors as members of the same racial people's community.[38] In the view of the RBWK organizers, the event was not meant to be divisive but rather an experience that contributed to "community formation" (*Gemeinschaftsbildung*). In typical Nazi fashion, community spirit was also fostered through the stigmatization of "racial" aliens: Jews, social outsiders, and people with hereditary illnesses were all excluded.[39]

The RBWK competitor was not an enemy but a respected adversary who had to be admired for his endeavours as a people's comrade even if he or she lost. Every participant deserved respect: "This competition does not determine winners and losers." What counted was everybody's "contribution to the community" (*gemeinschaftsgebundene Leistung*).[40] If someone was not successful, they should acknowledge the achievements of others without envy and try to become a better contestant the next time around. The judges of the competitions provided feedback to individual participants about their strengths and weaknesses, but the competitions also encouraged permanent self-scrutiny on the part of the participant. Like athletes, they were to make the effort "to work on themselves throughout the year and train in order to emerge as a winner the next time."[41]

In keeping with the lofty amateur ideals professed by the official discourse, the awards and recognitions for participation and achievements in the RBWK were mostly symbolic. Each competitor received a formal certificate of appreciation that certified that they had committed themselves to the ideals of work and performance.[42] Participation testified to a worker's physical fitness, character, and willingness to compete against others. Usually, only the district or national winners received something more tangible. While there were only a couple of hundred national winners in 1937, there were about 100,000 winners on the local and district levels.[43] This proliferation of winners was deliberate because the contest was, as we have observed, intended to mobilize young people. A 1934 report by a psychological consultant on the RBWK warned organizers that recognition of only the best performers could discourage widespread participation.[44] Recognition of competitors was to be spread as widely as possible. In the RBWK 1938/39, there were over 140,000 male and female competitors in the Gau Baden, among them 35 national, 303 Gau, and 1,480 local winners. They were not the only ones who received an official recognition. There were 29,877 participants who received commendations for outstanding performances. Almost a quarter of the competitors thus received official recognition.[45] While it was considered important to give special rewards to the very best, the RBWK distributed symbolic rewards more widely because it wanted to give the broad mass of people incentives to perform well. As Axmann put it: "It is good when 1,000 people make 10 steps forward, it is even better for our Volk when 100,000 make one step forward at the same time."[46]

By spreading recognition beyond the numerous local winners through minor gifts or simple commendations, the organizers tried to convey to young people the idea that the contest could be a rewarding experience even if they did not become local, Gau, or national champions. In many ways this concern about the appropriate distribution of rewards mirrored the tensions between high performance sport and sport for the masses more generally. Before 1933 there was already recognition among the promoters of sport for the masses that an emphasis on the best performances could discourage wider participation in sport. Recognizing many above-average achievers through medals, certificates, or minor gifts encouraged mass participation in sport, as well as in the RBWK. The SA sport medal is a good example of such an approach. People who demonstrated a fairly modest competency in sport received the award, which was handed out to approximately three million adults.[47] In mass sport, as well as in the sporting and vocational competitions conducted within the framework of the RBWK, people had to demonstrate minimum achievements in order to be recognized as worthy contributors to the racial community.

II. The Meanings of *Leistung*

The various meanings of Nazi *Leistung* propaganda can only be understood by reference to Nazi ideas about class and race. The regime expended a great deal of energy in conveying to a sceptical and potentially hostile working class that workers had finally become respectable members of a new racial community. This effort included the symbolic bridging of divisions of social class and political power; for example, the leader of the German Labour Front and other Nazi leaders insisted on shaking the hands of workers at the workplace, while Hitler (falsely) claimed that he had worked as a simple construction worker in Vienna.[48] The epitome of the recognition of workers' honour was the annual National Day of Labour on 1 May. Originally the date on which international socialists demonstrated for their cause and celebrated their achievements, the occasion was hijacked by the Nazis and turned into a day that celebrated the new respectability of German workers as members of the racial community.[49] The first of May was also the symbolic high point of the RBWK because Hitler personally received a selection of the national winners. When he addressed them in the newly built Reich Chancellery building in 1939, he claimed that the new building "was not destined for diplomats alone, but it also had to serve for the gathering of the Führer with his best workers."[50] The day before, the *Reichssieger* were invited to a reception in the propaganda ministry where they had the opportunity to talk with Goebbels, Schirach, and Ley.[51]

In Nazi ideology, the value of a people's comrade depended solely on his or her performance for the community. However, the notion of *Leistung* was, I argue, a multifaceted and polysemic notion also inherently ambiguous: it could connote a set of measurable achievements but also refer to a performance ethic that was expressed in a specific attitude to creativity and work (*Arbeitsgesinnung*).[52] This means that different attitudes and normative commitments played (and still play) a role in the use and understanding of the term. *Leistung* meant different things to different people. Its very ambiguity invoked certain meanings and obscured others depending on the context in which people employed the term. This section will analyse the different meanings of *Leistung* in relation to cultural notions of work performance and explore how Nazi officials presented the relationship between a person's performance, economic rewards, race, and social recognition as a respected member of the *Volks- und Leistungsgemeinschaft*.

On one level, the RBWK denied the significance of class differences. The sport metaphor underwriting this competition is important here. The RBWK organizers' claim that "character and performance" determined a person's social value and his suitability for leadership positions appealed to popular notions about the equalizing power of sport competitions.[53] In sport only performance counted. A person's social background and economic status was irrelevant. Axmann, for example, expressed his conviction that vocational performance could be measured as reliably as sporting performance: "The idea of competition can be perfectly realized in the same way in the vocational area as in sport."[54]

But if only performance mattered, what exactly counted as performance and constituted merit? Embedded in performance discourse were, I would argue, different notions of what constituted merit. Performance in terms of productivity could be measured; production targets and piece rates could be set that served as incentives for workers to be more productive. Wages and social rewards could then be determined based on a worker's objectively measured performance, which was considered fair because they corresponded to notions of economic reciprocity and were proportional to workers' contribution to productivity and national wealth. Hitler invoked such ideas of reciprocity in a speech in 1938: every German had to understand that the "value of his work must be equal to his wage." He justified this expression with reference to inflation fears: the German Reichsmark had to "remain an honest piece of paper that was an honest entitlement (*ehrliche Anweisung*) to the product of the honest labour of someone else."[55]

As Alf Lüdtke has pointed out, the discourse on quality work and performance had two layers. There was an official discourse shared by employers, work scientists, and many Nazi officials that emphasized productivity. At the centre of this was a notion of economic efficiency. Performance was judged in terms of the ratio between inputs of capital and labour and the quality and quantity of finished products.[56] This was the discourse of economic rationalizers and the four-year plan of 1936 that aimed to squeeze the highest productivity from limited human resources. After the integration of the unemployed into the labour force and the serious labour shortages that resulted from mobilization and rearmament drives, "the most thorough use of the performance capacity" of people became a top priority.[57] According to this view, wages and social benefits, such as the leisure activities promoted by the Labour Front, should be kept at a minimum since they compromised the productivity of the nation. As Hermann Göring, the plenipotentiary for the four-year plan, put it with reference to Labour Front support for KdF leisure activities: "the Labour Front should create more strength and less joy."[58] This type of performance discourse stressed pure productivity at the expense of material rewards and social welfare. It had limited appeal for workers who had to fear that they would be subjected to an austere efficiency regime.

As Lüdtke has shown, there was also an unofficial discourse on work performance whose measure was not productivity but the subjective experience of exhaustion and effort expended by the worker.[59] The RBWK organizers tried to acknowledge these attitudes. The decisive aspects of the performance campaign were not productivity or the outcome for participants, official proclamations claimed. After all, not everyone could be a winner. More important was the attitude with which competitors approached their work, the spirit in which they competed. Work only held true meaning through exertion and combative commitment for the community. As Schirach put it, the participants of the RBWK would realize "that the working human and not the capitalist shapes the fate of the nation" and "that not the money but the creative performance is decisive."[60] By competing and working on their skills, by their attempts to iron out weaknesses in their work performance, workers could demonstrate that their character and commitment to *Leistung* made them deserving members of the Aryan *Volksgemeinschaft*. I do not want to deny that the importance of *Leistungssteigerung* for the regime lay in an increase of productivity. Increased work productivity was a central goal of a dictatorship that tried to mobilize all resources for a future war. But defining *Leistung* as a set of subjective attitudes ultimately also constituted a means of raising productivity by giving encouragement to workers and diffusing fears that Nazi productivity drives were only based on an intensified exploitation of labour.

These fears were not without foundation. After the proclamation of the four-year plan in 1936, even some regime officials worried that long working hours might be unsustainable. The trustee of labour for the iron and steel industry, who was responsible for the setting of wage levels and the supervision of labour relations in the workplace, expressed concerns about the physical exhaustion of the labour force; the army economic inspectorate (*Wehrwirtschaftsinpektion*) attributed stagnating work productivity to exhaustion of workers; and the Nazi Party Gauleiter of the Saar area, Josef Bürckel, wondered whether it would not be better to return to the eight-hour shift because despite rationalization, modernization, and longer workdays, the mining output in his area still lagged behind the projections of the four-year plan.[61] Annual health reports by district medical officers also showed a rise in work-related illness and injuries as a result of longer workdays and intensified labour.[62]

Apart from concerns about the sustainability of the mobilization effort, there was some recognition that too much emphasis on productivity as a basis for acknowledging merit and distributing rewards was problematic. Distinctions among workers based on productivity alone could motivate some people but they could also undermine the motivation of those who did not receive such recognition.[63] This variation is another reason why performance was at least partially defined as an inner attitude, a set of value orientations. Mere participation in the RBWK was already described as honourable, because it demonstrated a person's commitment to the racial community. The message that performance in the sense of productivity was not everything was further reinforced by political criteria. The RBWK tried to disadvantage and eliminate people who might be very good in their vocation but who lacked the right inner attitude and character. The competition not only tested vocational skills and physical fitness, it also tested participants' commitment to the regime through a set of questions about Nazi politics and world view. Participants who could not answer these questions satisfactorily would lose significant points in the contest because the political section counted for a sixth of the final grade. The organizers emphasized that vocational performance and political commitment could not be separated while still claiming that vocational competence was indispensable to outstanding performance.[64]

Being conversant with the political issues of the day from a Nazi point of view was essential. This reality was not only true for participants in the RBWK but also for apprentices who had to undergo political assessments as part of their vocational examinations. If they did badly in the *Weltanschauung* part of their vocational tests, they could fail.[65] Victor Klemperer asserts as much in a story: an apprentice who answered the question "What comes after the Third Reich?" with "The Forth" would inevitably fail no matter how competent he was in his vocation. The correct answer was: "Nothing comes afterwards, because the Third Reich is the eternal Reich of the Germans."[66] While this story was probably based on a popular joke, the *Weltanschauung* questions for the RBWK at least were more open-ended and demanded longer essay-type answers; the political component of the RBWK was undoubtedly an integral part of the contest.

Defining *Leistung* at least in part in terms of political commitment allowed senior Hitler Youth officials to counter criticism that the myriad activities of the Hitler Youth kept young people from performing in schools and in the workplace.[67] In Axmann's view, the competition results clearly showed that Hitler Youth membership had a positive effect on performance. As evidence he produced data showing Hitler Youth members did better in the political *Weltanschauung* section of the competition than those who were not members of the Nazi movement. Given the extensive political indoctrination in the Nazi youth organization, this is hardly surprising. However, Axmann's claims that the political schooling also had a discernible effect on workplace performance was much less convincing, since he did not provide any evidence that showed that Hitler Youth members did better in the practical and theoretical vocational parts of the competition. It would not have been difficult to do this because the organizers could have correlated data from the questionnaire that each participant was asked to fill. Instead Axmann merely pointed out that 48 per cent of the RBWK *Reichssieger* had leadership positions in the HJ. Given the importance of *Weltanschauung* in the overall scoring in the competitions, this number tells us little about their professional competence compared to the other winners. Such claims might even have confirmed popular suspicion that members of party organizations were given preferential treatment in the competition. Axmann's failure to provide evidence, therefore, is a strong indication that the data did not bear out his claim that there was a significant positive correlation between Hitler Youth membership and job performance.[68]

Official proclamations always demanded that "the Reichssieger who presents himself to the Führer on May 1 has to combine *physical, vocational, and ideological fitness* (*weltanschauliche Tüchtigkeit*)" (emphasis in the original).[69] Due to this emphasis on the political commitment of the contestants, the propaganda for the RBWK tried to dismiss claims that the *Weltanschauung* part compromised the meritocratic principle of the competition, because this would have undermined the regime's claims about social fairness. For example, in the official account about his experience, the *Reichssieger* Heinz Kilian, a machine fitter in the second year of his apprenticeship, expressed only contempt for the "grumblers" (*Meckerer*) who complained that the *Weltanschauung* questions gave an unfair advantage to dedicated members of the Hitler Youth.[70]

The political component in the RBWK raised the question of what was more important, commitment to the Nazi world view or merit as determined by vocational skills, job performance, or, in the case of university students, academic performance? In examining the

German Research Foundation's practice of granting scholarships, one historian has claimed that ideological considerations (in the narrow sense of political allegiance to Nazism and its racial ideals) eclipsed meritocratic, academic considerations.[71] As seen from the above discussion about the political component of the RBWK, it was certainly advantageous for participants to demonstrate political knowledge and commitment to Nazism. This dedication was not only rewarded with points in the contest. From 1939 onwards, winners in the RBWK were supposed to fill out report cards on their political activism in the Hitler Youth and in the League of German Girls that were to be used to determine who would receive financial and educational support for his or her career development. "The often all too stormy competition for the good expert (*Fachmann*) may have led to a situation in which the political meaning of vocational education and support for the talented has been ... forgotten," the Hitler Youth declared. The stronger emphasis on political reliability was in part a response to a survey that found that only thirteen out of three hundred providers of stipends and other forms of vocational support had demanded an assessment of character and political attitude from their applicants. A planned support foundation for the talented (*Begabtenförderungswerk*) announced by the Reich Youth Leader promised to end such practices once and for all.[72]

It should be stressed, however, that rewards for political engagement and the determination of merit based on performance and skills in the workplace were not mutually exclusive. Both political commitment and vocational competence were demanded from the ideal people's comrade. Nazi ideologues did not see these two demands as contradictory. On the contrary, they argued that political commitment reinforced people's work ethic and commitment to improve their skills. In this view, "ideological attitude" (*weltanschauliche Haltung*) was the "*foundation of vocational performance*" (emphasis in the original).[73] This official discourse blurred distinctions and obscured tensions between political devotion to racial ideals and notions of merit based on performance and skills in the workplace. The performance assessment in the RBWK also demonstrates that determination of merit (or meritocracy for that matter) is not based on universal principles that operate outside specific political and social contexts. In this case meritocratic discourse and the determination of merit depended on historically specific cultural and political assumptions about the relationship between work performance and political commitment.

Both sets of non-vocational assessments in the RBWK – the political and sport tests – reinforced the message that performance would not be measured in terms of productive achievement alone but by the attitudes people brought to their work. This message was confirmed by the inclusion of people with physical disabilities. Those whose disabilities were not hereditary but were acquired later in life through an accident could participate if they demonstrated vocational talent and the will to perform. Disabled participants did not have to participate in the sporting contest and their vocational tests were adjusted according to their special needs. If they could cope with the intellectual requirements of the competition, the organizers argued, the principles of comradeship and mutual help demanded that people with heavy physical disabilities were to be encouraged through "joy in work" and even the occasional "helping hand." By contrast, all people with hereditary conditions were to be excluded. Youths in educational correctional facilities (*Erziehungsanstalten*) were to be excluded if their deviance was interpreted as hereditary and not as the result of environmental conditions.[74] This differentiation confirms that the experience of people with disabilities could vary in accordance with the racial hygienic policies of the regime. For the physically disabled, separate sections of the Hitler Youth existed. Those who were not seen as posing a threat to the hereditary health of the nation might theoretically still be accepted into the racial community – if they demonstrated their will to work for the community. In practice, however, the Nazi valorization of strength and the stigmatization of weakness created a hostile atmosphere for many.[75]

Defining *Leistung* as expression of an innate performance-orientation was meant to encourage people to participate in the RBWK. Participation was held to demonstrate that people had the will to work and become productive members of the community. The emphasis on subjective attitudes was also meant to quell suspicions that the stress on *Leistung* was nothing more than a productivity drive aimed at squeezing the last productive reserves out of the workforce. The promotion of the RBWK emphasized that people participated voluntarily because competition and struggle meant joy. Or, as Hitler put it when he greeted one of the national winners on 1 May 1937, "When work is struggle, work is beautiful."[76] Every participant could benefit because, as in sport, the RBWK only knew winners and participants who were "honourably defeated."[77] Whether such subtle semantics were enough to dispel people's performance anxieties remains doubtful. There was enough stigmatizing language in the RBWK promotional literature that conveyed contempt for those who could not meet minimum performance expectations. Failure to master tests was described with the term *versagen*, a word that in German has even more pejorative connotations than the English term "failing."[78] The terminological oscillation between encouragement, pressure, and denunciation was typical of a regime that made great promises of a future "social state" at the same time as it sought to enforce the cooperation of its citizens, whether through the pressure it applied on people to make "voluntary" contributions to the people's community or through terror.[79]

An examination of the *Leistung* discourse of the RBWK also provides an opportunity to explore how the regime's mobilization of human resources intersected with its racist propaganda. The RBWK presented the ideal people's comrade in racial terms. In doing so, the regime could draw on pre-Nazi ideological traditions that saw in the commitment to "quality" work an essential trait of Germanness.[80] By the 1920s, some of this discourse was already cast within the framework of Nordic racism. Racial scientists like Hans F. K. Günther and Ludwig Ferdinand Clauss, for example, argued that performance-orientation was an essential characteristic of the Nordic race.[81] As we have seen in the previous chapter, after 1933 anthropologists and physicians were keen on emphasizing similar links between race and sport performance.

For Hitler, work was not a path to the selfish fulfilment of individual needs. Rather, it was supposed to serve the community.[82] A similar understanding of work is also evident in the RBWK performance discourse. As Axmann put it: "The performance competition contributes to the strengthening of the work and vocational ethos. It shows the young workers in a tangible way that they do not work in order to live, but that they live in order to work."[83] Personal sacrifice and commitment to performance were explicitly cast as signs of racial superiority: "Unselfish sacrifice and performance for the community ... are unbetrayable signs of the value of the race."[84] Again, *Leistung* is defined here as a normative value orientation that had to be taught to workers. But if they committed themselves enthusiastically to this task, they also demonstrated their racial worth. In the *Leistung* concept, the concerns of economic rationalizers about labour productivity – be they employers, work scientists, or government bureaucrats – merged with Nazi attempts to define race in terms of innate attitudes and value orientations of the Aryan people's comrade.[85]

In Nazi performance discourse, the German people's comrade was presented as the "performance man" whose antithesis was the Jew.

Hitler denounced Jews as parasites and unproductive "drones" who undermined the performance capacity of the Aryan race in its struggle for survival. It goes without saying that Jews were excluded from the RBWK, which was presented as an authentic expression of the Aryan *Leistungsgemeinschaft*. An article headline such as: "Everybody is welcome – but no Jew" pointed to the Jew as the antithesis of the Aryan performance man.[86] The exclusion was based on the assumption that there was a particular German/Aryan work and performance ethos that would be corrupted by "racial aliens."

In the view of Ley, social and racial policies were inextricably linked. Jews were not even a race. Even "negroes" would protest if they were put into the same category as Jews. Jews were "tubercles and bacilli" who did not deserve pity. They were responsible for Marxism, a movement that, in contrast to Nazism, had not done anything for workers in practical terms.[87] By contrast, Nazism would liberate the German worker by turning him into a performer who willingly sacrificed himself for the Führer and the community. Work during the Weimar Republic was torture and a disgrace, while now it became life's fulfillment. In the view of the promoters of the RBWK, the German worker's voluntary commitment to performance stood in stark contrast to the Soviet slave system run by Jewish "parasites." While the Soviet worker was exploited by parasitic Jews and had no prospects, the son of a German worker could rise to the highest offices in the state based on his performance.[88] In this view, the RBWK were the antithesis to the Stakhanov system of labour intensification in the Soviet Union (see figure 4.7):[89] "By the most brutal means the Russian worker is forced to achieve this goal [the work norms of the Stakhanov system]. The Stakhanov-method is an undignified hurrier system. In Germany this is fundamentally different. Here the working people commit themselves ... to greater performance. This is proof of the high-mindedness (*Gesinnung*) of German youth and German workers."[90] This high-mindedness of the German worker was clearly wishful thinking since there is significant evidence of popular discontent with the intensification of work in Nazi Germany. It seems that the representation of the Stakhanov system was also a way of pre-empting popular criticism of "hurrying" (*Antreiberei*) by projecting it on the communist other.[91]

The Soviet Stakhanov campaign had its origins in the system of Socialist competition in the workplace. It emerged in the context of the first five-year plan designed to force the pace of Soviet industrialization from 1928 onwards. In contrast to the Nazi caricature of the Stakhanov

4.7 Stakhanov method vs *Reichsberufswettkampf*.
Printed with the permission of Bundesarchiv Berlin-Lichterfelde, NS 5 VI, Nr. 18794.

campaign, different types of socialist competition in the workplace were not simply crude exploitation drives. Like the educational efforts of the DINTA and the later ones of the Labour Front, Soviet performance campaigns tried to "develop th[e] independent initiative of workers ... as widely as possible," as Lenin put it in an article written in 1917 but published for the first time in 1929.[92] The Stakhanov campaign itself had its origins in the decision of a party committee to launch a competition for the best hewer in the Central Irmino mine in the Donbass in August 1935. The competition was meant to energize the workers, because the mine lagged behind in its plan fulfilment. As part of the competition the miner Aleksei G. Stakhanov was given the opportunity to set an example for outstanding productivity by cutting 102 tons of coal – more than 14 times his norm.[93] When the word of his achievement spread, his example was emulated in many other industries. 1936 was declared the year of Stakhanovites in which Stakhanov days, Stakhanov ten-day periods (dekadas), and Stakhanov months promoted productivity in industry. Workers who exceeded their work norms were declared "Stakhanovites," who in many enterprises made up more than a fourth of the workforce.[94] As historian Lewis Siegelbaum has shown, the political and social dynamics behind the campaign were complex and, for that reason, I cannot fully examine them here. What the RBWK and the Stakhanov campaign had in common was, however, the goal to change workers' subjectivity in order to promote virtues such as discipline, punctuality, sobriety as well as "mastery of technology." Both campaigns also promised workers better working opportunities, symbolic and material rewards, and, most importantly, skills development and thus upward mobility.[95]

The distinction RBWK organizers made between the Russians who were forced to work in an inhuman fashion to give everything for their five-year plans and the willing and enthusiastic German worker who gave everything for the success of the four-year plan pointed to the principle of "self education" (*Selbsterziehung*) that characterized the RBWK according to Nazi officials. While in the Soviet Union workers were allegedly forced to be productive, in Germany workers voluntarily educated themselves by exposing themselves to the joys of competition. In this process, the "high industriousness and creative spirit" of workers were mobilized – character traits that in the Nazi view were innate to the racial constitution of the German people's comrade.[96] The capacity for *Selbsterziehung* was racial. Its locus lay within the German worker who, according to Nazi educators, had a natural performance drive and affinity to Nazism. Political commitment and job performance, one writer claimed, were nurtured from the same racial root, which is why contestants in the RBWK were asked to demonstrate their knowledge of and commitment to the political ideals of Nazism in addition to their vocational skills.[97]

The construction of the German worker as a racially superior being, who demonstrated his or her superiority through "voluntary" performance in the workplace and the RBWK, is in some ways similar to Hitler's beliefs regarding the means by which a person's racial value could be determined. Hitler accepted the views of racial scientists on the different racial backgrounds of non-Jewish Germans but he rejected the notion that a person's race was always manifested in their physical appearance. Instead Hitler thought that a person's ability, performance, and achievement demonstrated his racial worth. *Leistung* was thus an expression of a person's racial background.[98] While such reasoning is clearly tautological – race determined ability, which in turn pointed to one's racial background – the peculiar inner logic of this claim was meant to encourage people to demonstrate their racial worth to the community through performance.

The notion of the peculiar nature of German attitudes to work might have been appealing to some workers. Historians like Alf Lüdtke and Ulrich Herbert have emphasized that German workers were proud of their own commitment to quality work. Such attitudes preceded Nazism and were part of a culture shared by organized labour in which "good work" stood for the identity and self-confidence of workers. Sometimes such views were combined with a rejection of American forms of rationalization that fostered the de-skilling of the labour force. Union representatives who had toured the US in the 1920s pointed in this respect to the differences between American workers whose poor training had made it necessary to make work processes foolproof and German workers whose skills allowed them to respond to changing work situations in a flexible way.[99] Similarities with more openly chauvinistic understandings of "German" work are apparent here.[100] Seen from this perspective, some workers might have considered an emphasis on the innate racial ability of the German worker as flattering, but it should be noted that this construction also carried a threat: those who were either incapable or unwilling to fulfil expected political and work commitments were readily denounced as racial inferiors who could be ostracized and fall victim to the regime's campaigns against antisocials.[101] Workers had to demonstrate that they were valuable members of the racial performance community. As Hitler put it: "the value of a human being ... and his value for the people's community are exclusively determined through the way in which he performs his assigned work."[102] People who showed "under performance" (*Minderleistungsfähigkeit*) over a long period of time could be stigmatized as racial inferiors. They became ineligible for social benefits, such as marriage loans, and could be victimized by Nazi eugenics policies and thrown into concentration camps.[103] In contemporary parlance, people had "to prove themselves" (*bewähren*) at work in order to gain acceptance into the community.

III. Performance, Merit, and the Promise of Social Mobility

In the 1930s, *Leistung* referred to notions of productivity and measurable achievements in the workplace. But *Leistung* also implied a broader set of attitudes and value orientations, which all German people's comrades were supposed to share. People were expected to demonstrate performance-orientation (*Leistungsbereitschaft*) through participation in sport, their commitment to work, and their willingness to sacrifice for the benefit of the racial community. In the view of the organizers, people's participation in the RBWK demonstrated their political commitment to the regime as well as their willingness to be productive citizens.

The propagation of the performance principle also carried the prospect of equal opportunity. The Nazi regime claimed to be meritocratic. While they did not create a classless society, many Nazis promoted a utopian vision that nonetheless aspired to change the ethos of social relations by doing away with unfair social privileges once and for all and rewarding people based on their innate abilities and their contribution to the racial community. This promise was meant to change workers' subjective understanding of their social situation through a process that historian Michael Schneider has called "unclassing" (*Ent-Klassung*).[104] Workers should cease to see themselves as members of a social class with distinct interests and accept that they were members of a racial performance community that offered them new opportunities based on their "natural" talents. In the opening quote of this chapter, Ley linked state support for the talented with the idea of building a stadium for the RBWK. The sport analogy that informed the competition is important here because it invoked a notion of sport as an arena of equal opportunity in which every German could demonstrate his or her abilities regardless of social background.

In the workplace, the discourse about performance legitimized the allocation (and denial) of social and material rewards. This practice is, for example, evident in the way in which employers and regime officials tried to change the wage structure in many industries by promoting the "performance wage" (*Leistungslohn*). Since the regime tried to keep the overall cost of wages down to protect its rearmament drive, officials attempted to foster workers' performance-orientation through wage structures that rewarded the most productive workers and penalized the least productive while keeping overall labour costs in check.[105] To use Adam Tooze's words, the Nazi racial community was a "people's community on a budget" with little room to significantly increase the real living standard of the mass of the German people.[106] Or as Jonathan Wiesen put it: "the regime could not reconcile the dream of creating a Nazi consumer economy with the push towards war."[107] Since the capacity to provide material rewards to workers was limited, performance pay and performance campaigns such as the RBWK were seen as cheap ways to reward workers selectively and raise productivity.[108]

But performance-based rewards also served another purpose. They conveyed the message that the regime was serious about changing social relations in order to create a better and fairer society that offered new opportunities for all people who were included in the racial people's community. The goal was to convince workers that Nazism, in contrast to previous political regimes, would be fair in its distribution of social recognition and economic opportunities.[109] By analysing how the promise of social mobility was presented in the RBWK and how these competitions articulated and reworked notions of fairness, rewards, and social merit, this section will examine the subtle semantics of the regime's attempt to rework people's self-understanding.

According to the social ideology promoted by Nazi leaders, individual talent and *Leistung* for the racial community were more important than a person's social (not "racial") background. Such meritocratic promises were already part of the 1920 program of the Nazi party, as Axmann liked to point out.[110] Point twenty demanded that every able and hard-working German should have the opportunity to pursue higher education and move into leading positions. It further demanded that talented children of poor parents should receive a state-sponsored education regardless of the social position and vocation of their parents.[111] After 1933, officials in the Reich education ministry tried to open up higher schooling for children from humble backgrounds. They wanted to abolish fees for secondary schools but their efforts were successfully opposed by the Reich finance minister Ludwig Graf von Schwerin von Krosigk for budgetary reasons.[112]

This outcome does not mean that Nazi leaders were not committed to meritocratic reforms. "No talented boy should be hindered in his upward mobility because of financial difficulties," Albert Holfelder, the departmental chief for education in the Reich education ministry, declared in 1940, and this commitment was shared by the Nazi Party.[113] As Rainer Zitelmann has shown in his study on Hitler's social and economic views, Hitler took meritocratic ideas very seriously. In Hitler's ideal world, social conventions, status, and a person's upbringing should not determine a person's economic and social position in society, unless of course the person was Jewish or belonged to other racial or social outsider groups that were ostracized and persecuted. Hitler was not motivated by ideas about social fairness. What mattered was an Aryan people's comrade's contribution to the national community. He believed in the economic necessity to exploit the performance potential of every German. In his view, the German nation could only succeed in the struggle for survival if it made the most efficient use of the best human resources.[114] In his own way, Hitler believed in the premises of a "human economy" that envisioned the total mobilization of all human resources for the national good in the most efficient way. Therefore it was imperative to find the "person born to it for every function in the life of ... [the] nation" based on a person's talent rather than his upbringing.[115] As the social climber par excellence, Hitler had little sympathy for traditional class hierarchies and ultimately wanted to see them replaced by new ones based on talent, race, and political commitment to the Nazi world view. Axmann enthusiastically subscribed to such meritocratic ideas, in large part because of his own humble upbringing in a working-class district in Berlin. Axmann's career path, from working-class student to senior official in the Hitler Youth and German Labour Front and, after 1940, Reich Youth leader, personified the promise of social upward mobility in the Third Reich.[116]

As historians have noted, the expansion of the military, the party, and numerous party organizations created new job opportunities for many people. The Labour Front alone had about 45,000 salaried employees at the beginning of the war.[117] All in all, the Nazi Party and its affiliates had 700,000 officials. By 1942, there were 2 million.[118] However, it should be noted that most of these were unpaid volunteers. In 1940, only 21,185 (about 2 per cent) of the 1,209,919 political leaders of the Nazi Party were paid.[119] For women, the Nazi Party organization NS *Frauenschaft*, the NS People's welfare (*Volkswohlfahrt*), the Labour Front's women's section, and the League of German Girls provided offices and career opportunities.[120] Whether a significant number of social climbers could take advantage of new professional chances or whether claims about such social opportunities were exaggerated to project the image of an open meritocratic society remains contested.[121] One area in which there was greater opportunity for promotion and upward social mobility was the army, which expanded significantly during the 1930s. By 1936 the army officer corps had more than doubled from 3,200 in 1932 to 8,400 men. By 1938 it had increased sevenfold to 21,700.[122]

Opportunities for careerism in NS organizations and the armed forces aside, historians have for the most part remained rather sceptical about the degree of social mobility during the Nazi period.[123] It should also be noted that changes in intergenerational social mobility only become discernible in the long term and the regime simply did not last long enough to be able to effect profound changes in this realm. Such developments are, furthermore, difficult to disentangle from the changes brought about by the war, population dislocations, and the postwar reconstruction of Germany.[124]

For those who could find employment in the new party bureaucracies, official claims about the opening up of new opportunities must have had a ring of truth.[125] There is a danger in overemphasizing the importance of such experiences of upward social mobility, however, since the growth of Nazi bureaucracies also gave rise to discontent about corruption and the parasitic nature of Nazi officials. Widespread preferential treatment of party members and bureaucrats cast doubt on the validity of the performance principle. As government and Gestapo reports attest over and over again, regime officials were keenly aware of workers' complaints on issues of distributive justice. They complained if employers gave the lie to Nazi claims about the equality of all people's comrades by giving preferential treatment to salaried employees, and they complained about the material privileges of employers, managers, foremen, and, most importantly, the corruption of Nazi officials.[126]

Labour Front officials in particular came under fire because their large bureaucracy was mostly financed by the membership contributions of workers.[127] Many workers were concerned about the lavish lifestyles of Labour Front leaders, which nourished justified rumours that officials misappropriated funds for their own purposes.[128] Such concerns were likely to undermine claims about the meritocratic basis of political hierarchies and social rewards. The RBWK organizers addressed these issues with claims that the competition would make it possible in the future to determine a "National Socialist rank order" based entirely on people's competence.[129]

Nazi propagandists never tired of drawing attention to unjust class prejudices in German society prior to 1933. The RBWK was hailed as a manifestation of the "Socialism of the Deed" that overcame petty class prejudices by giving everyone a chance to present his talents. Traditional class and status distinctions were dismissed as unimportant because, as in sport, the only thing that allegedly counted in the assessment of individuals was their performance. This push toward equality of opportunity, the organizers claimed, was not the case prior to 1933. Rather, there was a large discrepancy between the social structure of Germany and the "natural" hierarchy based on talent. Writers from the Hitler Youth administration complained that the performance of young people was not only limited by their innate "biological" capacity, as they argued it should be, but also by social circumstances that prevented them from reaching their full potential. Obstacles to performance were mostly "money, estate, and social conventions."[130] At the same time, higher schooling was mostly unaffordable for working-class youth. In addition, poor boys and girls often faced obstacles to their advancement because the financial situation of their parents and the needs of their siblings made it impossible for them to pursue formal training.[131] "Thousands of German junior workers had to enter their work life after basic schooling (*Volksschule*) as messengers or unskilled auxiliary workers (*Hilfsarbeiter*) only because the social situation of their parents did not allow for an apprenticeship," while "in the skilled vocations often those with mediocre talent [received] the privilege of thorough vocational training." This reality was not only unfair; it also constituted a "misallocation of national capital." [132]

Statistical evaluations of the social data collected in the RBWK supposedly demonstrated that many winners in the RBWK came from humble backgrounds and would now, for the first time, be given the opportunities for professional advancement they deserved. The RBWK was promoted as an instrument of talent diagnosis that provided disadvantaged youths with unprecedented opportunities for social upward mobility. Its stated goal was to identify those people with the greatest performance potential and give them the opportunity to develop that potential to the fullest. In terms of identifying specific talents, the contest continued the practices of Weimar psycho-technics with its attempts to identify the "right man for the right job."[133]

In the words of Axmann, the competition was like a giant magnet covering the entire Reich, a magnet that attracted all those people who had "the iron of performance" (*Eisen der Leistung*) in them.[134] This metaphor is interesting and its implications deserve further analysis. The term "iron" refers to some kind of innate performance potential, a resource that was hidden within the German population and that had to be recovered. Once discovered, it was up to the Nazi state to refine it – make steel out of it – for the benefit of the racial state. These ideas point to yet another justification for the RBWK: it provided an incentive for people to work on their vocational skills and upgrade them if the competition showed that they were deficient. The call for upskilling was in part a response to concerns voiced by industry, the labour administration, and the Labour Front about skills shortages in industries relevant to the four-year plan.[135] For employers and party and government officials, the shortage of semi-skilled and skilled labour posed a threat to productivity that needed to be addressed urgently.[136]

The RBWK responded to such concerns but it did not present the need for upskilling simply in terms of productivity. Since there was considerable stigma attached to being unskilled, the official propaganda turned the issue into a promise for opportunity by pledging to eliminate unskilled labour with Ley proclaiming: "We do not want to hear the word unskilled worker in Germany anymore."[137] The Nazi press claimed that the RBWK identified some of the best workers among the unskilled who deserved a chance to improve their skills.[138] From the perspective of the Labour Front and the Hitler Youth, the RBWK was to play a crucial role in this skill offensive because it encouraged every participant to work on the improvement of their vocational skills. The reward structure of the RBWK was linked to the promise of social "upward mobility" (*Aufstieg*) and "training" was to become the basis for that mobility. "*Education, training, and the right to move up (Aufstiegsrecht) lead to ... the real company community and the highest work performance*" (emphasis in the original).[139] By improving the performance and skills of working youth, "an individual faces the future of a guaranteed rise, in the atmosphere of a freedom that has once and for all overcome the confining fetters of being semi-skilled."[140]

There is some evidence that the drive to improve the skills of the workforce provided greater training opportunities for young people. Skills shortages meant that it became easier for people to leave the ranks of the unskilled and semi-skilled, while skilled workers found more opportunities for advanced technical training.[141] According to one study, the qualification drive in industry was so successful that there was a shortage of unskilled workers. Whereas in 1934 there were 200,000 school-leavers who entered the ranks of the unskilled, by 1938 there were only 150,000 and a year later the number had dropped to 30,000.[142]

The RBWK addressed the desire for occupational upward mobility while at the same time appealing to people's idealism and willingness to sacrifice for the common good. In keeping with the idealistic pretensions of the amateur principle in sport, winners in the RBWK were not encouraged to expect great material rewards. In 1937 every Reichssieger received 1,000 RM to be used not for private indulgence but for further professional training. The rewards that were given did not reflect a "humanitarian attitude towards the individual who received support," but served the "sober necessities of an economy serving the state," as an author from the Reich Youth leadership made clear.[143] The prizes given to local and district winners were mostly left to the discretion of employers and local officials. They included vocational excursions and trade books, promotions, training offered by the DAF or employers, or the opportunity to start an apprenticeship. Talented apprentices could accelerate their careers by shortening their training. Some could look forward to advanced educational opportunities at specialized trade and technical schools that trained master craftsmen, technicians, or engineers. Exceptionally talented people could receive a "Langemarck stipend" for study at universities. New vocational opportunities for people with demonstrated ability and ambition: this was presented as the main purpose of the reward structure of the RBWK.[144]

An article in *Der Angriff* emphasized that there were many workers with natural talents who deserved support to compensate for their social disadvantage. While education could not overcome the "hereditary limits of the blood," it had the "wonderful mission" to make sure that talented people could live up to their full hereditary value. This did not mean, however, that everybody was suited for advanced vocational training or university study.[145] The promise of social mobility was limited by what the assessors considered the "natural limit of talent" of individuals. Not every fitter had the ability to become an engineer and not every construction worker could become an architect.[146]

While the NS propaganda claimed that the Third Reich made it possible for even workers to get into the highest positions of the state, the reward structure of the contest played on the smaller social differentiations and distinctions that mattered in the real life worlds of employees and industrial workers. Most people could realistically hope for slight improvements in their lives by moving up one or two skill levels or rungs on the occupational ladder to become skilled workers or even low-level supervisors.[147] They might move from blue-collar to white-collar jobs, but very few could hope to make it into the ranks of the university educated. Despite high-sounding official proclamations, financial support for university students without means was virtually non-existent.[148]

Thus, the meritocratic performance ideology of Nazism did not challenge the class structure of German society in a fundamental way. Instead it tried to appeal to modest aspirations or exploit everyday discontent about preferential treatment of different categories of employees. It should be noted, however, that while the meritocratic ideology of Nazism may have had egalitarian tendencies in terms of the (unfulfilled) promise of equal opportunity, it was far from egalitarian in terms of the outcomes it intended. The racial people's community was to be hierarchical. It was to be based on individuals' natural abilities and loyalty to the regime. In many ways, the promise of upward mobility presupposed the continuing existence of class differences and social segmentation as a basis for status distinctions. Otherwise, social mobility would be meaningless. For those who could not improve their position in the occupational hierarchy, there was some consolation. They were reassured that they nevertheless fulfilled an important function in the economic life of the nation, "because the community ... invests even the smallest function with the prestige of social honour."[149]

The promise of equal opportunity was of course limited to hereditarily healthy Aryan Germans or, more specifically, the men of that group. While female apprentices and workers were encouraged to participate in the RBWK, the competition was careful not to challenge traditional expectations of gender roles in German society. Images of the contest reflected the gendered division of labour in German industry with young women working with textiles and young men dominating the metal trades. The organizers emphasized that women should be trained for jobs such as dressmaking that suited their "nature." Girls and women were also tested on their ability to cope with domestic chores (see figures 4.8, 4.9, 4.10, and 4.11). This system certainly accorded with a gender ideology dear to many Nazi leaders but it also reflected wider social expectations: for working women, *Leistung* meant that they had to demonstrate that they could cope with the double burden of paid work and household work.[150] The economic mobilization effort relied on women's work outside the home, which gave rise to calls for more thorough vocational education for women. At the same time, the gendered assessment structure of RBWK tried to bolster the traditional domestic division of labour "to make sure that every working woman can cope with the performance demands in each profession without having to renounce female characteristics that are of no lesser importance for our Volk."[151] Performance counted for both men and women, but the performance that counted for each gender was different. In some ways, this corresponded to the different performance expectations for boys and girls in sport. In the RBWK competitions, boys and girls had to prove themselves in running and in the long jump. But in the throwing contests boys had to throw clubs (mimicking hand grenades) and girls had to throw balls.[152]

While women were to receive better training in the interest of increased labour productivity, the promise of social upward mobility was not offered to them even though some companies, as for example

Der Wettkampf in der Gemeinschaft.

4.8 Young men competing in a metal trade. Artur Axmann, *Der Reichsberufswettkampf* (Berlin: Junker and Dünnhaupt, 1938), 232–3. Private collection.

in the electro-technical industry, provided women with specialized qualifications.[153] Young males were promised careers; for example, a fisher boy from Eastern Prussia became *Reichssieger* and was offered a place at a Nazi elite school (*Napola*) to prepare him for a career as a navy officer (see figure 4.12).[154] Women were steered towards vocations that were seen as particularly suited to their feminine nature. The reward structure of the RBWK demonstrates that women were not expected to be upwardly mobile in the same way as men. For one, women were not eligible for the Langemarck stipends that supported young men from humble backgrounds while they prepared for university.[155] According to a 1938 Labour Front survey of past winners, about 67 per cent of the male local and district winners received support to further their career aspirations, while only 47 per cent of the females did. Based on the

Wettkämpferinnen beim Plätten.

4.9 Female competitors ironing fabrics. Axmann, *Reichsberufswettkampf*, 104–5. Private collection.

assumption that boys and men wanted to move up in their profession, they were most of the time rewarded with various forms of additional training. They received support for attending specialized technical courses, their apprenticeship was accelerated, or, if unskilled, they were moved into regular apprenticeships. Others were moved to companies where they had better career prospects. Girls were more likely to be rewarded with small amounts of cash or paid travel.[156] According to the Labour Front survey, the only industry that gave female winners intensive support, presumably also in terms of additional training, was the textile industry, which was traditionally dominated by women. All the other sectors mentioned – wood, metal, commerce, textile, banking, and insurance – focused their support on men.[157]

In einer arteigenen Schulung werden die Mädels auf die besonderen

4.10 Vocational training in accordance with woman's nature.
Axmann, *Olympia der Arbeit*, 38. Private collection.

4.11 Domestic skills. Axmann, *Olympia der Arbeit*, 39. Private collection.

Für die spätere Ausbildung zum Seeoffizier besucht der Reichssieger 1935 Nährstand, der Fischerjunge aus Ostpreußen, die Nationalpolitische Erziehungsanstalt in Stuhm. Die Gemeinschaft fördert die Begabten! Leistung siegt!

4.12 Poor fisher boy and *Reichssieger* offered place at Napola in Stuhm to prepare for a career as a navy officer: "*The community supports the talented! Performance wins!*" Axmann, *Olympia der Arbeit*, 87 (emphasis in original). Private collection.

While there were almost twice as many boys as girls and three times as many men as women among the participants of the RBWK, the recruitment of women into the competition was an important goal for the Hitler Youth and the Labour Front. The importance of women's participation shows that the regime had no problem in accepting the full mobilization of working-class women in the interest of greater productivity as long as there were concessions to traditional notions of femininity and the sexual division of labour.[158] In doing this, the language of aspirationalism was mostly reserved for men. Women were rarely mentioned in a context that suggested they could overcome their social limitations. In their case, only their productivity, at home and at their paid work, was seen as important.

Scholars are divided about the degree to which the German working class was convinced by the social promises of the regime. Historians like Ian Kershaw, Timothy Mason, and Günther Morsch have pointed to the continuing importance of pre-1933 working-class perceptions. In their view, workers did not believe in the *Volksgemeinschaft* and continued to hold a dichotomous view of German society that separated workers from employers and managers but also from new Nazi bigwigs.[159] This argument has some merit. Populist Nazi officials appealed to a dichotomous understanding of class relations when they attacked antisocial employer behaviour. RBWK organizers publicly threatened employers and foremen who provided inadequate training. The RBWK was declared not only a test for apprentices but also for their supervisors who could lose the right to train apprentices if their charges underperformed.[160] Newspaper sometimes denounced "antisocial employers" who were arrested because they abused their employees, but it remains unclear how often employers had to face repercussions.[161] The main purpose of such proclamations was to convey to workers that the Labour Front took their concerns seriously by holding employers and managers accountable for their abuses. In this way the regime could substantiate its claims that it wanted to ensure fairness in the workplace.

Because of the populist strain in Nazism, some historians assume that at least aspects of the Nazi *Volksgemeinschaft* vision had considerable appeal for workers. Few go so far as Gunther Mai who seems to assume that workers took the propaganda of the regime seriously.[162] Others either point to the high priority given to the dignity of manual labour in public discourse or to promises of upward mobility as features that were popular with workers.[163] The main tenor of many studies is that workers' attitudes towards different aspects of Nazi society were not consistent.[164] Support for the Führer and hopes for social upward mobility might have been accompanied by a rejection of Nazi functionaries or resentment of stagnating wages, long work days, and the intensification of labour as rearmament picked up pace with the four-year plan. Official claims that the RBWK had nothing to do with a drive to intensify labour (*Antreiberei*) can be interpreted as a response to popular suspicions about the motivations behind performance campaigns.

Workers' attitudes towards their work also varied depending on its social prestige. Aircraft manufacturing was a new high-tech industry that offered more opportunities for professional advancement and higher wages than the mining or consumer goods industry. According to historian Frank Bajohr, this discrepancy led to an elitist avant-garde consciousness among many workers who became receptive to the regime's promises of social benefits and professional advancement.[165] But such attitudes were only characteristic for a minority of privileged workers in this industry, which grew very rapidly as a result of the armament drive. The number of employees increased from 3,800 in 1933 to about 325,000 in 1939. The centre of aircraft manufacturing was in middle Germany between Dessau and Magdeburg where population growth soon outstripped social infrastructure and led to significant housing shortages. Of the 150,000 workers employed by the Junkers aeroplane manufacturer, only about 21,000 permanent workers were among the privileged who received high wages and preferential treatment in housing. Despite the extensive *Werksgemeinschaft* propaganda and activities of the firm (including *Betriebssport* and a company foundation for the financial support of advanced schooling and higher education for the talented), the larger part of the workforce was unstable and fluctuated considerably, a development that caused great concern among management.[166]

The RBWK promoted a performance ideology in order to change people's attitudes towards their work. Scepticism about the effectiveness of the RBWK in this regard is reflected in the reports published by the Social Democratic Party in exile. One SOPADE report claimed that the sheer scale of the mobilization effort for the RBWK incited competitive fervour among participants even though they did not care very much about particular goals: "Most of these boys and girls do not care about calls for quality improvement and skilled workers. The fight itself and the ubiquitous activism sweep them away." The same report conceded that promises of upward social mobility might catch on with workers and apprentices, but it also expressed doubt about the sustainability of the regime's mobilization drives: such attempts would likely lead to "massive exhaustion of spiritual and mental strength which is sacrificed ... for a 'totalitarian demand' of dubious value."[167] A report from Württemberg claimed that participating apprentices made fun of the contest, which was a stark contrast to the moral earnestness propagated in official press reports.[168]

More direct evidence of the attitudes of participating apprentices is very rare and there is no way of knowing to what extent it is representative. Some of the apprentices of the shoe manufacturer Salamander, for example, failed to demonstrate the combative commitment and voluntary performance enthusiasm the competition tried to foster. Their answers in the theoretical and vocational parts of the contest suggest that their diligence at work was for the most part upheld by fear of their masters: "If I do not work exactly as my front man, then my foreman scolds me." Another missed the point of the performance campaign entirely when he claimed that he had to take care not "to work excessively fast, so that piece rates are not depressed."[169] Slowdowns in the interest of preserving income were certainly not part of the new National Socialist work culture that the Labour Front had in mind.

Defending one's autonomy in the workplace – either by asserting control of one's work pace or by creating distractions through horseplay – had for a long time been common in industrial workplaces. They were part of what Lüdtke has called "*Eigensinn*" (translatable as self-will or stubbornness), which allowed workers to protect a measure of personal autonomy at work. Such everyday practices in the workplace were difficult to eliminate even in a totalitarian dictatorship.[170] While their persistence tells us something about workers' attitudes at work, they are of limited value when assessing political attitudes towards the regime or Hitler. In any case, refusal to accept the demands of Nazi *Leistung* propaganda is not a form of active resistance against the regime. It can be seen, however, as an example of what the historian Martin Broszat has termed *Resistenz*: more or less effective attempts to reject, limit, or contain the totalitarian demands of the regime.[171] Whether propaganda and promises of upward social mobility engendered a more widespread performance mentality among workers and contributed to the regime's legitimacy has to remain an open question. It would be a mistake to make such claims based on a few scattered, contradictory sources.

During the war, the RBWK was suspended between 1940 and 1943. The reasons for this were twofold. First of all, the RBWK was a measure that tried to instil combative, competitive attitudes in the workforce during peacetime. With the beginning of the war, it seemed unnecessary to have a national mobilization drive on the scale of the RBWK given that it swallowed a large number of organizational and human resources that were needed for the war effort. The war, however, would pose serious challenges to the Nazi performance community. Labour shortages that had already become a serious problem during the rearmament drives of the 1930s were vastly exacerbated with the drafting of millions of German men into the military. After 1942 in particular, the regime tried to address these problems through the massive recruitment of foreign contract labour and the forced mobilization of Eastern European slave labour. But the shortage of human resources had implications for the members of the racial people's community as the regime tried to mobilize final "performance reserves" among the remaining workforce. The responses to these challenges are the subject of the final chapter.

Chapter Five

The Performance Community at War

The war was the ultimate test for the German performance community. As Robert Ley put it in a telegram to Hitler: "Millions of German workers ... in armament and war production improve their performances ... [demonstrating] tenacious will and faithful combative commitment ... They make up a thousand times for what they failed to do in 1918," which is why they deserved the socialist future promised by the regime.[1] Germany was again on the brink of collapse when Ley wrote these lines in November 1944, but during the first two years of the war it seemed that the war could have a different outcome. The Polish campaign ended after merely a couple of weeks in October 1939. In June 1940, France signed an armistice after a short campaign leaving only Britain at war with Germany. In August 1940, the regime started its economic preparations for the war against the Soviet Union in the following year.[2] When the German attack against the Soviet Union stalled during the winter of 1941/42, the regime managed to stave off defeat for more than three years. This prolongation was made possible not only through the ruthless exploitation of occupied territories but also the mobilization of the economic and human resources of the home front.

Throughout the war, the Labour Front, the Hitler Youth, and other sectors of the regime never wavered in their conviction that sport and other sporting-type contests were important for the psychological mobilization of Germans and the building and sustaining of social cohesion during the war. They believed that competition built character, promoted people's faith in their abilities, and strengthened their courage and willpower in the face of superior enemy resources and major defeats. The belief in the mobilizing power of competition was so deeply ingrained that the regime even revived the Reich Vocational Competition as *Kriegsberufswettkampf*.

Civilian sporting activities within Germany were not wound back when the war began. During the first half of the war, the German Labour Front still tried to activate adults and working youths through mass sport. Fitness campaigns, which promoted "*Einsatz*" in the sense of workers' and soldiers' combative commitment to the people's community in the workplace and at the front, were seen as providing a way to keep people in a constant mental state of mobilization. In the beginning these efforts tried to convey a message that the war would be short and require few sacrifices on the part of Germans.

But the disruptive force of the war would be increasingly felt after the attack on the Soviet Union failed. The mass mobilization of men for war and of men, women, youths, and foreign workers for work; excessive working hours; disruptions of civilian life through allied air raids; and the deaths and maiming of millions of soldiers gave lie to any ritualistic enactments of civil normalcy from 1942 onwards. Under the conditions of total war, the continuation of civilian sporting activities became more difficult. Still, authorities insisted that sport was a valuable means for the mobilization of working youths, and they tried to utilize sporting activities as well as vocational competitions to combat discipline problems in the workplace. From a health and fitness standpoint, forcing an overworked workforce to exercise made little sense. The desired effects were psychological, however: to sustain and further people's commitment to their work and instil a combative attitude among workers and soldiers.

The attempts of the regime to use sport as a form of mass mobilization and consensus building will be the subject of the first section of this chapter. Sport remained central to the regime's *Leistung* propaganda, which aimed to raise people's community-orientation, productivity, and military preparedness. Civilian sport was promoted as a strengthening of the "inner front," as a way to preserve national unity in the face of a national emergency that demanded great sacrifices from all members of the community. Labour shortages gave rise to calls for the mobilization of all available human resources including soldiers who had suffered disabling injuries in the course of the war. Sport was used to reintegrate the maimed and wounded into the workforce through exercise therapies and rehabilitation regimes that had already been developed by those like Gebhardt in the 1920s and early 1930s. While using the labour of the disabled served an immediate practical purpose, the symbolic aspect of the rehabilitation discourse was even more important. The regime had made every effort to stigmatize non-productive people but it could not afford to do the same with soldiers who had become disabled in service to their country. Exercise therapy and sport for the disabled affirmed that those who had lost their health and their limbs in service to the fatherland could still be valuable members of the "performance community."

Taking occupied Poland as a case study, the second part of this chapter will look at the promotion of sport among the German occupiers in order to create a sense of community and colonial mission. At the same time as they prepared to murder and exploit millions of Jews and Poles, the new rulers of Poland poured considerable resources into sport facilities for Germans, which reveals again the importance of sport for Nazi ideological projects. Sport was seen as furthering both a sense of social coherence and a sense of racial superiority among the occupiers who came from all over Germany and from different walks of life. Combative commitment for the colonial task was to be fostered in German sport communities, which were modelled after the company sport communities established by the Labour Front in the Reich.

The final section of this chapter will look at workplace competitions. In war, as in peace, these competitions were seen as technologies for "*Leistungssteigerung*." The most important one of these was the "*Kriegsberufswettkampf*" in 1943/44. This last national performance campaign was meant to mobilize the final physical and mental performance reserves of the home front and combat war weariness and lack of discipline among German youths who worked in industry.

I. Sport, Social Mobilization, and Rehabilitation

In October 1939, Robert Ley called upon all employers to use communal sporting activities as a means to "erect a performance and work community for the strengthening of the inner front."[3] Sport was to create a "reservoir of people's strength for combative commitment in all areas: ... at the front [and] in the production process."[4] The German Labour Front tried to use KdF company sport communities (BSGs) to mobilize employees for better work performance and exert tighter control over their leisure activities. Since regime officials were still haunted by the memory of the German defeat of 1918, which they attributed to a betrayal by the home front, they felt the need to emphasize the high degree of social cohesion that National Socialism had allegedly brought about.[5] According to NS sport propaganda, Germany was successful in cultivating physical fitness and strength of character not just among the social elite but also among the broad mass of people. Communal sporting activities organized by the BSGs were credited with minimizing social tensions between employers and employees as well as among different types of employees. Mass sport in Germany constituted a "proof of performance (*Leistungsnachweis*) of an entire people," in contrast to England where many sports were allegedly still confined to the social elites educated in places like Eton and Oxford. As Heinrich Satter, the editor of the illustrated sport weekly *Reichssportblatt*, put it, Germans were a unified "eighty million people [in which] almost every man and almost every woman has gone through a school of physical steeling and fortification, and at the same time through a character schooling for courage, discipline, sacrifice, and the spirit of comradeship."[6] In other words, the unity and performance-orientation brought about by sport was to guarantee the stability of the inner front and prevent a recurrence of the disastrous events of November 1918.

In the view of some employers, sport-centred activities could play an important role in fostering a corporate community spirit between employees and managers. In response to a questionnaire by the Reich Group Industry (RGI), the corporate representation of German industry, the personnel department of the large chemical conglomerate IG Farben emphasized the importance of such factors for productivity: "community formation [runs] absolutely parallel with performance increase in the sense of productivity." The company sent workers of all ages for rest cures where they were supposed to further their sense of comradeship and corporate community in communal sporting activities and workshops that focused on the history and future tasks of the corporation. During the war, over five thousand workers were sent on such vacations in the company-owned rest home Kohlhof, and they allegedly shared a common bond based on their experience as "*Kohlhofkameraden*."[7]

Until late 1941, the Labour Front and the KdF tried to convey the impression that the war had little impact on the domestic situation and would not require major sacrifices on the part of the civilian population. The regime tried to project the image of a "peace-like war economy" (*friedensähnliche Kriegswirtschaft*) in which rationing would be unnecessary because the war would soon be over.[8] This scenario might still have been plausible for many Germans before the attack on the Soviet Union in June 1941. Up to this point the Wehrmacht had achieved quick and, from the German point of view, relatively painless victories. In October 1941, the *Reichsbahn* (national railroad) company paper maintained that there was still "*Reichsbahnsport* as during peace time," suggesting that the war would soon be over and things would be going back to normal.[9] When the Wehrmacht's attack on the Soviet Union stalled in the winter of 1941/42, the tone of such reports became defiant: "Company sport during the war even more!" a Labour Front circular from Baden proclaimed in January 1942.[10]

Company sport was meant to promote social cohesion among Germans in difficult times, but as the war dragged on the regime's fitness campaigns seemed to have achieved the opposite. An increasing proportion of the overworked and exhausted workforce appears to have resented such mobilization attempts, participated unenthusiastically, or shirked participation altogether (see below). Nonetheless, regime officials were so convinced of the educational value of sport for character formation and *Einsatzbereitschaft* that propaganda for mass sport continued unabated. This practice was true for the old Reich and for those territories that were annexed by the regime after 1938: Austria, the Sudetenland, and, after 1939, the western parts of Poland. Furthermore, the BSG model was also transferred to the civilian employees of the occupation administration of the General Government in Poland to foster an esprit de corps among the colonizers (see next section).

For the period of the war it is very difficult to give a realistic assessment of people's participation in sport. According to a 1941 report, sporting activities in the workplace continued to grow after the outbreak of the war. There were supposedly 13,700 company sport communities (up from 10,421 in 1938) at the beginning of the war, already by the end of 1939 there were 16,000, and in mid-1941 there were allegedly between 2 and 3 million members in 21,000 BSGs.[11] Compared with previous reports on KdF sporting activities that gave detailed figures in order to suggest accuracy, a rough estimate of 2 to 3 million members seems rather vague. Furthermore, it is hard to believe that these numbers referred to regular participants in sporting activities. As shown in chapter 3, even before the war many members of BSGs participated only irregularly in exercise sessions and the statistics cited in the press were deliberately inflated.

There is no reason to believe that this practice was discontinued. If anything, the mendacity of the Nazi press grew worse during the war. For the Leverkusen IG Farben works, for example, there is evidence that its official BSG membership numbers were exaggerated by including the men who had been drafted into the army.[12] Consequently, published numbers for sport participation most likely reflected the mobilization aspirations of the Labour Front rather than the actual extent of people's participation. Official claims of 23,000 BSGs with 4 million members by the end of 1942 and 5.2 million regular participants in company sporting activities in late 1943 lacked credibility.[13]

Whether new BSGs really managed to generate more enthusiasm for sporting activities remains arguable, even for the first half of the war. Leaving aside the dubious accounting practices of the KdF, it is simply not plausible that a growing number of people committed to exercise at a time when their burden of work and the length of their workdays increased significantly. Between 1935 and 1943, the average weekly work time in all industries rose from 44.4 hours to 48.7 hours for both men and women. During the same period, the average working week for men increased from 45.6 to 51.4 hours. For women, the average industrial working week declined, but only because many of the women who entered industrial workplaces could only work part-time.[14] By September 1940, the working week in the armaments industry lasted 60 hours. In some cases people had to work up to 70 hours, with deleterious consequences for workplace discipline.[15] As historian Wolfgang Werner has shown, even some of the Labour Ministry's trustees of labour understood the situation of overworked workers and only responded with formal reprimands to violations of work discipline.[16]

Official sport propaganda rejected the notion that long and tiring workdays might lead to sport weariness among employees. While admitting that war work in the armaments industry demanded a commitment that went to the limit of people's performance capacity, sport officials claimed that the "tension" (*Spannung*) demanded by such work could only be eased through the "relaxation" (*Entspannung*) provided by communal sporting activities. "Regeneration, the permanent renewal of capital in strength and elasticity" through sport would produce "happiness and carefree cheerfulness." At least during the first year of the war, all practical obstacles to sporting commitment, such as forced blackouts, and the lack of heating materials, sport teachers, and leisure time, were simply dismissed as insignificant.[17] The common sense claim that exercise could actually increase fatigue and decrease people's working capacity even further was denounced as "an old fairy tale" that was proven wrong by the experience of company sport.[18]

The dismissive tone of such responses suggests concern about people's lack of commitment to communal sporting activities. To make up for regular participation in sport, special one-day fitness events, such as the previously mentioned "company sport appeals," were heavily promoted. The national company sport appeal of 1941 allegedly mobilized 3.7 million employees, a number that should also be viewed with scepticism. Reports were intended to suggest that Germany still had an untapped reservoir of human resources because more and more people were stirred into action each year. In 1940, the same event had only mobilized 2.3 million workers who had to undergo a much less rigorous sport program;[19] in 1943, a report alleged that 4 million workers had participated in the national company sport appeal.[20]

Contrary to such widely trumpeted successes, there is evidence that special fitness campaigns actually backfired and undermined official attempts to promote social cohesion. Sport appeals were intended as a ritualistic affirmation of people's commitment to the performance community – an "appeal of good will" (*Appell des guten Willens*) as NS propaganda called them – but it remains questionable whether they generated enough joy and enthusiasm in workers to re-energize them for long and dreary work days under the conditions of total war. During the second half of the war, such events often encountered outright hostility. According to an SD report from October 1942, "company sport appeals prompted ... for the most part a negative reception" among workers, even though there were always some "sport enthusiastic retinue members" who welcomed the event. Many workers tried to leave the workplace before the appeal or participated unenthusiastically. Workers argued that sport did more harm than good, given their nutritional situation and the length of their workdays.[21]

In a large plant in the Halle area "outbreaks of negative moods" (*negative Stimmungsausbrüche*) occurred when company security tried to prevent workers from leaving the company grounds before a sport appeal. Despite intimidation by security officials, who registered their names, many workers still left. From a shift of 250 men and women, of whom 10 per cent did not show up in the first place because they were sick, about 70 persons left. According to the SD, retinue members in other plants described such heavy-handed pressure as "voluntary coercion" (*freiwilliger Zwang*) by employers who wanted to impress political authorities with large numbers of participants in order to receive official performance awards for their companies. Under these circumstances one could not talk about an "appeal of good will."[22]

Given the work pressures and long working hours – and the resulting negative attitude of many employees – some promoters of company sport realized that there was little hope of getting people to do sport during their diminishing leisure time, which is why they tried to integrate sporting events into the workday.[23] One propaganda image, for example, showed a manager and blue-collar workers doing a 1000-metre run around their factory building with the subtitle defiantly proclaiming that "despite the war and the exertion of all energies company sport continues" in order "to strengthen joy in work and increase performance strength" (see figure 5.1).[24] One particularly zealous KdF sport

5.1 Workers and management: 1000 metres around the factory. Printed with the permission of Bundesarchiv Berlin Lichterfelde, NS 5 VI, Nr 19480, Bl. 24.

warden created a furniture obstacle in the hallway of an office building, which workers had to climb over on their way to the toilet. While "company hallway and stair case sporting competitions" were not recommended as universal models for company sport, they were commended as attempts "to mobilize ... the capital of good will, fantasy, and practical inventiveness that can be found in every company community."[25]

In many businesses, wariness about playing sport during working hours seems to have prevailed. Given the frenzied productivity drives during the second half of the war, this attitude met with understanding: "It goes entirely without saying that during this time [November 1942] production-related technical necessities are more important than ... company sport," the author of an article in an economics paper proclaimed. Citing the experience of the company leader Friedrich Träger from Pirna in Saxony, the same author conceded that integrating short exercise sessions into the workday could lead to gains in work morale and productivity. But in many war-relevant industries stopping machines and interrupting work simply might not have been feasible.[26]

In the second half of 1943, the economic situation had become so dire that Ley prohibited company roll calls and other mobilization events during working hours: "As important as the political and ideological education of the workforce is ... these events have to be carried out outside working hours ... so that production performance is not compromised." In September 1943, the armaments ministry and the RGI reiterated the prohibitions with explicit reference to company sporting events including company sport for youths.[27] The armaments ministry, however, soon reversed the prohibition of youth sport because it was worried about the declining work discipline of adolescent workers.[28] Since the war had diminished the disciplinary influence of parents, school, and Hitler Youth, it was all the more important that "companies kept up the working discipline of youths," as Nazi Party guidelines for company youth care explained. The guidelines suggested positive measures to restore working discipline, such as sport during working hours, youth roll calls, and company based social evenings, as well as punishments ranging from public rebukes to fines and imprisonment.[29]

Company sport was to be limited to German members of the racial people's community. In the context of growing numbers of foreign and forced labourers living in Germany from 1942 onwards, participation in company sport was closely policed. Foreign workers from Eastern Europe were not allowed to take part in sporting activities for Germans. The few instances in which Polish workers were enjoined to participate led to strong official reactions because common activities among Germans and Eastern European foreign workers violated the sacrosanct principle of racial segregation both in the workplace and social life. The district administration of the Labour Front Gau Württemberg-Hohenzollern denounced company announcements in German and Polish that called for common participation in company sport: "Such a nonsensical measure has to be absolutely ... prevented."[30] Affirmations of racial segregation were given greater urgency when the gender composition of the German workforce changed. As more German women became part of the industrial workforce and German men were called to the front, the participation of foreign workers in company sport could have only exacerbated concerns about racial pollution through "*Rassenschande*."[31]

While the Labour Front objected to the social mingling of Germans with foreigners, it was not opposed to foreign workers taking up sport. To the contrary, it encouraged sport among them as part of "meaningful recreational activities." In May 1943, a Labour Front circular from the Office for Work Deployment (*Amt für Arbeitseinsatz*), which was responsible for the administration of work camps for foreign workers, called upon the German camp leaders to organize a "Sport Day for Foreign Workers" in order to encourage them to take up sport. The office cited the same reasons that were given for the promotion of sport among Germans: "Sporting activity is one of the best means to preserve and enhance working power and joy in work." This rationale explains why the Labour Front wanted to "carry sport *into the broad mass* of foreign workers (emphasis in original)." The circular insisted there was no excuse for German camp commanders who refused to provide sporting opportunities for foreign workers – not even a lack of sporting equipment in the camps – since foreign workers could be called upon to build the necessary equipment themselves.[32]

There is no evidence about the attitude of foreign workers towards such initiatives. While some might have seen events like the sport day as a welcome distraction from bleak camp life, it remains doubtful that the promotion of sport had the desired effect on productivity and work morale. Foreign workers were even more overworked than their German counterparts and had even less energy to spare. Still, the tenacity with which Nazi officials held onto their belief that sport could mobilize psychological reserves is remarkable. The SS even introduced soccer games in concentration camps in order to raise the working power and morale of concentration camp inmates.[33]

The war also brought profound changes and tensions in gender relations. Women replaced men in industrial work, were drafted into the labour service, served as auxiliaries in the armed forces, and played an important role in the protection against air raids (*Luftschutz*).[34] In the process, they were subjected to militarized forms of discipline, which, according to historian Sybille Steinbacher, contributed to a "leveling of gender differences."[35] The absence of men on the home front, due to their service in the military, also led to a feminization of sport both in terms of participants and of "exercise leaders." In the teaching year 1940/41, 1,967 women were trained as exercise leaders at the Reich Academy for Physical Exercise as compared to only 1,455 men.[36] The last ideological remnants concerning the propriety of performance sport for women were thrown overboard. Critics of women's sport were denounced as "prudish representatives ... of a pacifist, caring attitude towards life (*schonungsbetonten Lebensauffassung*), which in the meantime has given way to a fighting, combat ready National Socialist world view grounded in a heroic attitude." The new Nazi woman was to combine masculine soldierly attributes with her calling as propagator of the race because "only intellectually qualified, strong, physically fit and performance capable women will bear healthy children."[37]

Some of the female exercise leaders supervised mixed-sex exercise sessions because of a shortage of male sport teachers, which some men found hard to accept. (As many historians have pointed out, the regime systematically excluded women from political power over German men.)[38] An editorial in the *Reichssportblatt* exhorted men to accept that exercising "under female command" was "the most natural thing." There was no room for "petty inhibitions." "It is a disgrace for a healthy German man not to exercise at all." "To fail (*versagen*) in an honest if not so successful endeavour in the eyes of a more advanced and sporty female course leader" was by comparison much less disgraceful.[39] Whether such reasoning calmed male fears of physical failure in the eyes of a woman remains questionable. It is more likely that the editorial tried to foster such fears in order to spur inactive men to become physically fit or risk public embarrassment. The use of the stigmatizing term "*versagen*" could hardly have been reassuring in a society in which images of hypermasculine physical prowess and soldierly values of combativeness were closely linked.

The *Reichssportblatt* heralded the "sport-steeled German soldier" and published images of "our iron-hard trained pioneers" who put their sport training to military use during the war against Poland (see figure 5.2).[40] In Nazi sport discourse, the success and failure of soldiers and sportsmen were linked. Fighter personalities were drawn to sport because the goal of sport and war was to "break resistance." Only someone "who has been knocked to the floor in a boxing contest, who saw the world as through a veil, whose legs did not take commands, whose spirit tried to refuse to serve ... knows this massive power of the will, to stand up again, to fight on in order to break the resistance of the

DEUTSCHER VERLAG

Berlin, den 12. September 1939

Nr. 37 / 6. Jahr / 20 Pfennig

Reichsſportblatt

Unſere eiſenhart trainierten Pioniere wuchten neue Träger für einen Flußübergang ein. Die Brücke ſprengten die Polen auf ihrem fluchtartigen Rückzug

5.2 Iron-hard trained pioneers building a bridge during the war against Poland. *Reichssportblatt*, 12 September 1939. Printed with the permission of Universitätsbibliothek Tübingen.

adversary. In these moments, the idea of sport breeds the true virtues of the soldierly fighter."[41] The war was presented here as a gigantic sporting contest in which the virtues of soldiers and athletes merged. To surrender in the face of the adversary's or the enemy's resistance was not an option for either of them.

As the war progressed, endurance in sport and sporting prowess became metaphors for the courage and indomitable will of the German people who could overcome any obstacle in the face of the material and military superiority of the enemy. "The will to defeat fate," so Ley argued in September 1942, "makes us realize that for a man of the will the impossible cannot exist."[42] Josef Goebbel never tired in propagating this cult of the will in the face of major defeats. After the disaster of Stalingrad in early 1943, he picked up the by now familiar boxing topos in one of his speeches: "We wipe the blood from our eyes, so that we can see clearly, and when the next round starts, then we again stand firmly on our legs." In another speech he invoked the untapped fighting potential of the German nation: "A people that until now has only boxed with its left hand and is still busy bandaging its right hand to use it ruthlessly in the next round, has no reason to give in."[43] In another one of his sporting metaphors, Goebbels equated the trials of the war with a marathon run: "It is not decisive in which condition ... the marathon runner *penetrates the finishing tape in the final seconds,* decisive is *that* he destroys – penetrates it (*daß er es zerstö*[rt]- *durchstößt*) (emphasis in original)."[44] While a marathon run and a war were both easy to start, "the colossal pressures on physis and psyche ... only come during the twentieth, thirtieth, or fortieth kilometre" when it was important to "keep one's nerves and remain steadfast ... and not to surrendre to a feeling of weakness."[45]

According to this logic, sport was the best training for the "relentless overcoming of the self" (*unerbitterliche Selbstüberwindung*) that was demanded of the Nazi soldier who had to overcome fear, fatigue, and any other limitations of the self that might have hindered his performance.[46] The impact of this type of propaganda on soldiers is difficult to assess. An analysis of soldiers' letters to a sport club official in Southwestern Germany suggests, however, that some soldiers described their sport training in terms of the physical and mental conditioning required by their anticipated or actual roles as combat soldiers. In their view, a true sportsman was also a better soldier.[47] The work of German soldiers was certainly exhausting – long marches and sleep deprivation were quite common and put them under significant strain – especially so in an army that was plagued by manpower shortages. Apart from physical training, there were also experiments with pharmacological forms of performance enhancement to cope with the physical demands of war work. Some soldiers and officers resorted to the methamphetamine Pervitin to combat fatigue and exhaustion. In a way, pharmacological doping and substance abuse was a logical consequence of Nazi performance campaigns that were intent on increasing people's physical and mental performances at any cost in order to sustain the war effort.[48]

Team or "*Mannschaft*" sports such as soccer, rugby, hockey, and handball were supposed to cultivate "a sense of community" that promoted commitment towards one's fighting comrades: "The true sport team is united by fighting and nobody sins more heinously against its spirit than the person who abandons it." "[A] sense of community, the selfless commitment to the great cause, the subordination of one's personal interests," these were the virtues demanded by any *Mannschaftssport* and crucial for the fighting soldier. "He who has become a true fighter in a real team sport is also the insuperable soldier we need now."[49] From such a point of view, the German sporting and community spirit explained in part the quick victory over Poland: "This war could only be won so quickly and thoroughly by a thoroughly trained Volk, a team of well-trained sportsmen ... Not to individual performances but to the performance of the *Mannschaft* we owe the great and fast successes (emphasis mine)."[50]

As a consequence of the emphasis the regime put on health, physical fitness, and productivity, war casualties and particularly maimed and seriously disabled soldiers posed a difficult challenge to the "performance community." This fact was highly problematic for the regime because the first phase of the euthanasia program, which included the murder of about 70,000 mostly mentally disabled people, had led to rumours that the regime tried to eliminate all people who were not able to contribute to the performance community, including old people and seriously disabled soldiers.[51] These reports threatened to undermine support for the home front as well as morale at the front, which is why the regime had to be careful about how it represented the fate of seriously disabled soldiers. Since performance propaganda and calls for *Leistungssteigerung* became more urgent as the war dragged on, the representation of seriously disabled soldiers became an evermore sensitive issue.

Attempts to negotiate tensions between performance discourse and disability gave rise to an extensive public discourse about rehabilitation.

Official proclamations had to reassure people that the physically disabled could still find a respectable place in the performance community. But in a society that assigned value to people based on their physical performance and productivity as well as race, the disabled needed to prove their worth for the people's community by demonstrating their will to perform. By participating in sport, the disabled could show their performance potential and *"feel that they have fully the same value"* as their healthy counterparts (emphasis in original).[52]

Before the war people with physical disabilities were not systematically excluded from the people's community. Physically disabled First World War veterans were hailed as the first citizens of the Reich, and apprentices with physical disabilities were encouraged to participate in the RBWK. Furthermore, there were special units of the Hitler Youth for people with different disabilities: those in Bann B for the Blind, Bann G for the deaf and hearing impaired (*Gehörlose und Gehörgeschädigte*), and Bann K for the physically disabled (*Körperbehinderte*) underwent the same kind of ideological schooling and physical training as the regular HJ. Their sporting activities consisted of paramilitary training (*Wehrsport*), including marching, scouting games, and shooting exercises, as well as track and field disciplines and gymnastics games. These units also participated in HJ sporting competitions.[53]

As in the case of non-disabled Germans, such as the "weaklings" who were "up-schooled" by Gebhardt to become productive members of the community, official acceptance and support was not granted as a form of welfare (*Fürsorge*). It was conditional upon people's willingness to contribute to and make sacrifices for the community. Despite signals that suggested that the regime welcomed deserving people with physical disabilities into the racial people's community, the actual situation of the physically impaired was quite ambiguous. Not only were physically disabled members of the Hitler youth segregated from regular units but members of the Bann K could only wear their uniforms with special permission. Furthermore, they also had special insignia that emphasized their difference. As historian Carol Poore has argued, such policies were "obviously meant to preserve the healthy, strong image of the HJ and BDM by preventing young people with obvious disabilities from appearing in their ranks."[54]

In celebrating physical strength and ruthlessness, the regime fostered contempt for the physically weak and disabled. Stigmatizing language betrayed scornful attitudes; for example, *"versagen"* was used for those who could not meet minimum standards in one or another of the sporting performance tests in which people's comrades were asked to demonstrate a minimum degree of physical fitness.[55] Minimum fitness requirements for university students fell into that category as did the sport tests for participants in the RBWK and the fitness tests for the Hitler youth. A 1935 decree of the Reich Education Ministry clearly implied that people who lacked physical aptitude and fitness were lesser human beings. In accordance with Hitler's condemnation of the "intellectual weakling" (*geistreicher Schwächling*) in *Mein Kampf*, physical ability and character were cited as important criteria for admission to university: "Institutions of higher education will not accept young people with severe ailments, whose vitality is seriously weakened and whose condition cannot be expected to improve, or carriers of hereditary diseases, for they are unsuitable."[56]

Still, there was a big difference in official attitudes towards "hereditarily healthy" people with physical disabilities and people who were stigmatized because they were suspected of being hereditarily inferior. People with intellectual disabilities were ostracized and stigmatized in public campaigns involving film and other mass media.[57] By contrast, the physically disabled and the weak were on probation: they could prove themselves by raising their performance levels and show that they were respectable members of the community. In this way, disability sport provided some of the physically disabled with an opportunity to distinguish themselves from people with mental disabilities who were considered as biologically inferior. Through sport they could affirm that they were still part of the people's community, a claim that the regime recognized with its support for disability sport. The military, for example, hired sport teachers for disability sport, the KdF offered disability sport courses where the disabled could find new "*Leistungskraft*," and public displays of disability sport – as during the Leipzig disability sport festival of 1943 – showcased the performances of disabled athletes.[58]

In November 1939, the army medical inspector (*Heeressanitätsinspektor*) Siegfried Handloser ordered that army hospitals use sport and work to rehabilitate wounded soldiers.[59] By participating in sport wounded and disabled soldiers were supposed to demonstrate their full value to the community: "Fit for sport equals 'full value' (*vollwertig*)," as one *Reichssportblatt* editorial put it rather bluntly.[60] The term *vollwertig* was of course the opposite of "*minderwertig*" (of lesser value), a designation for all those who were outside the people's community because they were considered unproductive, antisocial, hereditarily diseased, and/or racial aliens. For wounded soldiers, communal sport was designed to foster a sense of *Kameradschaft* – a nurturing and supportive atmosphere that gave the wounded a sense of belonging to the people's community, which was important for their reintegration as productive members of society. As a navy physician put it: "The people's community, however, must learn to receive these comrades into its circle just as they were discharged from the circle of *Frontkameraden*, as comrades of full value."[61]

"Full value" did not simply refer to the rehabilitation of a wounded or physically disabled person in the medical or physical sense. It also referred to the attitude of the affected person. The sport therapy developed by Gebhardt in Hohenlychen was meant to have a positive effect on people's psyches. During the war Hohenlychen became a treatment and rehabilitation centre for wounded Wehrmacht soldiers and SS men. Sport therapy was meant to assure them that they could again become fully valued members of the national community despite their disabilities. It aimed at building up the self-confidence of the wounded and disabled through exercises that were tailored to their particular disabilities. Through participation in sporting competitions, they could demonstrate their "worth" to the community. In this way "inferiority complexes" and other "forms of depressive states," especially among those who suffered amputations, would be prevented and the "will to live" and the "will to perform" would be restored.[62] Gebhardt drew on his experience with the treatment of sport and work injuries to develop a therapeutic model for the treatment of war injuries. Medical gymnastics that aimed at restoring lost bodily functions were to be supplemented by what he called "gymnastica aesthetica" – games and team sports that tried to raise the spirit and joy of the wounded. After this was achieved, the "gymnastica ascetica" would enforce strict training discipline to restore people's performance capacities, while the "gymnastica bellica" instilled manly hardness and team discipline for the return to the battlefield, or, if this was not possible, to the workforce.[63] As the First World War veteran of German sport rehabilitation Arthur Mallwitz put it, sport therapy was to foster the "*joyful affirmation of life*" that changed people's psychological attitude through a "*turning back from an inner feeling as a cripple to a human being of full value in the German performance state.*" In this way, sport in army hospitals fostered the acceptance of the "performance principle and its transfer onto the inner attitude of the sick" (emphases in original).[64]

Because the regime's performance propaganda reinforced popular anxieties about war injuries and disabilities, regime officials always had to be particularly careful how they represented soldiers who had been injured in the service for *Führer* and fatherland. In the beginning, official representations of the wounded followed a strategy of denial. A 1939 article included images of wounded soldiers preparing for a swimming exercise as well as injured soldiers who played soccer and basketball. None of them showed visible injuries or disabilities and the headline of the article proclaimed: "Soldiers play themselves healthy."[65]

Another article on a rehabilitative exercise session for wounded soldiers on the Reich sport field in Berlin emphasized the playful ease with which soldiers overcame their adversity. According to its author it was almost impossible to recognize that those who participated in sport for the wounded were actually injured: "There is no difference in the way in which sport for the wounded and other sport is conducted." Wounded limbs would be caught up in the movements of the healthy parts of the body and reactivated: "Sport is performed from the totality of the body, and the wounded limbs move along on their own, because they are forced by the required task." While there were limits to what individuals could actually do due to their injuries, "each of the wounded soldiers *strives to achieve the best possible performance*" by pushing the limits set by his injury. The language of the article reveals the tension between pressures put on the soldiers to become as fit as possible as quickly as possible and the psychological mobilization that this type of exercise therapy was supposed to achieve. On the one hand, the article claimed that "*the character of the task* [the exercise] *forces the seriousness of commitment.*" On the other hand, such commitment "emerges out of the free will; here *no external command* is helpful but the *inner command* of those who exercise is decisive" (emphases in original). In other words, exercise therapy was to engineer free will, commitment, and enthusiasm. Sport was to foster a "gain of psychological strength" to support the healing process.[66]

As during the peace period of the regime, the emphasis on voluntary and joyful participation was illusory. Those who did not want to participate in rehabilitation activities were treated with suspicion and seen as inferior. Direct threats were made regarding their financial support. A senior navy physician raised the possibility of notifying army welfare and support offices when a wounded soldier refused to participate in sport.[67] There is no evidence that this actually happened, but the threat again illustrates that Nazi welfare was contingent upon people's ability – or at least their demonstrated will – to become productive citizens.

If the defeat of 1918 and its aftermath was an obsession with Nazi leaders, who blamed the German collapse on the betrayal by the home front, so was the concern about those who were non-productive who evoked earlier worries about "pension-seeking" during and after the First World War. Any suggestion of resignation or "pension neurosis" was to be nipped in the bud in the interest of the total mobilization of the disabled and the people's community as a whole.[68] Or as Robert Ley had already put it prior to the war: "We do not want a people of pensioners, but a people of human beings, who can live from the labour of their own hands."[69] In the view of Nazi rehabilitation experts, "psychological treatment and cheering up of the wounded" had been neglected during the First World War, which explained the large number of "pension neurotics" who tried to claim support from the state. This claim is of course untrue. During that war, military physicians were very much concerned about psychological factors in rehabilitation (see chapter 1). To combat pension dependency, Nazi physicians and sport therapists tried to foster positive attitudes among the disabled. Laughter, joy, and the awakening of "fighting ambition" were considered psychological elements of the "greatest importance" that were best promoted through disability sport.[70]

Permanent disabilities became a more frequent topic in the Nazi press when the duration and ferocity of the war made disability a problem that was difficult to deny. Some reports still played down the severity of people's injuries. A reporter detailing a swimming exercise session of severely disabled men claimed that he "encountered such joyful laughter and shouting that one might presume that a group of children was frolicking in the water in joyful exuberance, had it not been for the voices" of the men. The injuries did not seem to matter, so committed were the men to their sport training, which was supervised by an "experienced swimming teacher, himself an old front soldier who has lost his left leg during World War I." In this story, dismemberment became almost irrelevant for the individuals concerned; it was only important as part of a legacy of sacrifice across generations.[71]

"To be considered full and performance-strong (*leistungsstarke*) members (*Glieder*) of our community": this idea was supposed to be the aspiration of the disabled who were expected to make every effort to vindicate themselves in the eyes of their national comrades.[72] The awkward choice of metaphor in this passage – implying that those who had lost a limb had to aspire to become fully functional limbs of the *Volkskörper* – pointed to the regime's attempts to make everyone, even seriously disabled soldiers, into productive contributors to the war economy.

The Reich Group Industry actively participated in efforts to reintegrate disabled soldiers. In November 1942, the RGI founded a Committee for the Reintegration of the War Disabled (*Ausschuss für die Wiedereingliederung von Kriegsversehrten*), which was chaired by Wolf Dietrich von Witzleben, a member of the Board of Directors of the electrical company Siemens & Halske. The committee was to provide guidance and coordination for existing industry initiatives in the field. It also served as liaison between industries and the military, and labour and welfare offices concerned with the occupational placement of disabled veterans. Practical concerns about the appropriate placement of the injured in jobs that were compatible with the nature of their injuries as well as their prewar training were to be resolved by a special working group of the RGI for the retraining of the disabled, which was headed by the former DINTA engineer Johannes Riedel.[73]

According to statistics assembled by the RGI, the attempts to reintegrate disabled soldiers into the industrial workforce were fairly successful. By June 1943, 36,068 disabled veterans had found jobs in industry, the largest numbers in the machine building industry (5,118) and the aircraft building and related industries (4,378).[74] While these numbers are significant, they have to be compared to the millions of labourers from Western and Eastern Europe who were forced to work in German industry at the same time. However, the recruitment of disabled veterans promised to solve a significant problem for German industry: the lack of reliable low-level supervisors (*Unterführer*) for foreign forced labour (see final section). As the RGI recognized, the efforts to reintegrate the disabled into the workforce were political as well as economic. Great care was taken to counter the impression that the disabled would have to suffer from social disadvantages or income losses because of their injuries.[75] Employers were legally required to ensure that disabled veterans would be placed in jobs that provided them with work that was comparable to their former posts in terms of income and career opportunities.[76] Since NS officials and employers had previously promoted notions of individual advancement among workers in an effort to break up class loyalties, they now had to make sure that disabled soldiers did not feel socially déclassé. Reintegration of the disabled has "to be considered important for the war effort, because the soldier at the front needs to have the consciousness that his vocational future is also secured in the case of disability."[77] From the official point of view, symbolic recognition of people's sacrifices was as important as economic reassurances, but it is not clear how many of the disabled themselves shared this view.

During Goebbels' famous total war speech after the battle of Stalingrad, the first row in the Berlin sport palace was occupied by disabled soldiers: "Before me sit rows of German wounded from the Eastern front ... leg and arm amputees with shot-up limbs, the war blind who have come with their Red Cross nurses, men in the blossom of their years ... [with] their crutches standing before them." They were all invited as a part of a "cross section of the entire German people in the best sense of the word" in order to emphasize their exemplary sacrifice for the community.[78] In November 1942, the Reich Sport Leader Tschammer introduced a national sport badge for the disabled (*Versehrtensportabzeichen*) to give public recognition to those who demonstrated through their sporting achievements their "performance capacity for their own good and for national power."[79] The performance criteria for the disability sport badge were developed by Gebhardt and based on his work with different types of physical disabilities at Hohenlychen. There were two broad performance categories for the *Versehrtensportabzeichen*. For group A, the criteria were tailored to different kinds of disabilities; for example, amputations of legs or lower legs, or permanent stiffness of joints, etc. For those in group B with multiple debilitating injuries, performance criteria were decided on a case-by-case basis.[80]

The bestowal of the first awards in December 1942 provided another opportunity to emphasize the theme of cross-generational sacrifice and obligations. Tschammer, who had suffered a permanent injury to his right hand during the First World War, handed the award to one of his disabled young assistants. A "tradition rich soldierly past and a soldierly present worthy of tradition" met on that occasion.[81] The sacrifice of generations past was a recurring theme that emphasized the obligation of the younger generation to make great sacrifices. When the Reich Commissioner for the Occupied Netherlands Arthur Seyß-Inquart received his disability sport badge from Tschammer und

Osten in December 1942, he was initially celebrated on the cover of the *Reichssportblatt* as another FirstWorld War veteran who had suffered permanent injuries.[82] In reality, he suffered from a lack of mobility in his left leg caused by a mountain climbing accident. Since he continued to ski and climb mountains, the sport weekly *NS-Sport* presented him as a model invalid who was *"vollwertig"* because he surpassed many of his healthy contemporaries with his exceptional sporting ability.[83]

While NS disability sport aimed at making the disabled productive again, influencing people's attitudes or morale was considered equally important, particularly during the second half of the war. The disability sport badge did not just reward sport performance. It rewarded "the spirit that gave soul to the deed" because "history did not judge what a nation has endured during her hardest time, she judges only how she has endured it."[84] Those awarded the disability sport badge were recognized for their sacrifice and for demonstrating through their sporting achievements that they were willing to overcome their physical limitations. Frequent reports on the sporting successes of disabled soldiers were supposed to inspire everyone to give their best in sport and at work. Stories about amputees who ran 5 kilometres in 53 or 46 minutes, or a sergeant (*Unterscharführer*) of the *Waffen SS* with an amputated leg who jumped 3.1 metres and swam 300 metres in 6.6 minutes were parables for the dormant will and performance potential of individuals and the nation as a whole that could be mobilized in the face of adversity.[85] The inspirational value of such reports was so attractive that it led to pressure on disabled veterans to exercise excessively. This practice went so far that the Reich Ministry of the Interior had to condemn "the propagandistic exhibition of record performances," which enticed the disabled to overexert themselves and compromise their health.[86]

As during the First World War, the reasons for mobilizing people's performance reserves were often cast in a language of care. Paul Kellner, a writer in *NS-Sport*, maintained that "in the National Socialist state man constitutes the highest good of our Volk. Therefore the war injured and physically disabled ... can count on the very best care and ... support. The restoration of his physical-mental working strength and full integration into the economic and vocational life of the Volk is the task of honour of the nation."[87] While some disabled war veterans might have been unenthusiastic about the prospect of being forced into industrial production and preferred what they considered their well-deserved pensions, in Nazi discourse the disabled soldier was always performance-oriented and willing to work and sacrifice for the community: "For the German war-disabled terms such as 'cripple' or 'invalid' are a grave insult. He does not want to belong with those people who open their hands and expect special financial support from the state. He expects no 'alms' at all, but he demands to be one hundred per cent integrated into the work process of the people's community."[88]

National Socialist Germany stood for a radical departure from the practices of the Weimar Republic, which fobbed off war victims with a pittance: "Just as the disabled front soldier does not want pity, but demands respect, so he does not want charity but the furtherance and support he deserves, in order to ... work for his people and build his life out of his own strength," the *Völkischer Beobachter* declared.[89] This perspective towards disabled veterans was not only opposed to the attitudes and practices of the Weimar years but also to the system in Anglo-Saxon countries where the physically disabled received small amounts of financial support from the state but were otherwise abandoned to their fate. Pensions were frowned on by the Nazi regime, and seen as something that would undermine any desire on the part of the invalid to engage in useful work, leaving him "to accept the charity of the tax payers" until the end of his life. The denunciation of Anglo-Saxon practices might be regarded as another version of the old theme that contrasted hard-working Germans with English rentiers and pension seekers (see chapter 1). But, as Deborah Cohen has shown, there were real differences in the ways in which Britain and Germany dealt with disabled veterans in the 1920s and '30s. While the British state paid minor pensions and forced its veterans to rely on private charities, the Weimar and Nazi states emphasized rehabilitation and reintegration into the workforce.[90]

The emphasis on economic productivity is evident in the writings of military physicians concerned with exercise therapy: "In accordance with national socialist economic thinking, according to which the human being is the most valuable good of our people, the care for the physically disabled is given much more emphasis than previously" – a task that was important for the "preservation of the working strength of every individual."[91] As a senior physician of the air force explained, exercise and "exemplary strength of will" could compensate for the most serious impairment, as in the case of a pilot who had learned, after the loss of both legs, to walk on his prostheses without crutches and to drive an automobile.[92] In this view, disability was no excuse for a lack of performance in life or in sport. As a swimming teacher for disabled veterans at the Reich Academy for Physical Exercise explained, superior amputees could often swim as well as or even better than weak or even average healthy swimmers. This showed that "swimming is not a question of limbs, but a matter of the will."[93] In the embattled Nazi universe the will could compensate for everything.

II. German Sport in Occupied Poland

After the defeat of Poland, the Germans embarked upon a radical transformation of the ethnic composition of Eastern Europe that culminated in massive programs of ethnic cleansing and mass murder. These policies were based on a racist vision of a settler society that created new social and cultural institutions for a German-dominated Eastern Europe. In this context, sport was supposed to foster a shared sense of German identity and racial superiority among the colonizers. As a result German occupation authorities devoted considerable energy to building sport facilities and setting up sport communities (*Sportgemeinschaften*) for what they envisioned as an emerging racial community of Germans.

The territories occupied by the Nazis after the defeat of Poland were divided into Western districts (including the new German districts "*Danzig-Westpreußen*" and "*Warthegau*" as well as those parts of "Upper Silesia" that had become part of Poland as a result of the treaty of Versailles) and an Eastern part called General Government (GG). Starting in late 1939, German SS and police under the command of the Reich Commissioner for the Consolidation of the German Volk *Reichsführer SS* Heinrich Himmler sought to expel Jews and Poles from the Western territories that had been annexed by the Reich. In these districts, the occupiers tried to merge disparate populations of people designated as Germans into a homogenous racial community. These people included German administrators and settlers from Germany, members of the German ethnic minority in Poland, as well as "*Volksdeutsche*" settlers, that is, people of German ethnic origin from the Baltic countries or from the now Soviet-occupied Eastern territories of Poland who often had only a faint familiarity with German language and culture. Another group consisted of the minority of Poles who became objects of Germanization policies because they were deemed to be of valuable racial stock. According to the logic of the racial planners of the SS, such a draining of "good stock" from the Polish population would discourage resistance against the occupiers.[94]

Merging these groups into a *Volksgemeinschaft* of Germans was a task for racial nation-building. Young German women volunteers from Germany were charged with the task of "civilizing" new rural settlers from Eastern Europe as well as turning "racially valuable" Poles into acceptable Germans. Building German communities in the East was a daunting task, which, as Elizabeth Harvey has shown, met with only limited success.[95] After 1939, sport was to become an important part of this German cultural mission. The basis for community building through sport was the German gymnastics associations in Poland, some of which had been focal points for German nationalist activities in Poland prior to the war.[96]

From March 1939, the main executive of the German Gymnasts (*Deutsche Turnerschaft* or DT) in Eastern Upper Silesia mainly consisted of members of the Young German Party for Poland, which was "the political fighting organization of the German *Volk* in Poland," as a Nazi paper claimed shortly after the end of the Polish campaign.[97] Already in October 1939, Dr. Georg Niffka, the Gauleiter for Silesia of the Young German Party and club leader of the German Men's Gymnastics Association 1861 of Myslowitz, claimed responsibility for all German sport and gymnastics in occupied Poland.[98] While German gymnasts (whether they lived inside or outside Germany's borders) had always seen themselves as defenders of the German nation, it seems to have been the DT's younger members who had become particularly susceptible to Nazi ideas.[99]

According to the editor of the *Reichssportblatt*, Heinrich Satter, sport and gymnastics clubs were "among the main carriers of active Germandom" in Poland during the interwar years, which is why they had become objects of Polish retribution in the aftermath of the German attack in September 1939. If German colonization meant turning "the new, old German *Gaue* into German land, inhabited by German men," this could not be achieved through force and orders alone. It required the mobilization of "powerful inner forces which lay dormant in true racial movements (*Volkstumsbewegungen*)" and that could be awakened through sport. In the case of the formerly Polish areas of Upper Silesia, which were to be integrated into the old Reich Gau Silesia, German efforts of *Volksgemeinschafts*-building could rely on a relatively well-developed infrastructure of German sport and cultural associations on both sides of the former German-Polish border. The integration of the new territories was furthered in a practical way, for example, by the composition of the Silesian Gau team selected for a football match against the Gau Berlin: allegedly more than half of the Silesian team consisted of ethnic Germans who had previously played for the Polish national team.[100]

Because of the pre-existing German infrastructure in Upper Silesia, the build-up of German sporting structures started from there. In *Danzig-Westpreußen* and in the *Warthegau* the situation was more complex because, with the exception of Danzig, Germans constituted only a small minority in these areas. Organizational structures had to be created there from scratch. Through the exchange of sport teams and secondment of sport teachers from other German districts, the new *Gaue* were supposed to be integrated with the sporting structures of prewar Germany. Collaboration between the new districts under the "sport friendly *Gauleiter* Greiser and Forster" was considered a crucial part of a process that aimed at the consolidation of the German racial base in these territories. Sporting events were promoted as "manifestations of German custom, German life style" – as a means to redeem "'polonized' people's comrades," who had more or less assimilated into prewar Polish society.[101]

The territory of the General Government posed in some ways a quite different challenge to the German occupiers. In contrast to the new districts in Western Poland, initially it was not conceived as a settler colony but served instead as a dumping ground for all those people whom the Nazis considered racially undesirable. Until May 1941, about half a million Poles and Jews had been deported to the General Government, which would mainly serve as an exploitable reservoir of cheap labour and food for the Reich. Over one million Poles were sent as forced labourers to Germany by March 1943.[102] But from 1941, German plans for the GG were based on the assumption that the territory would also be ethnically cleansed and turned into a German settler colony within fifteen to twenty years.[103]

As in Western Poland, the German authorities of the GG attempted to create a sense of social cohesion among the occupiers. Organized sport was considered as particularly suited to this task. Given the isolation of the relatively small number of Germans in a hostile environment, GG officials considered it important to build institutions that provided a semblance of the civilian – if regimented and militarized – lives to which people from Germany were accustomed.[104] Governor General Hans Frank handed responsibility for supervising sporting activities in the GG to the Nazi Party of the satellite state. While a conference of the Leadership Ring for German Sport in the GG emphasized that participation in sport was to be voluntary, the goal was to integrate every German into sporting activities, including women who worked in the GG. This task was mostly attempted through the founding of sporting communities that were modelled after the BSGs in the Reich. The German Post Office (East), for example, founded company sport communities for its workforce, and there were similar *Sportgemeinschaften* for other civilian employees in the GG administration. As in the Reich, "character formation" (*Erziehung zur Persönlichkeit*) and performance enhancement were cited as key objectives. In the view of GG officials, common sporting activities were also important because Germans in the GG worked "often in exposed positions under difficult circumstances," which made it necessary to do everything "to preserve the freshness and health of our working power." The relatively older age of civilian employees in the GG made this endeavour even more important.[105]

In promoting sport, GG officials articulated notions of an innate German work and performance ethic in order to legitimize German racial superiority. From a Nazi point of view, performance-orientation as expressed in a peculiar German work and sport ethic was part of a German racial mentality that the "racially inferior" Poles lacked. Shortly after the end of the Polish campaign, the Nazi press attributed the quick collapse of the Polish army to the lack of physical fitness of the mass of the Polish people. While the Polish nation had always been obsessed with its elite athletes, so the argument went, it neglected to care for the fitness of the general population. Only about 0.75 per cent of the population participated in organized sporting activities in prewar Poland, it was claimed. Taken together with the utter neglect of sport in rural areas, the low national participation rate in sport was presented as an indictment of Polish fitness and culture more generally.[106] The situation reflected a "primitivity that almost no other European country shows to this extent. Here the term Polish mess (*polnische Wirtschaft*) finds its truest meaning."[107] Responsible for this mess was not only the Polish sport officials who neglected to promote the fitness of the masses but the Polish mentality more generally. Polish athletes were deemed to be lazy. Compared to German athletes they lacked independent motivation and "work enthusiasm." This was the logic behind the ideas that "the Polish athlete had to be driven" and that he was most successful when Germans coached him.[108] The Nazis did not invent such stereotypes but were served well by them in fostering master race or "*Herrenmenschen*" attitudes that justified the relentless exploitation and harassment of Poles.

Since the GG was officially not part of the Reich but a formally separate political entity, often referred to somewhat awkwardly as "territory situated next to the Reich" (*Reichsnebenland*), the NS Reich League for Physical Exercise (NSRBL) insisted that all contacts and agreements between sport officials from the Reich and the GG were to be conducted via the official NSRBL department for foreign contacts (*Gau Ausland*).[109] At the same time, sporting events involving athletes from Germany and the GG affirmed that Germans in the GG were still part of the larger German racial community. The soccer and handball championship teams of the GG could thus participate in the Great German championships. In 1941, eight GG sport teams competed with sport teams from the Reich at the elite level. In soccer, four of the top teams, among them the SS and Police Sport Community Warsaw and the German Gymnastics and Sport Community Cracow, could qualify for the Tschammer Cup, the equivalent of today's German Soccer Federation cup. In 1941, Cracow, the capital of the GG, hosted the first national canoe race of the season on the Vistula river.[110] These sporting events were supposed to create a sense of civic normalcy in a situation that was quite extraordinary. These efforts were not confined to entertainment and spectator sports, however. Every German man and woman was expected to participate in sport.

As Harvey has shown, women played an important role in the German cultural mission in the occupied East. In the Wartheland and Danzig-Westpreußen, they served as settlement advisers and social workers for ethnic German settlers who had to be turned into respectable German racial comrades.[111] In this context it is not surprising that the GG regime tried to exploit the star appeal of one of Germany's most well-known women athletes: the 1936 Olympic discus-throwing gold medalist Gisela Mauermeyer, an ideal representative of fit Aryan womanhood (see again figure 3.2), led well-publicized track and field training camps for German women. The success of such fitness drives, the Nazi press claimed, could be seen from the success of male and female GG sporting teams that in summer 1942 defeated a selection of athletes from Upper Silesia in Cracow.[112]

While the *Krakauer Zeitung* liked to trumpet the sporting success of the best GG sport teams, it had to admit that the comprehensive sport mobilization of German employees in the GG was not always successful. In the German administration Wednesday afternoons were reserved for sport but participation was mixed. In the district capital of Radom, only four people showed up one afternoon, while the GG capital Cracow could report several hundred participants in leisure sport activities in one afternoon. There was an issue with gender here too. Out of seventy participants from the German Gymnastics and Sport Community/DTSG Krakau (the official sport organization of the civilian administration) about fifty were women. Most male members of the DTSG did not participate, something that was noted as a major problem that needed to be addressed through sport propaganda.[113]

In designating an entire afternoon for sporting activities among its employees, the GG administration gave more support to sport in the workplace than state bureaucracies in the Reich. In 1941, the Reich Ministry of the Interior banned the practice of government offices and public institutions in the Reich setting aside Wednesday afternoons for sport because the "needs of war" (*Kriegsnotwendigkeiten*) demanded that this time was used for work,[114] but top GG administrative leaders continued to push for sporting activities during working hours. Why was this so? The answer lies in the importance assigned to sport as an instrument for building a sense of community and racial superiority in a hostile environment.[115] The governor of Warsaw, Ludwig Fischer, justified the build-up of a sporting infrastructure since the spring of 1940 as part of a comprehensive cultural task in the German-dominated East. While sporting activities in the East had started out as a diversion for German soldiers, in Fischer's view, the participation of German civilians in the GG was desirable for several reasons. Sport was to socialize a special type of human suited for the colonization of the East. "In a foreign racial environment (*fremdvölkischen Umgebung*) high demands are placed on ... [the colonizer's] manner and attitude. The East demands the type of the fighting human. Fighters, however, are not educated through theory, but only through combative commitment," which, according to NS sport ideology, was best cultivated through sport, in particular fighting sports (*Kampfsport*). Given the burdens imposed on GG employees, the preservation and strengthening of people's working and performance capacity was another reason Fischer thought sport was advantageous. Keeping Germans productive into old age was a central goal of Nazi biopolitics that also applied in the occupied East: "Due to its continental and colonial tasks of the future, the Great German Reich cannot afford to do without the work of individuals who have reached the traditional age limit."[116]

The rulers of the GG were very worried about the image that the colonizers presented to the Poles. The "prestige of Germandom" could not be compromised, because this would have encouraged resistance.[117] Sport was meant to instil the attitude of the "*Herrenmensch*" with a habitus that signified natural authority over the native population. "Every German working in the General Government for the occupied Polish territories is a representative of the sovereign authority (*Hoheit*) of the Great German Reich. As such he must be fresh, upright, physically fit and joyfully committed," Dr. Otto Wächter, the Governor of the Cracow district, proclaimed during the dedication of the Cracow sport stadium in 1940. The use of the large sport complex (a renovation of pre-existing Polish facilities) was restricted to Germans who needed to be fit and committed to the guarantee of "security and order" in the new territories.[118] As in the Reich, sport in the GG was strictly segregated. Competitions against Poles were not tolerated because a German defeat could pose a challenge to claims of racial superiority.[119]

German occupation authorities also believed that sport had a much-needed disciplinary effect on administrative personnel. Germans in the East were mostly left to their own devices thus increasing the "danger of undesirable ways of living." This danger could only be eliminated through organized leisure activities. This is why, in summer 1940, Fischer made sport participation obligatory for all "retinue members" of the German administration of Warsaw, even though later proclamations insisted that sport in the GG always had to be voluntary in order to foster people's enthusiasm.[120] Fischer did not indicate what he meant by undesirable ways of living. But people's opportunities and temptations to participate in activities that ran counter to the political and economic goals of the GG government were numerous in a situation where the power to control the abuse of executive power was quite limited. Black market activities and corruption were widespread.[121] Such abuses were endemic to the administration of the GG. Frank enriched himself shamelessly, for example, as did his governors. Karl Lasch, governor of Radom and then Galicia, was even arrested and executed upon Himmler's orders.[122] Corruption and abuse of power for personal enrichment in the GG were so widespread that the GG was popularly referred to as the "Gangster Gau."[123]

Being isolated in a foreign land also meant that the occupiers had to rely on each other for company and amusement during their leisure time. The abuse of alcohol was a favourite past-time, as were sexual excesses involving brothels, street prostitutes, and informal relations with local women. While they might have violated racial segregation, sexual relations between Germans and Poles (if they were not Jewish) were tacitly tolerated for pragmatic reasons as long as they were pursued discreetly and did not compromise German prestige and honour.[124] Social relations with locals and alcohol abuse posed serious disciplinary problems for the occupation authorities, who, therefore, tried to structure the leisure activities of their employees as much as possible. Entertainment evenings for work comrades (*Kameradschaftsabende*), movies, theatre events, and organized sporting activities served such purposes.[125] Whether these activities were really suited to curb "undesirable" behaviour is disputable given that such behaviour and corruption were rampant at the highest administrative levels.

By October 1940, a year after the founding of the GG, a significant administrative support structure for sporting activities had been created. There were seventy-one German sport communities in the GG's four districts: twenty-eight in Cracow, twenty-six in Warsaw, eleven in Radom, and six in Lublin. By the end of the year there were about eighty altogether. Each district had its own civilian sport commissioner, and every sub-district (*Kreis*) had a sport leader. The SS, the police, and different administrative units (civilian administration, railroad, and post) had their own sport leaders. The *Deutsche Volksgemeinschaft*, the organization of ethnic Germans in the GG, created new sport and gymnastics clubs of its own. Both Cracow and Warsaw had large sport complexes. In Cracow's case, it had track and field and soccer stadiums, each with spectator stands. There were three other soccer pitches, a target shooting range, ten tennis courts, two outdoor pools (one with diving platform), and changing rooms for 2,400 guests. A fencing school, a gymnastics school, a table tennis facility, and an indoor tennis centre, in which instructors from the DTSG Cracow would give lessons in winter, were planned. In the former YMCA swimming pool, courses promised to make "every German a swimmer." All of this was meant to serve a population of less than 25,000 Germans.[126]

In Warsaw, the infrastructure of the former Polish capital was used to stage major soccer competitions with thousands of spectators. The Germans could utilize the large sporting facilities there, among them a large stadium for 40,000 spectators, swimming pools, and numerous tennis courts including an exclusive facility with clubhouse reserved for government civil servants of the Sport Community Palais Brühl, the seat of its patron Governor Fischer. The governor had a preference for socially elitist sports such as sailing, which were out of reach for ordinary Germans in the GG. Hunting licences were usually only given to officers and high-ranking employees and civil servants. In Warsaw at least, elitist sports served as an open marker of social distinction among Germans, which contradicted the egalitarian claims of Nazi sport ideologues.[127]

In Lublin there were plans to build a new sport park. All district and sub-district capitals were to receive outdoor swimming pools. For the spring of 1941, the GG sport commissioner Georg Niffka wanted to hire sport teachers for the training of exercise leaders, and he tried to ensure that the health department of the GG provided experienced sport physicians for athletes. Whether all of this eventually happened remains unclear. But the sport administration of the GG was clearly in an expansionist mood. To give German sporting activities a patina of high culture, Carl Diem, now director of the International Olympic Institute in Berlin, was invited to Cracow, Warsaw, Radom, and Lublin in order to present slide presentations on German excavations in ancient Olympia.[128]

German sport was part of a range of cultural activities designed to promote Germandom in the GG and at the same time provide the master race with a sense of privilege and privileges to come. In July 1940, Frank created the Philharmonic Orchestra of the GG and in September of the same year he opened the German Theatre in the presence of Goebbels; almost until the end of the GG's existence he invited renowned German orchestras, singers, and actors to perform in Cracow. A scientific society, a cultural association, art exhibitions, and a multitude of prizes for cultural and sporting achievements were all part of the Governor General's vision of a future German East.[129] In May 1942, these practices culminated in the preposterous claim by the German News Office (*Deutsches Nachrichtenbüro*) that Cracow, with its 24,800 German inhabitants, was now a purely German city that served as "a display window of German performance in the East."[130] The 275,000

Polish inhabitants of the city were not part of this German future and the remaining 18,000 Jews of Cracow lived in a ghetto awaiting their murder.

Exercise for civilian and party employees continued into 1942 as did sporting contacts between sport associations in the Reich and the GG. Some sport clubs tried to continue their activities almost until the end of the German occupation. As late as August 1944 the Cracow section of the German Alpine Club promised Frank that it would do everything to keep mountaineering activities alive, defiantly declaring "we will not give in" (*wir lassen uns nicht unterkriegen*).[131] Sport was considered significant enough to become the object of conflicts between GG civilian administrators and SS officials that necessitated the attention of the Governor General and higher SS leaders. In June 1942, SS Hauptsturmführer (Captain) Oppitz was appointed as Sport Leader of the GG and leader of the NS-League for Physical Exercise in the General Government. His deputy, Frank's former sport commissioner, Georg Niffka, remained responsible for the supervision of sport within the state administration. Niffka, who had started out as Commissioner for German Physical Exercise in occupied Poland before becoming GG sport commissioner in March 1940, now had to be content to be the deputy of SS Captain Oppitz.[132] While Niffka had been admitted to the SS as an Untersturmführer (lieutenant) in November 1940, his superiors thought that he was not suitable as an SS officer because he had used his position to give support to Poles.[133] Niffka's demotion also indicated the extent to which the real power in the GG had shifted from the civilian administration under Frank to the SS.[134]

It is important to keep in mind the wider context in which German cultural and sporting activities took place. At around the same time (1942), the handball team of the Order Police of the central German city of Magdeburg was celebrated for winning the German handball championship by defeating the team from Waldhof-Mannheim 6:5 (see figure 5.3),[135] while members of other Order Police units were conducting mass shootings of Jews or rounding them up for deportation into extermination centres.[136] Between 22 July and 21 September 1942 more than 250,000 Jews were deported from the Warsaw Ghetto to the Treblinka extermination camp and murdered as part of *Aktion Reinhardt*. The remaining 60,000 Jews were murdered during and after the Warsaw ghetto uprising in April 1943.[137] On some occasions, sport provided a diversion for some of those undertaking these tasks. The SS and Police leader of Warsaw, Dr. Ferdinand von Sammern-Frankenegg, along

Was strahlt uns hier so lustig entgegen? Eine ganze Reihe von Meistern, die eine Meisterschaft errungen haben: eine ste Kameradschaft, der deutsche Handballmeister 1942, Ordnungspolizei Magdeburg!

POLIZEI ganz in Ordnung.

Ordnungspolizei MAGDEBURG deutscher Handballmeister

Rechts: Ein Torrichter, der ganz bei der Sache ist

Dieser saftige Wurf setzt selbst einen so tüchtigen Mann wie Müller-Waldhof in Schrecken. Darüber im Bild die Wirkung auf die begeisterungsfähige Jugend

5.3 "Polizei - ganz in Ordnung." Order Police Magdeburg German Handball champion. *Reichssportblatt*, 21 Juli 1942. Printed with the permission of Universitätsbibliothek Tübingen.

with Governor Fischer and many members of the SS and police, was among 2,000 spectators who experienced "two stimulating and entertaining hours" during a boxing tournament of the SS and police in September 1942 (see figure 5.4). Boxing was not surprisingly a favourite sport of the SS and police as it was credited by Himmler with instilling "harshness and decisiveness" (*Härte und Entschlossenheit*) in his men, character traits that they certainly needed in their murderous work.[138]

DEUTSCHER VERLAG

Copyright 1942 by Deutscher Verlag, Berlin

Berlin, den 15. September 1942

Nr. 37 / 9. Jahr / 20 Pfennig

Für die Zustellung ortsübliche Gebühr

Reichssportblatt

SS
und Polizei
warben in
Warschau
für den
Boxsport

Der hat gesessen!
Unter der Wucht des
Schlages weicht
Pietsch betroffen
zurück. K.o.-Sieger:
Kleinholdermann

Wie der begeisterte Sport-
kamerad (Bild oben) die
Boxkämpfe in Warschau
weiter verfolgte, sehen Sie
auf der fünften Seite des
Blattes

Sonderaufnahmen
für das Reichssportblatt
von Herbert Berger

Der
deutsche Sport
sammelt am
Sonnabend und
Sonntag für das
Kriegs-WHW.!

5.4 SS and police promoted boxing. *Reichssportblatt*, 15 September 1942. Printed with the permission of Universitätsbibliothek Tübingen.

III. Activating the Workforce: The Competition Principle during Total War

The formation of politically reliable, active, and performance-oriented subjects was at the core of Nazi sport discourses. This is not only evident in relation to the promotion of physical fitness as a means to foster people's combative commitment to the racial community. As shown in chapter 4, the fostering of political reliability and performance-orientation was also the rationale behind the extension of the sporting principle to the realm of work through the *Reichsberufswettkampf*. While the Olympics of Labour were suspended from 1940 to 1943, the difficult war situation put such forms of psychological mobilization back on the agenda.

In industry, productivity was to be increased through rationalization of production processes, the mobilization of money, labour and raw materials, and the rational allocation of these resources.[139] But, as Adam Tooze has argued, the significance of Albert Speer's so-called armaments miracle – the tripling of armaments production between February 1942 and July 1944 – lay not only in the actual increase of armaments production but in the psychological reassurance and mobilization of the population: "The armaments miracle was one more Triumph of the Will. The genius of the Nazi leadership combined with the iron determination of the German people would overcome any adversity."[140] This section will examine one aspect of the psychological mobilization of Germans in the workplace. It will analyse the use of workplace competitions to activate the German labour force during the war by looking at three examples that owed much to the lessons learned from the RBWK before the war: a system of workplace competitions put in place by a medium-sized machine building firm in Württemberg, a pilot project for company competitions organized by the German Labour Front in consultation with Speer's armaments ministry in Austria, and finally the revival of the RBWK as *Kriegsberufswettkampf* in 1943/44.

From 1942 onwards, the war crisis led to pressure for an increase in performance in many areas. The regime tried to squeeze as much productivity as possible from forced labourers, POWs, and concentration camp inmates by ruthlessly exploiting them.[141] In the case of German workers, officials resorted to a combination of threats, terror, and performance incentives to extract productive reserves from the labour force. Absenteeism and malingering were prosecuted. Offending workers were denied wages and food rations, and in severe cases they were imprisoned, deported to work education camps, or even sent to concentration camps. Workers also had to fear being drafted into the army, which was a frightening prospect given the scale of human loss on the Eastern front.[142] Sick workers faced close scrutiny by company physicians or so-called "trust physicians" (*Vertrauensärzte*) working for the Reich Labour Ministry who identified malingerers and forced them back to work. In some companies the number of people on the sick rolls was halved, which, as Winfried Süß has pointed out, could have hardly been the result of the therapeutic abilities of these physicians.[143]

Yet, the methods by which the regime tried to draw productivity from the German workers were not all negative. As important as repression was for putting pressure on the workforce, it was not an effective tool for the mobilization of people's enthusiasm and fighting spirit. Since the regime depended for its survival on the active support of a large section of the German population, it had to be careful not to erode the popular support that it still enjoyed. In the iron and metal industry, a new performance-based wage structure was meant to provide positive incentives.[144] There was symbolic recognition of particularly productive armaments workers. They received the "war service cross," which was awarded across Germany with much public fanfare.[145] When the situation worsened the regime drew on experiences from the prewar period in order to mobilize the final psychological reserves. The RBWK was revived in 1943 to address problems of war weariness and disciplinary problems at the workplace. The re-launched competition, now called War Vocational Competition (*Kriegsberufswettkampf*), invoked memories of the normalcy of the prewar period and rearticulated social promises of fairness and upward social mobility.

There were employers as well as regime officials who thought that the peacetime competitions had generated a genuine competitive enthusiasm among the workforce that was well worth exploiting. The machine-building company Heller Brothers in the Württemberg city of Nürtingen, for example, created an intramural performance competition for its workforce to awaken and strengthen the "will to perform" among its employees. "The will for performance and sacrificial commitment in the human being is in a constant fight with his egoism, comfort and indifference," the company paper declared. From July 1942 the company addressed the apathy among its workforce through quarterly vocational competitions. Winners became members of the "shock troops of labour" and were declared "co-workers of the company leader." Employees with above average performance were awarded the "Honour Book of Labour." In October 1943, Ley personally expressed his appreciation of the initiative at the "Performance show of NS-Model and War-Model Companies" in Stuttgart.[146] In the eyes of the Labour Front, the firm was a model enterprise. It received a couple of awards for its social commitment (including an award for the support of Strength through Joy), and from 1938 to 1943 the "Gau Diploma for Exceptional Performances" in the "Performance Competition for German Companies." On 1 May 1942, the company was named an "NS-Model Company" (*Nationalsozialistischer Musterbetrieb*), and on 1 May 1943 it became a "War-Model Company" (*Kriegsmusterbetrieb*) because of its contribution to the war economy.[147]

Competitions among German workers were just one element in a total work system that aimed at maximizing the work commitment and productivity of the German workforce. An "Honour Board" with pictures of those "work comrades" who died at the front "so that we can live" might have instilled a sense of obligation in some workers. But since workers whose work was not considered essential to the war effort were drafted into the army, such commemorations also served as a stark reminder of what one could expect if one's home front performance was judged insufficient.[148] The Heller Bros. company paper left no doubt that the workplace competition would uncover substandard performances without fail and reward those who performed well: "It is astonishing what kinds of insights have been gained … through these assessments. Many a boaster has ... been recognized for his real value, while some work comrade who has quietly and unassumingly gone beyond the call of duty . . . has moved into the right light." The paper expressed confidence that the proportion of those who were willing to give their best was far larger than the small number of those who were indifferent or even hostile and who "eventually will have disappeared."[149]

According to postwar testimony, assessment in the performance competition was often based on estimates and it rewarded political attitudes and denunciations, which is why the winners always came from the same group of people. German workers who complained were branded as "bad performers" (*Leistungs-Schlechte*) and they could be fined, arrested, or drafted. Punishments were announced on a public message board to intimidate the rest of the workforce.[150] In order to facilitate the control of foreign labour, the wages of German workers were tied to the performance of the forced labourers assigned to their work group. If they did not perform, foreign workers (about 44 per cent of the workforce in 1943) were beaten, arrested, and imprisoned in one of the notorious work education camps.[151]

There is no way of knowing whether intramural workplace competitions were widespread or whether the Heller Bros. initiative was unique. In any case, workplace competitions accorded well with the Labour Front's emphasis on psychological mobilization of the workforce. In February 1942, Hitler ordered Ley to abandon all Labour Front initiatives dealing with the technical rationalization of work processes and focus on the psychological preparation of company leaders and workers.[152] This order from Hitler was meant to keep the Labour Front from interfering with organizational and technical aspects of the war economy. Economic management and rationalization were now the preserve of the armaments ministry under the newly appointed minister Albert Speer in collaboration with the technical and organizational experts of industry. The Labour Front, therefore, had to content itself with its educational mission and foster the combative commitment and performance attitude of the workforce in its campaigns.

A good example of such a campaign was an Austrian company competition that was conducted within the framework of the War Performance Competition of German Companies (*Kriegsleistungskampf der deutschen Betriebe*). The *Kriegsleistungskampf* rewarded companies for productivity increases as well as success in mobilizing the productive reserves of their workforce. The Austrian competition, a pilot project drawing on a proposal by Josef Petterka, the District Social Warden (*Gausozialwalter*) of the Labour Front Gau Vienna,[153] was taken up by the DAF leadership and submitted to Speer. Initially Speer was sceptical because neither the Labour Front nor the armaments ministry had enough staff to direct a national competition, but he agreed to a limited trial in the *Gaue* Vienna and Steiermark under the direction of Petterka.[154] The contest lasted six months between October 1943 and April 1944. Five plants in Vienna and three in the Gau Steiermark eventually participated.[155] The purpose of the competition was "to activate every retinue member so that he commits himself voluntarily and energetically ... to achieve his [performance] optimum." Company leaders and their followers were urged to explore "every ... possible means to secure ... the greatest performance capacity and the strongest performance will of every individual for the highest performance of the company."[156] The event could be conducted as a contest between two companies, between different plants of the same company, or as an intramural competition between different departments of the same plant. Companies or departments could challenge each other directly to foster the ambition and determination of their workforce. During the six months of the contest, workers were continuously informed about the incoming results as well as the contribution of different departments. In this way, they could observe the contest like a sport match and increase their efforts if their firm fell behind. Management and workers had to demonstrate their performance in ten areas, such as leadership, work discipline, overcoming of performance obstacles, enhancement of working power, care for women and youths, advanced training opportunities, organization of work (*Arbeitseinsatz*), wage structure, and productivity. Representatives of the Labour Front and the Reich Ministry for Armaments and War Production under Speer conducted the assessment jointly.[157]

The Austrian company competition was intended to influence the inner attitude of workers and their superiors. This attitude was referred to as "*Haltung*," a military term that, in the context of the competition, meant that workers and their immediate superiors accepted their respective roles in the productive community and actively contributed to the success of the enterprise. The guidelines for the contest impressed upon the industrial masters, foremen, and department heads who worked as sub-leaders (*Unterführer*) that they were role models for their subordinates and had to demonstrate leadership through their impeccable *Haltung* to inspire confidence in workers and spur them on. Vocational competence alone was not enough. Sub-leaders were warned that their authority was based on their ability to lead men and it was expected that they would create a positive attitude in the workplace that was conducive to high performances. Like their workers, sub-leaders were on probation. They had to prove their *Haltung* and demonstrate that they deserved their higher rank and salaries and were not simply "unworthy beneficiaries of the people's community." They were encouraged to see themselves as the backbone of the fighting company community: "Like the officers and NCOs at the front, the company sub-leaders have to form the firm framework ... [for the] retinue."[158]

Company leaders motivated their retinue with explicit references to the competitive sport logic that informed the contest: "As on the sport field," the team with "the best capabilities and the toughest fighting spirit" would prevail. Exceptional performances could only be achieved through "the sporting and fighting spirit of all work comrades ... Like in a soccer team every work comrade has his place and his task in the company contest where he has to fulfil his duty."[159] Loudspeaker announcements on the company grounds informed workers about where their performance was lacking. People who came too late to work were admonished because this would cause the company to lose points in the contest.[160] Individual workers who distinguished themselves in the contest were awarded "war service crosses" or "war service medals." The Labour Front put forward eighty-four workers for such distinctions, which were awarded by the armaments ministry.[161]

If one believes the reports sent by participating firms to the Labour Front, the Austrian initiative was a big success. The Viennese automobile firm Gräf & Stift reported a 30 to 35 per cent increase in productivity in one of their plants. The company attributed a 20 per cent rise to the new system of performance pay introduced in mid-1943. The remaining 15 per cent, the firm claimed, could only have been achieved through the company competition.[162] The plant director of the Steyr-Daimler-Puch A. G. in Vienna, another automobile manufacturer, reported a 55 per cent increase in productivity between November 1943 and the beginning of March 1944 even though the workforce had only grown by 6 per cent. He estimated that this amounted to thirty thousand working hours per month and claimed that this success was in large part due to the "mobilization of the performance will of the retinue."[163] Whether any such increases in productivity can really be attributed to a rise in performance due to the competition can hardly be measured. Firms also wanted to demonstrate their efficiency and indispensability for the war effort so as to ensure continued allocation of scarce resources and labour by the Speer ministry and the "Plenipotentiary for Work Deployment" Fritz Sauckel.[164] Despite the positive assessment the experiment was not repeated. The Labour Front blamed this on a shortage of qualified personnel who could organize such competitions.[165] From the second half of 1944, however, the allied bombing campaigns, disruptions of transport networks, war losses, and shortages of manpower and raw materials made such campaigns pointless.[166]

On a national level, vocational competitions were resumed on Hitler's orders in late 1943 as *Kriegsberufswettkampf*.[167] Like the RBWK, the wartime competition was designed as a collaborative endeavour of the Hitler Youth, the Labour Front, and business.[168] In practice the driving forces were the Hitler Youth and the Labour Front. The corporate representative of business (*Organisation der gewerblichen Wirtschaft* or OgW) was not properly consulted despite pronouncements to the contrary. The competitions tried to mobilize all male and female apprentices, young workers in training, and unskilled workers born in 1926 or earlier. The participants competed on the local, Gau, and Reich levels in six separate performance classes. They had to demonstrate their practical skills, their theoretical knowledge, and their ideological rectitude. The competitions took place between February and April 1944. Winners were formally honoured on the first of May, the Day of National Labour.[169] The victors at the Gau and Reich levels as well as participants who demonstrated "above average performance combined with good natural predisposition (*Veranlagung*)" could be drafted for a Reich Selection Camp (*Reichsausleselager*) where they were further assessed. The best could look forward to advanced vocational training and schooling.[170]

The War Vocational Competition was for the most part a response to the declining work discipline among the young workforce, which was a clear indication of the fragility of people's performance enthusiasm if it ever existed. During the war apprentices had to be integrated into the production process in order to address the labour shortage. Along with the intensification of labour, this amalgamation led to significant disciplinary problems that Nazi officials explained in terms of the desire of young men to serve at the front: As a "regrettable consequence of the lack of compatibility between vocation and the urge for military deployment a loosening of work discipline may appear," one writer claimed.[171]

As the war progressed, work discipline among German women and youth became worse. The disciplinary problems of German youths, however, were not necessarily the result of an overwhelming desire to serve at the front, even though officials liked to present it that way. In the case of youths and women, the regime could not mete out the same types of retribution as it did in the case of German male adult workers, who could be thrown into work education camps, concentration camps, or sent to the front, though work education camps were a means of last resort in the case of particularly recalcitrant youths who broke their contracts or repeatedly missed work.[172] Reports by the Security Service of the SS complained that people did not accept that they had a "duty to perform." They pointed out that the slackness of young workers increased as soon as they received their draft notice; many quit their jobs altogether. This suggests that work discipline among older youths was to some extent sustained by the fear of being drafted. Lack of parental supervision, the scarcity of Hitler Youth leaders, the inability of workplace superiors to assert their authority, and the persistence of materialist and Marxist attitudes in bigger cities and industrial areas were all cited as factors contributing to the declining work performance of youths. From the perspective of the SD, the situation seemed to deteriorate rapidly.[173]

It is remarkable that when in 1943 the Labour Front suspended most non-production related workplace activities (including company appeals and sport events) to minimize disruptions of the production process, social and sporting activities for youths were excluded at the request of Speer's Ministry for Armaments and War Production. Even late in the war sport was regarded as an effective instrument to ensure the work discipline and productivity of youths.[174]

From this point of view, the revival of the competitive spirit through vocational competitions also made sense. In the view of KBWK organizers, the lack of work commitment of young people did not only lead to a "total breakdown of performance." Apprentices also failed to acquire basic vocational skills and knowledge, since vocational training and productive work were closely intertwined under wartime conditions. The task of the competition was to build "a bridge between the soldierly mentality of the young and their obligatory fitness in their vocation" and demonstrate the soldierly nature of work during the war. The revival of the RBWK under wartime conditions was praised in this context as a "psychologically and pedagogically extremely fortunate artifice (*glücklicher Kunstgriff*)."[175]

More than 2.5 million apprentices allegedly participated in the KBWK, which demanded considerable scarce resources in terms of organization, manpower, and assessment. To meet these requirements, the organization of the event had to be "elastic," or, in other words, flexible enough to adjust to scarcities and difficulties under wartime conditions. Despite considerable difficulties, the organizers insisted that "the competition [was] not a burden on the total war effort but to the contrary one of its most important consequences" because it was a valuable initiative for the full vocational mobilization of the young generation.[176] About one hundred thousand of the participants were selected for additional vocational training in 1944, while an unspecified number were further scrutinized to determine their leadership capacities in Reich Selection Camps. But in contrast to the peacetime competitions, which emphasized the selection of above-average vocational talents, the KBWK aimed at mobilizing everyone. Even "the average and below-average performances ... were scrutinized" in an attempt to provide "all possibilities and means for performance enhancement."[177]

If one looks at the KBWK as a productivity drive in terms of a means-ends rationality, one must conclude that it was an odd use of resources. For these reasons, business circles were critical of the campaign. The district chamber of commerce of Hanau pointed out that it had regarded the war competition as a mistake from the beginning. Its fears were confirmed by the way the contest was conducted. Apprentices were supposed to demonstrate their skills on work pieces that were part of the regular production process. Most of the time this was not possible because mass production pieces were not suitable for assessment purposes. As a result separate assessment tasks had to be developed and examined. All of this cost precious working time of both management and workers and it disrupted the much more important qualifying examinations for apprentices.[178] According to the industrial department of the district chamber of commerce of Düsseldorf, many of the assessment questions were ambiguous and badly formulated, which is another indication of the hasty improvisation of the competition.[179] The Reich Group Industry noted these problems and expressed its irritation that the Hitler Youth leadership had not consulted with the OgW when it embarked on the campaign.[180]

Given the hopeless war situation in early 1944, the main significance of the KBWK lay in the last mobilization of psychological resources for the war effort. For this purpose promises of upward social mobility were reiterated. Employers were interested in the "broad base of average talents," who could serve in supervisory positions as "sub-leaders."[181] In other words, the KBWK tried to identify those workers who could be entrusted with the supervision of foreign contract and slave labour. While a large company such as the chemical BUNA works of IG Farben relied on its psychological testing and vocational training departments to select German workers for leadership positions, a smaller company like the Heller works saw in workplace competitions the best "value indicator for performance and attitude."[182]

Because of the growing number of foreign labourers, the skills of the sub-leaders were deemed less important than their reliability and soldierly *Haltung*. Disabled soldiers were considered as particularly reliable in this respect because their front experience gave them the "firmness and harshness" required in dealing with "racially alien work forces." Promoting disabled veterans to supervisor positions could be presented as a reward for their sacrifices, but this was also a rather devious way to channel people's personal bitterness into the repression of an increasingly restless slave labour force.[183]

To make German workers (whether disabled or not) into supervisors of foreign labourers was also consistent with the racial performance ideology that attributed a particular German work ethic to Germans. A order from December 1942 by the Reich Security Main Office of the SS had already emphasized the need to maintain or create hierarchies in the workplace that were based on racial criteria, with German workers on top and foreign forced labourers and Soviet POWs at the bottom: "The fact that foreign workers often comprise the majority of the work force ... lays a special task on Germans. The aim must be to imbue the German worker with a sense of joint responsibility. He must feel he is being called upon as a member of the German people and, for example, must not be placed in a position subordinate to the foreign worker. It must be easier for him than for a foreigner to advance to a more skilled position in the firm as a result of training."[184] As late as December 1944, KBWK propagandists reiterated such promises of upward social mobility by announcing "far-reaching support for the talented," who had proven themselves in the contest.[185] Given the disorganization of German society and the crumbling of the war economy under the conditions of sustained allied bombings, these promises must have had a very hollow ring.

Conclusion

"*Leistung* – a bourgeois not a fascist principle": this is how Paul Nolte, one of Germany's most vocal historians, explained his understanding of performance. Nazism might have "picked up elements of a '*Leistungskultur*' and instrumentalized" them, but for Nolte "performance is in many ways inseparable from an open liberal society."[1] Nolte's claim has some merit. Notions of performance and achievement were closely connected with the emergence of bourgeois society in the eighteenth and nineteenth centuries. As we saw in chapter 1, at the beginning of the twentieth century anxieties about the future performance capacity of the German nation state were for the most part articulated by members of liberal bourgeois elites. Liberal reformers were worried about what they saw as the declining health and productivity of the German population, and they looked to new strategies to raise the military fitness and working power of Germans. The promotion of mass sport was an important element in these strategies. It was part of a whole series of initiatives including social hygiene, continuing education schools, and organized leisure activities for school-leavers, and it culminated in the Prussian youth care decree of 1911. The decree provided money for sport and youth games to promote health and joy in work among young males. Liberals and conservatives hoped that such wholesome leisure activities would immunize young people against the temptations of organized socialism and build social cohesion. As I have argued throughout the book, the support for mass sport was not only about raising the physical fitness of people. It often had an ideological element in that promoters of sport tried to foster values and attitudes that would change people's subjective understanding of themselves and their role in society.

The First World War exacerbated concerns about the physical and psychological fitness of the German population. There were millions of wounded and seriously disabled soldiers who threatened to become a major burden on the German welfare state. A civilian population seriously weakened by hunger and disease made matters worse. All of this gave great urgency to demands for renewed biopolitical interventions to restore and increase the performance capacity of people. Ensuring the physical, mental, and social fitness of young people was an important goal for Weimar governments at all levels and they responded by expanding welfare services and sporting opportunities for school children, youths, and adults. Through these efforts they could build on initiatives emerging from civil society: the rapidly expanding sport and gymnastics movement was part of a leisure culture that was quite compatible with utilitarian approaches that emphasized the need to raise people's physical fitness and will to work.

Weimar was a pluralistic society. The large Socialist labour movement and the existence of a socialist and Catholic Centre coalition government in Prussia, the largest state, meant that Weimar biopolitics was tempered by a strong element of social care or *Fürsorge*. Promoters of sport often emphasized the remedial aspects of sport and exercise and they were careful to avoid the impression that they were primarily interested in raising productivity. Work and sport scientists who were committed to economic rationalization emphasized the need to conserve as well as enhance people's working power, and they denounced American forms of rationalization as unsuitable for German conditions because they allegedly raised productivity at the expense of the health and well-being of workers. But as I have pointed out, there was another strand in Weimar biopolitics whose advocates were primarily interested in turning people into productive citizens who were willing to work and knew their place in the social hierarchy. Supporters of company sport hoped that sport would change workers' attitudes to their work and create a "company community" committed to the productivity of the enterprise. DINTA engineers saw in sport a tool to educate young workers for work, and physicians like Karl Gebhardt thought that his boot camps could turn young apprentices into healthy performance-oriented workers who willingly submitted to the requirements of the hierarchically organized industrial workplace. After 1930 the military and conservatives looked to sport as a means to foster people's acceptance of a new authoritarian political order that was supposed to end class conflict and restore the "defensive will" of the nation. Sport should teach young people to "to obey, shut up ... [and] accept authority," as the conservative surgeon and director of the DHfL Ferdinand Sauerbruch put it in late 1932.

The authoritarian thrust in Weimar *Jugendertüchtigung* should lead us to question Nolte's claim that the high esteem of performance is inextricably linked to open liberal societies. Nolte proposes a normative, almost ontological understanding of performance and bourgeois culture or "*Bürgerlichkeit*" that is quite problematic. For one, the meaning of cultural concepts can change significantly depending on the historical context in which such concepts circulate. During the Weimar period concerns about the declining performance capacity of individuals and the nation were expressed within the framework of a liberal and democratic society, but the end of the republic demonstrates that these issues were also central to visions of an authoritarian and anti-democratic transformation of Germany. It was Nazism that drew the most radical conclusions from these concerns by turning *Leistungssteigerung* into the raison d'être of the racial people's community preparing for war. To avoid any misunderstandings here: *Leistung* does not have to be a fascist concept, though it can be, and in the case of Nazism, which demanded that German citizens demonstrate their racial value to the community through performance in sport and at work, it clearly was. Performance was one of the core values of Nazism. The regime propagated a new social order in which a person's worth and social status was supposed to be based on race and individual achievement. People who performed well were promised rewards and upward social mobility, while those who did not were denounced as antisocial and work-shy and terrorized.

While Nazi performance ideology emphasized increased work productivity, the consensus building aspect was equally important. As I have argued, sport discourse functioned as a technology of subjectivation to shape the ideal citizen of the national community: competitive, combative, ruthless, and ambitious. This kind of citizen was performance-oriented and ready to seize any of the new social and economic opportunities that the regime promised to those who were willing to work and sacrifice for the racial community. Although such opportunities were limited, there were certainly instances in which they manifested in a more tangible way; for example, when apprentices were rewarded with additional training or study opportunities for their performance in the RBWK or when labour shortages made it possible for workers and disabled veterans to move into supervisory positions for foreign workers.

Yet one should not conclude from the ubiquitous performance discourse and performance rituals that such motivational technologies were successful in fostering a widespread performance-orientation among the workers, salaried employees, and apprentices who were the targets of this propaganda. The Nazis certainly expended great energy to promote the performance will and combativeness of the average German people's comrade. As we have seen, the promotion of sport in Nazi mass organizations and in the workplace was central to this project. But while the Nazi press trumpeted the great success of company sport – claiming that millions of people participated in KdF company sport communities – in reality, people's regular participation in company sport remained limited. The fact that the regime resorted to annual performance campaigns such as the company sport appeal was a sign that despite the relentless promotion of sport for fun, health, and increased productivity, most people were probably not much more active in sport than during the Weimar period. Given the growing length of the average workweek in many industries, this lack of participation is not really surprising.

The effect of annual performance campaigns on the psychological mobilization of people is difficult to establish. Some people might have been caught up in the immediate excitement. For others events such as the company sport appeal or the Olympics of Labour might have been relatively meaningless rituals in which they participated to demonstrate compliance. When the Labour Front and Hitler Youth suspended the RBWK after 1939, they hoped that the sense of national emergency generated by the war would make such resource-intensive performance campaigns unnecessary. But the war emergency, repression, and continued performance propaganda in the Nazi press did not erase official anxieties about labour productivity and declining workplace discipline whether real or imagined. The fact that from 1942 onwards, some employers and the German Labour Front saw the need to revive different types of workplace competitions to foster a performance mentality among young workers points to the limited impact of Nazi performance propaganda.

By the end of the war, performance campaigns had lost most of their effectiveness. Evidence from the 1944 War Vocational Competitions points to growing apathy among young working people. In the state administration of Württemberg, many of the apprentices who trained to become land surveyors participated in the competition as might be expected of people who would eventually have to seek employment within state or city administrations. The assessment of the local competitions in Stuttgart was sobering for the Nazi authorities. As an official report from February 1944 noted, many put the competition behind them "without any ambition, with indifference, and thoughtlessness." If the vocational commitment was worrisome, the ideological firmness of the participants caused even greater concern. The answers were so bad that they were "almost beyond description" and a "sad testimony" to the competence of educators in the Hitler Youth.[2] This result was a far cry from the "increase of the performance will," the "impeccable behaviour at work," and the "soldierly sense of duty" that the competition was meant to foster.[3]

Performance rituals such as vocational competitions were designed as technologies of power to increase the productivity of people. The mostly symbolic rewards for success in these competitions were meant to compensate for the absence of more tangible material incentives in an economy geared towards rearmament and later on total war. To some extent one can discern here a partial identity of interests between the German Labour Front and employers who both sought to raise the productivity and the performance-orientation of the workforce. Employers who participated in these endeavours lent their support to Nazi performance drives that aimed at raising the productivity of their workers as long as they did not compromise their managerial prerogatives or interfere with production.

Nazi performance propaganda was directed at salaried employees, workers, and apprentices. It was meant to foster people's will to work and prevent a recurrence of the 1918 collapse of the German home front. For the most part it was not aimed at people in leadership positions who in any case thought that they were high achievers with no need for artificial incentives. Hans Kühne, the company leader of the IG Farben branch Leverkusen, for example, considered himself as being in a "permanent . . . performance competition" whether his branch participated in the Performance Competition of German Companies organized by the German Labour Front or not.[4]

Still, it is plausible that Nazi policies and performance discourse left a mark on the attitudes of business managers and army officers. Michael Geyer has argued that an emerging new elite of ideological, industrial, and military technocrats proved eager to seize opportunities in the course of Nazi expansionism after 1938.[5] MacGregor Knox has pointed out that the regime provided new chances for aspiring soldiers and army officers because of the rapid expansion of the officer corps before and especially during the war. While elite school diplomas such as the *Abitur* were still important for a successful career as an officer before 1939, this focus on academic credentials changed as the war progressed. By 1942 Hitler and the chief of army personnel Rudolf Schmundt had pushed through new criteria for officer promotion that emphasized the national socialist *Leistungsprinzip*. Battlefield performance was now a more important criterion for promotion than seniority or formal *Bildung*. This shift created new performance incentives for NCOs and junior officers and fostered loyalty towards the regime.[6] In the final volume of his history of German society, Hans-Ulrich Wehler has gone so far as to argue that Nazism's emphasis on competition and new social opportunities fostered a "performance fanaticism" that had a profound impact on the mentality of the economic elites of West German society: the "unbridled competitiveness and passionate professional engagement which characterized the West German economy and society since 1948 stemmed from the dark sources of the National-socialist past." The de-Nazified version of this performance mentality then became the "vehement driving force" of the "social market economy" of the economic postwar miracle, a bold if rather speculative argument.[7]

The end of the war did not put an end to performance discourse, but at least in West Germany it put an end to state-driven performance campaigns in the service of greater productivity and ideological indoctrination. Company sport and even in some instances vocational competitions were revived but these were private initiatives by employer organizations or white-collar employee unions. In 1950, the German Employees Union (*Deutsche Angestelltengewerkschaft*), for example, revived vocational competitions for apprentices in white-collar professions, which drew criticism from the youth organization of the German Trade Union Federation (*Deutscher Gewerkschaftsbund*) because of alleged similarities with their Nazi predecessors.[8] But such postwar competitions were not part of an overarching biopolitical vision to raise the performance capacity of German society and they certainly lacked the militaristic and viciously racist ideological elements of Nazi performance discourse.

The same can be said of the promotion of conventional sport. While various postwar West German governments were supportive of both elite and mass sport, support was comparatively modest and not a high priority. It was certainly no substitute for the enormous promotion of sport through the state and Nazi mass organizations before the war. The Nazi regime, nevertheless, did have a significant impact on West Germany's sporting landscape. The ideologically motivated division between bourgeois sport organizations and socialist working-class clubs so characteristic of the socio-political milieus of the Weimar years was thoroughly destroyed by Nazism, and Socialist working-class clubs were not revived.

In West Germany, sport propaganda was mostly left to the flourishing sector of private sport associations organized in the German Sport League (*Deutscher Sportbund* or *DSB*) and its State Sport Leagues (*Landessportbünde*). In the 1960s, the DSB promoted "sport for everyone" to encourage people to join one of its affiliated sport clubs. The big national fitness campaigns of the 1970s and '80s – starting with the "*Trimm Dich*" campaign in 1970 – were also initiated by the DSB. These campaigns emphasized the health benefits of exercise and tried to encourage people to take up sport or fitness activities during their leisure time. They were not based on a pedagogical agenda designed to foster psychological performance-orientation, responsible citizenship, or national productivity.[9] The character of company sport had changed as well. The employees themselves, who often received support from their employers, now organized their own leisure activities. While many employers still might have hoped that company sport fostered loyalty to the enterprise, it was not tied to a totalitarian system of *Leistungssteigerung* anymore.[10]

The situation in East Germany was quite different. The East German government was committed to a Soviet-style reorganization of the East German economy and society. As in West Germany, the old socialist sporting associations, which had served as one of the organizational backbones of a socialist alternative culture during the Imperial and Weimar period, were not revived. The East German government instead built up a company-centred sport system of company sport communities (*Betriebssportgemeinschaften*) based on the Soviet model. Rather than providing a framework for an independent associational life, the activities of these BSGs, such as participation in national fitness campaigns or sporting competitions, were centrally determined by the summer and winter sport plans of the State Committee for Physical Culture and Sport.[11] This system was in some ways similar to the work-centred sport system of BSGs built up by the German Labour Front. The point here is not to draw simplistic parallels and misguided comparisons between Nazi and East Germany because – although both regimes were dictatorial in nature – they were quite different and pursued divergent social and political goals. There were, however, some striking functional similarities in the promotion of mass sport and productivity in both regimes. The *Leistung* concept did not function solely in liberal bourgeois or fascist contexts; it had a communist history as well.

The East German sport system is best known for the success of its elite athletes at world championships and Olympic games. GDR officials believed that international success in elite sport would strengthen the legitimacy of the regime and raise international recognition of the East German state. But the massive support for elite sport at the expense of mass sport was for the most part a phenomenon of the 1970s and '80s. During the 1950s and early '60s, the East German government emphasized the importance of mass sport as a means to raise people's productivity and paramilitary skills. By participating in their company sport communities, East German citizens were also supposed to demonstrate their active commitment to the building of socialism and the principles of socialist citizenship.[12] The centrepiece of East German sport promotion was the state-sponsored BAV sport medal, which was introduced in 1950. Recipients of the medal (which was modelled after the Soviet GTO badge) had to demonstrate that they were "prepared for work and defence" (*Bereit zur Arbeit und Verteidigung* or BAV) by participating in a series of fitness tests and an ideological exam. Questions asked about the relationship between sport, work productivity, the defence of the socialist homeland, and the development of socialist morality.[13]

The East German state emphasized the link between sport, care of the body, and productivity. Sport was conceived as part of a rational care for the productive forces of the human body and mind, which fit nicely with the goal of creating a planned central command economy that aimed at a systematic development of productive forces.[14] In this framework, the rational development of human resources through sport and workplace competitions was supposed to foster work productivity for the building of socialism. Sport was meant to raise productivity in two ways. First, GDR sport and work scientists claimed that sport would help workers to conserve their energy and improve their time management during work. Second, advocates of company sport believed that workplace sport would increase people's loyalty to their enterprise and promote bonds of solidarity among workers, which would benefit productivity.[15] On a purely pedagogical level, these approaches were not that different from the methods of DINTA pedagogy of the 1920s and early '30s, but the political goals (easing tensions and building trust between employers and workers in the case of DINTA; fostering loyalty and commitment to the building of socialism in the case of East Germany) were quite different.

Where Nazi Germany had its vocational competitions with their symbolic rewards and promises of social upward mobility as substitutes for more tangible material rewards, East Germany had a system of socialist competition to foster the performance-orientation and productivity of the workforce. The 1950 Law of Labour provided the legal framework for the competitions that (similar to the RBWK) constituted pedagogical rituals meant to foster performance-orientation at work and political loyalty to regime goals. In the GDR, productivity goals were determined by central planning. The socialist competition between companies, departments, and work brigades was to provide a social mechanism to engineer better economic performances. The Free German Trade Union League (*Freier Deutscher Gewerkschaftsbund*), the mass organization that tried to foster socialist consciousness and performance-orientation among the working population, organized the competitions. Unlike the RBWK, the socialist competitions were directly tied to material rewards in terms of premiums and flexible components of performance or productivity wages. Given the limited consumption opportunities for East German citizens compared to their West German counterparts, such material incentives had only a limited effect on work mobilization and productivity.[16]

This book has traced the various ways in which sport was used or sporting principles were invoked to foster performance-orientation and productivity of people in German history. While the sport-related aspects of performance discourse might have lost much of their currency and persuasiveness today, concerns about the quality and productivity of the German workforce are still very much alive. Post-unification Germany has developed its own reform campaigns to activate people in order to turn them into performance-oriented subjects. The neoliberal labour market reforms of the Schröder government, for example, which were informed by visions of a social state that activated the unemployed in order to turn them into useful and productive citizens, could in this context be interpreted as part of a larger modern history of biopolitical interventions. But the detailed exploration of such links is beyond the scope of this book.

Notes

Introduction

1 Robert Ley, *Die grosse Stunde. Das deutsche Volk im totalen Kriegseinsatz. Reden und Aufsätze aus den Jahren 1941-1943* (München: Franz Eher, 1943), citation 27.

2 Emil von Schenckendorff, "Wehrkraft und Jugenderziehung," *Jahrbuch für Volks- und Jugendspiele* 9 (1900): citation 14.

3 There is no social and cultural history of *Leistung* in twentieth-century Germany. Henning Eichberg examined nineteenth-century understandings of performance in German physical culture and sport, see: Henning Eichberg, *Leistung, Spannung, Geschwindigkeit. Sport und Tanz im gesellschaftlichen Wandel des 18./19. Jahrhunderts* (Stuttgart: Klett Cotta, 1978). John Hoberman's work looks at the history of performance enhancement in sport, see John Hoberman, *Mortal Engines: The Science of Performance and the Dehumanization of Sport* (New York: Free Press, 1992). His book *Testosterone Dreams: Rejuvenation, Aphrodisia, Doping* (Berkeley: University of California Press, 2005) examines pharmacological performance enhancement in the West.

4 For references to the large historiography on each of these issues see the individual chapters.

5 On Goldscheid and his concept of *Menschenökonomie*, see: Uwe Bröckling, "Menschenökonomie und Humankapital. Eine Kritik der bio-politischen Ökonomie," *Mittelweg* 36, no. 12.1 (2003): 3–22.

6 On the notion of the human motor in contemporary physiology, see: Anson Rabinbach, *The Human Motor: Energy, Fatigue, and the Origins of Modernity* (New York: Basic Books, 1990).

7 The notion of technologies of subjectivation that aim at transforming the understanding of collectives and populations goes back to Michel Foucault and his intellectual circle of the Collège de France Seminar. See: Michael C. Behrendt, "Accidents Happen: François Ewald, the 'Antirevolutionary' Foucault, and the Intellectual Politics of the French Welfare State," *Journal of Modern History* 82 (2010): 585–624. In the German context, this concept has been fruitfully applied by sociologists in their attempts to outline the "economization of social life": Thomas Lemke, Susanne Krasmann, and Ulrich Bröckling, "Gouvernementalität, Neoliberalismus und Selbsttechnologien," in *Gouvernementalität der Gegenwart. Studien zur Ökonomisierung des Sozialen*, ed. Ulrich Bröckling et al. (Frankfurt: Suhrkamp, 2000), 7–40; Thomas Lemke, *Gouvernementalität und Biopolitik*, 2nd. ed. (Wiesbaden: VS-Verlag, 2008).

8 For a work that advocates a similar synthesis of cultural, social, and political history, see: Geoff Eley and Keith Nield, *The Future of Class in History: What's Left of the Social?* (Ann Arbor: University of Michigan Press, 2007).

9 Edward Ross Dickinson, "Citizenship, Vocational Training, and Reaction: Continuation Schooling and the Prussian 'Youth Cultivation' Decree of 1911," *European History Quarterly* 29 (1999): 109–47. On the important role of sport in Prussian youth care, see: Ralf Schäfer, *Militarismus, Nationalismus, Antisemitismus: Carl Diem und die Politisierung des bürgerlichen Sports im Kaiserreich* (Berlin: Metropol, 2011), 193–203.

10 Nikolas Rose, *Inventing Our Selves: Psychology, Power, and Personhood* (Cambridge: Cambridge University Press, 1996).

11 Götz Aly, *Hitler's Beneficiaries: Plunder, Racial War, and the Nazi Welfare State*, trans. Jefferson Chase (London: Metropolitan/Holt, 2007).

12 Ulrich Bröckling, *Das unternehmerische Selbst. Soziologie einer Subjektivierungsform* (Frankfurt: Suhrkamp, 2007), 14 and 22–3.

13 For the notion of ideological work, see: Mary Poovey, *Uneven Developments: The Ideological Work of Gender in Mid-Victorian England* (Chicago: University of Chicago Press, 1988), 1–3. See also: Kathleen Canning, *Gender History in Practice: Historical Perspectives on Bodies, Class, and Citizenship* (Ithaca and London: Cornell University Press, 2006), 109–11.

14 In many Foucault-inspired governmentality studies power does not only work in a negative way by constraining people's possibilities of action. It also has a productive element that encourages people to think about themselves and their possibilities in new ways. For an excellent summary of these issues, see: Behrendt, "Accidents Happen," 595–604.

15 Vernon Lidtke, *The Alternative Culture: Socialist Labor in Imperial Germany* (New York and Oxford: Oxford University Press, 1985).

16 Dieter Langewiesche, "The Impact of the German Labor Movement on Workers' Culture," *Journal of Modern History* 59 (1987): 506–23; Detlev Peukert, *The Weimar Republic: The Crisis of Classical Modernity*, trans. Richard Deveson (New York: Hill and Wang, 1987), chap. 7.
17 Pierre Bourdieu, *Distinction: A Social Critique of the Judgment of Taste*, trans. Richard Nice (Cambridge: Harvard University Press, 1984).
18 Hajo Bernett, *Der Weg des Sports in die nationalsozialistische Diktatur* (Schorndorf: Hofmann, 1983), chap. 4.
19 Arno Klönne, *Jugend im Dritten Reich. Die Hitlerjugend und ihre Gegner* (Köln: Papyrossa, 2003), 57–8.
20 Hajo Bernett, *Sportunterricht an der nationalsozialistischen Schule. Der Schulsport an den höheren Schulen Preußens 1933-1940* (Sankt Augustin: Hans Richarz, 1985), 48–52.
21 Wolfgang Buss, "Die Entwicklung des deutschen Hochschulsports vom Beginn der Weimarer Republik bis zum Ende des NS-Staates. Umbruch, Neuanfang, oder Kontinuität?" (PhD diss., Göttingen, 1975), 164–8.
22 Lorenz Peiffer, "Der Ausschluss der deutschen Juden 1933 aus deutschen Turn- und Sportvereinen und das Beschweigen nach 1945. Alte und neue Perspektiven deutscher Sporthistoriografie," *Zeitschrift für Geschichtswissenschaft* 59, no. 3 (2011): 217–19. On anti-Semitism in the German sport movement during the Weimar Republic, see: Jacob Borut, "Jews in German Sports during the Weimar Republic," in *Emancipation through Muscles. Jews and Sports in Europe*, ed. Michael Brenner and Gideon Reuveni (Lincoln: University of Nebraska Press, 2006), 77–92.

1. *Wehrkraft* and *Volkskraft*

1 There is a large literature on health and social reformers, who advocated social and self-reform because they were worried about the declining fitness of the population. See : John Alexander Williams, *Turning to Nature in Germany: Hiking, Nudism, and Conservation* (Stanford: Stanford University Press, 2007); Michael Hau, *The Cult of Health and Beauty in Germany: A Social History 1890-1930* (Chicago: University of Chicago Press, 2003); Kevin Repp, *Reformers, Critics, and the Path of German Modernity: Anti-Politics and the Search for Alternatives, 1890-1914* (Cambridge: Harvard University Press, 2001).
2 Emil von Schenckendorff, quoted in Hermann Raydt, "Bericht über den XIII. Deutschen Kongreß für Volks- und Jugendspiele in Heidelberg," *Körper und Geist* 21 (1912/13): 137–45, citation 138.

3 Ralf Schäfer, "Der Zentralausschuß für Volks- und Jugendspiele und seine Stellung in der deutschen Sportgeschichte," in *mens sana in corpore sano*, ed. Krüger (Hamburg: Czwalina, 2008), 41–56, especially 46–53.
4 Ibid., 51.
5 Christiane Eisenberg, *'English Sports' und deutsche Bürger: Eine Gesellschaftsgeschichte 1800–1939* (Paderborn: Ferdinand Schöningh, 1999), 263–70.
6 Ferdinand Hueppe, *Deutschlands Volkskraft und Wehrfähigkeit* (Berlin: August Hirschwald, 1916), 4–5, 16–19, 42–3 and 46–7, citation 42.
7 On Goldscheid's understanding of *Menschenökonomie*, see: Ulrich Bröckling, "Menschenökonomie," 3–22, citation 6; Jochen Fleischhacker, "Menschen und Güterökonomie. Anmerkungen zu Rudolf Goldscheid's demoökonomischem Gesellschaftsentwurf," in *Wissen, Politik, und Öffentlichkeit. Von der Wiener Moderne bis zur Gegenwart*, ed. Mitchell G. Ash (Wien: WUV, 2002), 207–29, especially 222–5.
8 Rabinbach, *Human Motor*, 262. On the history of the institute, see: Theo Plesser and Hans-Ulrich Thamer ed., *Arbeit, Leistung, Ernährung. Vom Kaiser-Wilhelm-Institut für Arbeitsphysiologie in Berlin zum Max-Planck-Institut für molekulare Physiologie und Leibniz Institut für Arbeitsforschung in Dortmund* (Stuttgart: Franz Steiner, 2012).
9 Corinna Treitel, "Max Rubner and the Biopolitics of Rational Nutrition," *Central European History* 41 no. 1 (2008): 1–25, especially 6.
10 Rabinbach, *Human Motor*, 182–8 and 208–10, citation 210.
11 The term biopolitics was coined by Michel Foucault but my use of the term is slightly different. Foucault made a distinction between what he called the "anatomo-politics of the human body," which aimed at the disciplining and optimization of people's capacities and productivity, and biopolitics proper, which aimed at the regulation of procreation and sexuality. In my view, the enhancement of people's performance capacities and the regulation of procreation including eugenics were supplementary biopolitical projects that aimed to foster the productivity and efficiency of a population. Michel Foucault, *The History of Sexuality*, vol. 1 (London: Penguin, 2008), 139–41.
12 On the discourse of the will in German literature and the training of people's will through physical culture and education, see: Michael Cowan, *Cult of the Will: Nervousness and German Modernity* (University Park: Pennsylvania State University Press, 2007), especially chaps. 3 and 4.
13 Philipp Osten, *Die Modellanstalt. Über den Aufbau einer "modernen Krüppelfürsorge" 1905-1933* (Frankfurt: Mabuse, 2004), citation 10.
14 Eisenberg, "English Sports," chap. 4.

15 Svenja Goltermann, *Körper der Nation. Habitusformierung und die Politik des Turnens* (Göttingen: Vandenhoeck & Ruprecht, 1998); Michael Krüger, *Körperkultur und Nationsbildung: Die Geschichte des Turnens in der Reichsgründungsära – eine Detailstudie über die Deutschen* (Schorndorf: Hofmann, 1996).

16 Frank Becker, *Den Sport gestalten. Carl Diems Leben (1882-1962)*, vol. 1 *Kaiserreich* (Duisburg: Universitätsverlag Rhein-Ruhr, 2009), 180. The 1916 games were cancelled because of the First World War. For a discussion of the elaborate opening ceremony, see: Noyan Dinçkal, *Sportlandschaften. Sport, Raum und (Massen-)Kultur in Deutschland 1880-1930* (Göttingen: Vandenhoeck & Ruprecht, 2013), 107–21.

17 Kaiser Wilhelm II, *Körper und Geist* 23 (1913/14), citation 65. On the Emperor's public support for sport, see also: Schäfer, *Militarismus*, 323.

18 Eisenberg, "English Sports," 215–33.

19 Becker, *Sport gestalten*, vol. 1, 124–9.

20 Schäfer, *Militarismus*, 234–8.

21 On the widespread concerns about the attitudes of young workers, see: Derek S. Linton, *"Who Has the Youth, Has the Future." The Campaign to Save Young Workers in Imperial Germany* (Cambridge: Cambridge University Press, 1991); Derek S. Linton, "Preparing German Youth for War," in *Anticipating Total War: The German and American Experiences, 1871-1914*, ed. Manfred F. Boemeke, Roger Cickering, and Stig Förster (Cambridge: Cambridge University Press, 1999), 167–87.

22 On German workers' sport, see: Hans Joachim Teichler and Gerhard Hauk, eds., *Illustrierte Geschichte des Arbeitersports* (Berlin: Dietz, 1987). On the Socialist labour movement's alternative culture, see: Lidtke, *Alternative Culture*. On sport as part of the Weimar Socialist culture, see: Wilhelm L. Guttsman, *Workers' Culture in Weimar Germany. Between Tradition and Commitment* (New York: Berg, 1990), chap. 5.

23 Paul Weindling, "Hygienepolitik als sozialintegrative Strategie im späten deutschen Kaiserreich," in *Medizinische Deutungsmacht im sozialen Wandel*, ed. Alfons Labisch and Reinhard Spree (Bonn: Psychiatrie-Verlag, 1989), 37–55; Detlev Peukert, *Grenzen der Sozialdisziplinierung. Aufstieg und Krise der deutschen Jugendfürsorge, 1878-1932* (Köln: Bund-Verlag, 1986); Ute Frevert, *Krankheit als politisches Problem. Soziale Unterschichten in Preussen zwischen medizinischer Polizei und staatlicher Sozialversicherung* (Göttingen: Vandenhoeck & Ruprecht, 1984).

24 Larry Frohman, "Prevention, Welfare and Citizenship: The War on Tuberculosis and Infant Mortality in Germany, 1900-1930," *Central European History* 39 (2006): 431–81; Larry Frohman, *Poor Relief and Welfare*

in Germany from the Reformation to World War I (Cambridge: Cambridge University Press, 2008); Edward Ross Dickinson, "Biopolitics, Fascism, Democracy: Some Reflections on Our Discourse about Modernity," *Central European History* 37, no. 1 (2004): 1–47.

25 See also Noyan Dinçkal's argument about sport events as ritualized enactments of emotions separate from everyday experiences (*ausseralltägliche Affekthandlungen*) that served to foster people's performance-orientation. Dinçkal, *Sportlandschaften*, 288.

26 Becker, *Sport gestalten*, vol. 1, 131–4. There is some debate about the league's effectiveness in attracting new groups of young people who had not already been members of bourgeois youth and sport organizations. The impressive membership numbers were for the most part based on the membership of its affiliated organizations. Whether one considers the league a success or not, the organizing effort still tells something about official attitudes towards male youths. For a critical assessment of the debate on the league's impact, see: Dickinson, "Citizenship," 137–8.

27 Schäfer, *Militarismus*, 193–203 and 214–31. Diem did not only have an important role in the DRAFOS, DSBA, and the JDB. Since 1908 he was also a member of the Main Committee for Physical Exercise and Youth Care of Greater Berlin where he lobbied for an expanded role for sport in youth care and the creation of sporting facilities in the capital.

28 Anon., "Einladung zu dem 14. Deutschen Kongreß für Volks- und Jugendspiele in Stettin," *Körper und Geist* 22 (1913/14): 33–5, citation 34.

29 Hermann Raydt, "Leibesübungen und kaufmännische Fortbildungsschule," *Körper und Geist* 22 (1913/14): 39–46, citation 46.

30 Willi Cuno, "Reichstag speech," (139th session, 2 March 1911), citations 5110, accessed on 2 February 2012, www.reichstagsprotokolle.de/index.html. Cuno's contribution was part of an unsuccessful *Freisinnigen* initiative that demanded shorter military service and preferential treatment in promotions for drafted soldiers who could demonstrate that they were excellent gymnasts.

31 Klaus Prange, "Der Zentralausschuß und die Finanzierung von Leibesübungen, Spiel und Sport," *Sportwissenschaft* 24 (1994): 45.

32 Stephan Wassong, *Playgrounds und Spielplätze. Die Spielbewegung in den USA und Deutschland 1870-1930* (Aachen: Meyer & Meyer, 2007).

33 H. Roeder, "Muskelarbeit und Gewichtsansatz," *Körper und Geist* 22 (1913/14): 61–73, citation 67.

34 "Ministerial-Erlaß zur Jugendpflege," *Körper und Geist* 20 (1911/12): 59–63, citation 60. For the historical background to youth care or the youth

cultivation decree, see also: Dickinson, "Citizenship;" Williams, *Turning to Nature*, 115–16.

35 "Grundsätze und Ratschläge für Jugendpflege," *Körper und Geist* 20 (1911/12): 63–6, citation 63.

36 Dickinson, "Citizenship," 130 and 141.

37 Cuno, "Reichstag," 2 March 1911.

38 Ute Frevert, *Women in German History: From Bourgeois Emancipation to Sexual Liberation* (Oxford and New York: Berg, 1989), chap. 10.

39 "Ministerial-Erlaß," 62.

40 Kathleen Canning, *Languages of Labor and Gender: Female Factory Work in Germany, 1850-1914* (Ithaca: Cornell University Press, 1996).

41 Emil von Schenckendorff, "Über Jugendpflege," *Körper und Geist* 21 (1912/13): 18.

42 Ferdinand August Schmidt, "Zur Ertüchtigung des weiblichen Geschlechts," *Körper und Geist* 21 (1912/13): 49–52, citation 52.

43 J. Krieg, "Über die Notwendigkeit einer Reform in der Körpererziehung des weiblichen Geschlechts," *Körper und Geist* 22 (1913/14): 377–83, citation 381.

44 Canning, *Languages of Labor*, citation 14.

45 Ausschuß für die Ertüchtigung des weiblichen Geschlechts, "Thesen," *Körper und Geist* 21 (1912/13): 49.

46 Krieg, "Körpererziehung," citations 383.

47 Alice Profé, "Die Ertüchtigung unserer Frauen," *Körper und Geist* 21 (1912/13): 193–205, especially 198–9.

48 Ibid., 200–2.

49 Dorothea Meinecke, "Zur Jugendpflege für das weibliche Geschlecht," *Körper und Geist* 21 (1912/13): 89–94, citations 90–1. In Britain, supporters of physical culture were for the most part concerned about the physical fitness of women as "mothers of the race." Ina Zweiniger-Bargielowska, *Managing the Body: Beauty, Health, and Fitness in Britain, 1880-1939* (Oxford: Oxford University Press, 2011), chap. 3.

50 Eva Brinkschulte, *Körperertüchtigung(en). Sportmedizin zwischen Leistungsoptimierung und Gesundheitsförderung* (Habilitation: FU Berlin, 2002), 40–4. Profé, "Ertüchtigung," citation 193.

51 Profé, "Ertüchtigung," citation 194.

52 Ibid., citation 197. While promoters of sport generally accepted women's sport, there were people who thought that women needed more protection from excessive competitiveness and overexertion than men. See, for example: F. P. Wiedemann, "Die Grenzen des Frauensports," *Körper und Geist* 27 (1918/1919): 71–2. The author thought it was important not to

neglect aesthetics in the quest for performance because it compromised women's special nature (*Eigenart*).

53 Erik N. Jensen, *Body by Weimar: Athletes, Gender, and German Modernity* (Oxford: Oxford University Press, 2010).

54 Sebastian Conrad, *Globalisierung und Nation im deutschen Kaiserreich* (München: C. H. Beck, 2006), citation 100.

55 Conrad, *Globalisierung*, chap. 6.

56 Joan Campbell, *Joy in Work, German Work: The National Debate, 1800-1945* (Princeton: Princeton University Press, 1989), citation 35.

57 Michael Wildt, "Der Begriff der Arbeit bei Hitler," in *Arbeit im Nationalsozialismus*, ed. Marc Buggeln and Michael Wildt (Berlin: De Gruyter, 2014), 3–24.

58 Conrad, *Globalisierung*, 288.

59 Ignaz Kaup, "Die Ertüchtigung unserer erwerbstätigen Jugend," *Körper und Geist* 21 (1912/13): 225–37, citation 225. Kaup was the first professor for social hygiene in Germany. On his career, see: Andrea Raupach, "Ignaz Kaup (1870-1944). Hygieniker zwischen Sozial- und Rassenhygiene" (PhD diss., Mainz, 1989), 35.

60 Paul Hagemeister, "Die körperliche Ertüchtigung der werktätigen Jugend," *Körper und Geist* 23 (1914/15): 75–81. Hagemeister was a member of the Prussian House of Deputies and first mayor of the Thuringian city Suhl.

61 There is a large literature on Wilhelmine nationalism and imperialism, see for example: Dirk Bönker, *Militarism in a Global Age: Naval Ambitions in Germany and the United States before World War I* (Ithaca: Cornell University Press, 2012); Roger Chickering, *"We Men Who Feel Most German": A Cultural Study of the Pan-German League* (Boston: Allen & Unwin, 1984); Geoff Eley, *Reshaping the German Right: Radical Nationalism and Political Change After Bismarck* (1980; repr., Ann Arbor: University of Michigan Press, 1991).

62 Thomas Etzemüller, *Ein immerwährender Untergang. Der apokalyptische Bevölkerungsdiskurs im 20. Jahrhundert* (Bielefeld: Transcript, 2007); Thomas Bryant, *Friedrich Burgdörfer (1890-1967). Eine diskursbiographische Studie zur deutschen Demographie im 20. Jahrhundert* (Stuttgart: Franz Steiner, 2010); Matthias Weipert, *"Mehrung der Volkskraft." Die Debatte über Bevölkerung, Modernisierung und Nation 1890-1933* (Paderborn: Ferdinand Schöningh, 2006).

63 Raupach, *Kaup*, 33–4.

64 Kaup, "Ertüchtigung," citation 226. On the assessment of military recruits before the First World War, see: Heinrich Hartmann, *Der Volkskörper bei der Musterung. Militärstatistik und Demographie in Europa vor dem Ersten Weltkrieg* (Göttingen: Wallstein Verlag, 2011).

65 Kaup, "Ertüchtigung," 225–6.

66 Paul Lerner, *Hysterical Men: War, Psychiatry, and the Politics of Trauma in Germany* (Ithaca: Cornell University Press, 2003); Andreas Killen, *Berlin Electropolis: Shock, Nerves, and German Modernity* (Berkeley: University of California Press, 2006).
67 Kaup, "Ertüchtigung," 226–7.
68 Ibid., 228–30.
69 Zweiniger-Bargielowska, *Managing the Body*, 66, 72–3.
70 Ibid., 84–5, citation 85.
71 Ibid., 64, 82–4, citation 74.
72 On the role of recruitment statistics in controversies about Germany's future as an agrarian or industrial society, see: Hartmann, *Volkskörper bei der Musterung*, 48–58.
73 Kaup, "Ertüchtigung," citation 232.
74 Emil von Schenckendorff, "Denkschrift betreffend die Notwendigkeit einer geregelten Körperpflege für die Jugend des Volkes im 14. und 18. Lebensjahre," *Körper und Geist* 21 (1912/13): 257–60.
75 Ibid., 259–60. In 1912, the ZA conducted a survey among German cities and towns with more than 6000 inhabitants in order to find out how much was done for physical education in the existing *Fortbildungsschulen*. 726 cities and towns responded in the survey, and less than a fourth of these continuing education schools offered mandatory or voluntary gymnastics or sport subjects themselves. Others often outsourced such educational offerings to local gymnastics and sport clubs, or to the *Jungdeutschlandbund*. Alexander Dominicus, "Die Einführung des Turnens und Spielens in der Fortbildungsschule," *Körper und Geist* 21 (1912/13): 261–3.
76 For the prewar period, there are no data for girls. In 1921 about 10 per cent of girls attended such schools: Klaus Harney, "Fortbildungsschulen," *Handbuch der deutschen Bildungsgeschichte*, vol. 4, *1870-1918: Von der Reichsgründung bis zum Ende des ersten Weltkriegs*, ed. Christa Berg (München: C. H. Beck, 1991), 380–8, especially 386.
77 Ernst Kohlrausch, "Bericht über den XV. Deutschen Kongreß für Volks- und Jugendspiele in Altona," *Körper und Geist* 22 (1913/14): 69–75, especially 70. Since many of these schools were run by municipalities or by private associations funded by local employers, the Prussian state had to show some restraint in interfering with their affairs. This is probably the reason why the state minister only left it at a recommendation. Harney, "Fortbildungsschulen," 384.
78 Kaup, "Ertüchtigung," 236–7.
79 Noyan Dinçkal, "Das gesunde Maß an Schädigung. Die Inszenierung von Sport als Wissenschaft während der Dresdner Hygiene-Ausstellung

1911," *Historische Anthropologie* 17 (2009): 17–37; Jürgen Court, *Deutsche Sportwissenschaft in der Weimarer Republik und im Nationalsozialismus*, vol. 1, *Die Vorgeschichte 1900-1918* (Münster: LIT Verlag, 2008), 71–87.

80 Between May and October, there were many more sporting events for spectators such as the German university championships in many sport disciplines, the German tennis championship, hockey, and cycling competitions etc. For the full calendar of sporting events, see: Nathan Zuntz, Carl Brahm, Arthur Mallwitz, eds., *Sonderkatalog der Abteilung Sportausstellung der internationalen Hygieneaustellung Dresden 1911* (Dresden: Verlag der Internationalen Hygieneausstellung, 1911), 81–7.

81 In 1900 and 1904, the organizers of the Olympic games tried to use the publicity of the world exhibitions to promote Coubertin's project. This approach backfired. Since the sporting competitions were drawn out over several months, they failed to promote the Olympics as a coherent event and were not considered a great success. Hans Langenfeld, "Die ersten beiden Jahrzehnte," in *Deutschland in der Olympischen Bewegung. Eine Zwischenbilanz*, ed. Manfred Lämmer (Frankfurt: NOK, 1999), 41–83.

82 Zuntz et al., *Sonderkatalog der Abteilung Sportausstellung*, citation 6.

83 Ibid.

84 Dinçkal, "Schädigung," 24–5, citation 25.

85 On the concept of "personal efficiency" a popular term in the Progressive Era in the US, see: Jennifer Karns Alexander, *The Mantra of Efficiency: From Water Wheel to Social Control* (Baltimore: Johns Hopkins University Press, 2008), 92–9.

86 The desire to enhance personal capacities was also reflected in the discourse of contemporary health and life reformers: Hau, *Cult of Health*, chap. 1.

87 Court, *Sportwissenschaft*, vol. 1, chap. 3.

88 Hanns-Christian Gunga, *Nathan Zuntz: His Life and Work in the Fields of High Altitude Physiology and Aviation Medicine* (Amsterdam and London: Academic Press, 2009); Ferdinand August Schmidt, "N. Zuntz," *Körper und Geist* 29 (1920): 28. On Mosso's and Zuntz's research on high altitude physiology, see: Philipp Felsch, *Laborlandschaften. Physiologische Alpenreisen im 19. Jahrhundert* (Göttingen: Wallstein, 2007), 103–7.

89 Nathan Zuntz, "Zur Physiologie der Spiele und Leibesübungen," *Körper und Geist* 20 (1911/12): 145–55.

90 Peter Tauber, *Vom Schützengraben auf den grünen Rasen. Der erste Weltkrieg und die Entwicklung des Sports in Deutschland* (Berlin: LIT Verlag, 2008), 71–93.

91 Michael Hau, "Volksertüchtigung, Wehrbereitschaft und Volkskraft. Debatten vor und nach 1914," *Limbus. Australisches Jahrbuch für germanistische Literatur- und Kulturwissenschaft* 7 (2014): 181–96.
92 Becker, *Sport gestalten*, vol. 1, 72 and 118–19; Tauber, *Schützengraben*, 133–4.
93 Tauber, *Schützengraben*, 141–3, citation 142. On the America journey, see: Becker, *Sport gestalten*, vol. 1, 186–94. Wassong, *Playgrounds*, 212–42.
94 Tauber, *Schützengraben*, 243–5 and 429.
95 Becker, *Sport gestalten*, vol. 1, 259–60.
96 Richard Bessel, *Germany after the First World War* (Oxford: Clarendon Press, 1995), 88.
97 Ulrich von Oertzen, "Deutsche Turner und Sportsleute!" *Stadion-Kalender für das Deutsche Reich*, 3rd, 4th, and 5th year, 5, no. 1 (1917), citation 1.
98 "Körperliche Ausbildungspflicht der Jugend," *Stadion-Kalender*, 3rd, 4th, and 5th-year, 5, no. 1 (1917), citation 6. The law was drafted by Carl Diem and passed on to the Prussian War and Education (*Kultus*) Ministries in 1916.
99 Oertzen, "Deutsche Turner," citation 1.
100 "An unsere Förderer," *Stadion-Kalender*, 3rd, 4th, and 5th year, 5, no. 2 (1917): 25.
101 "Ergänzte Tagesordnung zur Hauptversammlung. Antrag des Vorstandes," *Stadion-Kalender*, 3rd, 4th, and 5th year, 5, no. 1 (1917): 18–20, citation 20.
102 Ernst Müller-Meiningen, *Wir brauchen ein Reichsjugendwehrgesetz*. Flugschriften des ZA für Volks- und Jugendspiele, Heft 1 (Leipzig: Teubner, 1915), citation 11.
103 Bessel, *Germany*, 12–14; Lerner, *Hysterical Men*, 129.
104 Otto von Schjerning, quoted in Arthur Mallwitz, "Exzellenz von Schjerning über Kinder- und Jugendpflege und ihre Bedeutung für die Volks- und Wehrkraft," *Stadionkalender* 6, no. 3 (1918): 11–13, citations 11.
105 "Ergänzte Tagesordnung," 18.
106 Carl Diem, "Die Zukunft der Leibesübungen und der Reichsausschuß," *Stadion-Kalender*, 3rd, 4th, and 5th year, 5, no. 2 (1917): 26–30, especially 29.
107 Diem, "Zukunft," 26–7.
108 Müller-Meiningen, *Reichsjugendwehrgesetz*, 9–10, 20–2 and 39–40. Shortly before the war, the Reichstag had rejected a liberal proposal to provide national support for sport and gymnastics associations.
109 Turninspektor Edelhoff, "Kursus zur Ausbildung der weiblichen Jugendpflege in Barmen," *Körper und Geist* 25 (1916/17): 35–40, citation 37.

110 Fritz Winther and Hanna Winther-Feldten, "Frauendienst und Körperbildung," *Körper und Geist* 25 (1916/17): 34–5, citations 34.
111 Dorothea Meinecke, "Die körperliche Ertüchtigung der Mädchen und Jungfrauen," *Körper und Geist* 24 (1915/16): 353–60, especially 358.
112 Spielinspektor Münzer, "Lehrkurse zur Ausbildung von weiblichen Spielleitern," *Körper und Geist* 24 (1915/16): 360–1. Münzer reports about two such courses in the government district of Oppeln in which 332 women participated.
113 Dorothea Meinecke, "Weshalb sind Leibesübungen in Kriegs- und Friedenzeiten eine Notwendigkeit für das weibliche Geschlecht?" *Körper und Geist* 24 (1915/16): 52–6, citation 53.
114 Diem, "Zukunft," citation 28.
115 Carl Diem, "Körperübung – Bürgerpflicht," *Stadion-Kalender* 6, no. 10 (1918), citations 55. This article also appeared in the liberal daily *Vossische Zeitung*.
116 Diem, "Zukunft," citation 30.
117 Diem, "Körperübung –Bürgerpflicht," citation 56.
118 Deutscher Reichsausschuß für Leibesübungen, *Spielplatz-Gesetz. Entwurf eines Reichs- und Landesgesetzes* (Berlin: DRAL, 1917), citation 5. A copy of this draft can be found in the bound volumes of the Stadion-Kalender 1917 in the library of the Deutsche Sporthochschule Köln.
119 "An unsere Förderer," *Stadion-Kalender* 5, no. 2 (1917), 25.
120 "Bericht über die Sitzung des Wettkampf-Ausschusses," Stadion-Kalender 5, no. 5 (1917): 66–7.
121 Carl Diem, "Aufgaben des Ausschusses für wissenschaftliche Forschung," *Stadion-Kalender* 6, no. 10 (1918), citation 57.
122 Diem, "Aufgaben," 57.
123 Lerner, *Hysterical Men*, chap. 4, citation 122.
124 Otto Baumgarten, "Erziehung zu einem wehrkräftigen Volk," *Körper und Geist* 26 (1917/18): 19–25. See also: Otto Baumgarten, *Erziehungsaufgaben des Neuen Deutschland* (Tübingen: Mohr, 1917).
125 On medico-mechanical therapies for war injuries, see: Noyan Dinçkal, "Medikomechanik. Maschinengymnastik zwischen orthopädischer Apparatebehandlung und geselligem Muskeltraining, 1880-1918/19," *Technikgeschichte* 74, no.3 (2007): 227–50, especially 243–9.
126 Johannes Rissom, "Leibesübungen der Einarmer und Einbeiner," *Körper und Geist* 25 (1916/17): 306–10, especially 306; Matthew Price, "Bodies and Souls. The Rehabilitation of Maimed Soldiers in Germany and France during the First World War." (PhD. diss., Stanford University, 1998), 141–2.

127 Osten, *Modellanstalt*, 151, 159–62, citation 162; Carol Poore, *Disability in Twentieth-Century German Culture* (Ann Arbor: University of Michigan Press, 2007), 49–51.
128 Poore, *Disability*, 8–13; Price, "Bodies and Souls," 130–4, citation 131.
129 Rissom, "Einarmer und Einbeiner," citations 305 and 308.
130 "Turnübungen für Einarmige und Einbeinige in Kiel," *Körper und Geist* 25 (1916/17): 317–9, citation 318.
131 Josef Schäfer, "Ministerialrat Dr med. Arthur Mallwitz 1880-1968. Ein Leben für Sport, Sportmedizin und Gesundheitsfürsorge" (PhD diss., Bonn, 2003), 278–87. Mallwitz was also one of organizers of the Dresden sport exhibition.
132 "Wettkämpfe Kriegsbeschädigter in Görden bei Brandenburg," *Stadion-Kalender* 5, no. 9 (1917), 103–4. Schäfer, "Mallwitz," 282–3.
133 The first of these competitions took place in June 1917 and still included hand grenade throwing competitions. "Wettkämpfe Kriegsbeschädigter," *Stadionkalender* 5, no. 7 (1917): 89–90, citation 89; Arthur Mallwitz, "Körperübungen für Kriegsbeschädigte,"*Athletik-Jahrbuch* 11 (1919): 49–55. On the Ettlingen competitions, see: Johannes Rissom, "Wettkämpfe der Kriegsbeschädigten im Reservelazarett Ettlingen i. Baden," *Körper und Geist* 27 (1918/19): 134–9.
134 Cited after Sabine Kienitz, *Beschädigte Helden. Kriegsinvalidität und Körperbilder 1914-1923* (Paderborn: Ferdinand Schöningh, 2008), 194.
135 Kienitz, *Beschädigte Helden*, 54, 201–2, 253–5, and 285–6.
136 "Wettkämpfe Kriegsbeschädigter," citation 89.
137 Wolfgang Kohlrausch, "Heilturnanstalt und Sonnenbad eines Feldlazaretts," *Körper und Geist* 25 (1916/17): 200–2.
138 H. Kuhr, "Die Notwendigkeit von Lazarettspielplätzen," *Körper und Geist* 27 (1918/19): 131–4, citation 134.
139 German compulsion contrasts with the situation in France, where wounded soldiers were considered civilians who were not subject to military authorities and who for the most part could refuse medical treatments. Susanne Michl, *Im Dienste des "Volkskörpers." Deutsche und französiche Ärzte im Ersten Weltkrieg* (Göttingen: Vandenhoeck & Ruprecht, 2007), 76–7.
140 Rissom, "Einarmer und Einbeiner," citations 309.
141 Rissom, "Wettkämpfe," citation 135.
142 Kohlrausch, "Heilturnanstalt," citation 202.
143 People who suffered from mental impairment due to physical brain injuries had a somewhat ambiguous position. Some gymnastics teachers and physicians emphasized empathy, personal encouragement, and

patience in their treatment, while the neurologist Walter Poppelreuther forced soldiers with head injuries to perform painful exercises in order to assess their remaining physical performance capacity. W. Samel, "Heilpädagogisches Turnen bei Kopfschutzverletzten," *Körper und Geist* 27 (1918/19): 162–5; Michael Hagner, "Verwundete Gesichter, verletzte Gehirne. Zur Deformation des Kopfes im Ersten Weltkrieg," in *Gesichter der Weimarer Republik*, ed. Gilman and Schmölders (Köln: DuMont, 2000), 87–93.

144 Lerner, *Hysterical Men*, 122.

145 Thomas Kühne, *Kameradschaft. Die Soldaten des nationalsozialistischen Krieges und das 20. Jahrhundert* (Göttingen: Vandenhoeck & Ruprecht, 2005).

146 Kienitz, *Beschädigte Helden*, 269–70.

147 Ibid., 288–90, citations 289.

2. Conditioning Bodies and Minds

1 Theodor Lewald, *Sport, Wirtschaft, Volksgesundheit* (Berlin: Georg Stilke, 1926), 3–4. On the DRAL and the organizational framework of the Weimar sport movement, see Eisenberg, *"English Sports,"* chap. 7.

2 Lewald, *Sport, Wirtschaft*, 4–9.

3 Peukert, *Weimar Republic*, citation 131.

4 Christiane Eisenberg, "Massensport in der Weimarer Republik. Ein statistischer Überblick," *Archiv für Sozialgeschichte* 33 (1993): 137–77, especially 147–8. These figures include sport and gymnastic clubs whose members actively pursued some form of physical exercise whether it was competitive sport or gymnastics. It does not include organizations that promoted tourism – such groups had more than one million members during the period.

5 Carl Diem, the general secretary of the DRAL, was deeply impressed by the popular enthusiasm for sport in the United States. He attributed the greater contentment and happiness of American workers compared to their German counterparts to the "healthy human mind" (*gesunder Menschenverstand*) and character that was formed through physical activity and play. In 1913, Diem was part of a DRAFOS delegation that toured the United States in preparation for the ill-fated Berlin Olympic Games planned for 1916. In spring 1929, Carl Diem and Theodor Lewald led a government-endorsed informational tour of American sporting facilities. Carl Diem, *Sport in Amerika. Ergebnisse einer Studienreise* (Berlin: Weidmannsche Buchandlung, 1930), 1–2.

6 Eisenberg, *"English Sports,"* chap. 7; Frank Becker, *Amerikanismus in Weimar. Sportsymbole und politische Kultur* (Wiesbaden: DUV, 1993). On sport and gender relations, see Jensen, *Body by Weimar.* On the worker sport movement, see Teichler and Hauk, eds., *Illustrierte Geschichte des Arbeitersports* and Guttsmann, *Worker's Culture.*

7 Eisenberg, *"English Sports,"* 380–87. Michael Baker Barrett, "Soldiers, Sportsmen, and Politicians. Military Sport in Germany, 1924–1935" (PhD diss., University of Massachusetts, 1977).

8 Exceptions are studies on company sport: Andreas Luh, *Betriebssport zwischen Arbeitgeberinteressen und Arbeitnehmerbedürfnissen. Eine historische Analyse vom Kaiserreich bis zur Gegenwart* (Aachen: Meyer & Meyer, 1998); Sebastian Fasbender, *Zwischen Arbeitersport und Arbeitssport. Werksport an Rhein und Ruhr 1921–1938* (Göttingen: Cuvillier, 1997).

9 To cite just a few of the works that deal with Weimar eugenics, see Hans Walter Schmuhl, ed., *Rassenforschung an Kaiser-Wilhelm-Instituten vor und nach 1933* (Göttingen: Wallstein, 2003); Ute Planert, "Der dreifache Körper des Volkes. Sexualität, Biopolitik und die Wissenschaften vom Leben," *Geschichte und Gesellschaft* 26 (2000): 539–76; Michael Schwartz, *Sozialistische Eugenik. Eugenische Sozialtechnologien in Debatten und Politik der deutschen Sozialdemokratie 1890–1933* (Bonn: Dietz, 1995); Sheila Faith Weiss, "The Race Hygiene Movement in Germany, 1904–1945," in *The Wellborn Science: Eugenics in Germany, France, Brazil, and Russia,* ed. Mark B. Adams (New York and Oxford: Oxford University Press, 1990), 8–68; Paul Weindling, *Health, Race, and German Politics between National Unification and Nazism, 1870–1945* (Cambridge: Cambridge University Press, 1989).

On qualitative aspects of Wilhelmine and Weimar biopolitics other than eugenics, see: Geoffrey Cocks, *The State of Health: Illness in Nazi Germany* (Oxford: Oxford University Press, 2012), 26–8 and 61–2; Treitel, "Max Rubner"; Frohman, "Prevention, Welfare, and Citizenship"; Edward Ross Dickinson, *The Politics of German Child Welfare from the Empire to the Federal Republic* (Cambridge: Harvard University Press, 1996), chaps. 6–8; Elizabeth Harvey, *Youth and the Welfare State in Weimar Germany* (Oxford: Clarendon, 1993).

10 On the DHfL, see: Court, *Sportwissenschaft,* vol. 2, *Die Geschichte der deutschen Hochschule für Leibesübungen 1919–1925* (Berlin: Lit Verlag, 2014); Noyan Dinçkal, "Der Körper als Argument. Die Deutsche Hochschule für Leibesübungen und die Produktion wissenschaftlicher Gewissheiten über den Nutzen des Sports," in *Der Sport auf dem Weg in die Moderne. Carl Diem und seine Zeit,* ed. Michael Krüger (Berlin: Lit Verlag, 2009), 173–97;

Brinkschulte, *Körperertüchtigung(en)*, 74–101; Eisenberg, "*English Sports*," 352–57.

11 Carl und Liselott Diem Archiv (CULDA), Sachakten, Nr. 185. The promotion of *Breitensport* was one of the main purposes of the *Hochschule* from the outset. It was more than a compensation for the lack of a good research profile, as Eisenberg has suggested. Eisenberg, "*English Sports*," 362.

12 On Diem's role during the Weimar Republic, see: Becker, *Sport gestalten*, vol. 2, *Weimarer Republik*, Duisburg: Universitätsverlag Rhein-Ruhr, 2011.

13 Carl Diem, *Die Deutsche Hochschule für Leibesübungen* (Berlin: DHfL, 1924), 5–6.

14 CULDA, Sachakten, Nr. 203.

15 The DRAL's socialist counterpart, the Central Commission for Worker Sport and Physical Care (*Zentralkommission für Arbeitersport und Körperpflege*, or ZAK) was significantly smaller, in part because many workers were members in the *bürgerliche* sport associations. In 1929, the ZAK represented about 1.2 million workers practicing sport, gymnastics, and/or other forms of physical exercise such as hiking. Fritz Wildung, *Arbeitersport* (Berlin: Bücherkreis, 1929), 43–6.

16 Alfred Schiff, "Zehn Jahre äussere Entwicklung," in *Die Deutsche Hochschule für Leibesübungen, 1920-1930*, ed. Alfred Schiff (Berlin: DHfL, 1930), 17–18. In 1924/25 almost 34 per cent of the budget came from the Reich, in 1928/29 almost 48 per cent, in 1929/1930 about 44 per cent. On DHfL funding in the early 1920s see: Court, *Sportwissenschaft*, vol. 2, 83–93.

17 Arthur Mallwitz, "Arbeit und Sport," in *Arbeit und Sport* (Zentralblatt für Gewerbehygiene: Beiheft 21), ed. Hermann Gerbis (Berlin: Julius Springer, 1931), 8–18, especially 13–14.

18 Ibid., 14; Landesarchiv Berlin (LAB) A Rep 001-02, Nr. 585 (continued), 77.

19 Erich Beyer, "Sport in der Weimarer Republik," in *Geschichte der Leibesübungen*, vol. 3.2, *Leibesübungen und Sport in Deutschland vom Ersten Weltkrieg bis zur Gegenwart*, ed. Horst Ueberhorst (Berlin: Bartels und Wernitz, 1982), 657–700, especially 670–1.

20 Eisenberg, "*English Sports*," 368.

21 *Deutsches Archiv für Leibesübungen* 3 (1929/30), 11; 5 (1931/32), 246.

22 Archiv Humboldt Universität (AHU) Charité Direktion, Nr. 868, Bl., 57–9.

23 CULDA, Sachakten, Nr. 16. The survey lists all in all 123 municipalities that either had a *Stadtamt für Leibesübungen* or smaller committees or departments of youth welfare offices concerned with the support and administration of local sporting activities. It also listed twenty-four cities that planned to create such offices or departments.

24 Dr. Wagner, in "Wörtliches Stenogramm," negotiations in Breslau, October 14, 1924, 2, in CULDA Sachakten, Nr. 16.

25 Carl Diem, in "Wörtliches Stenogramm."

26 Theodor Lewald, "Leibesübungen und Volksgesundheit," in *Die deutschen Leibesübungen. Grosses Handbuch für Turnen, Spiel und Sport*, ed. Edmund Neuendorff (Berlin and Leipzig: Wilhelm Andermann, 1927), 35–40.

27 The DRAL commissioned expert reports by sixteen leading medical professors and public health officials in support of such claims. Among them were the surgeons August Bier (Berlin), Ferdinand Sauerbruch (Munich), Kümmell (Hamburg), the city medical councilor of Berlin Karl von Drigalski, the Berlin medical professors for hygiene Hahn and Max Rubner (the director of the first medical clinic of the Charité and the KWIA), Wilhelm His, and the Hamburg neurologist Max Nonne. Bier and Sauerbruch were among the most well-known medical professors in Germany. Both also lent their reputation to the DRAL by serving as *Rektor* of the DHfL from 1920 to 1932 (Bier) and 1932 to 1934 (Sauerbruch). Lewald, *Sport, Wirtschaft*, 9–23. In the view of Max Nonne sport would strengthen people's ability and will to work. Nonne, best known for his hypnotic treatment of war neurotics, evaluated nervous and disability claims in Hamburg. He was committed to exposing false pension claims by so-called pension neurotics. Lerner, *Hysterical Men*, 229; Killen, *Berlin Electropolis*, 207; Hans Hoske, *Arbeit und Erholung im Lehrlingsalter* (Hamburg: Deutschnationaler Handlungsgehilfenverband, n.d.), 4, 14, and 18–19. Hoske cited statistics from the Reichspost and a large Berlin company that, in his view, demonstrated that exercise breaks significantly reduced sick days.

28 Lewald, "Leibesübungen und Volksgesundheit," 37–9.

29 LAB A Rep 001-02, Nr. 585 (continued), citations 19 and 21.

30 Ibid., citation 106 front.

31 Ibid., 53, 77, 78, and 110 front. At stake were the 3 million RM within the Youth Welfare Fund mentioned above. The Landtag provided these funds unanimously, which is an indication of the high priority given to the support of *Leibesübungen* among all political parties. Böß himself was a member of the German Democratic Party (DDP).

32 Ernst Poensgen, "Die wirtschaftliche Bedeutung der Ge-So-Lei," in *GE-SO-LEI. Grosse Ausstellung Düsseldorf 1926 für Gesundheitspflege, Sozialfürsorge und Leibesübungen*, ed. Arthur Schlossmann and Martha Fraenkel (Düsseldorf: Schwann, 1927), 15–17. On the Ge-So-Lei and other Weimar hygiene exhibitions, see Hau, *Cult of Health*, 125–49.

33 Horst Jerrmann, "Die sportlichen Veranstaltungen während der Gesolei," in *GE-SO-LEI*, ed. Schlossmann and Fraenkel (1927), 321–55. Most of the exhibitions were by men. Women, however, demonstrated their skills in apparatus gymnastics, horseback riding, waterskiing, swimming, and rhythmic gymnastics.
34 Luh, *Betriebssport*, citation 98.
35 There is already a quite extensive literature on European physiology and work physiology. See, for example, Philipp Sarasin, *Geschichtswissenschaft und Diskursanalyse* (Frankfurt: Suhrkamp, 2003), 61–99; François Vatin, "Arbeit und Ermüdung. Entstehung und Scheitern der Psychophysiologie der Arbeit," in *Physiologie und industrielle Gesellschaft. Studien zur Verwissenschaftlichung des Körpers im 19. und 20. Jahrhundert*, ed. Philipp Sarasin and Jakob Tanner (Frankfurt: Suhrkamp, 1998), 347–68; Rabinbach, *Human Motor*. On the relationship between physiology and elite sport, see Hoberman, *Mortal Engines*.
36 Archiv zur Geschichte der Max-Planck-Gesellschaft (AGMPG), I. Abt., Rep 1a, Nr. 1444, 11f. On the collaboration, see also Frank Becker, "Rationalisierung – Körperkultur – Neuer Mensch. Arbeitsphysiologie und Sport in der Weimarer Republik," in *Arbeit, Leistung*, ed. Plesser and Thamer (2012), 149–70; Gertrud Schottdorf, *Arbeits- und Leistungsmedizin in der Weimarer Republik* (Husum: Matthiesen, 1995), 107–17.
37 Diem, *Hochschule*, 29–31. As the following discussion shows, however, the relationship between labour rationalization and sport was more complicated than a simple association between piecework rates (*Akkord*) and sport records (*Rekord*) would suggest. Frank Becker, "Revolution des Körpers. Der Sport in Gesellschaftsentwürfen der klassischen Moderne," in *Der neue Mensch. Utopien, Leitbilder und Reformkonzepte zwischen den Weltkriegen*, ed. Alexandra Gerstner, Barbara Könczöl, and Janina Hentwig (Frankfurt: Peter Lang, 2006), 103–4.
38 *Arbeitsphysiologie. Zeitschrift für die Physiologie des Menschen bei Arbeit und Sport* 1 (1928/1929)–12 (1943/1944).
39 Otto Schmith, "Zur Physiologie der Sportbewegungen. Untersuchungen zur Frage einer allgemeinen und speziellen angewandten Bewegungslehre der Sportbewegungen," *Arbeitsphysiologie* 5 (1932): 394–423.
40 Michael Mackenzie, "The Athlete as Machine: A Figure of Modernity in Weimar Germany," in *Leibhaftige Moderne. Körper in Kunst und Massenmedien 1918-1933*, ed. Michael Cowan and Kai Marcel Sicks (Bielefeld: Transcript, 2005), 48–62, especially 54–5.
41 On the goals of work physiology research at the KWIA, see Bundesarchiv Berlin-Lichterfelde (BABL) R 1501, 108970/6, Bl. 298 and 299; Richard

Hanisch, "Wirtschaft und Leibesübungen," *Die Leibesübungen* 3, no. 22 (1927): 532–3.

42 Diem, *Hochschule*, 31.

43 AGMPG Archiv, I. Abt. Rep. 1 a, Nr. 1353, Bl. 135–6 and 201–3.

44 In a 1925 report to Friedrich Glum, the director of the general administration of the Kaiser Wilhelm Society, Atzler claimed that industry did already make use of his results without providing any concrete examples. AGMPG Archiv, I. Abt. Rep. 1 a, Nr. 1353, Bl. 136. There were firms that sought the KWIA's advice, see: Alexander Neumann, "Das KWIA und der Kampf gegen die Ermüdung" in *Arbeit, Leistung*, ed. Plesser and Thamer (2012), 171–95, especially 177. But according to Frank Becker the objective outcome of the research remains unclear: Becker, "Rationalisierung – Körperkultur – Neuer Mensch," 169.

45 Edgar Atzler, "Rationalisierung der menschlichen Arbeit vom physiologischen Gesichtspunkt," in *Anatomie und Physiologie der Arbeit*, ed. Edgar Atzler and Gunther Lehmann (Halle: Marhold, 1930), 273–89, especially 276.

46 Carl Diem, "Vom Wandel der Praxis," in *Deutsche Hochschule*, ed. Schiff (1930), 79–80.

47 Robert Herbst, "Sport und Arbeit," in *Körper und Arbeit. Handbuch der Arbeitsphysiologie*, ed. Edgar Atzler (Leipzig: Georg Thieme, 1927), 730–2.

48 BABL, R 1501, Nr. 126782/1, Bl. 178h.

49 Herbst, "Sport und Arbeit," 716–33, especially 716–18 and 727–9.

50 Edgar Atzler, "Das Ermüdungsproblem vom arbeitsphysiologischen Standpunkt," in *Anatomie und Physiologie der Arbeit*, ed. Atzler and Lehmann (1930), 290–313. Here I would disagree with John Hoberman who has characterized medical opposition to exaggerated performance enhancement in sport as part of a premodern attitude. In my opinion, this depiction is not helpful because the "modernity" of such attitudes depends on their context. By adhering to hygienic prescriptions of moderation in exercise, scientists such as Herbst did not express premodern scepticism about the possibilities of scientific performance enhancement in sport. John M. Hoberman, "The Early Development of Sports Medicine in Germany," in *Sport and Exercise Science: Essays in the History of Medicine*, ed. John W. Berryman and Roberta J. Park (Urbana: University of Illinois Press, 1992), 233–82, especially 243–49.

51 Edgar Atzler, "Physiologische Rationalisierung," in *Körper und Arbeit*, ed. Atzler (1927), 407–87, especially 409–20. Schottdorf, *Arbeits- und Leistungsmedizin*, 88–90.

52 Edgar Atzler, "Aufgaben und Ziele der Arbeitsphysiologie," *Die Arbeit: Zeitschrift für Gewerkschaftspolitik und Wirtschaftskunde* 3 (1926): 541–50 and 622–29.

53 Richard Wetzell has shown for German criminology that German psychiatrists did not always adhere to a strict genetic determinism; see Richard F. Wetzell, *Inventing the Criminal: A History of German Criminology, 1880-1945* (Chapel Hill: University of North Carolina Press, 2000); Richard F. Wetzell "Kriminalbiologische Forschungen an der DFA für Psychiatrie," in *Rassenforschung an Kaiser-Wilhelm-Instituten*, ed. Schmuhl (2003), 68–98.

54 Herbst, "Sport und Arbeit," citation 729.

55 On Kohlrausch, see Angelika Uhlmann, "'Der Sport ist der praktische Arzt am Krankenlager des deutschen Volkes.' Wolfgang Kohlrausch und die Geschichte der deutschen Sportmedizin" (PhD diss., University of Freiburg, 2004), https://www.freidok.uni-freiburg.de/volltexte/1590/.

56 Wolfgang Kohlrausch, "Zusammenhänge von Körperform und Leistung. Ergebnisse der anthropometrischen Messungen an Athleten der Amsterdamer Olympiade," *Arbeitsphysiologie* 2 (1929): 187–203. On Kretschmer's constitutional typology and Weimar culture, see Michael Hau, "The Holistic Gaze in German Medicine, 1890-1930," *Bulletin of the History of Medicine* 74 (2000): 495–524.

57 Herbst, "Sport und Arbeit," 730.

58 During the Weimar years, the renowned German Psychiatric Institute in Munich, which would become notorious after 1933 for its promotion of Nazi racial hygiene under its director Ernst Rüdin, received considerable sums of Rockefeller Foundation money, as did the Brain Research Institute of the Kaiser Wilhelm Society in Berlin. Because of the prevalence of hereditarian assumptions in psychiatry, the research at both institutions had strong eugenic implications. Paul Weindling, "The Rockefeller Foundation and German Biomedical Sciences, 1920-1940: From Educational Philanthropy to International Science Policy," in *Science, Politics, and the Public Good*, ed. Nicolaas A. Rupke (London: Macmillan, 1988), 119–40. On Rockefeller support for the biomedical sciences in Europe, see William H. Schneider, *Rockefeller Philanthropy and Modern Biomedicine: International Initiatives from World War I to the Cold War* (Bloomington: Indiana University Press, 2002).

59 Volker Roelcke, "Programm und Praxis der psychiatrischen Genetik an der Deutschen Forschungsanstalt für Psychiatrie unter Ernst Rüdin," in *Rassenforschung an Kaiser-Wilhelm-Instituten*, ed. Schmuhl (2003), 54–5.

60 Prof. Rautmann an Dekan der Berliner Medizinischen Facultät, Prof. Gocht, 4 March 1933, in AHU, Med. Fak. Nr. 275, Bl. 37; Fritz Duras, "Die

ärztliche Überwachung der Studierenden an der Universität Freiburg i. B.," AHU, Med. Fak. Nr. 275, Bl. 40–4; Edmund Schlink, "Über den Einfluss der Leibesübungen auf den Atemtypus," *Arbeitsphysiologie* (1932): 596–604, especially 598–9.

61 This distinction between Weimar and Nazi practices is important. During the Nazi period these surveys were part of the admission process, and they were used to exclude students from university studies if they were considered "physically inferior"; see Béla Bodó, "The Medical Examination and Biological Selection of University Students in Nazi Germany," *Bulletin of the History of Medicine* 76 (2002): 719–48. This is not to say that the physicians cited here rejected eugenics. According to Rautmann, eugenics (*Rassenhygiene*), better living conditions, and physical exercise were all important factors for the improvement of the physical performance potential of German students in the long run because some physical deficits were based on hereditary predispositions. Rautmann's main emphasis, however, was on programs of remedial or therapeutic exercise. He did not specify how racial hygiene was supposed to improve the physical condition of students. Hermann Rautmann, "Zur ärztlichen Untersuchung der Deutschen Studentenschaft, Sonderdruck," *Deutsche Medizinische Wochenschrift* 18 (1924): 12, AHU, Med. Fak. Nr. 275, Bl. 78.

62 Duras, "Ärztliche Überwachung," citation Bl. 44.

63 Ibid., citation Bl. 41.

64 Ibid., Bl. 42.

65 Diem, *Hochschule*, 28–9.

66 Herta Beck, *Leistung und Volksgemeinschaft. Der Sportarzt und Sozialhygieniker Hans Hoske, 1900-1970* (Husum: Matthiesen Verlag, 1991), 14–37.

67 Ibid., 42–7. On life reform and popular hygiene during the Weimar Republic, see Hau, *Cult of Health*, chap. 6.

68 Judith Hahn, *Grawitz, Genzken, Gebhardt. Drei Karrieren im Sanitätsdienst der SS* (Münster: Klemm & Oelschlaeger, 2008).

69 Karl Gebhardt, "Lehrlings-Übungslager," *Münchener Medizinische Wochenschrift* 74 (1927): 1223–6. Hahn, *Grawitz, Genzken, Gebhardt*, 59–64.

70 Gebhardt, "Lehrlings-Übungslager," 1224–5.

71 Karl Gebhardt, "Praktische sportärztliche Tätigkeit," *Münchener Medizinische Wochenschrift* 72 (1925): 1521–2.

72 Karl Gebhardt, "Beitrag zur Übungsfürsorge," *Münchener Medizinsche Wochenschrift* 76 (1929): 1251–5 and 1298–1303, citation 1254.

73 Atzler estimated that there would be a shortage of 2 million full-time workers by 1937 because of the lower birth rate during the war. In

labour-intensive industries such as mining the aging workforce had to be treated with great care to prevent physical attrition and declining productivity. Edgar Atzler, Bericht über Bergwerksexpedition (1926), AGMPG I. Abt. Rep 1a, Nr 1354, Bl. 91–5, especially 92.

74 Alfons Gersbach, ed., *Die Ergebnisse der Sportbiologischen Untersuchungen bei der ersten Internationalen Arbeiterolympiade in Frankfurt am Main im Juli 1925* (Frankfurt: Zentralkommission für Sport- und Körperpflege, 1927), 6 and 9. On the Frankfurt Workers Olympics, see Nadine Rossol, *Performing the Nation in Interwar Germany: Sport, Spectacle and Political Symbolism, 1926–1936* (New York: Palgrave Macmillan, 2010), 35–42.

75 Georg Heinrich Schneider, "Blutgruppenuntersuchungen," in *Ergebnisse*, ed. Gersbach (1927): 31–54, especially 47.

76 Ernst Schwarz, "Körpermessungen," in *Ergebnisse*, ed. Gersbach (1927): 55–66, especially 64–6.

77 See, for example, Gabriela Wesp, *Frisch, Fromm, Fröhlich, Frau. Frauen und Sport in der Weimarer Republik* (Frankfurt: Ulrike Helmer, 1998), 161–3; Gertrud Pfister, "Neue Frauen und weibliche Schwäche. Geschlechterarrangements und Sportdiskurse in der Weimarer Republik," in *Sport auf dem Weg*, ed. Krüger (2009): 285–310; Gertrud Pfister, "The Medical Discourse on Female Physical Culture in Germany in the 19th and early 20th Centuries," *Journal of Sport History* 17 (1990): 183–98, especially 191–3.

78 Wolfgang Kohlrausch, "Körperbau und Wachstum," in *Deutsche Hochschule*, ed. Schiff (1930), 53.

79 Brinkschulte, *Körperertüchtigung(en)*, 109 and 117–18.

80 Carla Verständig, "Frauensport," in *Deutsche Hochschule*, ed. Schiff (1930), 83–6.

81 Franz Kirchberg, "Die Tätigkeit des Sportlehrers im Dienste der allgemeinen Körperpflege," in *Deutsche Hochschule*, ed. Schiff (1930), 41. Böß denounced "sentimental and unnatural" beauty ideals as well as the prudish "coddling" (*Verzärtelung*) of women and urged them to work on their health and beauty by pursuing sports. He was also the driving force behind the building of a dormitory for female sport students at the DHfL. LAB A Rep 001-02, Nr. 585 (continued), 20–1. On the contemporary debate about the suitability of particular sports for women, see: Jensen, *Body by Weimar*, 124–30. For examples of a greater emphasis on women's productivity, see also Planert, "Körper des Volkes," 573–5.

82 Carl Diem, "Frauenstudium" in *Deutsche Hochschule*, ed. Schiff (1930), 89; Kohlrausch, "Körperbau und Wachstum," 53–4.

83 David Meskill, "Characterological Psychology and the German Political Economy in the Weimar Period (1919-1933)," *History of Psychology* 7,

no. 1 (2004): 3–19. On German psycho-technics, see also: David Meskill, *Optimizing the German Workforce: Labor Administration from Bismarck to the Economic Miracle* (New York: Berghahn Books, 2010); Ulfried Geuter, *The Professionalization of German Psychology in Nazi Germany* (Cambridge: Cambridge University Press, 1992); Alexandré Métraux, "Die angewandte Psychologie vor und nach 1933 in Deutschland," in *Psychologie im Nationalsozialismus*, ed. Carl Friedrich Graumann (Berlin: Springer, 1985), 222–62.

84 On sport psychology at the DHfL, see also Jürgen Court, "Sportanthropometrie und Sportpsychologie in der Weimarer Republik," *Sportwissenschaft* 32 (2002): 401–14, especially 403–5.

85 Schulte an Diem, 4 March 1931, in CULDA, Sachakten, Nr. 28. On Schulte, see Helmut Lück, "'Und halte Lust und Leid und Leben auf meiner ausgestreckten Hand.' Zu Leben und Werk von Robert Werner Schulte," in *Arbeiten zur Psychologiegeschichte*, ed. Horst Gundlach (Göttingen: Hogrefe, 1994), 39–48.

86 As a psycho-technician Schulte had a reputation in both fields. He worked regularly as a consultant for private industry. See, for example, Robert W. Schulte, *Eignungsprüfungen im Schreibmaschinenbau* (Stuttgart: Ferdinand Enke, 1926). He was also responsible for the Psycho-technical Main Laboratory for Sport and Vocational Science of the Prussian police and counseled municipal welfare, health, youth, and work offices in matters of social welfare and sport. See the following works by Schulte: *Eignungs- und Leistungsprüfung im Sport. Die psychologische Methodik der Wissenschaft von den Leibesübungen* (Berlin: Guido Hackebeil, 1925), 7; *Leistungssteigerung in Turnen, Spiel und Sport. Grundlinien einer Psychobiologie der Leibesübungen* (Oldenburg: Gerh. Stalling, 1926); *Die Psychologie der Leibesübungen. Ein Überblick über das Gesamtgebiet* (Berlin: Weidmannsche Buchhandlung, 1928). In addition to working for the DHfL, Schulte directed the psycho-technical laboratory at the Prussian College for Physical Exercise in Berlin-Spandau (*Preussische Hochschule für Leibesübungen*), a school that mostly trained gymnastics teachers for Prussian schools. The *Preussische Hochschule* was the former *Preussische Landesturnanstalt* whose director Edmund Neuendorff was not on friendly terms with the DHfL, because he favored German gymnastics over sport. On the tensions between sport and gymnastics during the Weimar Republic, see Eisenberg, "*English Sports*," 374–80. On the activities of the Preussische Hochschule, see Edmund Neuendorff, *Bericht über die Arbeit der Preussischen Hochschule für Leibesübungen in den Jahren 1925–1931* (Berlin: PHfL, 1932).

87 Schulte, *Eignungs- und Leistungsprüfung*, 12.

88 Ibid., 46–7.
89 Ibid., 13 and 30.
90 Diem, *Hochschule*, 32–4.
91 Schulte, *Eignungs und Leistungsprüfung*, 26.
92 Ibid., 131–2 and 44–5.
93 Schulte an Diem, 4 March 1931, in CULDA, Sachakten, Nr. 28. In this letter, Schulte also refers to personal tensions with other staff members at the DHfL that made him leave.
94 Carl Diem, "Aufzeichnungen für den Besuch von Ministerialdirektor Richter in der DHfL am 13. Januar 1930," CULDA, Sachakten Nr. 191, 6–7.
95 Ibid., 4–5.
96 Eisenberg, "*English Sports*," 360.
97 Hanns Sippel, *Leibesübungen und geistige Leistung* (Berlin: Weidmannsche Buchhandlung, 1927).
98 Ibid., 16–19.
99 Ibid., 21–9.
100 Ibid., 103.
101 Tätigkeitsbericht DHfL WS 1925/26, CULDA, Sachakten Nr. 188.
102 Hanns Sippel, *Körper – Geist – Seele. Grundlage einer Psychologie der Leibesübungen* (Berlin: Weidmannsche Buchhandlung, 1926), 7–13; Sippel, "Psychologie der Leibesübungen," in *Deutsche Hochschule*, ed. Schiff (1930), 72–5.
103 Sippel, *Leibesübungen und geistige Leistung*, 124–8.
104 Diem, *Hochschule*, 6. The psychological transformation of individuals through sport was a major theme running through Diem's theoretical writings on physical education.
105 On the role of sport in DINTA work pedagogy, see Fasbender, *Arbeitersport und Arbeitssport*, 46–8. and 83–90. On the history of DINTA and its vision of a New Worker, see Mary Nolan, *Visions of Modernity: American Business and the Modernization of Germany* (New York and Oxford: Oxford University Press, 1994), 185–96.
106 Max Mengerinhausen, "Die Erziehung des Arbeiters zur Arbeit," *Die Umschau* 31 (1927): citations 1010–12.
107 Fasbender, *Arbeitersport und Arbeitssport*, 49.
108 Ibid., 53 and 63.
109 Hans Riedel, "Sport und Turnen in der technischen Arbeitsschulung," *Arbeitsschulung* 1 (1929): 8–11.
110 Gebhardt, "Praktische sportärztliche Tätigkeit," 1522.
111 Gebhardt, "Lehrlings-Übungslager," 1225.

112 Friedrich Wilhelm von der Linde, "Arbeitgeber und Leibesübungen," in *Arbeit und Sport*, ed. Gerbis (1931): 43–62, especially 51.
113 Gebhardt, "Lehrlings-Übungslager," 1225.
114 Gebhardt, "Beitrag zur Übungsfürsorge," 1299.
115 Ibid., 1254.
116 Ibid., citations 1299–1303.
117 Linde, "Arbeitgeber und Leibesübungen," 59–62.
118 Ibid., citations 47 and 51.
119 Ibid., 49. According to Linde, the requirement varied according to the employer between one and four hours per week.
120 Luh, *Betriebssport*, 111.
121 BABL NS 5 VI, Nr. 19422, Bl. 21–3 and 29, citation Bl. 21. The observer, a Mr. Dähn, was most likely from the German National Union of Commercial Employees, which was invited to send a representative to the conference. While the union was also right wing it was quite critical of the promotion of company union ideals by employers. Larry Eugene Jones, "The German National Union of Commercial Employees from 1928 to 1933," *Journal of Modern History* 48, no. 3 (1976), 462–82, especially 464–5. See also the letter by Walter Preuss, who was editor of the union's journal *Deutsche Handelswacht*, in BABL NS 5 VI, Nr. 19422., Bl. 27–9.
122 Dr Bartels und Dr Koehler, "Rundschreiben an Mitglieder und Interessenten der Gesellschaft betreffend Tagung des Unterausschusses für Gesundheitswesen," 30 Mai 1928, BABL NS 5 VI, Nr. 19422, Bl. 24 back and front.
123 On Bartels' role in the GWS, see Karl-Peter Reeg, *Friedrich Georg Christian Bartels (1892-1968). Ein Beitrag zur Entwicklung der Leistungsmedizin im Nationalsozialismus* (Husum: Matthiesen Verlag, 1988), 19–32.
124 Bartels as cited in ibid., 22.
125 The RAG tried to enlist the financial help of the GWS for this expansion, but by its own admission it was not able to achieve its ambitious goals. Walter Preuss, "Betr. Reichsarbeitsgemeinschaft der Behörden- und Firmensportverbände und Gesellschaft für deutsche Wirtschafts- und Sozialpolitik," 15 Juni 1928, BABL NS 5 VI, 19422, Bl. 27–9. Paul Duysen, "Aus eigenem Hause," 10 November 1931, BABL NS 5 VI, 19422, Bl. 14. According to Luh, the RAG (from 1929 renamed *Reichsverband deutscher Firmensportvereine*) had about twenty-two thousand members in 1929. Nationwide there were more than three hundred thousand people organized in company sport clubs, some of which were organized in the DRAL. Luh, *Betriebssport*, 117–20 and 189–94. In addition, there were

many clerical employees and manual workers who were organized in DRAL affiliated "bourgeois" sport clubs.

126 Paul Zobel, *Werksport und Arbeitersport* (Berlin: Märkische Spielvereinigung, 1926), 18–31; Cornelius Gellert, *Unsere Gegner*, 2nd. ed. (Leipzig: Arbeiter-Turnverlag, 1927); BABL NS 5 VI, 19422, Bl. 13 and 20; Fasbender, *Arbeitersport*, 198–202; Luh, *Betriebssport*, 194–9.

127 Walter Maschke, "Arbeiter und Leibesübungen," in *Arbeit und Sport*, ed. Gerbis (1931), 63–7. Maschke was the youth secretary of the socialist-leaning free trade union league *Allgemeiner Deutscher Gewerkschaftsbund* (ADGB).

128 Hanns Sippel, "Psychologische Überlegungen zur Frage der Sportpause," in *Arbeit und Sport*, ed. Gerbis (1931), 34–42.

129 Fasbender, *Arbeitersport und Arbeitssport*, 119.

130 Uhlmann, "Sport ist der praktische Arzt," 4.

131 On such preventive and rehabilitative trends in German welfare and social work, see Young-Sun Hong, *Welfare, Modernity, and the Weimar State, 1919–1933* (Princeton: Princeton University Press, 1998), especially 58–65 and 203–5.

132 Gerald R. Gems, "Welfare Capitalism and Blue-Collar Sport: The Legacy of Labor Unrest," *Rethinking History* 5, no. 1 (2001): 43–58; Richard Holt, *Sport and Society in Modern France* (London: MacMillan, 1981), 202–4.

133 Joan Tumblety, *Remaking the Male Body: Masculinity and the Uses of Physical Culture in Interwar and Vichy France* (Oxford: Oxford University Press, 2013); Ina Zweiniger-Bargielowska, *Managing the Body*.

134 In Britain state-supported fitness campaigns only became important in the late 1930s and they do not seem to have played a role in countries such as Australia or the US. Zweiniger-Bargielowska, *Managing the Body*; Ana Carden-Coyne, *Reconstructing the Body: Classicism, Modernism, and the First World War* (Oxford: Oxford University Press, 2009).

135 Nikolaus Katzer, "Körperkult und Bewegungszwang. Zur gesellschaftlichen Dynamik des frühen sowjetischen Sportsystems," in *Sport auf dem Weg*, ed. Krüger (2009), 257–83.

136 John Read, "Physical Culture and Sport in the early Soviet Period," *Australian Slavonic and East European Studies* 10 (1996): 59–84, especially 63–8 and 79–81; Alison Rowley, "Sport in the Service of the State: Images of Physical Culture and Soviet Women, 1917-1941," *The International Journal of the History of Sport* 23, no. 8 (2006): 1314–40, especially 1330–2; Barbara Keys, *Globalizing Sport: National Rivalry and International Community in the 1930s* (Cambridge: Harvard University Press, 2006), 160–5.

137 Katzer, "Körperkult," 274–5; Barbara Keys, "The Body as Political Space: Comparing Physical Education under Nazism and Stalinism," *German History* 27, no. 3 (2009): 395–413, especially 401–2. As Keys points out, there were also important cultural differences between Germany and Russia or the Soviet Union, which could not draw on an established gymnastics movement or on intellectual traditions emphasizing the importance of exercise for personal development.

138 Killen, *Berlin Electropolis*, especially 207.

139 Greg Eghigian, *Disability, Insurance, and the Birth of the Social Entitlement State in Germany* (Ann Arbor: University of Michigan Press, 2000); Hong, *Welfare*, 250–6 and 271–6.

140 "Notizen zur Frage der Wehrhaftmachung der Jugend," 4 March 1931, BABL R 43 II, Nr 519, Bl. 43. Before 1929, the Reich supported sport with 1.5 Million RM per year. For 1929 the sum was reduced to 1 million. In 1930 there were 800,000 RM and for 1931 750,000.

141 Fasbender, *Arbeitersport*, 149–51; Luh, *Betriebssport*, 135–6.

142 "Abkommen des Reichsverbands der Firmensportvereine mit den Paten," 15 June 1931, BABL NS 5 VI, Nr. 19422, Bl. 15f. The Reichsverband was the successor of the RAG. Many clubs were not directly controlled by employers and the sponsorship has to be seen as an attempt by employers to assert more control over business-based sporting activities. The sponsorship committee was founded by six firms who tried to solicit further support from other employers. The initiative was to remain confidential to avoid public suspicion. The scheme came to an end in late 1931 because of protests by the DnHV whose sport association was a member of the Hamburg Reichsverband subsidiary the *Sportsverband der Geschäftsmannschaften Hamburgs*. As in the case of the GWS's attempt to take control, the DnHV was concerned that there might be too much employer influence over the umbrella league. 15 June 1931, BABL NS 5 VI, Nr. 19422, Bl. 17.

143 Johannes Hürter, *Wilhelm Groener. Reichswehrminister am Ende der Weimarer Republik* (München: Oldenbourg, 1993), 139–45.

144 Becker, *Sport gestalten*, vol. 2, 201–4; Rüdiger Bergien, *Die bellizistische Republik. Wehrkonsens und "Wehrhaftmachung" in Deutschland, 1918–1933* (München: Oldenbourg, 2012), 366–7. On the relationship between the Reichswehr and the *Volkssportschulen*, see also: Barrett, "Soldiers, Sportsmen, and Politicians," chap. 2.

145 Reichswehrminister Groener an Reichskanzler Brüning, 18 October 1930, BABL R 43 II, Nr. 519, citations Bl. 2 back.

146 Groener an Brüning, 18 October 1930, citation Bl. 4; Groener an Reichsminister of the Interior, 1 August 1930, BABL R 43 II, Nr. 519, Bl. 18–20. Groener invoked here what Bergien has called the "*republikanischen Wehrkonsens*" (shared by many republicans including Social Democrats), which combined support for military preparedness with a commitment to the republic, see: Bergien, *Republik*, 187–8.
147 "Notizen Wehrhaftmachung," BABL R 43 II, Nr. 519, Bl. 32.
148 Ibid., Bl. 43.
149 Ibid., Bl. 44.
150 "Erlaβ des Reichspräsidenten über die körperliche Ertüchtigung der Jugend," BABL R 43 II, Nr. 519, citations Bl. 97; Becker, *Sport gestalten*, vol. 2, 220–4.
151 Cited after Becker, *Sport gestalten*, vol. 2, 225.
152 Ibid., 229–30.
153 Bergien, *Republik*, 383.
154 Becker, *Sport gestalten*, vol. 2, 30.

3. Conditioning People's Comrades

1 Hans Hoske, "Die Leibesübungen als Mittel der aufbauenden Bevölkerungspolitik," *Archiv für Bevölkerungswissenschaft und Bevölkerungspolitik* 4 (1934): 241–51, citation 241.
2 On Gebhardt's career during the Nazi period, see: Hahn, *Grawitz, Genzken, Gebhardt*.
3 Hans Hoske, "Leibesübungen als Entwicklungsreiz," in *Konstitutions- und Erbbiologie in der Praxis der Medizin*, ed. Walther Jaensch (Leipzig: Ambrosius Barth, 1934), 351–65; Karl Gebhardt, "Körperschule der Schwächlichen," in *Konstitutions- und Erbbiologie*, ed. Jaensch (1934), 357–9.
4 AHU, UK Personalia Karl Gebhardt, G 031, Vol. 3, Bl. 3–5; Frohwalt Heiss, H 187, Vol. 2, Bl. 2–4.
5 Susanne Heim, *Kalorien, Kautschuk, und Karrieren: Pflanzenzüchtung und landwirtschaftliche Forschung in Kaiser-Wilhelm-Instituten, 1933–1945* (Göttingen: Wallstein, 2003), 91–3.
6 Philipp Felsch, "Volkssport. Zur Ökonomie der körperlichen Leistungsprüfung im Nationalsozialismus," *SportZeit* 1, no. 3 (2001): 5–29.
7 Thomas Beddies, "*Du hast die Pflicht gesund zu sein." Der Gesundheitsdienst der Hitlerjugend 1933–1945* (Berlin: be.bra. Wissenschaft, 2010), 132–6, 174. Boys and girls had to undergo fitness assessments for their performance medals, but the criteria were different. Young girls, for example, were not asked to participate in shooting exercises: Reichsjugendführung, ed., *Mädel*

im Dienst. Jungmädelsport, 2nd. ed. (Potsdam: Ludwig Voggenreiter, 1940), 150–6.

8 Because of its location in the industrial centre of Germany, Dortmund offered better opportunities to obtain "worker material" (*Arbeitermaterial*) from mining, industry, and agriculture for research purposes. The Kaiser Wilhelm Society also thought the new location made it easier to propagate its research results among industry. The city of Dortmund promised to build a new building for the institute and support it with 20,000 RM. AGMPG Abt. I, Rep 1a, Nr. 1391, Bl. 8 and 9. The relocation was primarily a response to the chronic funding shortages of the institute: Sören Flachowsky, "'Das Institut erfreut sich in den Kreisen der Industrie des Ruhrbezirks ganz besonderer Beliebtheit.' Das Kaiser-Wilhelm-Institut für Arbeitsphysiologie und die Montanindustrie 1913–1945," in *Arbeit, Leistung*, ed. Plesser and Thamer (2012), 357–424.

9 Deutsche Hochschule für Leibesübungen, *Tätigkeitsbericht 1930/31*, 31; Eisenberg, "*English Sports*," 365–6.

10 AHU UK Personalia Frohwalt Heiss, vol. 3, Bl. 9. Deutsche Hochschule für Leibesübungen, *Tätigkeitbericht 1929/30*, 52; *Tätigkeitsbericht 1930/31*, 54; *Tätigkeitsbericht 1931/32*, 38.

11 Because of his involvement with the Nazi regime Diem remains a very controversial figure to this day. While some see him as a conservative who tried to keep his distance from the regime, others emphasize his active engagement for the regime whenever he received the opportunity. For detailed analysis of the complicated transformational process of the German sport administration during the first year of Nazism and the role of Carl Diem, see: Becker, *Sport gestalten*, vol. 3, *NS-Zeit* (2009), chaps. 1 and 2. On the founding of the Reichsbund für Leibesübungen, see: Hajo Bernett, *Der Weg des Sports in die nationalsozialistische Diktatur. Die Entstehung des Deutschen (Nationalsozialistischen) Reichsbund für Leibesübungen* (Schorndorf: Karl Hofman, 1983).

12 Bernett, *Weg des Sports*, 8–10. A small number of workers' sport clubs were coordinated like their bourgeois counterparts and survived. On the fate of worker soccer clubs, see: Eike Stiller, "Fußball in der organisierten Arbeitersportbewegung," in *Hakenkreuz und rundes Leder. Fußball im Nationalsozialismus*, ed. Lorenz Peiffer and Dietrich Schulze-Marmeling (Göttingen: Die Werkstatt, 2008), 166–77.

13 On Lewald, see Arnd Krüger, *Theodor Lewald. Sportführer ins Dritte Reich* (Berlin: Bartels & Wernitz, 1975). On Diem's and Lewald's roles in the organization of the 1936 games, see Becker, *Sport gestalten*, vol. 3 (2009), chap. 3; David Clay Large, *Nazi Games: The Olympics of 1936* (New York:

Norton, 2007); Hans Joachim Teichler, *Internationale Sportpolitik im Dritten Reich* (Schorndorf: Hofmann, 1991). In 1938, Diem became acting director of the International Olympic Institute, a research institute on the history of the Olympic idea, which was financed by the Reich and officially recognized by the IOC. On Diem's career after 1936, see Becker, *Sport gestalten*, vol. 3 (2009).

14 BABL R 4901, Nr. 126336, Bl. 2 and 3. Both Lexer and Sauerbruch were Gebhardt's superiors while he was at the University of Munich.

15 Ibid.

16 "Aktennotiz Diem," 14 März 1934, CULDA Sachakten, Nr 29. On the political significance of Carl Krümmel, see: Horst Ueberhorst, *Carl Krümmel und die nationalsozialistische Leibeserziehung* (Berlin: Bartels & Wernitz, 1976). On the Reich Sport Leader, see: Dieter Steinhöfer, *Hans von Tschammer und Osten. Reichssportführer im Dritten Reich* (Berlin: Bartels & Wernitz, 1973).

17 "Erlass des Führers und Reichskanzlers über die Reichsakademie für Leibesübungen," 7 April 1937, CULDA Sachakten, Nr. 29.

18 "Erklärung des Kuratoriums für Leibesübungen zur neuen Reichsakademie für Leibesübungen," CULDA Sachakten, Nr. 565a.

19 Patrizia Dogliani, "Sport and Fascism," *Journal of Modern Italian Studies* 5, no. 3 (2000): 328–30.

20 Hajo Bernett, *Nationalsozialistische Leibeserziehung. Eine Dokumentation ihrer Theorie und Organisation* (Schorndorf: Karl Hofmann, 1966), 171; Bernett, *Weg des Sports*, 53–62. These unresolved conflicts were also discussed in the SD report for 1938: "Jahreslagebericht 1938 des Sicherheitshauptamtes," in *Meldungen aus dem Reich. Die geheimen Lageberichte des Sicherheitsdienstes der SS 1938-1945*, ed. Heinz Boberach, vol. 2 (Herrsching: Pawlak, 1984), 148–50.

21 Heinz Wetzel, "Reichsakademie für Leibesübungen. Die politischen Grundlagen," *Reichssportblatt* 3, no. 18 (1936): 587.

22 Wolf Strache, "Die Reichsakademie für Leibesübungen," *Reichssportblatt* 3, no. 19 (1936): 618–21, citation 621.

23 On Nerz' career, see: Nils Havemann, *Fussball unterm Hakenkreuz. Der DFB zwischen Sport, Politik und Kommerz* (Frankfurt: Campus, 2005), especially 149–55.

24 AHU UK Personalia, N 022 Otto Nerz, Vol. 1, Bl. 1 and 32; Vol 2, Bl. 1 and 5.

25 AHU NS Doz 195 Otto Nerz, Bl. 5–7 and 22.

26 Havemann, *Fussball*, 160.

27 AHU UK Personalia, Sch 288 Bruno K. Schultz, Vol 2, Bl. 8 and 39–41.

28 Bruno K. Schultz, "Rassenkundliche Untersuchungen bei Olympiakämpfern," *Volk und Rasse* 11, no. 9 (1936): 363–8.
29 Bruno K. Schultz, "Die rassenbiologische Bedeutung der Leibesübungen," *Volk und Rasse* 11, no. 8 (1936): 339–47.
30 Jacob Borut, "Jews in German Sports," 78. The Zionist promotion of muscular Judaism was in part a response to these stereotypes, see: Todd Samuel Presner, *Muscular Judaism: The Jewish Body and the Politics of Regeneration* (London: Routledge, 2007).
31 Walther Jaensch, and Auguste Hoffmann, "Rasse, Konstitution, und Höchstleistung bei den Siegern des XI. Olympia." *Münchener Medizinische Wochenschrift* 4, no. 1 (1937): 16–22, citations 22.
32 Gebhardt to Ministerialrat Dr Barthels in RdI, BABL R 4901, Nr. 126336, Bl. 6–7.
33 Hong, *Welfare*, especially 60–4, 250–6, and 271–6.
34 The notion of "*rassische Generalprävention*" was used by Ulrich Herbert to describe the changing priorities of the SS/police security complex after 1936: Ulrich Herbert, *Best. Biographische Studien über Radikalismus, Weltanschauung, und Vernunft 1903-1989*, 2nd ed. (Bonn: Dietz, 1996), 170–7.
35 Gebhardt, "Beitrag zur Übungsfürsorge," 1300.
36 Gebhardt, "Lehrlings-Übungslager," 1224.
37 Karl Gebhardt, "Soziale Medizin und Hygiene," *Münchener Medizinische Wochenschrift* 80 (1933): 1256. On the compulsory Reichsarbeitsdienst, see: Kiran Klaus Patel, *Soldiers of Labor: Labor Service in Nazi Germany and New Deal America, 1933–1945* (Cambridge: Cambridge University Press, 2005).
38 Gebhardt, "Soziale Medizin," citation 1257.
39 Karl Gebhardt, "Grenzen und Gegenanzeigen der Übungsbehandlung," *Verhandlungen der deutschen orthopädischen Gesellschaft*, vol. 29, *Beilagenheft der Zeitschrift für orthopädische Chirurgie* 62 (1935), 45–8.
40 Gebhardt, "Soziale Medizin," citation 1257.
41 Wilfried Zeller, "Konstitution und Berufsberatung," in *Konstitutions- und Erbbiologie*, ed. Jaensch (1934), 280–99, especially 297.
42 Wetzell, "Kriminalbiologische Forschung," 75–90 and 97–8.
43 Dagmar Herzog, *Sex after Fascism: Memory and Morality in Twentieth Century Germany* (Princeton: Princeton University Press, 2007), 34–6; Geoffrey Cocks, *Psychotherapy in the Third Reich: The Göring Institute*, 2nd ed. (New Brunswick: Transactions, 1997).
44 Walther Jaensch, "Konstitution als Struktur und Formbildung, Wachstum und Entfaltung ererbter Anlagen," *Leibesübungen und Körperkonstitution*," ed. Walther Jaensch (Berlin: Alfred Metzner, 1935): 14–36; Walther Jaensch, "Nachwort des Kursleiters und Herausgebers," in *Konstitutions- und*

Erbbiologie, ed. Jaensch (1934): 380–5, citation 383. On Jaensch, see: Michael Hau, "Constitutional Therapy and Clinical Racial Hygiene in Weimar and Nazi Germany," *Journal of the History of Medicine and Allied Sciences* (2015), doi: 10.1093//jhmas/jrv034.

45 Arno Arnold, "Konstitution und ihr Einfluß auf die Leistung," in *Normale und pathologische Physiologie der Leibesübungen*, ed. Wilhelm Knoll und Arno Arnold (Leipzig: Ambrosius Barth, 1933): 20–43, especially 28.

46 Martin Brustmann, "Das Gesetz des Trainings," *Deutsche Sportlehrer-Zeitung*, May 1937, BABL NS 5 VI, Nr. 19398, citation Bl. 128 (back).

47 An Gruppenführer Schmitt, 18 November 1938, BABL SS Führerpersonalakten (formerly BDC) Martin Brustmann, Nr. 112; Brustmann an Reichsarzt SS Grawitz, 14 May 1939, BABL SS Führerpersonalakten, Nr. 112.

48 "Personalangaben 22 October 1938," BABL SS Führerpersonalakten, Nr. 112.

49 Leonardo Conti, "Ziel und Organisation des deutschen Sportes im Nationalsozialistischen Deutschland," *Leibesübungen und körperliche Erziehung* 52 (1933): 473–5.

50 Angelika Ebbinghaus und Karl Heinz Roth, "Kriegswunden. Die kriegschirurgischen Experimente in den Konzentrationslagern und ihre Hintergründe," in *Vernichten und Heilen. Der Nürnberger Ärzteprozess und seine Folgen*, ed. Angelika Ebbinghaus and Klaus Dörner (Berlin: Aufbau, 2001), 177–218; Ulf Schmidt, *Justice at Nuremberg: Leo Alexander and the Nazi Doctor's Trial* (New York: Palgrave, 2004), 259–61.

51 Heinrich Epping, *Das Sportarztwesen* (Leipzig: Georg Thieme, 1936), 48.

52 AHU, UK Personalia Gebhardt, Vol. 3, Bl. 8

53 AHU, UK Personalia Gebhardt, Vol. 3, Bl. 3–5.

54 Gebhardt, "Lehrlings-Übungslager," 1226

55 AHU, UK Personalia Gebhardt, Vol. 3, Bl. 3–5.

56 AHU, UK Personalia Gebhardt, Volume 1, Bl. 8, 11, 23; Vol 3, Bl. 8.

57 On Gebhardt's career in the Waffen SS, see: Hahn, *Grawitz, Genzken, Gebhardt*, 332–56.

58 Hahn, *Grawitz, Genzken, Gebhardt*, 166–70.

59 AHU, UK Personalia Gebhardt, vol. 3, Bl. 3–5, 44–5.

60 AHU, UK Personalia Gebhardt, vol. 1, Bl. 51, vol. 3, Bl. 33, 34. Among the 400 physicians were one hundred recently graduated physicians (*Jungärzte*) and many assistant physicians who underwent some form of extended training at Hohenlychen each year. AHU, UK Personalia Gebhardt, vol. 3, Bl. 39 and 40; Hahn, *Grawitz, Genzken, Gebhardt*, 191–2.

61 Ernst Eick, "Mehr Härte," *Leibesübungen und körperliche Erziehung* 54, no. 19 (1935): 405–6, citation 406.

62 Bernett, *Sportunterricht*, 56–7.
63 K. Hannak, "Erste Erfahrungen im Schulboxen," *Leibesübungen und körperliche Erziehung* 55, no. 3 (1936): 41–2, citations 42.
64 Hans Groh as cited by Bernett, *Nationalsozialistische Leibeserziehung* (1966), 92–5, citation 95.
65 Hans Bartsch as cited by Bernett, *Nationalsozialistische Leibeserziehung* (1966), citation 95.
66 Margarete Knipper as cited by Bernett, *Nationalsozialistische Leibeserziehung* (1966) 96.
67 AHU Personalia Auguste Hoffmann, vol. 1, Bl. 70–1. On the Hitler Youth medical service, see: Beddies, *Pflicht gesund zu sein*, especially 39–52.
68 AHU Personalia Auguste Hoffmann, vol. 3, Bl. 6 (back).
69 AHU Personalia Auguste Hoffmann, vol. 1, Bl. 73.
70 Tagebucheintrag vom 2 Juli 1936, *Die Tagebücher von Joseph Goebbels. Teil I: Aufzeichnungen 1923–1941*, Band 3/II: März 1936–Februar 1937, ed. Jana Richter. Im Auftrag des Instituts für Zeitgeschichte und mit Unterstützung des Staatlichen Archivdienstes Rußlands, ed. Elke Fröhlich (München: K. G. Saur 2001).
71 Cocks, *State of Health*, 75–6.
72 Brustmann an Kranefuss, 16 September 1939, BABL Führerpersonalakten Brustmann, Nr. 112. Brustmann also criticized the company sport roll calls during which six people had died.
73 AHU Personalia Frohwalt Heiss, vol. 3, Bl. 23.
74 "Das deutsche Turn- und Sportfest in Breslau feierlich eröffnet," *Völkischer Beobachter*, 28 July 1938, BABL NS 5 VI, Nr. 19424, Bl. 31–2, citation 31 back.
75 AHU Personalia Hans Hoske, vol. 2, Bl. 23.
76 Ibid., Bl. 31.
77 Hans Hoske, *Die menschliche Leistung als Grundlage des totalen Staates* (Leipzig: S. Hirzel, 1936), 26–7.
78 Karl Gebhardt, *Übungsbehandlung* (Jena: Gustav Fischer, 1934), 6.
79 Hoske, *Leistung*, citations 14–15.
80 Ibid., 15.
81 Lerner, *Male Hysteria*; Killen, *Berlin Electropolis*.
82 Hoske, *Leistung*, 24.
83 Hoske, *Leistung*, 28–30, citation 30.
84 Gebhardt, *Übungsbehandlung*, 8.
85 Heinrich Meusel, "Einheitliche körperliche Grundschulung, eine Forderung des Dritten Reiches," *Deutsche Sportlehrer-Zeitung*, July 1937, BABL NS 5 VI, Nr. 19398, Bl. 110.

86 Heinrich Meusel, *Körperliche Grundausbildung*, 2nd ed. (Berlin: Weidmannsche Verlagsbuchhandlung, 1938), 8.
87 Berno Bahro, *Der SS-Sport. Organisation – Funktion – Bedeutung* (Paderborn: Schöningh, 2013), 106–23, 299–301.
88 Jaensch and Hoffmann, "Rasse, Konstitution, und Höchstleistung," citation 22.
89 In Baeumler's thinking, the term *Mannschaft*, which is generally used for women's teams as well, was to be understood in its original gendered meaning with resonances of a homosocial bond of men (*Männerbund*). Only a *Männerbund* with a soldierly attitude was of real political significance for the community. Winfried Joch, *Politische Leibeserziehung und ihre Theorie im nationalsozialistischen Deutschland* (Frankfurt: Lang, 1976), 95–7 and 120; Alfred Baeumler, *Männerbund und Wisssenschaft* (Berlin: Junker und Dünnhaupt, 1940), 66–7 and 162–5. On Baeumler, see also: Nitzan Lebovic, *The Philosophy of Life and Death: Ludwig Klages and the Rise of Nazi Biopolitics* (New York: Palgrave Macmillan, 1913).
90 In the original the final sentence was a pun on Merkens' name, which in German also means remember: "*das wollen wir uns alle fein merken.*" "Toni Merkens Olympiasieger. Wieder Drei Goldene für Deutschland," *Völkischer Beobachter*, 8 August 1936, BABL NS 5 VI, Nr. 19411, citations Bl. 33 back and front.
91 "Merkens herrlicher Sieg," *Der Angiff*, 8 August 1936, BABL NS 5 VI, Nr. 19411, citation Bl. 23 back.
92 As translated by Lewis Erenberg, *The Greatest Fight of Our Generation: Louis vs. Schmeling* (Oxford: Oxford University Press, 2006), 95 and 119, citation 95.
93 Ibid., citation 148.
94 Robert Ley, *Durchbruch der sozialen Ehre. Reden und Gedanken für das schaffende Deutschland* (Berlin: Mehden Verlag, 1935).
95 "Wehrgeist und Idealismus," *Berliner Lokalanzeiger*, 19 Juli 1938, BABL, NS 5 VI, Nr. 19426, Bl. 18.
96 BABL, NS 5 VI, Nr. 19426, Bl. 4, 11, 13, and 49.
97 "Kampfspiele 1938 in Nürnberg. Die Leistungsschau der wehrhaften Mannschaft," *VB* 7 August 1938, BABL NS 5 VI, Nr. 19426, citation Bl. 17.
98 BABL NS 5 VI, Nr. 19426, 46.
99 BABL NS 5 VI, Nr. 19426, citations Bl. 18 and 23.
100 "Die Jugend ruft zum größten Sportfest der Welt," *Der Angriff*, 18 May 1938, BABL NS 5 VI, Nr. 19426, citations Bl. 27.
101 Reichskuratorium für Wirtschaftlichkeit, ed., *Der Mensch und die Rationalisierung*, vol. III, *Eignung und Qualitätsarbeit* (Jena: Gustav Fischer, 1933), citations 47–8. On the RKW, see Nolan, *Visions of Modernity*, 133–7.

102 On the DAF and its leader Ley, see: Rüdiger Hachtmann, "Arbeit und Arbeitsfront: Ideologie und Praxis," in *Arbeit im Nationalsozialismus*, ed. Buggeln and Wildt (2014), 87–106; Rüdiger Hachtmann, ed., *Ein Koloß auf tönernen Füßen. Das Gutachten des Wirtschaftsprüfers Karl Eicke über die Deutsche Arbeitsfront vom 31. Juli 1936* (München: Oldenbourg, 2006), 9–92; Ronald Smelser, *Robert Ley: Hitler's Labor Front Leader* (Oxford: Berg, 1988). On the discourse on social honor in Labour Front propaganda, see: Alf Lüdtke, "The 'Honor of Labor': Industrial Workers and the Power of Symbols under National Socialism," in *Nazism and German Society, 1933-1945*, ed. David F. Crew (London: Routledge, 1994), 67–109.

103 On the role of sport in the KdF organization, see: Hajo Bernett, "Nationalsozialistischer Volkssport bei 'Kraft durch Freude,'" *Stadion* 5 (1979): 89–146; Luh, *Betriebssport*, chap. 4.

104 Karl Lorch, "Jeder Sport steht jedem offen," *Deutsche Arbeitskorrespondenz*, 23 November 1938, BABL NS 5 VI, Nr 19427, Bl. 31.

105 *Leibesübungen mit Kraft durch Freude* 1 (1935) Sportprogramm Gau Groß-Berlin April-Juni 1935, 2.

106 Luh, *Betriebssport*, 236–9.

107 "Betriebssport für den deutschen Arbeiter!," *Drei Werke – ein Wille*, July 1937, BABL NS 5 VI, Nr. 19422, Bl. 5.

108 BABL NS 5 VI, Nr. 19427, citations Bl. 31–2.

109 "Leibesübungen treiben mit der KdF.-Jahressportkarte," *Deutsche Arbeitskorrespondenz*, December 1938, BABL NS 5 VI, Nr. 19427, Bl. 28.

110 "Der Sport in der Arbeitsfront," *Völkischer Beobachter*, 29 November 1933, BABL NS 5 VI, Nr. 19427, Bl. 76.

111 BABL NS 5 VI, Nr. 19398, Bl. 10.

112 Kalle, *Der Betriebssport bei Kalle & Co. Aktiengesellschaft Wiesbaden-Biebrich* (Wiesbaden, 1940), 7–15.

113 Bernett, "NS-Volkssport," 110–12.

114 "Bisher 21 Millionen Teilnehmer am KdF-Sport," *Völkischer Beobachter*, 13 April 1938, BABL NS 5 VI, Nr. 19428, Bl. 7.

115 Bernett, "NS-Volkssport," 110.

116 Jürgen Reulecke, "Die Fahne mit dem goldenen Zahnrad: Der Leistungskampf der deutschen Betriebe," in *Die Reihen fast geschlossen. Beiträge zur Geschichte des Alltags unterm Nationalsozialismus*, ed. Detlev Peukert and Jürgen Reulecke (Wuppertal: Peter Hammer, 1981), 245–69; Matthias Frese, "Vom 'NS-Musterbetrieb' zum 'Kriegsmusterbetrieb'. Zum Verhältnis von deutscher Arbeitsfront und Großindustrie," in *Der Zweite Weltkrieg. Analysen, Grundzüge, Forschungsbilanz*, ed. Wolfgang Michalka (München: Piper, 1997), 382–401.

117 "Sozialer Leistungsbericht 1940/41 auf den Gebieten Berufserziehung und Betriebsführung, Kraft durch Freude, Gesundheits- und Volksschutz," WA BaWü B 144 J. F. Adolff AG, Nr. 300, 72–82. In 1937/38, the firm did not provide any financial support for company sport but in 1938/39 it provided 23,266.63 RM, in 1939/40 31,712 RM, and in 1940/41 5042.83 RM mostly for the company sport ground.

118 "Betriebssport für den deutschen Arbeiter," *Drei Werke – ein Wille*, July 1937, BABL NS 5 VI, Nr. 19422, Bl. 5.

119 Bernett, "NS-Volkssport," 111–12.

120 BSG an Direktor Hans Kühne, "Jahresbericht der Wettkampfgruppen in der B.S.G. Farbenindustrie A.G. Leverkusen, 22. Januar Leverkusen," 22 January 1942, Bayer Corporate Archive (BCA), Betriebssport 236/069.

121 Wirtschaftsberichte Arbeitswissenschaftliches Institut der DAF Ende August 1939. Teil 1, Nr. 29: "Die Tätigkeit des Sportamtes der NS-Gemeinschaft 'Kraft durch Freude' im Jahre 1938," BABL NS 5 VI, Nr. 19428, Bl. 1–3. The total membership for all of the BSGs in the Reich must have been higher than the 506,687 members confirmed in the report because numbers for four *Gaue* with a total of 1,059 BSGs were missing. Since these represented only about 10 per cent of all BSGs in the Reich, it seems unlikely that there were many more than 550,000 members altogether. The report mentions more than 20 million participants for all KdF sporting events combined including sport courses open to the families of Labour Front members, and exercise sessions for apprentices and working youths. The remaining 10 million were participants of such events. Given the KdF accounting practices, this number is certainly also inflated through multiple counts.

122 Ibid., Bl. 2.

123 "Sozialer Leistungsbericht 1940/41," WA Ba Wü B 144 J. F. Adolff AG, Nr. 299, 9–15 and Nr. 300, 72.

124 "Kraft durch Freude" Sportamt, *Sportappell der Betriebe 1938*, Berlin: Deutsche Arbeitsfront, 1938, citation 9.

125 On the scoring system, see: "Kraft durch Freude" Sportamt, *Sportappell*, 24–7.

126 The 1938 report of the public savings bank *Girokasse Öffentliche Bank und Sparkasse Stuttgart*, proudly declared that the bank's BSG had finished tenth among sixty companies in its competition class III. "Geschäftsbericht der städtischen Sparkasse Stuttgart und der städtischen Girokasse Stuttgart 1938," WA BaWü B 102. Girokasse Öffentliche Bank und Sparkasse Stuttgart, Bü 823, 20.

127 Leistungskampf der deutschen Betriebe: An die Mitarbeiter und Mitarbeiterinnen, 16 August 38, WA BaWü B 144 J. F. Adolff AG, Bü 379.

128 "Rundschreiben Nr. 527 Sozialabteilung," 14. Okt. 1938. At least this was the number that the Nazi press reported: "Leverkusen meldet: 9000 I. G. – Kameraden beim Betriebssport," *Bergische Post*, 20 October 1938, BCA, Betriebssport 236/069.
129 Hans Kühne, "Betr.: Sportappell der Betriebe," 1 July 1939, BCA, Betriebssport 236/069.
130 "Voranmeldung Sportappell der Betriebe 1939," 1 May 1939, BCA, Betriebssport 236/069.
131 Kühne, "Sportappell," 1 July 1939, BCA, Betriebssport 236/069.
132 KdF Betriebssportamt I. G. Farben, "Sportappell der Betriebe 1939," 15 August 1939, BCA, Betriebssport 236/069. The alternative event scheduled for the 29th of August was never held because of the impending war.
133 Betriebssportgemeinschaft an Dir. Kühne, 10 May 1940, BCA, Betriebssport 236/069. The announcement by the Reichssportführer had an unfortunate timing because it coincided with the start of the Western campaign against France and the Benelux states.
134 Karl Lorch, "Der Sommersporttag der Betriebe," *Die Innere Front*, 21 July 1940, BABL NS 5 VI, Nr. 19422, Bl. 1.
135 Betriebsführer Direktor Dr Weber, "Waldlauf der Betriebe," 6. Juni 1940, WA BaWü B 70 WMF, Bü 1300.
136 On the historical debate about *Volksgemeinschaft*, see: Michael Wildt, "'Volksgemeinschaft'. Eine Antwort auf Ian Kershaw," *Zeithistorische Forschungen/Studies in Contemporary History* 8 (2011): H. 1. http://www.zeithistorische-forschungen.de/16126041-Wildt-1-2011; Ian Kershaw, "'Volksgemeinschaft'. Potential und Grenzen eines neuen Forschungkonzepts, *Vierteljahreshefte für Zeitgeschichte* 59 (2011): 1–17; Frank Bajohr and Michael Wildt, *Volksgemeinschaft. Neue Forschungen zur Gesellschaft des Nationalsozialismus* (Frankfurt: Fischer, 2009).
137 "Zum Betriebssport angetreten," *Rheinische Landeszeitung*, 8 May 1940, BCA, Betriebssport 236/069.
138 Luh, *Betriebssport*, 144–5, citation 145.
139 "Schnösel kannte keine Volksgemeinschaft," *Jungvolk am Bau*, Febr. 1936, BABL NS 5 VI, Nr. 18793.
140 Shelley Baranowski, *Strength through Joy: Consumerism and Mass Tourism in the Third Reich* (Cambridge: Cambridge University Press, 2004), 66–72 and 121.
141 "Schluß mit den 'feudalen' Sportarten," *Westdeutscher Beobachter*, 22 December 1936, BABL NS 5 VI, Nr. 19398, citations Bl. 151.
142 Luh, *Betriebssport*, 238.

143 Kalle, *Betriebssport*, 9.
144 Ibid., 39 and 41. In a concession to social equity, horseback riding was subsidized for workers. White-collar employees paid 1 RM.
145 Baranowski, *Strength through Joy*, 121.
146 Victoria de Grazia, *The Culture of Consent: Mass Organization of Leisure in Fascist Italy* (Cambridge: Cambridge University Press, 2002), 35–6, 66–7, 74–6, citations 152, 170–9.
147 Ibid., 78–9 and 170–9.
148 Susan Grant, *Physical Culture and Sport in Soviet Society: Propaganda, Acculturation, and Transformation in the 1920s and 1930s* (New York: Routledge, 2013), 25–7 and 37–44.
149 David L. Hoffmann and Annette F. Timm, "Utopian Biopolitics. Reproductive Policies, Gender Roles, and Sexuality in Nazi Germany and the Soviet Union," in *Beyond Totalitarianism: Stalinism and Nazism Compared*, ed. Michael Geyer and Sheila Fitzpatrick (Cambridge: Cambridge University Press, 2009), 87–129, citation 87.
150 Tumblety, *Remaking the Male Body*, chap. 3.
151 Ibid., 179–89.
152 Ibid., 75–84.
153 Ibid., 206. In 1940, the Vichy commissioner for sport had a budget twenty times larger than Léo Legrange's under the Popular Front.
154 Ina Zweiniger-Bargielowska, "Building a British Superman: Physical Culture in Interwar Britain," *Journal of Contemporary History* 41 (2006): 595–610, especially 606–10; Eadem, *Managing the Body*, 309–30.
155 Kalle, *Betriebssport*, citation 15.
156 "Betriebssport als eine Betriebsgemeinschafts-Aufgabe," *Mercedes Gefolgschaft* Nr., 7 Juli 1937, BABL NS 5 VI, Nr. 19478, Bl. 44. The Mercedes Bureau Maschinen GmBH in Zehla-Mehlis (Thuringia) produced typewriters and calculating machines, see: "Museen der Stadt Zella-Mehlis," accessed 1 July 2011, http://www.beschussanstalt.zella-mehlis.de/?Ausstellungen:Mercedes-B%FCromaschinen.

4. The Olympics of Labour

1 "Schrittmacher des deutschen Sozialismus," *Hamburger Fremdenblatt*, 30 April 1938, BABL NS 5 VI, Nr. 6056.
2 Artur Axmann, *Olympia der Arbeit. Arbeiterjugend im Reichsberufswettkampf* (Berlin: Junker und Dünnhaupt, 1937).
3 For a summary of the debates on consumerism in Nazi Germany, see: Hans-Werner Niemann, "'Volksgemeinschaft' als Konsumgemeinschaft?,"

in *"Volksgemeinschaft": Mythos, wirkungsmächtige soziale Verheißung oder soziale Realität im "Dritten Reich"?*, ed. Detlef Schmiechen-Ackermann (Paderborn: Ferdinand Schöningh, 2012): 87–109. Most of the new consumer products, which the Nazi regime promised to the average people's comrade, were either not produced for private consumption (as in the case of the *Volkswagen*) or if they became available were unaffordable for most workers (as in the case of the radio *Volksempfänger*). On the Volkswagen project and other *"Volksprodukte,"* see: Wolfgang König, *Volkswagen, Volksempfänger, Volksgemeinschaft. "Volksprodukte" im Dritten Reich: Vom Scheitern einer nationalsozialistischen Konsumgesellschaft* (Paderborn: Ferdinand Schöningh, 2004). On the KdF, see: Baranowski, *Strength through Joy*, especially 98–9 and 155–61. On Prora, see: Hasso Spode, "Fordism, Mass Tourism and the Third Reich: The 'Strength through Joy' Seaside resort as an Index Fossil," *Journal of Social History* 38, no. 1 (2004): 127–55.

4 Moritz Föllmer, "Was Nazism Collectivistic? Redefining the Individual in Berlin, 1930–1945," *Journal of Modern History* 82, no. 1 (2010): 61–100, especially 67–8, 73–4, and 96–9; Moritz Föllmer, *Individuality and Modernity in Berlin: Self and Society from Weimar to the Wall* (Cambridge: Cambridge University Press, 2013), chap. 4. On the collectivist ethic of Nazism, see: Claudia Koonz, *The Nazi Conscience* (Cambridge, Mass.: Harvard University Press, 2005).

5 Artur Axmann, *Der Reichsberufswettkampf* (Berlin: Junker und Dünnhaupt, 1938), 19–20. The first competitions for the *"Kaufmannsjugend"* were held in Southwestern Germany in 1921, see: "Reichsberufswettkampf der werktätigen deutschen Jugend," *Deutsche Kaufmannspraxis*, January 1936, BABL NS 5 VI, Nr. 6053.

6 Wirtschaftsgruppe Chemische Industrie an angeschlossene Firmen, 11 January 1938, BCA 059/268, vol. 2.

7 On the dialectic between the fostering of popular expectations and the push for greater productivity, see: Michael Schneider, *Unterm Hakenkreuz. Arbeiter und Arbeiterbewegung 1933–1939* (Bonn: J. H. W. Dietz, 1999), 227–34.

8 Poovey, *Uneven Developments*, 1–3.

9 Klaus-Michael Mallmann and Gerhard Paul, *Herrschaft und Alltag. Ein Industrierevier im Dritten Reich. Widerstand und Verweigerung im Saarland*, vol. 2 (Bonn: J. H. W. Dietz, 1991), 114 and 160–3.

10 Michael Wildt has argued for an inter-actionist "practice-centred" (*praxeologisch*) approach to analyse the practices by which notions of community were constituted in Nazi Germany. Wildt, "'Volksgemeinschaft'. Eine Antwort auf Ian Kershaw," 4.

11 The RBWK have already received some attention in the historiography of labour relations, vocational education, and the mobilization of youths. None of these studies analyse the relationships between sport discourse, performance ideology, and meritocratic appeals. Michael Buddrus discusses these contests as part of youth mobilization for total war, see: *Totale Erziehung für den totalen Krieg. Hitlerjugend und nationalsozialistische Jugendpolitik* (München: K. G. Saur, 2003), 513–41. The significance of the contests for vocational education is discussed in Theo Wolsing, *Untersuchungen zur Berufsausbildung im Dritten Reich* (Kastellaun: Aloys Henn, 1977), 496–545. Torsten Schaar discusses the competitions with reference to Axmann's career, see: "Vom Hitlerjungen zum Reichsjugendführer der NSDAP. Eine nationalsozialistische Karriere" (PhD diss., Universität Rostock, 1998), 133–45, 156–63, and 388–91. Matthias Frese briefly discusses them in his book on NS company politics, see: *Betriebspolitik im Dritten Reich. Deutsche Arbeitsfront, Unternehmer und Staatsbürokratie in der westdeutschen Großindustrie* (Paderborn: Ferdinand Schöningh, 1991), 411–20.
12 Patel, *Soldiers of Labor*, especially 193–215.
13 Michael Kater, "The Reich Vocational Contest and Students of Higher Learning in Nazi Germany," *Central European History* 7 (1974): 225–61.
14 For a list of the *Wettkampfgruppen*, see: Axmann, *Reichsberufswettkampf*, 49–66.
15 Ibid., 117.
16 "Ortswettkampfunterlagen der Wettkampfgruppe Leder 1938," WA BaWü B 150 Salamander, Nr. 613.
17 Axmann, *Reichsberufswettkampf*, 103.
18 Ibid., 26 and 236–7.
19 Schneider, *Unterm Hakenkreuz*, 215–17; Günter Kaufmann, *Das kommende Deutschland. Die Erziehung der Jugend im Reich Adolf Hitler's*, 2nd ed. (Berlin: Junker und Dünnhaupt, 1940), 190.
20 "Aufruf Adolf Hitler's zum Reichberufswettkampf der Hitlerjugend, 30 October 1943," in *Deutsche Jugend 1933–1945. Eine Dokumentation*, ed. Karl Heinz Jahnke and Michael Buddrus (Hamburg: VSA-Verlag, 1989), 372–3.
21 "Kriegsberufswettkampf beendet," 29 April 1944, BABL NS 5 VI, 6047.
22 Schwarz und Dr. Kühne an Abteilungsvorstände, Betriebsführer und Bürovorsteher, 15 November 1938, BCA 074–001–010.
23 Title image from *Von Werk zu Werk. Monatsschrift der Werksgemeinschaft der I. G. Farbenindustrie Aktiengesellschaft*, May 1938, Leverkusen edition, from: BCA.

24 Kühne as cited by Peter Hayes, *Industry and Ideology: IG Farben in the Nazi Era* (Cambridge: Cambridge University Press, 2001), 97. In late 1934, Kühne was expelled from the Nazi Party because he had been a Freemason but he continued to support the RBWK and other DAF initiatives. Freemasons were pardoned by Hitler and he was readmitted in July 1939. BABL 3200 (formerly BDC), Hans Kühne M 0037; Hayes, *Industry*, 102.
25 Deutscher Metallarbeiter-Verband. Kreisleitung Opladen an Kühne, 23 April 1934, BCA 059–268, vol. 1. The "District Youth Warden" (*Kreisjugendwart*) of the DAF expresses here his gratitude to Kühne for his "extraordinary obligingness."
26 Wirtschaftsgruppe Chemische Industrie an angeschlossene Firmen, 11 January 1938, BCA 059/268, vol. 2, citation 2.
27 Ibid.
28 Ibid., 2; Sozialabteilung Leverkusen I. G. Werk an Abteilungsvorstände etc., 4 February 1936, BCA 059–268.
29 Salamander Geschäftsleitung an Gauobmann der DAF, 26 January 1938, WA BaWü B 150 Salamander, Nr. 613. That the firm had short work even in 1938 indicates that the company did not share in the armaments boom.
30 Gauobmann Berufswettkampf: Sonderanweisung an Kreisobmänner und Kreisbeauftragte, 24 Februar 1938, WA BaWü B 150 Salamander, Nr. 613.
31 Axmann, *Reichsberufswettkampf*, 26 and 31.
32 Fasbender, *Zwischen Arbeitersport und Arbeitssport*, 109–14.
33 Axmann, *Reichsberufswettkampf*, 30; Hachtmann, *Koloß*, 297–8. Arnhold ran the office between 1935 and 1940 and for a short time in 1942 before he had a personal falling-out with Ley.
34 Karl Arnhold, "Mobilisierung der Leistungsreserven unserer Betriebe. Vortrag gehalten im Berliner Sportpalast, 1939," HSAS J 150 533/56, citations 5 and 8.
35 There are strong continuities here with the social rationalization and human resource management during the Weimar Republic, see chap. 2 of this book and: Nolan, *Visions of Modernity*, 179–205; Peter Hinrichs, *Um die Seele des Arbeiters. Arbeitspsychologie, Industrie- und Berufssoziologie in Deutschland, 1871-1945* (Köln: Pahl Rugenstein, 1981), chap. 2.
36 J. B., "Die sportlichen Leistungsprüfungen im RBWK 1937," *Reichsjugendpressedienst*, 18 March 1937, BABL NS 5 VI, Nr. 6045; "Neue Menschen – ganze Menschen," *Berliner Tagblatt*, 28 April 1937, BABL NS 5 VI, Nr. 6045.
37 "Aufstieg muß die Leistung lernen," *N.S.K.*, 8 May 1937, BABL NS 5 VI, Nr. 6046, Bl. 122.

38 Peter von Werder, "Erziehung zum Wettkampf," *Völkischer Beobachter*, 22 April 1938, BABL NS 5 VI, Nr. 6056.
39 Axmann, *Reichsberufswettkampf*, 69–70.
40 Hans Wiese, "Leistungsteigerung im deutschen Arbeitsleben," *Zeitschrift für Organisation*, 25 July 1938, BABL NS 5 VI, Nr. 6047, Bl. 67–70, citations Bl. 68.
41 Axmann, *Reichsberufswettkampf*, citation 26.
42 Ibid., 340–2.
43 Ibid., 309.
44 The report was commissioned by the DAF and written by the Berlin psychologist Hans Rupp based on lessons drawn from the first RBWK in 1934. About three hundred copies of the report were circulated among Labour Front officials. It was also published in the leading psychotechnical journal, see: Hans Rupp, "Über den Reichsberufswettkampf," *Psychotechnische Zeitschrift* 9, no. 2 (1934): 29–34 and 9, no. 3 (1934): 61–74.
45 DAF Gauwaltung Baden, *Der Reichsberufswettkampf aller schaffenden Deutschen. Grundlage der Begabtenförderung* (1939, brochure), p. 5, BABL NS 5 VI, Nr. 6044.
46 Ibid., citation 5.
47 Felsch, "Volkssport," 5–29.
48 Lüdtke, "The 'Honor of Labor,'" 69–71 and 74–5.
49 Eberhard Heuel, *Der umworbene Stand. Die ideologische Integration der Arbeiter im Nationalsozialismus* (Frankfurt/New York: Campus, 1989), especially 61–6.
50 "Die Kampfgruppe 'Gesundheit' im Reichsentscheid des RBWK in Köln," *Volksgesundheit* Mai 1939, BABL NS 5 VI, Nr. 6058. See also: Heuel, *Stand*, 136–8. He describes how already in 1933 selected workers were flown to Berlin and received by Goebbels, Hitler, and Hindenburg in the old Reich Chancellery building.
51 "Als Reichssieger der Dentisten beim Führer. Der Reichssieger Rachinger erzählt," *Volksgesundheit* Mai 1939, BABL NS 5 VI, Nr. 6058.
52 This term is used by Rupp, "Reichsberufswettkampf." Axmann uses the term "*Arbeitsauffassung*." Axmann, *Reichsberufswettkampf*, 28.
53 Axmann, *Reichsberufswettkampf*, citations 19.
54 Ibid., citation 29.
55 Hitler as quoted in Ibid., 24.
56 Lüdtke, "Honor of Labor," 89.
57 Axmann, *Reichsberufswettkampf*, citation 22–3.
58 Göring as translated by Timothy Mason, *Social Policy in the Third Reich: The Working Class and the 'National Community'* (Oxford: Berg, 1993), 216.
59 Lüdtke, "Honor of Labor," 89.

60 Schirach as cited by Axmann, *Reichsberufswettkampf*, citations 29.
61 Mallmann and Paul, *Herrschaft und Alltag*, 59–61.
62 Cocks, *State of Health*, 135–8.
63 Rupp, "Reichberufswettkampf," 32.
64 Axmann, *Reichsberufswettkampf*, 103, 107, and 121. The tests consisted of three parts for male apprentices and workers: The practical vocational test was worth seventy points, vocational theory thirty points, and the political part on *Weltanschauung* was worth twenty. For girls and women the practical and theoretical tests were shorter because they had to demonstrate skills in 'domestic economics' (*Hauswirtschaft*), worth thirty points.
65 The economics ministry, which was interested more in vocational performance and a general performance-orientation (*Arbeitsgesinnung*), considered this as excessive. Frese, *Betriebspolitik*, 304.
66 Victor Klemperer, *LTI. Notizbuch eines Philosophen*, 20th ed. (Leipzig: Reclam, 2005), 143–5.
67 "Hindert HJ-Dienst die Berufsleistung?," *N.S.K.*, 15 November 1938, BABL NS 5 VI, Nr. 6057. The negative impact of Hitler Youth activities on students was a great concern for officials in the Reich Education Ministry including the minister Bernhard Rust. Anne C. Nagel, *Hitler's Bildungsreformer. Das Reichsministerium für Wissenschaft, Erziehung und Volksbildung 1934–1945* (Frankfurt: S. Fischer, 2012), 198, 225–6, and 335.
68 Axmann, *Reichsberufswettkampf*, 134–6 and 147.
69 "Reichsberufswettkampf 1936," *Kölnische Zeitung*, 3 December 1935, BCA 059–268.
70 Heinz Kilian, "Wie ich den Reichsberufswettkampf erlebte," München Reichskampf 1937, BCA 059–268.
71 Lothar Mertens, *"Nur politisch Würdige." Die DFG-Forschungsförderung im Dritten Reich 1933–1937* (Berlin: Akademie Verlag, 2004), 347.
72 "Politisches Dienstzeugnis im Reichsberufswettkampf," 21 November 1938, BABL NS 5 VI, Nr. 6047, Bl. 43.
73 G. H. C., "Bestleistungen aus weltanschaulicher Festigkeit," *N.S.K.*, 22 Dezember 1937, BABL NS 5 VI, Nr. 6046, citations Bl. 43.
74 Axmann, *Reichsberufswettkampf*, 69–70, citations 70. "Teilnahme der Körperbehinderten am Berufswettkampf," Deutsche Arbeitsfront to Gauwaltung, 21 December 1937, BABL NS 5 VI, Nr. 6046, Bl. 46.
75 Poore, *Disability*, 125–32.
76 Rudolf Richter, "Wenn die Arbeit Kampf ist, dann ist die Arbeit schön," München Reichskampf 1937, BCA 059–268.
77 Friedrich Nebauer, "Alle machen mit!," *Arbeitertum*, 15 October 1937, BABL NS 5 VI, Nr. 6046, citation Bl. 98.

78 "Wie vollzieht sich der Reichsberufswettkampf," *Graphische Jugend*, Dezember 1937, BABL NS 5 VI, Nr. 6056. The article refers to failure in the sport and ideological parts of the test: "Anyone who fails (*versagt*) in these two tests will never qualify as a winner."
79 One only needs to think of the "voluntary" membership in the DAF or of the ways in which people were enjoined to make "voluntary" contributions to the NS welfare organization or to the "Winter Aid" (*Winterhilfswerk*). These proved to be so unpopular that the regime stopped them for a while in the summer of 1935. Günter Morsch, *Arbeit und Brot. Studien zur Lage, Stimmung, Einstellung und Verhalten der deutschen Arbeiterschaft 1933–1936/37* (Frankfurt: Peter Lang, 1993), 328.
80 Campbell, *Joy in Work*; Morsch, *Arbeit und Brot*; Alf Lüdtke, "German Work and German Workers: The Impact of Symbols on the Exclusion of Jews in Nazi Germany. Reflections on an open question," in *Probing the Depth of German Antisemitism. German Society and the Persecution of Jews, 1933–1945*, ed. David Bankier (New York: Berghahn Books, 2000), 296–311.
81 Hau, *Cult of Health*, 156 and 163.
82 Morsch, *Arbeit und Brot*, 33–8.
83 Axmann, *Olympia der Arbeit*, 13.
84 Ibid., citation 7.
85 Morsch, *Arbeit und Brot*, 36.
86 "Reichsberufswettkampf 1938 eröffnet," *Völkischer Beobachter*, 12 February 1938; "Jeder ist gern gesehen – aber kein Jude," *Der Angriff*, 15 January 1938, BABL NS 5 VI, Nr. 6046, Bl. 3 and 14.
87 "Im Sandkasten der Wirtschaft," *Der Angriff*, 19 November 1938, BABL NS 5 VI, Nr. 6041.
88 Pohle-Vetter, "Leistung gegen Sklaverei!," *N.S.K.*, 13 October 1936 BABL NS 5 VI, Nr. 6045. On the condemnation of Stakhanovism see also Föllmer, "Was Nazism Collectivistic," 78.
89 BABL NS 5 VI, Nr. 18794.
90 Axmann, *Reichsberufswettkampf*, citation 28.
91 In the Saar area, for example, workers compared the intensification of labour to conditions in German concentration camps. Mallmann and Paul, *Herrschaft und Alltag*, 59; Timothy Mason, *Nazism, Fascism and the Working Class*, ed. Jane Caplan (Cambridge: Cambridge University Press, 1995), 118–19; Ian Kershaw, *Popular Opinion and Political Dissent in the Third Reich: Bavaria 1933–1945* (Oxford: Clarendon, 1983), 99.
92 Lewis H. Siegelbaum, *Stakhanovism and the Politics of Productivity in the USSR, 1935-1941* (Cambridge: Cambridge University Press, 1988), 40–1, citation 41.

93 Siegelbaum, *Stakhanovism*, 67–76.
94 Ibid., 156.
95 Ibid., 200, 225–36 and 267–73. Emphasizing similarities between the two productivity campaigns does not imply acceptance of a simplistic totalitarianism model. Recent comparative scholarship on the two regimes has tried to move beyond such approaches. See: Geyer and Fitzpatrick, eds., *Beyond Totalitarianism.*
96 DAF Gauwaltung Baden, "Reichsberufswettkampf. Grundlage der Begabtenförderung," (1939, brochure), p. 4, BABL NS 5 VI, Nr. 6044; Albert Müller, "Selbsterziehung zur Leistung," *Kölnische Zeitung*, 20 April 1936, BABL NS 5 VI, Nr. 6044.
97 "Blick auf den Wettkampf aller Schaffenden," *Frankfurter Volksblatt*, 8 December 1937, BABL NS 5 VI, Nr. 6046, Bl. 69 and "Ley: Berufswettkampf für alle Lebensalter," *Der Angriff*, 3 November 1937, BABL NS 5 VI, Nr. 6046, Bl. 91.
98 Rainer Zitelmann, *Hitler: The Politics of Seduction*, trans. Helmut Bogler (London: London House, 1999), 375–9.
99 Ulrich Herbert, "'Die guten und die schlechten Zeiten'. Überlegungen zur diachronen Analyse lebensgeschichtlicher Interviews," in *"Die Jahre weiß man nicht, wo man die heute hinsetzen soll." Faschismuserfahrungen im Ruhrgebiet. Lebensgeschichte und Sozialkultur im Ruhrgebiet 1930–1960*, ed. Lutz Niethammer (Bonn: J. H. W. Dietz Nachf. 1983), 89–90; Lüdtke, "Honor of Labor," 86.
100 Alf Lüdtke, "'Deutsche Qualitätsarbeit' – ihre Bedeutung für das Mitmachen von Arbeitern und Unternehmern im Nationalsozialismus," in *Firma Topf & Söhne: Hersteller der Öfen für Auschwitz. Ein Fabrikgelände als Erinnerungsort?*, ed. Aleida Assmann, Frank Hiddemann, and Eckhard Schwarzenberger (Frankfurt: Campus, 2002), 128–30.
101 On the relationship between Nazi work ideology and the persecution of "anti-socials," see: Morsch, *Arbeit und Brot*, 168–76 and 315–20. On the persecution of anti-socials in particular "Action Work-shy" of 1938, see: Wolfgang Ayaß, *"Asoziale" im Nationalsozialismus* (Stuttgart: Klett-Cotta, 1995), especially 138–79.
102 Hitler as cited by Irmgard Weyrather, "'Deutsche Arbeit' – Arbeitskult im Nationalsozialismus," *Zeitschrift für Religions- und Geistesgeschichte* 56, no. 1 (2004): 18–36, citation 34.
103 Julia Hörath, "'Arbeitsscheue Volksgenossen'. Leistungsbereitschaft als Kriterium der Inklusion und Exklusion," in *Arbeit im Nationalsozialismus*, ed. Buggeln and Wildt (2014), 309–28; Rüdiger Hachtmann, *Industriearbeit im "Dritten Reich"* (Göttingen: Vandenhoeck & Ruprecht, 1989), 161–2

and 243–4; Ulrich Herbert, "'The Real Mystery in Germany': The German Working Class during the Nazi Dictatorship," in *Confronting the Nazi Past: New Debates on Modern German History*, ed. Michael Burleigh (London: Palgrave MacMillan, 1996), 27–8.

104 Schneider, *Unterm Hakenkreuz*, 769.

105 Ibid., 519 and 584–6; Hachtmann, *Industriearbeit*, 161–7. Changing the wage structure could have serious negative implications for social cohesion, since there were winners and losers. The Work Science Institute of the DAF noted this when it weighed the advantages and disadvantages of a "national wage order" (*Reichslohnordnung*) that was never introduced. "Denkschrift des arbeitswissenschaftlichen Instituts der DAF. Zur Problematik einer Reichslohnordnung" (Dezember 1940) in *Arbeiterklasse und Volksgemeinschaft*, ed. Timothy Mason (Opladen: Westdeutscher Verlag, 1975), 822–9.

106 Schneider, *Unterm Hakenkreuz*, 519–20 and 585–6; Tilla Siegel, *Leistung und Lohn in der nationalsozialistischen Ordnung der Arbeit* (Opladen: Westdeutscher Verlag, 1989), 126–42. On Nazi economic policies generally and the emphasis on containing wages, see: Adam Tooze, *The Wages of Destruction: The Making and Breaking of the Nazi Economy* (London: Allen Lane, 2006), chap. 5.

107 S. Jonathan Wiesen, *Creating the Nazi Marketplace: Commerce and Consumption in the Third Reich* (Cambridge: Cambridge University Press, 2011), citation 38.

108 Schneider, *Unterm Hakenkreuz*, 585.

109 Siegel, *Leistung und Lohn*, 122–4.

110 Axmann, *Reichsberufswettkampf*, 309–10.

111 "25-Punkte-Programm der NSDAP," accessed on 11 December 2011, http://www.dhm.de/lemo/html/dokumente/nsdap25.

112 Nagel, *Hitler's Bildungsreformer*, 99.

113 Party representatives and ministry officials might disagree about specific reforms, but they shared the commitment to open up new opportunities for the talented from the lower classes. Nagel, *Hitler's Bildungsreformer*, 350–1, citation 350.

114 Zitelmann, *Politics of Seduction*, 99–121, especially 104.

115 Hitler as translated by Helmut Bogler in Zitelmann, *Politics of Seduction*, 108. Weimar advocates of the human economy would have referred to this as "the right man for the right job."

116 Schaar, *Vom Hitlerjungen zum Reichsjugendführer*.

117 Hachtmann, *Koloß*, 19.

118 Hans-Ulrich Wehler, *Deutsche Gesellschaftsgeschichte*, vol. 4, *Vom Beginn des ersten Weltkriegs bis zur Gründung der beiden deutschen Staaten 1914–1945* (München: C. H: Beck, 2008), 688.
119 Armin Nolzen, "The NSDAP, the War, and German Society," in *Germany and the Second World War*, ed. Jörg Echternkamp, vol. 9.1, *Politicization, Disintegration, and the Struggle for Survival* (Oxford: Clarendon Press, 2008), 121.
120 Sybille Steinbacher, "Differenz der Geschlechter? Chancen und Schranken für die Volksgenossinnen," in *Volksgemeinschaft*, ed. Bajohr and Wildt (2009), 95; Claudia Koonz, *Mothers in the Fatherland: Women, the Family, and Nazi Politics* (New York: St. Martin's Press, 1987).
121 Schneider, *Unterm Hakenkreuz*, 778.
122 MacGregor Knox, *Common Destiny: Dictatorship, Foreign Policy, and War in Fascist Italy and Nazi Germany* (Cambridge: Cambridge University Press, 2000), 209.
123 Hartmut Berghoff, "Did Hitler create a new society? Continuity and change in German social history before and after 1933," in *Weimar and Nazi Germany: Continuities and Discontinuities*, ed. Panikos Panayi (Harlow: Longman, 2001), 74–104, especially 92–8.
124 Schneider, *Unterm Hakenkreuz*, 776–9. Studies on social mobility in twentieth-century Germany have examined long-term developments over several decades. Ruth Federspiel's book on the Berlin district Neukölln looks at the period from 1905 to 1957, see: *Soziale Mobilität im Berlin des zwanzigsten Jahrhunderts. Frauen und Männer in Berlin-Neukölln 1905–1957* (Berlin: de Gruyter, 1999). In his study of Hamburg and Schleswig-Holstein, sociologist Hans Martin Bolte has focused on the years between 1927 and 1953, see: *Sozialer Aufstieg und Abstieg. Eine Untersuchung über Berufsprestige und Berufsmobilität* (Stuttgart: Ferdinand Enke, 1959).
125 David Schoenbaum, *Hitler's Social Revolution: Class and Status in Nazi Germany, 1933–1939* (New York and London: W. W. Norton, 1980), 273–4.
126 Morsch, *Arbeit und Brot*, 357–8 and 386–7; Schneider, *Unterm Hakenkreuz*, 721; Kershaw, *Popular Opinion*, 84–5 and 104–5.
127 Morsch, *Arbeit und Brot*, 224–5.
128 There is no doubt about the corruption of Nazi officials, and workers and the general public also perceived them as very corrupt, see: Frank Bajohr, *Parvenüs und Profiteure. Korruption in der NS-Zeit* (Frankfurt: Büchergilde, 2001), 49–62 and 177–87. Official reports by the regime were very much concerned about the low reputation of Nazi organizations, in particular the Labour Front. Morsch, *Arbeit und Brot*, 376–80.

129 G. H. C., "Bestleistungen aus weltanschaulicher Festigkeit," *N. S. K.*, 22 December 1937, BABL NS 5 VI, Nr. 6046, citation Bl. 43.
130 "Der Aufstieg des deutschen Jungarbeiters," *Reichsjugendpressedienst* Nr. 108, 19 May 1937, BABL NS 5 VI, Nr. 6046, Bl. 116.
131 Ibid.
132 H. Freudenberg, "Das politische Ergebnis des Reichberufswettkampfes" BABL NS 5 VI, Nr. 18795, p. 359.
133 Katja Patzel-Mattern, *Ökonomische Effizienz und sozialer Ausgleich. Die industrielle Psychotechnik in der Weimarer Republik* (Stuttgart: Franz Steiner Verlag, 2010), especially chap. 4; David Meskill, *Optimizing the German Workforce*.
134 Axmann, *Reichsberufswettkampf*, 309.
135 Hachtmann, *Industriearbeit*, 86–9.
136 Ibid., 42–3 and 54–63.
137 "Schrittmacher des deutschen Sozialismus," *Hamburger Fremdenblatt*, 30 April 1938, BABL NS 5 VI, Nr. 6056.
138 "Lehren des RBWK. Beste Kräfte unter den Ungelernten," *Deutsche Zeitung*, 28 April 1936, BABL NS 5 VI, Nr. 6044.
139 "Aufstieg muß die Leistung lohnen," *N.S.K.*, 8 Mai 1937, BABL NS 5 VI, Nr. 6046, citations Bl. 122.
140 "Aufstieg des deutschen Jungarbeiters," BABL NS 5 VI, Nr. 6046, citation Bl. 116.
141 Hachtmann, *Industriearbeit*, 86–9.
142 John Gillingham, "The 'Deproletarianization' of German Society: Vocational Training in the Third Reich," *Journal of Social History* 19 (1986): 423–32, especially 427.
143 "Aufstieg des deutschen Jungarbeiters," BABL NS 5 VI, Nr. 6046, Bl. 116.
144 DAF Gauwaltung Baden, "Reichsberufswettkampf. Grundlage der Begabtenförderung," (1939, brochure), p. 9-11, BABL NS 5 VI, Nr. 6044.
145 "Die Arbeiterschaft ist reich an Begabungen," 12 July 1938, BABL NS 5 VI, Nr. 18794.
146 DAF Gauwaltung Baden, "Reichsberufswettkampf. Grundlage der Begabtenförderung," (1939, brochure) p. 8, BABL NS 5 VI, Nr. 6044.
147 The highly segmented German workforce included many vocational differentiations and social distinctions with different levels of income, social status, and prestige. The difference between white- and blue-collar employees was not the only distinction that was important. The large industrial work force included the skilled, semi-skilled, and unskilled, supervisors, foremen, and other lower management positions, which in official parlance were hailed as "sub-leaders of the economy" (*Unterführer*

der Wirtschaft). Qualification structures varied from industry to industry but in general there was a greater demand for skilled and semi-skilled qualifications in the 1930s. For example, in the chemical industry whose work force had been dominated by unskilled workers, new production processes required workers with specialized training. In the electro-technical industry, greater demands for highly qualified workers opened up new opportunities for skilled workers, while semi-skilled workers moved into the skilled workers' old positions and were in turn replaced by unskilled workers who had to be trained for their new work. On the differentiation of qualifications and new opportunities for some workers in the chemical, electro-technical, steel, and coal industry, see: Wolfgang Zollitsch, *Arbeiter zwischen Weltwirtschaftskrise und Nationalsozialismus. Ein Beitrag zur Sozialgeschichte der Jahre 1928 bis 1936* (Göttingen: Vandenhoeck & Ruprecht, 1990), 41–71; Schneider, *Unterm Hakenkreuz*, 330–2.

148 Historian Michael Grüttner comes to the conclusion that despite the rhetoric of equal opportunity, there was little change in the social background of university students. At the beginning of 1939, there were only 155 men with a Langemarck stipend preparing for university. How many of them were first discovered in the RBWK remains unclear. According to official sources, at most 8 to 10 per cent of university students came to university through non-traditional avenues such as aptitude tests, Langemarck stipends, or the "special maturity test" (*Sonderreifeprüfung*) available for gifted graduates of higher technical schools. Circumstantial postwar evidence suggests that the percentage was even less than 2 per cent. Michael Grüttner, *Studenten in Dritten Reich* (Paderborn: Schöningh, 1995), 146–54 and 477.

149 "Wege zum Aufstieg," *Der Angriff*, 23 April 1936, BABL NS 5 VI, Nr. 6039.

150 "Wettkampfaufgaben für 300 Frauenberufe," *Völkischer Beobachter*, 16 December 1937, BABL NS 5 VI, Nr. 6056.

151 "Sinnvolle Berufsgestaltung für die Frau," *Hamburger Fremdenblatt*, 13 December 1937, BABL NS 5 VI, Nr. 6056.

152 "Gute Leistungen der Jungarbeiter. Sportkämpfe der Berufsbesten im Reichsberufswettkampf," *Völkischer Beobachter*, 27 April 1936, BABL NS 5 VI, Nr. 6044.

153 Zollitsch, *Arbeiter*, 55–7.

154 Axmann, *Olympia der Arbeit*, 87. The Napolas combined political indoctrination with advanced schooling, physical toughening, and military discipline to create a new Nazi elite, see: Christian Schneider, Cordelia Stillke, and Bernd Leineweber, *Das Erbe der Napola: Versuch einer*

Generationengeschichte des Nationalsozialismus (Hamburg: Hamburger Edition, 1996), 33–46.

155 DAF Gauwaltung Baden, "Reichsberufswettkampf. Grundlage der Begabtenförderung," (1939, brochure) p. 11, BABL NS 5 VI, Nr. 6044.

156 "Wie der Wettkampfsieg gelohnt wurde," *N.S.K.* 7 January 1938, BABL NS 5 VI, Nr. 6046, Bl. 29 front.

157 Ibid., 29 back.

158 This becomes particularly evident during the war (see chap. 5). Sybille Steinbacher argues that the mobilization of women led in some instances to a levelling of gender differences, see: "Differenz," 99.

159 Kershaw, *Popular Opinion*, 373–5; Morsch, *Arbeit und Brot*, 374–5; Timothy Mason, "'The Workers' Opposition in Nazi Germany," *History Workshop Journal* 11 (1981): 120–37.

160 Axmann, *Olympia der Arbeit*, 12.

161 Morsch, *Arbeit und Brot*, 167–8; Mallmann and Paul, *Herrschaft und Alltag*, 152–3. See also the case of the Salamander shoe manufacturer cited above whose management was publicly pilloried for its antisocial attitude towards workers who participated in the RBWK.

162 Gunther Mai, "Arbeiterschaft zwischen Sozialismus, Nationalismus und Nationalsozialismus," in *Der Schatten der Vergangenheit*, ed. Uwe Backes, Eckhard Jesse, and Rainer Zitelmann (Frankfurt/Berlin: Propyläen, 1990), 195–217.

163 Lüdtke, "Honor of Labor," 69–89.

164 Dick Geary, "Working Class Identities in the Third Reich," in *Nazism, War, and Genocide*, ed. Neil Gregor (Exeter: University of Exeter Press, 2005), 42–55; Tilla Siegel, "Whatever was the Attitude of German Workers? Reflections on Recent Interpretations," in *Fascist Italy and Nazi Germany: Comparisons and Contrasts*, ed. Richard Bessel (Cambridge: Cambridge University Press, 1996), 61–77, especially 68; Herbert, "Real Mystery in Germany," 23–36; Mary Nolan, "Rationalization, Racism, and Resistenz: Recent Studies of Work and the Working Class in Nazi Germany," *International Labor and Working-Class History* 48 (1995): 131–51.

165 Frank Bajohr, "Dynamik und Disparität. Die nationalsozialistische Rüstungsmobilisierung und die 'Volksgemeinschaft,'" in *Volksgemeinschaft*, ed. Bajohr and Wildt (2009), 78–93.

166 Lutz Budraß, *Flugzeugindustrie und Luftrüstung in Deutschland 1918–1945* (Düsseldorf: Droste, 1998), 460–4; Junkers Flugzeug- und Motorenwerke A. G., *Vier Jahre Sozialer Aufbau*, 1938, 68–70, and 84–5. The foundation focused its support on apprentices but other talented retinue members could also apply.

167 *Deutschlandbericht der Sopade* 5 (1938), 550–1.
168 *Deutschlandbericht der Sopade* 3 (1936), 1328.
169 "Berufskundliche Fragen (1937). Antworten von Jungen," WA BaWü B 150 Salamander, Nr. 613 Reichberufswettkämpfe.
170 Alf Lüdtke, "What Happened to the 'Fiery Red Glow,'" in *The History of Everyday Life: Reconstructing Historical Experiences and Ways of Life*, ed. Alf Lüdtke (Princeton: Princeton University Press, 1995), 226–8.
171 Martin Broszat, "Resistenz und Widerstand. Eine Zwischenbilanz des Forschungsprojekts 'Widerstand und Verfolgung in Bayern 1933–1945,'" in *Nach Hitler. Der schwierige Umgang mit unserer Geschichte*, ed. Hermann Graml and Klaus-Dietmar Henke (München: Oldenbourg, 1987), 68–91, especially 75–6.

5. The Performance Community at War

1 Ley to Hitler, BABL NS 5 I, Nr. 341.
2 Tooze, *Wages of Destruction*, chap. 13.
3 Ley as cited in Bernett, "NS Volkssport," 135.
4 "Front der Leibesübungen," *NS-Sport*, 1 October 1939, citation 1.
5 Throughout his work Timothy Mason has emphasized how Nazi leaders worried about the repeat of another 1918, which explains their concern with integrating the working class into the new Germany and their persistent worries about social cohesion during the war. Whether the working class really posed a threat to the regime during the war is of course a different matter altogether. Mason, *Arbeiterklasse und Volksgemeinschaft*, xix–xxi.
6 Heinrich Satter, "Nicht nur in Eton und Oxford . . . In Deutschland ist das ganze Volk sportlich gehärtet und bereit," *Reichssportblatt*, 5 September 1939, 1128 and 1130.
7 "'Gemeinschaftsbildung' im Betrieb," 14 September 1944, BABL R 12 I, Nr. 312, 1–7, citations 1 and 6. On the IG Farben's human resource development efforts during the war, see: Johannes Platz, Lutz Raphael, and Ruth Rosenberger, "Anwendungsorientierte Betriebspsychologie und Eignungsdiagnostik," in *Wissenschaften und Wissenschaftspolitik. Bestandsaufnahmen zu Formationen, Brüchen und Kontinuitäten im Deutschland des 20. Jahrhunderts*, ed. Rüdiger vom Bruch and Brigitte Kaderas (Stuttgart: Franz Steiner, 2002), 291–309, especially 304–5.
8 Hans Dietrich Schäfer, *Das gespaltene Bewußtsein. Vom Dritten Reich bis zu den langen Fünfziger Jahren* (Göttingen: Wallstein, 2009), 71.

9 Carl Johannes Rummel, "Reichsbahnsport wie im Frieden," *Die Reichsbahn* Nr. 15. 22, 29 October 1941, BABL NS 5 VI, Nr. 19480, Bl. 35–6.
10 "Betriebssport im Krieg erst recht!," Gaubrief der DAF, 30 Janurary 1942, BABL NS 5 VI 19480, Bl. 28 front and back.
11 "Trotz Krieg: Vormarsch des Betriebssports," *Neuer Wirtschaftsdienst* No. 144, 25 July 1941, BABL NS 5 VI, Nr. 19480, Bl. 50.
12 "Betriebssportgemeinschaft: Jahresbericht der Wettkampfgruppen in der B.S.G. Farbenindustrie A. G. Leverkusen," 22 January 1942, BCA 236/069, 3. There were 1,800 members of whom 955 served in the Wehrmacht.
13 Bernett, "NS-Volkssport," 116; "Betriebssport auch im Kriege. 5.2 Millionen nehmen teil," 22 September 1943, BABL NS 5 VI, 19480, Bl. 6.
14 For details on the increasing length of the workweek, see: Hachtmann, *Industriearbeit*, 50–3, especially table 1, 51. On the intensification of labour, fatigue, and declining health, see: Hachtmann, *Industriearbeit*, 229ff.
15 Wolfgang Franz Werner, *"Bleib übrig!" Deutsche Arbeiter in der nationalsozialistischen Kriegswirtschaft* (Düsseldorf: Schwann, 1983), 147.
16 Werner, *"Bleib übrig,"* 147. See also: Mallmann and Paul, *Herrschaft und Alltag*, 59–60.
17 H. S., "Entspannung nach ernster Arbeit," *Reichssportblatt*, 6 February 1940, citations 128–9.
18 Heinrich Satter, "Kleiner Aufwand – großer Nutzen. Phantasie und angeborener Frohsinn beleben den Betriebssport," *Reichssportblatt*, Weihnachten 1939, citation 1490.
19 "Der Betriebssport setzte sich durch," *Der Angriff*, 7 February 1942, BABL NS 5 VI, 19480, Bl. 27.
20 "Betriebssport auch im Kriege. 5.2 Millionen nehmen teil," 22 September 1943, BABL NS 5 VI, 19480, Bl. 6.
21 "Stimmen zur Aufnahme des Betriebssportappells durch die Arbeiterschaft," in *Meldungen aus dem Reich. Die geheimen Lageberichte des Sicherheitsdienstes der SS 1938–1945*, ed. Heinz Boberach, vol. 11 (Herrsching: Pawlak, 1984), Nr. 323 (5. 10. 1942), citation 4290.
22 Ibid., citations 4291.
23 "Betriebssport auch im Kriege," *Wirtschaftspolitischer Dienst*, 17 June 1942, BABL NS 5 VI, Nr. 19480, Bl. 19.
24 BABL, NS 5 VI, Nr 19480, Bl. 24.
25 Heinrich Satter, "Kleiner Aufwand," citations 1490.
26 "Betriebssport in der Arbeitszeit?," *Wirtschaftspolitischer Dienst*, 7 November 1942, BABL NS 5 VI, Nr. 19480, citation Bl. 13.
27 Reichsgruppe Industrie an Gauwirtschaftskammern, 23 September 1943, BABL R 12 I, Nr. 337.

28 Reichsminister für Rüstung und Kriegsproduktion, 4 January 1944, BABL R 12 I, Nr. 337.

29 "Arbeitsdisziplin der Jugend," 16 July 1943, BABL R 12 I, Nr. 337.

30 BABL NS 5 VI, Nr. 19480, Bl. 40.

31 Ulrich Herbert, *Hitler's Foreign Workers: Enforced Foreign Labor in Germany under the Third Reich*, trans. William Templer (Cambridge: Cambridge University Press, 1997), 75–7, 131–3, 268–70; Alexandra Przyrembel, *"Rassenschande." Reinheitsmythen und Vernichtungslegitimation im Nationalsozialismus* (Göttingen: Vandenhoeck & Ruprecht, 2003); Mark Spoerer, "Die soziale Differenzierung der ausländischen Zivilarbeiter, Kriegsgefangenen und Häftlinge im Deutschen Reich," in *Das Deutsche Reich und der Zweite Weltkrieg*, ed. Jörg Echternkamp, vol. 9. 2, *Die Deutsche Kriegsgesellschaft 1939–1945* (München: DVA, 2005), 485–576, especially 562–5.

32 Fleischmann an Gauwaltungen der DAF: "Sporttag der ausländischen Arbeiter in den Lagern," 28 May 1943, BABL NS 5 I, Nr. 271, citations 1. It is not clear from this document whether the sport day was only intended for workers from Western Europe. The cultural welfare initiatives of the Labour Front usually excluded Poles and workers from Eastern Europe for racial reasons. Spoerer, "Soziale Differenzierung," 560–1; Achim Nolzen, "The NSDAP, the War, and German Society," in *Germany and the Second World War*, ed. Echternkamp, vol. 9.1 (2008), 161-3.

33 Veronika Springmann, "Fußball im Konzentrationslager," in *Hakenkreuz und rundes Leder*, ed. Peiffer and Schulze-Marmeling (2008), 498–503, especially 502.

34 Nicole Kramer, *Volksgenossinnen an der Heimatfront. Mobilisierung, Verhalten, Erinnerung* (Göttingen: Vandenhoeck & Ruprecht, 2011); Franka Maubach, *Die Stellung halten. Kriegserfahrungen und Lebensgeschichten von Wehrmachtshelferinnen* (Göttingen: Vandenhoeck & Ruprecht, 2009); Jörg Echternkamp, "At War, Abroad and at Home: The Essential Features of German Society in the Second World War," in *Germany and the Second World War*, ed. Echternkamp, vol. 9.1 (2008), 40–9. For an in-depth analysis of the debate about the mobilization of German women for work, see: Eleanor Hancock, "Employment in Wartime: The Experience of German Women during the Second World War," *War and Society* 12, no. 2 (1994), 43–68.

35 Steinbacher, "Differenz der Geschlechter," 99–101, citation 99.

36 Heinrich Meusel, "Der Übungsleiter," *Reichssportblatt*, 16 December 1941.

37 Joseph Ruppert, "Ärztliches zum Frauensport," *NS-Sport*, 28 March 1943, 2.

38 Frevert, *Women in German History*, 217; Koonz, *Mothers in the Fatherland*, 219. On women's role in the Nazi sport system, see: Michaela Czech,

Frauen und Sport im nationalsozialistischen Deutschland. Eine Untersuchung zur weiblichen Sportrealität in einem patriarchalischen Herrschaftssystem (Berlin: Tischler, 1994).

39 Satter, "Kleiner Aufwand," citations 1490.

40 The citations are from the covers of *Reichssportblatt*, 5 September 1939 and 12 September 1939.

41 G. St., "Der kämpferische Sport," *Reichssportblatt*, 12 September 1939, citations 1139.

42 Ley, *Die grosse Stunde*, citation 103. The German discourse on the will in the face of adversity and enemy superiority goes back to the First World War, see: Alexander Meschnig, *Der Wille zur Bewegung. Militärischer Traum und totalitäres Programm. Eine Mentalitätsgeschichte vom Ersten Weltkrieg zum Nationalsozialismus* (Bielefeld: Transcript, 2008), 73–4, 102, 180, and 325.

43 Joseph Goebbels as cited in Klemperer, *LTI*, 299.

44 Joseph Goebbels, "Appell der Kasseler Amtswalter, 5 November 1943," in *Goebbels – Reden*, ed. Helmut Heiber, vol. 2, *1939–1945* (Düsseldorf: Droste, 1972), 259–86, citation 268. Whether the awkward reference to destruction (*Zerstörung*) was deliberate or a Freudian slip needs to remain open.

45 Goebbels, "Appell," citations 268–9.

46 St., "Der kämpferische Sport," citation 1139.

47 Klaus Cachay, Steffen Bahlke, and Helmut Mehl, *"Echte Sportler" – "Gute Soldaten." Die Sportsozialisation des Nationalsozialismus im Spiegel von Feldpostbriefen* (Weinheim and München: Juventa, 2000), 239–42.

48 Peter Steinkamp, "Pervitin (Methamphetamine) test, use, and misuse in the German Wehrmacht," in *Man, Medicine, and the State: The Human Body as an Object of Medical Research in the 20th Century*, ed. Wolfgang Eckart (Stuttgart: Franz Steiner Verlag, 2006): 61–71; Cocks, *State of Health*, 142, 165–9.

49 St., "Der kämpferische Sport," citations 1139 and 1146.

50 Wilhelm Ritter von Schramm, "Sportgeist und Kriegserfolg," *Reichssportblatt*, 31 October 1939, citation 1306.

51 Ulf Schmidt, *Karl Brandt: The Nazi Doctor. Medicine and Power in the Third Reich* (London: Hambledon Continuum, 2007), 147–8; Winfried Süß, *"Volkskörper" im Krieg. Gesundheitspolitik, Gesundheitsverhältnisse und Krankenmord im nationalsozialistischen Deutschland, 1939–1945* (München: Oldenbourg, 2003), 301–3. German POWs occasionally referred to these rumours in their secretly taped conversations, see: Sönke Neitzel and Harald Welzer, *Soldaten On Fighting, Killing, and Dying: The Secret World War II Transcripts of German POWS* (Melbourne: Scribe, 2011), 162.

52 Alfred Kramer, "Verwundetensport – Weg zur Leistung," *NS-Sport*, 13 December 1942, 3–4, citation 4. The author was a navy physician (*Marinestabsarzt*).
53 Poore, *Disability*, 69–75; Wedemeyer-Kolwe, "Aussonderung oder Förderung," 131–3; Bernd Wedemeyer-Kolwe, *Vom "Versehrtenturnen" zum Deutschen Behindertensportverband (DBS). Eine Geschichte des deutschen Behindertensports* (Hildesheim: Arete Verlag, 2011), 29–30.
54 Poore, *Disability*, citation 133; Wedemeyer-Kolwe, *Vom "Versehrtenturnen,"* 29.
55 "Der Unsportliche verschwindet," *Der Angriff*, 24 April 1938, BABL NS 5 VI, Nr. 18795.
56 As translated by Poore, *Disability*, 83; Adolf Hitler, *Mein Kampf* (München: Franz Eher, 1933), citation 452.
57 Ulf Schmidt, *Medical Films, Ethics, and Euthanasia in Nazi Germany* (Husum: Matthiesen, 2002); Poore, *Disability*, 99–116.
58 Wedemeyer-Kolwe, "Aussonderung oder Förderung," 135–6; "263 Kriegsversehrte als Sportler," *Deutsche Allgemeine Zeitung*, 17 February 1943, BABL NS 5 VI, Nr. 19425, Bl. 3; "Kriegsversehrte treiben Sport bei KdF," *Der Angriff*, 6 April 1943, BABL NS 5 VI, Nr. 19427, Bl. 1.
59 Wedemeyer-Kolwe, *Vom "Versehrtensport,"* 37.
60 Heinrich Satter, "Sporttüchtig = 'vollwertig'" *Reichssportblatt*, 21 November 1939, 394.
61 Kramer, "Verwundetensport – Weg zur Leistung," *NS-Sport*, 13 December 1942, 3–4, citation 4. On the emotional and nurturing aspects of Kameradschaft, see: Kühne, *Kameradschaft*, chap. 4.
62 Satter, "Sporttüchtig = 'vollwertig,'" citation 1394; Hahn, *Grawitz, Genzken, Gebhardt*, 333–40. There were about four hundred beds for Wehrmacht soldiers and three hundred for the SS.
63 Karl Gebhardt, "Gedanken zum Verwundetensport und dem Versehrtensportabzeichen," *NS-Sport*, 6 December 1942, 4–5, citations 4.
64 Arthur Mallwitz, "Verwundetensport im Weltkrieg und jetzt," *NS-Sport*, 6 December 1942, 5–6, citation 6. At the time Mallwitz was the "chief physician" (*Chefarzt*) of reserve army hospital 124 in Berlin.
65 R. L., "Soldaten spielen sich gesund," *NS-Sport*, 19 November 1939, 3.
66 "Besuch beim Verwundetensport," *NS-Sport*, 21 July 1940, citations 5.
67 Admiralarzt Dr Lange, "Warum Sport mit Verwundeten?" *NS-Sport*, 13 December 1942, 3.
68 "Besuch beim Verwundeten-Sport," citations 5.
69 "Vier Jahre Sportamt Kraft durch Freude," *Der Angriff*, 14 April 1938, BABL NS 5 VI, Nr. 19427, Bl. 40.

70 Lange, "Warum Sport mit Verwundeten?," citations 3.
71 "Versehrte als Rettungsschwimmer," *Völkischer Beobachter*, 29 April 1943, BABL NS 5 VI, Nr. 19435, Bl. 4 front and back.
72 Ibid., Bl. 4 back.
73 Herbert Studders, "Die Wiedereingliederung von Kriegsversehrten in die Industrie," 7 January 1943, BABL R 12 I, Nr. 316. The special working group (*Arbeitsstelle der Reichsgruppe Industrie für Wiedereinschulung von Kriegsversehrten*) existed since May 1942.
74 Reichsgruppe Industrie Statistik und Wirtschaftsbeobachtung, "Kriegsversehrte des gegenwärtigen Krieges am 31. 5. 1943 im Altreich (Vorkriegsumfang)," BABL R 12 I, Nr. 80, Bl. 13. The numbers seem to refer to the old Reich before 1939 including Austria and the Sudetenland but excluding the Western Polish territories annexed after 1939. After May 1943, the numbers continued to rise but there are no statistics, see: Reichsgruppe Industrie an die Industrieabteilung der Gauwirtschaftskammer, 22 December 1943, BABL R 12 I, Nr. 80, Bl. 8.
75 "Das Versehrtenproblem und die Industrie. Standardvortrag 1," BABL R 12 I, Nr. 316; "Entlohnung des Versehrten," 7 March 1944, BABL R 12 I, Nr. 318.
76 "Der Weg des Versehrten," BABL R 3101, Nr. 10273.
77 "Grundsätze für die Eingliederung von versehrten Wehrdienst- und Einsatzbeschädigten," BABL R 12 I, Nr. 316.
78 Joseph Goebbels, "Kundgebung des Gaues Berlin der NSDAP. Berlin, Sportpalast, 18 February 1943," in *Goebbels – Reden*, ed. Heiber, 172–208, citation 203.
79 "Reichssportabzeichen für Versehrte und Körperbehinderte," BABL NS 5 VI, Nr. 19459, Bl. 13 back and front; "Verleihung des Versehrtensportabzeichens." RdErl. D. RmdI, 22 December 1943, BABL NS 5 VI, Nr. 19459, Bl. 2.
80 "Ein Reichssportabzeichen für Kriegsversehrte," *Deutsche Allgemeine Zeitung*, 1 December 1942, BABL NS 5 VI, Nr. 19459, Bl. 16; RdErl. D. RmdI, 22 December 1943, BABL NS 5 VI, Nr. 19459, Bl. 2.
81 H. Beutrer, "Eine Feierstunde des deutschen Sports. Erste Verleihung des Versehrten-Sportabzeichens in Berlin," *Reichssportblatt*, 8 December 1942.
82 "Das Versehrten-Sportabzeichen für Reichsminister Dr. Seyß-Inquart," *Reichssportblatt* 15 December 1942.
83 "Durch Leibesübungen vollwertig," *NS-Sport*, 7 March 1943, 1.
84 Beutrer, "Feierstunde," *Reichssportblatt*, 8 December 1942.
85 BABL NS 5 VI, Nr. 19459, Bl. 7 and 9.
86 RdErl. D. RmdI, 22 December 1943, BABL NS 5 VI, Nr. 19459, Bl. 2.

87 Paul Kellner, "Die Leistungen von kriegsverletzten Schwimmern und Rettungsschwimmern," *NS-Sport*, 21 December 1941, citation Der Sportwart, Nr. 51.
88 Walter Hulek, "Der Verwundetensport," *NS-Sport*, 25 October 1942, citations 1–2.
89 *Völkischer Beobachter*, 20 July 1943, BA-BL NS 5 VI, Nr. 19459, citation Bl. 7.
90 On the different treatment of disabled First World War veterans in Britain and Germany, see: Deborah Cohen, *The War Come Home: Disabled Veterans in Britain and Germany, 1914–1939* (Berkeley: University of California Press, 2001).
91 Peter Schenkel, "Amputierte und Schwimmsport," *Umschau in Wissenschaft und Technik* 17, 27 April 1941, BABL NS 5 VI, Nr. 19435, citation Bl. 15 front.
92 Ibid., Bl. 16 front and back.
93 Kellner, "Leistungen von kriegsverletzten Schwimmern," Sportwart, Nr. 51.
94 Götz Aly and Susanne Heim, *Vordenker der Vernichtung. Auschwitz und die deutschen Pläne für eine neue europäische Ordnung* (Hamburg: Hoffmann und Campe, 1991), 125–68. On Nazi Germanization and occupation policies, see also: Czeslaw Madajczyk, *Die Okkupationspolitik Nazideutschlands in Polen, 1939–1945*, transl. Berthold Puchert (Köln: Pahl-Rugenstein, 1988), chaps. 19–25; Martin Broszat, *Zweihundert Jahre deutsche Polenpolitik*, 2nd rev. ed. (Frankfurt: Suhrkamp, 1978), 272–306.
95 Elizabeth Harvey, *Women and the Nazi East: Agents and Witnesses of Germanization* (New Haven and London: Yale University Press, 2005), especially chap. 6.
96 Helma Kaden and Helmut Westphal, "Der Missbrauch des Sports zur Formierung der faschistischen V. Kolonne in Polen (1934–1938)," *Theorie und Praxis der Körperkultur* 21 (1972): 581–5.
97 Georg Bartosch, "Die große Aufgabe der Deutschen Turnerschaft in Polen," *NS-Sport*, 24 September 1939, 3. While the *Jungdeutsche Partei* claimed to have been the only legitimate pro-Nazi organization in Poland, the statement in *NS-Sport* is a gross simplification. There were vocal Nazi sympathizers in other German organizations. The complexity of this issue cannot be fully explored here. On the activities of the pro-Nazi *Jungdeutsche Partei für Polen* and German nationalist activities in Poland, see: Richard Blanke, *Orphans of Versailles: The Germans in Western Poland, 1918–39* (Lexington: University of Kentucky Press, 1993), especially 170–182; Winson Chu, "*Volksgemeinschaften unter sich.* German Minorities and Regionalism in Poland, 1918–39," in *German History from the Margins*, ed. Neil Gregor, Niels H. Roemer, and Mark Roseman (Bloomington: Indiana University Press, 2006): 104–26.

98 Georg Bartosch, "Heimkehr von polnischer Verschleppung. Dr. Niffka, Beauftragter für deutsche Leibesübungen im ehemaligen Polen erzählt," *NS-Sport*, 15 October 1939, 4; "Abwicklungsstelle der Jungdeutschen Partei für Polen Bielitz," 26 June 1940, BABL SS Führerpersonalakten, Georg Niffka, Nr. 350 A.

99 Bartosch talks of the rejuvenation of the DT leadership as a result of the takeover by the *Jungdeutsche Partei*. Bartosch, "Aufgabe der Turnerschaft," 3. On the German DT's attitude towards Nazism during the Weimar Republic and the early years of the regime, see: Lorenz Peiffer, "'Auf zur Gefolgschaft und zur Tat!': Deutsche Turnerschaft und Nationalsozialismus – zwischen Selbstgleichschaltung und Selbstbehauptung," *IWK: Internationale wissenschaftliche Korrespondenz zur Geschichte der deutschen Arbeiterbewegung* 35 (1999): 530–48; Lorenz Peiffer, *Die deutsche Turnerschaft. Ihre politische Stellung in der Zeit der Weimarer Republik und des Nationalsozialismus* (Ahrensburg: Czwalina, 1976).

100 Hermann Satter, "Die neuen Gaue. Zu den Ost-Problemen der deutschen Leibeserziehung," *Reichssportblatt*, 23 January 1940, citations 90. Not all of these players necessarily identified as ethnic Germans prior to the German occupation. In occupied Poland, racial designations also served to brush aside any ambiguities of ethnic identification. On the ambiguities of German Polish soccer relations, see: Thomas Urban, *Schwarze Adler, weiße Adler. Deutsche und polnische Fußballer im Räderwerk der Politik* (Göttingen: Die Werkstatt, 2011).

101 Satter, "Die neuen Gaue," citations 90.

102 Dieter Schenk, *Hans Frank. Hitler's Kronjurist und Generalgouverneur* (Frankfurt: S. Fischer, 2006), 205–20; Broszat, *Polenpolitik*, 293–8.

103 Madajczik, *Okkupationspolitik*, 76–8.

104 On the experiences of the German occupiers in Warsaw, see: Stephan Lehnstaedt, *Okkupation im Osten. Besatzeralltag in Warschau und Minsk 1939–1944* (München: Oldenbourg, 2010).

105 E. Horn, "Der 1. Schritt zum Sport," *Krakauer Zeitung*, 4/5 May 1941, BABL NS 5 VI, Nr. 19402, Bl. 38.

106 Georg Bartosch, "Das war der polnische Sport," *NS Sport*, 8 October 1939, 3; *NS-Sport*, 15 October 1939, 6.

107 Bartosch, "polnische Sport," *NS Sport*, 15 October 1939, citation 6.

108 Bartosch, "polnische Sport," *NS-Sport*, 22 October 1939, citation 6.

109 NSRLB Führungsabteilung: "Rundschreiben betr.: Generalgouvernement," 12 June 1942, CULDA, Sachakten 29. It might be due to the ambiguous status of the GG that Teichler's book on

international sport politics does not deal with GG relations with the Reich, see: Teichler, *Internationale Sportpolitik*.

110 Dietrich Redeker, "Und nun Alle! Das Sportleben des Generalgouvernements am Wendepunkt," *Krakauer Zeitung*, 12 May 1941, BABL NS 5 VI, Nr. 19402, Bl. 39 front.

111 Harvey, *Women in the Nazi East*, chaps. 4 and 6.

112 "GG: auch im Sport schon ein Begriff. Leibesübungen im General Gouvernement in hoher Blüte," *Reichssportblatt*, 8 September 1942.

113 Redeker, "Und nun alle," Bl. 39 back.

114 "Rundschreiben des Reichsarbeitsminister, Betriebssport während der Arbeitszeit," 11 August 1941, BABL R 3901, Nr. 20516, Bl. 73 (back). For public administrations in the Reich the ban seems to have been enforced. Public officials who did not comply were ordered to do so. See the correspondence about the director of the municipal health insurance (AOK) in Graz in BABL R 3901, Nr. 20516, Bl. 114, 115, and 119.

115 Lehnstaedt, *Okkupation*, 190.

116 Gouverneur Dr. Fischer, "Verpflichtung zum Sport," *Krakauer Zeitung*, 12 April 1941, BABL NS 5 VI, Nr. 19402, citation Bl. 40.

117 Lehnstaedt, *Okkupation*, 200–10.

118 "'Deutsche Kampfbahn Krakau," *NS-Sport*, 16 June 1940, 2.

119 Lehnstaedt, *Okkupation*, 133.

120 Fischer, "Verpflichtung zum Sport,", citation Bl. 40. On compulsory sport in the GG, see also: Dietrich Redeker, "Generalgouvernement – Vorbild der Breitenarbeit," *Warschauer Zeitung* 15/16 1940, BABL NS 5 VI, Nr. 19402, Bl. 44.

121 Schenk, *Frank*, 241.

122 Ibid., 243–8.

123 Ibid., 242.

124 Lehnstaedt, *Okkupation*, 180–7 and 237–42.

125 Ibid., chap. 2.

126 "Deutsche Leibesübungen im Generalgouvernement," *NS-Sport*, 10 November 1940, 2–3; Georg, Niffka, "Sport im Generalgouvernement," *NS-Sport*, 8 December 1940, 1.

127 Lehnstaedt, *Okkupation*, 137–8; Niffka, "Sport."

128 "Deutsche Leibesübungen im Generalgouvernement," 2–3; Niffka, "Sport."

129 Schenk, *Frank*, 193–7.

130 Deutsches Nachrichtenbüro as cited in Schenk, *Frank*, 226.

131 Deutscher Alpenverein Zweig Krakau to Frank, 18 August 1944, BABL R 52 II, Nr. 1, Bl. 42.

132 NSRLB Führungsabteilung: "Rundschreiben,", 12 June 1942, CULDA, Sachakten 29. Before his demotion Niffka claimed responsibility for all German sport and gymnastics. This included civil servants of the GG administrations, the German railroad, and the German Post as well as organized sport for the police, Wehrmacht, the SS, and ethnic Germans in the GG. "Deutsche Kampfbahn Krakau," *NS-Sport*, 16 June 1940, 2.

133 Befehlshaber der Sicherheitspolizei und des SD im Generalgouvernement Schöngarth an den Höheren SS und Polizeiführer Ost Krüger, 6 March 1941, SS Führerpersonalakten Niffka.

134 Schenk, *Frank*, 274–6.

135 "Polizei - ganz in Ordnung. Ordnungspolizei Magdeburg deutscher Handballmeister," *Reichssportblatt*, 21 July 1942.

136 As explored in great detail in the course of the controversy between Christopher Browning and Daniel Goldhagen, see: Christopher Browning, *Ordinary Men: Reserve Police Battalion 101 and the Final Solution in Poland* (New York: Harper Collins, 1992); Daniel Goldhagen, *Hitler's Willing Executioners: Ordinary Germans and the Holocaust* (New York: Vintage, 1997).

137 Lehnstaedt, *Okkupation*, 287–97.

138 "Hier wurde was gezeigt! SS und Polizei werben für den Boxsport," *Reichssportblatt*, 15 September 1942.

139 Tooze, *Wages of Destruction*, 576–8.

140 Ibid., citation 554. The armaments indexed increased from 100 in February 1942 to 330 in July 1944; Tooze, *Wages of Destruction*, 627.

141 Ulrich Herbert, *Hitler's Foreign Workers*; Michael Thad Allen, *The Business of Genocide: The SS, Slave Labor, and the Concentration Camps* (Chapel Hill: University of North Carolina Press, 2002), chap. 5.

142 Werner, *"Bleib Übrig."*

143 Süß, *'Volkskörper' im Krieg*, 251–3.

144 Tilla Siegel and Thomas Freyberg, *Rationalisierung im Nationalsozialismus*, 107–14; Siegel, *Leistung und Lohn*, chap. 4.

145 Tooze, *Wages of Destruction*, 554–5; Robert Ley, *Schmiede des Schwertes. Der deutsche Arbeiter im Grossdeutschen Freiheitskampf* (München: Franz Eher, 1942), 137–41; Ley, *Die grosse Stunde*, 208.

146 *Die Heller-Betriebsgemeinschaft. Gebr. Heller Werkzeugmaschinenfabrik,1 no. 1,* December 1943, 3–4 in Stadtarchiv Nürtingen.

147 Ibid., 11.

148 Ibid., 13–5.

149 Ibid., citations 4.

150 Steffen Seischab, "Nürtingen im zweiten Weltkrieg," in *Nürtingen 1918–1950. Weimarer Republik, Nationalsozialismus, Nachkriegszeit*, ed. Petra Garski-Hoffmann, André Kaiser, Steffen Seischab, and Reinhard Tietzen (Nürtingen: Sindlinger-Burchartz, 2011), 336.
151 Petra Garski-Hoffmann, "Ausländische Zwangsarbeiter," in *Nürtingen 1918–1950*, ed. Garski-Hoffmann (2001): 306–8 and 312–14.
152 Reichsgruppe Industrie to Dr Grävell, 18. February 1942, BABL R 12 I, Nr. 400.
153 Josef Petterka to Pg. Keil DAF Amt Soziale Selbstverantwortung. Hauptabteilung Leistungskampf, 14 July 1944, BABL NS 5 I, Nr. 343.
154 "Notiz für Brief Dr Ley an Minister Speer," BABL NS 5 I, Nr. 342. Speer was approached by Theodor Hupfauer, the director of the DAF office *Soziale Selbstverantwortung* (Social Personal Responsibility) and who also worked for the Speer ministry. On Hupfauer's role in the Speer ministry, see: Hachtmann, *Koloß*, 62 footnote 120.
155 These were two plants from the large machine-building firm Simmering-Graz-Pauker, one plant from the car manufacturer Steyr-Daimler-Puch, the car manufacturer Gräf & Stift, and the machine-building firm Niessenwerke in Vienna. The Steiermark firms were one plant from Steyr-Daimler-Puch, one from Simmering-Graz-Pauker, and another firm (Elin A. G.). "Brief an Reichsminister Speer," BABL NS 5 I, Nr. 342.
156 Josef Petterka, "Wettstreit der Betriebe im Kriegsleistungskampf der deutschen Betriebe (1943)" BA-BL NS 5 I, Nr. 342, citations 1.
157 Ibid., 1–10.
158 Ibid., citations 11–13.
159 Ibid., citations 22.
160 Ibid., 23.
161 Petterka to Keil, 14. Juli 1944, BABL NS 5 I, Nr. 343; Keil to Petterka, 27 Juli 1944, in BABL NS 5 I, Nr. 343.
162 Gräf & Stift an Petterka, 25 May 1944, BABL NS V I, Nr. 342.
163 Betriebsführer Weithner to Petterka, 17 June 1944, in BABL NS V I, Nr. 342.
164 Neil Gregor, *Stern und Hakenkreuz. Daimler-Benz im Dritten Reich* (Berlin: Propyläen, 1998), 137–9; Tooze, *Wages of Destruction*, 604–5.
165 "Vermerk Hauptabteilung Leistungskampf," 28 August 1944, BABL NS 5 I, Nr. 343.
166 Ian Kershaw, *The End: Hitler's Germany 1944-1945* (London: Allen Lane, 2011), 134–42.
167 "Aufruf Adolf Hitlers zum Reichsberufswettkampf der Hitlerjugend, 30 Oktober 1943," in *Deutsche Jugend 1933–1944*, ed. Karl Heinz Jahnke and Michael Buddrus (Hamburg: VSA-Verlag, 1989), 372–3.

168 Deutsche Arbeitsfront, *Richtlinien für den Kriegsberufswettkampf der deutschen Jugend 1943/1944* (Berlin: Deutsche Arbeitsfront, 1943), 3.
169 Ibid., 12–16.
170 Ibid., 7–8 and 16, citation 16.
171 G. E. "Rüstzeug für die Rüstung," *Deutsche Allgemeine Zeitung*, 9 November 1943, BABL NS 5 VI, Nr. 6047, citation Bl. 14 front.
172 Gauwirtschaftskammer Wien an bezirkliche Stellen der Wirtschaftsgruppen und Fachgruppen, 21 Januar 1944, BABL R 12 I, Nr. 308.
173 Boberach, ed. *Meldungen aus dem Reich* vol. 11, Nr. 324, 8. 10.1942, 4304–06, citation 4304; Vol. 12, Nr. 342, 10. 12. 1942, 4558–4564.
174 "Leibesübungen der berufstätigen Jugend innerhalb der Arbeitszeit," 4 January 1944, BABL R 12 I, Nr. 337; "Merkblatt für die Betriebe zur Erhaltung der Arbeitsdisziplin der Jugend," in BABL R 12 I, Nr. 337.
175 G. E. "Rüstzeug für die Rüstung," citation Bl. 14 front.
176 Ibid., citation Bl. 14 back.
177 "Ausbildung entscheidend für die Leistung," *VB* 14 December 1944, BABL NS 5 VI, Nr. 6047, Bl. 1 (front).
178 Dr von Albedyhll to Reichswirtschaftskammer, 14 April 1944, BABL R 12 I, Nr. 308.
179 Gauwirtschaftskammer Düsseldorf Abteilung Industrie to Reichsgruppe Industrie, 20 May 1944, BABL R 12 I, Nr. 308.
180 Geschäftsführung Reichsgruppe Industrie to Reichswirtschaftskammer, 6 June 1944, BABL R 12 I, Nr. 308.
181 G. E., "Rüstzeug für die Rüstung," citation Bl. 14 back.
182 "Das Leistungsertüchtigungswerk der DAF. In der Betriebsgemeinschaft Gebr. Heller, Nürtingen 1944," BABL R 12 I, Nr. 312, citation 4; "Buna-Werke an RGI," 17 March 1944, BABL R 12 I, Nr. 312.
183 G. Messarius, "Die fachliche Betreuung der Kriegsversehrten und ihre Leistungsertüchtigung. Vortrag gehalten vor der deutschen Fördergemeinschaft für Kriegsbeschädigte am 29 Juni 1944 in Berlin," BABL R 3101, Nr. 10274, Bl. 66 back.
184 As translated by William Templer in Herbert, *Hitler's Foreign Workers*, 230.
185 "Ausbildung entscheidend," BABL NS 5 VI, Nr. 6047, citation Bl. 1 back; "Siegerförderungen im Kriegsberufswettkampf 1944," *Die deutsche Post* 18 April 1944, BABL NS 5 VI, Nr. 6047, Bl. 2.

Conclusion

1 Paul Nolte, "Leistung -ein bürgerliches, kein faschistisches Prinzip," accessed 6 October 2012, originally at http://lesesaal.faz.net/wehler/

exp_forum.php?rid=9. Nolte's remarks were in response to an online discussion of Hans-Ulrich Wehler's *Gesellschaftsgeschichte* of postwar Germany in the *Frankfurter Allgemeine Zeitung*. His contribution was also published without its suggestive title, in: Patrick Bahners and Alexander Camman, eds., *Bundesrepublik und DDR. Die Debatte um Hans-Ulrich Wehlers "Deutsche Gesellschaftsgeschichte"* (München: C. H. Beck, 2009), 116.

2 "Bericht über den Ortswettkampf am 9. 2. 1944 der Lehrlinge der Innenverwaltung an 5 verschiedenen Orten," HSAS E 151/12 Bü 131, citations Bl. 10–12.

3 "Vortragsunterlage für den Kriegsberufswettkampf der deutschen Jugend," HSAS Stuttgart E 151/12 Bü 131, Bl. 2, citations 2 and 5.

4 Kühne to Kissel, 16 August 1937, BCA Nr. 061–060.

5 Michael Geyer, "Restorative Elites, German Society and the Nazi Pursuit of War," in *Fascist Italy and Nazi Germany*, ed. Bessel (1996), 150.

6 Knox, *Common Destiny*, 206–27.

7 Hans-Ulrich Wehler, *Deutsche Gesellschaftsgeschichte*, vol 5, *Bundesrepublik und DDR 1949-1990* (München: C. H. Beck, 2008), citations 214. Most historians have rejected Wehler's argument about the long-term effects of a Nazi performance mentality. They point to other motivational factors such as poverty, hunger, and later on new consumption opportunities that underpinned people's motivation for work in the postwar era, see: Bahners and Camman, eds., *Bundesrepublik und DDR*, 107–123. For a historical perspective on "performance society," see: Reinhold Reith, "Leistungsgesellschaft? Diskussionen über Leistungslohn in historischer Perspektive," in *"Arbeit": Geschichte, Gegenwart, Zukunft*, ed. Josef Ehmer (Leipzig: Akad. Verl.-Anst., 2002), 115–36.

8 Killat, "Berufswettkampf," *Aufwärts: Jugendzeitschrift des Deutschen Gewerkschaftsbundes (Brit. Zone)* 22 April 1950, 3, Nr. 8, 7, accessed 9 July 2012, http://digicoll.library.wisc.edu/cgi-bin/History/History-idx?type=div&did=History.auf1950April22.i0007&isize=M.

9 Verena Mörath, *Die Trimm-Aktionen des deutschen Sportbundes zur Bewegungs- und Sportförderung in der BRD 1970-1994 =* Veröffentlichungsreihe der Forschungsgruppe Public Health. Forschungsschwerpunkt Arbeit, Sozialstruktur und Sozialstaat (Berlin: Wissenschaftszentrum für Sozialforschung, 2005), 22–36.

10 Marie-Luise Klein, "Betriebssport in der Bundesrepublik Deutschland," in *Zwischen Arbeitnehmerinitiativen und Unternehmensinteresse. Zur Geschichte des Betriebssports in Deutschland*, ed. Gertrud Pfister (Sankt Augustin: Academia Verlag, 1999), 121–30.

11 Molly Wilkinson Johnson, *Training Socialist Citizens: Sports and the State in East Germany* (Leiden: Brill, 2008), 2, 35, 47, and 56–64.
12 Ibid., 16.
13 Ibid., 75–7.
14 On the Soviet-style central command economy of the GDR, see: André Steiner, *The Plans that Failed* (New York: Berghahn, 2010).
15 Johnson, *Training Socialist Citizens*, 80–5.
16 Friederike Sattler, "Arbeitsmobilisierung" and "Sozialistischer Wettbewerb" in *FDBG-Lexikon. Funktion, Struktur, Kader und Entwicklung einer Massenorganisation der SED (1945–1990)*, ed. Dieter Dowe, Karlheinz Kuba, and Manfred Wilke (Berlin: Friedrich-Ebert-Stiftung, 2009), accessed 3 July 2012, http://library.fes.de/FDBG-Lexikon.

Bibliography

Archival Sources

Archiv der Humboldt Universität, Berlin (AHU)

Charité Direktion

Nr. 868

Med. Fak.

Nr. 275

UK Personalia

G 031 Karl Gebhardt
H 187 Frohwalt Heiss
H 436 Hans Hoske
H 475 Auguste Hoffmann
N 022 Otto Nerz
Sch 288 Bruno K. Schultz

NS Doz

Nr. 195 Otto Nerz

Archiv zur Geschichte der Max-Planck-Gesellschaft, Berlin (AGMPG)

I. Abt., Rep 1a

Nr. 1353, 1354, 1391, 1444

Bayer Corporate Archives, Leverkusen (BCA)

Nr. 059/268, 061-060, 074–001–010, 236/069
Von Werk zu Werk. Monatsschrift der Werksgemeinschaft der I. G. Farbenindustrie Aktiengesellschaft 29 May 1938, Leverkusen edition.

Bundesarchiv Berlin-Lichterfelde (BABL)

Formerly Berlin Document Center (BDC)

3200 Hans Kühne M 0037
SS Führerpersonalakten Martin Brustmann, Nr. 112.
SS Führerpersonalakten, Georg Niffka, Nr. 350 A.

NS 5 I

Nr. 271, 341, 342, 343

NS 5 VI

Nr. 6039, 6041, 6044, 6045, 6046, 6047, 6053, 6056, 6057, 6058, 18793, 18794, 18795, 19398, 19402, 19411, 19422, 19424, 19425, 19426, 19427, 19428, 19435, 19459, 19478, 19480

R 12 I

Nr. 80, 308, 312, 316, 318, 337, 400

R 43 II

Nr. 519

R 52 II

Nr. 1

R 1501

Nr. 108970/6, 126782/1

R 3101

Nr. 10273, 10274

R 3901

Nr. 20516

R 4901

Nr. 126336

Carl und Liselott Diem Archiv, Köln (CULDA)

Sachakten

Nr. 16, 28, 29, 185, 188, 191, 203, 565a

Hauptstaatsarchiv Stuttgart (HSAS)

E 151/12 Bü 131
J 150 533/56

Landesarchiv Berlin (LAB)

A Rep 001–02, Nr. 585

Stadtarchiv Nürtingen

Die Heller-Betriebsgemeinschaft. Gebr. Heller Werkzeugmaschinenfabrik, 1. no. 1 (Dezember 1943).

Wirtschaftsarchiv Baden-Württemberg, Hohenheim (WA BaWü)

B 70 WMF

Bü 1300

B 102 Girokasse Öffentliche Bank und Sparkasse Stuttgart

Bü. 823

B 144 J. F. Adolff AG

Bü 299, 300, 379

B 150 Salamander

Bü. 613

Published Primary Sources

Anon. "Durch Leibesübungen vollwertig." *NS-Sport,* 7 March (1943): 1–2.
– "Das Versehrten-Sportabzeichen für Reichsminister Dr. Seyß-Inquart." *Reichssportblatt,* 15 Dezember 1942.

– "Hier wurde was gezeigt! SS und Polizei werben für den Boxsport." *Reichssportblatt*, 15 September 1942.

– "GG: auch im Sport schon ein Begriff. Leibesübungen im General Gouvernement in hoher Blüte." *Reichssportblatt*, 8 September 1942.

– "Polizei - ganz in Ordnung. Ordnungspolizei Magdeburg deutscher Handballmeister." *Reichssportblatt*, 21 July 1942.

– "Deutsche Leibesübungen im Generalgouvernement." *NS-Sport*, 10 November (1940): 2–3.

– "Besuch beim Verwundetensport." *NS-Sport*, 21 July (1940): 5.

– "'Deutsche Kampfbahn Krakau." *NS-Sport*, 16 June (1940): 2.

– "Front der Leibesübungen" *NS-Sport*, 1 October (1939): 1.

– "Wettkämpfe Kriegsbeschädigter in Görden bei Brandenburg." 5, No. 9 *Stadion-Kalender* (1917): 103–4.

– "Wettkämpfe Kriegsbeschädigter." *Stadion-Kalender* 5, no. 7 (1917): 89–90.

– "Bericht über die Sitzung des Wettkampf-Ausschusses," Stadion-Kalender 5, no. 5 (1917): 66–7.

– "An unsere Förderer." *Stadion-Kalender* 3rd, 4th, and 5th year, 5 no, 2 (1917): 25.

– "Ergänzte Tagesordnung zur Hauptversammlung. Antrag des Vorstandes." *Stadion-Kalender* 3rd, 4th, and 5th year, 5, no. 1 (1917): 18–20.

– "Körperliche Ausbildungspflicht der Jugend." *Stadion-Kalender* 3rd, 4th, and 5th year, 5, no. 1 (1917): 6.

– "Turnübungen für Einarmige und Einbeinige in Kiel." *Körper und Geist* 25 (1916/17): 317–19.

– "Einladung zu dem 14. Deutschen Kongreß für Volks- und Jugendspiele in Stettin." *Körper und Geist* 22 (1913/14): 33–5.

– "Grundsätze und Ratschläge für Jugendpflege." *Körper und Geist* 20 (1911/12): 63–6.

– "Ministerial-Erlaß zur Jugendpflege." Körper und Geist 20 (1911/12): 59–63.

Arnold, Arno. "Konstitution und ihr Einfluß auf die Leistung." In *Physiologie der Leibesübungen*, edited by Knoll and Arnold, 20-43, Leipzg: Johann Ambrosius Barth, 1933.

Atzler, Edgar and Gunther Lehmann, eds. *Anatomie und Physiologie der Arbeit.* Halle: Marhold, 1930.

Atzler, Edgar. "Das Ermüdungsproblem vom arbeitsphysiologischen Standpunkt." In *Physiologie der Arbeit*, edited by Atzler and Lehmann, 290–313. Halle: Marhold, 1930.

– "Rationalisierung der menschlichen Arbeit vom physiologischen Gesichtspunkt." In *Physiologie der Arbeit*, edited by Atzler and Lehmann, 273–80. Halle: Marhold, 1930.

– *Körper und Arbeit. Handbuch der Arbeitsphysiologie.* Leipzig: Georg Thieme, 1927.
– "Physiologische Rationalisierung." In *Körper und Arbeit*, edited by Atzler, 407–87. Leipzig: Georg Thieme, 1927.
– "Aufgaben und Ziele der Arbeitsphysiologie." *Die Arbeit: Zeitschrift für Gewerkschaftspolitik und Wirtschaftskunde* 3 (1926): 541–50 and 622–9.
Ausschuß für die Ertüchtigung des weiblichen Geschlechts. "Thesen." *Körper und Geist* 21 (1912/13): 49.
Axmann, Artur. *Der Reichsberufswettkampf.* Berlin: Junker und Dünnhaupt, 1938.
– *Olympia der Arbeit. Arbeiterjugend im Reichsberufswettkampf.* Berlin: Junker und Dünnhaupt, 1937.
Baeumler, Alfred. *Männerbund und Wissenschaft.* Berlin: Junker und Dünnhaupt, 1940.
Bartosch, Georg. "Das war der polnische Sport." *NS-Sport*, 8 October (1939): 3; 15 October (1939): 6 and 22 October (1939): 6.
– "Heimkehr von polnischer Verschleppung. Dr. Niffka, Beauftragter für deutsche Leibesübungen im ehemaligen Polen erzählt." *NS-Sport*, 15 October (1939): 4.
– "Die große Aufgabe der Deutschen Turnerschaft in Polen." *NS-Sport*, 24 September (1939): 3.
Baumgarten, Otto. "Erziehung zu einem wehrkräftigen Volk." *Körper und Geist* 26 (1917/18): 19–25.
– *Erziehungsaufgaben des Neuen Deutschland.* Tübingen: Mohr, 1917.
Beutrer, H. "Eine Feierstunde des deutschen Sports. Erste Verleihung des Versehrten-Sportabzeichens in Berlin." *Reichssportblatt*, 8 Dezember 1942.
Boberach, Heinz, ed., *Meldungen aus dem Reich. Die geheimen Lageberichte des Sicherheitsdienstes der SS 1938-1945.* Herrsching: Pawlak, 1984.
Conti, Leonardo. "Ziel und Organisation des deutschen Sportes im Nationalsozialistischen Deutschland." *Leibesübungen und körperliche Erziehung* 52 (1933): 473–5.
Deutsche Arbeitsfront, *Richtlinien für den Kriegsberufswettkampf der deutschen Jugend 1943/1944.* Berlin: Deutsche Arbeitsfront, 1943.
Deutsche Hochschule für Leibesübungen. *Tätigkeitsberichte.* Berlin: DHfL, 1920–32.
Deutscher Reichsausschuß für Leibesübungen. *Spielplatz-Gesetz. Entwurf eines Reichs- und Landesgesetzes.* Berlin: DRAL, 1917.
– "Bericht über die Sitzung des Wettkampf-Ausschusses." *Stadion-Kalender* 5, Nr. 5 (1917): 66–7.
Diem, Carl. *Sport in Amerika. Ergebnisse einer Studienreise.* Berlin: Weidmannsche Buchandlung, 1930.

– "Vom Wandel der Praxis." In *Deutsche Hochschule*, edited by Schiff, 79–82. Berlin: DHfL, 1930.
– "Frauenstudium." In *Deutsche Hochschule*, edited by Schiff, 87–91. Berlin: DHfL, 1930.
– *Die Deutsche Hochschule für Leibesübungen*. Berlin: DHfL, 1924.
– "Aufgaben des Ausschusses für wissenschaftliche Forschung." *Stadion-Kalender* 6, no. 10 (1918): 57.
– "Körperübung—Bürgerpflicht." *Stadion-Kalender* 6, no. 10 (1918): 55–6.
– "Die Zukunft der Leibesübungen und der Reichsausschuß." *Stadion-Kalender* 3rd, 4th, and 5th year, 5, no. 2 (1917): 26–30
Dominicus, Alexander. "Die Einführung des Turnens und Spielens in der Fortbildungsschule." *Körper und Geist* 21 (1912/13): 261–3.
Edelhoff. "Kursus zur Ausbildung der weiblichen Jugendpflege in Barmen." *Körper und Geist* 25 (1916/17): 35–40.
Eick, Ernst. "Mehr Härte." *Leibesübungen und körperliche Erziehung* 54, no. 19 (1935): 405–6.
Epping, Heinrich. *Das Sportarztwesen*. Leipzig: Georg Thieme, 1936.
Fröhlich, Elke, ed. *Die Tagebücher von Joseph Goebbels. Teil I: Aufzeichnungen 1923–1941.* Band 3/II: März 1936–Februar 1937 Editor(s): Jana Richter. Im Auftrag des Instituts für Zeitgeschichte und mit Unterstützung des Staatlichen Archivdienstes Rußlands (München: K. G. Saur, 2001).
Gebhardt, Karl. "Gedanken zum Verwundetensport und dem Versehrtensportabzeichen." *NS-Sport*, 6 December (1942): 4–5.
– "Grenzen und Gegenanzeigen der Übungsbehandlung." *Verhandlungen der deutschen orthopädischen Gesellschaft*, vol. 29, *Beilagenheft der Zeitschrift für orthopädische Chirurgie* 62 (1935): 45–8.
– *Übungsbehandlung*. Jena: Gustav Fischer, 1934.
– "Körperschule der Schwächlichen" In *Konstitutions- und Erbbiologie*, edited by Jaensch, 357–9. Leipzig: Johann Ambrosius Barth, 1934.
– "Soziale Medizin und Hygiene." *Münchener Medizinische Wochenschrift* 80 (1933):1256–8.
– "Beitrag zur Übungsfürsorge." *Münchener Medizinsche Wochenschrift* 76 (1929): 1251–5 and 1298–1303.
– "Lehrlings-Übungslager." *Münchener Medizinische Wochenschrift* 74 (1927): 1223–6.
– "Praktische sportärztliche Tätigkeit." *Münchener Medizinische Wochenschrift* 72 (1925): 1521–2.
Gellert, Cornelius. *Unsere Gegner*. 2nd. ed. Leipzig: Arbeiter-Turnverlag, 1927.
Gerbis, Hermann F., ed. *Arbeit und Sport* (Zentralblatt für Gewerbehygiene: Beiheft 21). Berlin: Springer, 1931.

Gersbach, Alfons, ed. *Die Ergebnisse der Sportbiologischen Untersuchungen bei der ersten Internationalen Arbeiterolympiade in Frankfurt am Main, im Juli 1925.* Frankfurt: Zentralkommission für Sport- und Körperpflege, 1927.

Goebbels, Josef. "Appell der Kasseler Amtswalter, 5. 11. 1943." In vol. 2 of *Goebbels—Reden,* edited by Heiber, 259–86. Düsseldorf: Droste, 1972.

– "Kundgebung des Gaues Berlin der NSDAP. Berlin, Sportpalast, 18. 2. 1943," In vol 2 of *Goebbels—Reden,* edited by Heiber, 172–208. Düsseldorf: Droste, 1972.

Hagemeister, Paul. "Die körperliche Ertüchtigung der werktätigen Jugend." *Körper und Geist* 22 (1913/14): 75–81.

Hanisch, Richard. "Wirtschaft und Leibesübungen." *Die Leibesübungen* 3, no. 22 (1927): 532–3.

Hannak, K. "Erste Erfahrungen im Schulboxen." *Leibesübungen und körperliche Erziehung* 55, no. 3 (1936), 41–2.

Heiber, Helmut, ed. *Goebbels–Reden.* 2 vols. Düsseldorf: Droste, 1972.

Herbst, Robert. "Sport und Arbeit." In *Körper und Arbeit,* edited by Atzler, 716–33. Leipzig, Georg Thieme, 1927.

Hitler, Adolf. *Mein Kampf.* München: Franz Eher, 1933.

Hoske, Hans. *Die menschliche Leistung als Grundlage des totalen Staates.* Leipzig: S. Hirzel, 1936.

– "Leibesübungen als Entwicklungsreiz." In *Konstitutions- und Erbbiologie,* edited by Jaensch, 351–6. Leipzig: Johann Ambrosius Barth, 1934.

– "Die Leibesübungen als Mittel der aufbauenden Bevölkerungspolitik." *Archiv für Bevölkerungswissenschaft und Bevölkerungspolitik* 4 (1934): 241–51.

– *Arbeit und Erholung im Lehrlingsalter.* Hamburg: Deutschnationaler Handlungsgehilfenverband, n.d.

Hueppe, Ferdinand. *Deutschlands Volkskraft und Wehrfähigkeit.* Berlin: August Hirschwald, 1916.

Hulek, Walter. "Der Verwundetensport." *NS-Sport,* 25 Oktober (1942): 1–2.

Jaensch, Walther and Auguste Hoffmann, "Rasse, Konstitution, und Höchstleistung bei den Siegern des XI. Olympia." *Münchener Medizinische Wochenschrift* 4, no.1 (1937): 16–22.

Jaensch, Walther, ed. *Leibesübungen und Körperkonstitution.* Berlin: Alfred Metzner, 1935.

– "Konstitution als Struktur und Formbildung, Wachstum und Entfaltung ererbter Anlagen." In *Leibesübungen und Körperkonstitution,* edited by Jaensch, 14–36. Berlin: Alfred Metzner, 1935.

– ed. *Konstitutions- und Erbbiologie in der Praxis der Medizin.* Leipzig: Johann Ambrosius Barth, 1934.

– "Nachwort des Kursleiters und Herausgebers." In *Konstitutions- und Erbbiologie,* edited by Jaensch, 380–5. Leipzig: Johann Ambrosius Barth, 1934.

Jerrmann, Horst. "Die sportlichen Veranstaltungen während der Gesolei." In *GESOLEI*, edited by Schlossmann and Fraenkel, 321–5. Düsseldorf: Schwann, 1926.

Junkers Flugzeug- und Motorenwerke A. G. *Vier Jahre Sozialer Aufbau*. 1938.

Kalle & Co. *Der Betriebssport bei Kalle & Co. Aktiengesellschaft Wiesbaden-Biebrich*. Wiesbaden: Kalle, 1940.

Kaufmann, Günter. *Das kommende Deutschland. Die Erziehung der Jugend im Reich Adolf Hitler's*. 2nd ed. Berlin: Junker und Dünnhaupt, 1940.

Kaup, Ignaz. "Die Ertüchtigung unserer erwerbstätigen Jugend." *Körper und Geist* 21 (1912/13): 225–37.

Kellner, Paul. "Die Leistungen von kriegsverletzten Schwimmern und Rettungsschwimmern." *NS-Sport*, 21 December (1941), Der Sportwart, Nr. 51.

Killat. "Berufswettkampf." *Aufwärts: Jugendzeitschrift des Deutschen Gewerkschaftsbundes (Brit. Zone)* 22 April 1950, 3, Nr. 8, 7. Accessed 9 July 2012. http://digicoll.library.wisc.edu/cgi-bin/History/History-idx?type=div&did=History.auf1950April22.i0007&isize=M.

Kirchberg, Franz. "Die Tätigkeit des Sportlehrers im Dienste der allgemeinen Körperpflege." In *Deutsche Hochschule*, edited by Schiff, 37–43. Berlin: DHfL, 1930.

Knoll, Wilhelm and Arno Arnold, eds. *Normale und pathologische Physiologie der Leibesübungen*. Leipzig: Johann Ambrosius Barth, 1933.

Kohlrausch, Ernst. "Bericht über den XV. Deutschen Kongreß für Volks- und Jugendspiele in Altona." *Körper und Geist* 22 (1913/14): 69–75.

Kohlrausch, Wolfgang. "Körperbau und Wachstum." In *Deutsche Hochschule*, edited by Schiff, 49–54. Berlin: DHfL, 1930.

– "Zusammenhänge von Körperform und Leistung. Ergebnisse der anthropometrischen Messungen an Athleten der Amsterdamer Olympiade." *Arbeitsphysiologie* 2 (1929): 187–203.

– "Heilturnanstalt und Sonnenbad eines Feldlazaretts." *Körper und Geist* 25 (1916/17): 200–2.

"Kraft durch Freude" Sportamt. *Sportappell der Betriebe 1938*. Berlin: KdF, 1938.

– *Leibesübungen mit Kraft durch Freude* no. 1. Sportprogramm Gau Groß-Berlin April-Juni 1935. Berlin: KdF, 1935.

Kramer, Alfred. "Verwundetensport–Weg zur Leistung." *NS-Sport* 13, December (1942): 3–4.

Krieg, J. "Über die Notwendigkeit einer Reform in der Körpererziehung des weiblichen Geschlechts." *Körper und Geist* 22 (1913/14): 377–83.

Kuhr, H. "Die Notwendigkeit von Lazarettspielplätzen." *Körper und Geist* 27 (1918/19): 131–4.

Lange. Warum Sport mit Verwundeten? " *NS-Sport*, 13 December (1942): 3.

Lewald, Theodor. "Leibesübungen und Volksgesundheit." In *Die deutschen Leibesübungen*, edited by Neuendorff, 35–40. Berlin und Leipzig: Wilhelm Andermann, 1927.

– *Sport, Wirtschaft, Volksgesundheit*. Berlin: Georg Stilke, 1926.

Ley, Robert. *Die grosse Stunde. Das deutsche Volk im totalen Kriegseinsatz. Reden und Aufsätze aus den Jahren 1941-1943*. München: Franz Eher, 1943.

– *Schmiede des Schwertes. Der deutsche Arbeiter im Grossdeutschen Freiheitskampf*. München: Franz Eher, 1942.

– *Durchbruch der sozialen Ehre. Reden und Gedanken für das schaffende Deutschland*. Berlin: Mehden Verlag, 1935.

Linde, Friedrich Wilhelm von der. "Arbeitgeber und Leibesübungen." In *Arbeit und Sport*, edited by Gerbis, 43–62. Berlin: Springer, 1931.

Mallwitz, Arthur. "Verwundetensport im Weltkrieg und jetzt." *NS-Sport*, 6 December (1942): 5–6.

– "Arbeit und Sport." In *Arbeit und Sport*, edited by Gerbis, 8–18. Berlin: Springer, 1931.

– "Körperübungen für Kriegsbeschädigte." *Athletik-Jahrbuch* 11 (1919): 49–55.

– "Exzellenz von Schjerning über Kinder- und Jugendpflege und ihre Bedeutung für die Volks- und Wehrkraft." *Stadionkalender* 6, no. 3 (1918): 11–13.

Maschke, Walter. "Arbeiter und Leibesübungen." In *Arbeit und Sport*, edited by Gerbis, 63–7. Berlin: Springer, 1931.

Meinecke, Dorothea. "Die körperliche Ertüchtigung der Mädchen und Jungfrauen." *Körper und Geist* 24 (1915/16): 353–60.

– "Weshalb sind Leibesübungen in Kriegs- und Friedenzeiten eine Notwendigkeit für das weibliche Geschlecht?" *Körper und Geist* 24 (1915/16): 52–6

– "Zur Jugendpflege für das weibliche Geschlecht." *Körper und Geist* 21 (1912/13): 89–94.

Mengerinhausen, Max. "Die Erziehung des Arbeiters zur Arbeit." *Die Umschau* 31 (1927): 1010–12.

Meusel, Heinrich. "Der Übungsleiter." *Reichssportblatt*, 16 December 1941.

– *Körperliche Grundausbildung*. 2nd ed. Berlin: Weidmannsche Verlagsbuchhandlung, 1938.

Müller-Meiningen, Ernst. *Wir brauchen in Reichs-Jugend-Wehrgesetz*. (=Flugschriften des ZA für Volks- und Jugendspiele, Heft 1). Leipzig: Teubner, 1915.

Münzer. "Lehrkurse zur Ausbildung von weiblichen Spielleitern." *Körper und Geist* 24 (1915/16): 360–1.

Nettelbeck, Petra, ed. *Deutschlandbericht der Sopade, 1934-1980.* Salzhausen and Frankfurt am Main: Zweitausendeins, 1980.

Neuendorff, Edmund. *Bericht über die Arbeit der Preussischen Hochschule für Leibesübungen in den Jahren 1925-1931.* Berlin: PHfL, 1932.

– *Die deutschen Leibesübungen. Grosses Handbuch für Turnen, Spiel und Sport.* Berlin and Leipzig: Wilhelm Andermann, 1927.

Niffka, Georg. "Sport im Generalgouvernement." *NS-Sport,* 8 December (1940): 1.

Oertzen, Ulrich von. "Deutsche Turner und Sportsleute!" *Stadion-Kalender für das Deutsche Reich,* 3., 4th, and 5th year, 5, no. 1 (1917): 1.

Poensgen, Ernst. "Die wirtschaftliche Bedeutung der Ge-So-Lei." In Vol. 1 of *GE-SO-LEI,* edited by Schlossmann and Fraenkel, 15–17. Düsseldorf: Schwann, 1927.

Profé, Alice. "Die Ertüchtigung unserer Frauen." *Körper und Geist* 21 (1912/13): 193–205.

R., L. "Soldaten spielen sich sich gesund." *NS-Sport,* 19 November (1939): 3.

Raydt, Hermann. "Leibesübungen und kaufmännische Fortbildungsschule." *Körper und Geist* 22 (1913/14): 39–46.

– "Bericht über den XIII. Deutschen Kongreß für Volks- und Jugendspiele in Heidelberg." *Körper und Geist* 21 (1912/13): 137–45

Reichsjugendführung, ed. *Mädel im Dienst. Jungmädelsport.* 2nd. ed. Potsdam: Ludwig Voggenreiter, 1940.

Reichskuratorium für Wirtschaftlichkeit, ed. *Der Mensch und die Rationalisierung.* Vol. 3 of *Eignung und Qualitätsarbeit.* Jena: Gustav Fischer, 1933.

Riedel, Hans. "Sport und Turnen in der technischen Arbeitsschulung." *Arbeitsschulung* 1 (1929): 8–11.

Rissom, Johannes. "Wettkämpfe der Kriegsbeschädigten im Reservelazarett Ettlingen i. Baden." *Körper und Geist* 27 (1918/19): 134–9.

– "Leibesübungen der Einarmer und Einbeiner." *Körper und Geist* 25 (1916/17): 306–10.

Roeder, H. "Muskelarbeit und Gewichtsansatz." *Körper und Geist* 22 (1913/14): 61–73.

Rupp, Hans. "Über den Reichsberufswettkampf." *Psychotechnische Zeitschrift* 9, no. 2 (1934): 29–34 and 9, no. 3 (1934): 61–74.

Ruppert, Joseph. "Ärztliches zum Frauensport." *NS-Sport,* 28 März (1943): 2.

Samel, W. "Heilpädagogisches Turnen bei Kopfschutzverletzten." *Körper und Geist* 27 (1918/19): 162–5.

Satter, Heinrich. "Die neuen Gaue. Zu den Ost-Problemen der deutschen Leibeserziehung." *Reichssportblatt,* 23 January 1940.

– "Entspannung nach ernster Arbeit." *Reichssportblatt,* 6 February 1940.
– "Kleiner Aufwand—großer Nutzen." *Reichssportblatt,* Weihnachten 1939.
– "Sporttüchtig = vollwertig." *Reichssportblatt,* 21 November 1939.
– "Nicht nur in Eton und Oxford ... In Deutschland ist das ganze Volk sportlich gehärtet und bereit." *Reichssportblatt,* 5 September 1939.
Schenckendorff, Emil von. "Denkschrift betreffend die Notwendigkeit einer geregelten Körperpflege für die Jugend des Volkes im 14. und 18. Lebensjahre." *Körper und Geist* 21 (1912/13): 257–60.
– "Über Jugendpflege." *Körper und Geist* 21 (1912/13): 18.
– "Wehrkraft und Jugenderziehung," *Jahrbuch für Volks- und Jugendspiele* 9 (1900): 14–66.
Schiff, Alfred. *Die Deutsche Hochschule für Leibesübungen, 1920-1930.* Berlin: DHfL, 1930.
– "Zehn Jahre äussere Entwicklung." In *Deutsche Hochschule,* edited by Schiff, 8–19. Berlin: DHfL, 1930.
Schlink, Edmund. "Über den Einfluss der Leibesübungen auf den Atemtypus." *Arbeitsphysiologie* 5 (1932): 596–604.
Schlossmann, Arthur and Martha Fraenkel, eds. *GE-SO-LEI. Grosse Ausstellung Düsseldorf 1926 für Gesundheitspflege, Sozialfürsorge und Leibesübungen.* 2 vols. Düsseldorf: Schwann, 1927.
Schmidt, Ferdinand August. "N. Zuntz." *Körper und Geist* 29 (1920): 28.
– "Zur Ertüchtigung des weiblichen Geschlechts." *Körper und Geist* 21 (1912/13): 49–52.
Schmith, Otto. "Zur Physiologie der Sportbewegungen. Untersuchungen zur Frage einer allgemeinen und speziellen angewandten Bewegungslehre der Sportbewegungen." *Arbeitsphysiologie* 5 (1932): 394–423.
Schneider, Georg Heinrich. "Blutgruppenuntersuchungen." In *Ergebnisse,* edited by Gersbach, 31–54. Frankfurt: Zentralkommission für Sport- und Körperpflege, 1927.
Schramm, Wilhelm Ritter von. "Sportgeist und Kriegserfolg." *Reichssportblatt,* 31 October 1939.
Schulte, Robert W. *Die Psychologie der Leibesübungen. Ein Überblick über das Gesamtgebiet.* Berlin: Weidmannsche Buchhandlung, 1928.
– *Leistungssteigerung in Turnen, Spiel und Sport. Grundlinien einer Psychobiologie der Leibesübungen.* Oldenburg: Gerh. Stalling, 1926.
– *Eignungsprüfungen im Schreibmaschinenbau.* Stuttgart: Ferdinand Enke, 1926.
– *Eignungs- und Leistungsprüfung im Sport. Die psychologische Methodik der Wissenschaft von den Leibesübungen.* Berlin: Guido Hackebeil, 1925.
Schultz, Bruno K. "Die rassenbiologische Bedeutung der Leibesübungen." *Volk und Rasse* 11, no. 8 (1936): 339–47.

– "Rassenkundliche Untersuchungen bei Olympiakämpfern." *Volk und Rasse* 11, no. 9 (1936): 363–68.

Schwarz, Ernst. "Körpermessungen." In *Ergebnisse*, edited by Gersbach, 55–66. Frankfurt: Zentralkommission für Sport- und Körperpflege, 1927.

Sippel, Hanns. "Psychologische Überlegungen zur Frage der Sportpause." In *Arbeit und Sport*, edited by Gerbis, 34–42. Berlin: Springer, 1931.

– "Psychologie der Leibesübungen." In *Deutsche Hochschule*, edited by Schiff, 72–5. Berlin: DHfL, 1930.

– *Leibesübungen und geistige Leistung*. Berlin: Weidmannsche Buchhandlung, 1927.

– *Körper–Geist–Seele. Grundlage einer Psychologie der Leibesübungen*. Berlin: Weidmannsche Buchhandlung, 1926.

St., G. "Der kämpferische Sport." *Reichssportblatt*, 12 September 1939.

Strache, Wolf. "Die Reichsakademie für Leibesübungen." *Reichssportblatt* 3, no. 19 (1936): 618–21.

Verständig, Carla. "Frauensport." In *Deutsche Hochschule*, edited by Schiff, 83–6. Berlin: DHfL, 1930.

Wetzel, Heinz. "Reichsakademie für Leibesübungen. Die politischen Grundlagen." *Reichssportblatt* 3, no. 18 (1936): 587.

Wiedemann, F. P. "Die Grenzen des Frauensports." *Körper und Geist* 27 (1918/1919): 71–2.

Wildung, Fritz. *Arbeitersport*. Berlin: Bücherkreis, 1929.

Winther, Hans and Hanna Winther-Feldten. "Frauendienst und Körperbildung." *Körper und Geist* 25 (1916/17): 34–5.

Zeller, Wilfried. "Konstitution und Berufsberatung." In *Konstitutions- und Erbbiologie*, edited by Jaensch, 280–99. Leipzig: Johann Ambrosius Barth, 1934.

Zobel, Paul. *Werksport und Arbeitersport*. Berlin: Märkische Spielvereinigung, 1926.

Zuntz, Nathan. "Zur Physiologie der Spiele und Leibesübungen." *Körper und Geist* 20 (1911/12): 145–55.

Zuntz, Nathan, Carl Brahm, and Arthur Mallwitz, eds. *Sonderkatalog der Abteilung Sportausstellung der internationalen Hygieneaustellung Dresden 1911*. Dresden: Verlag der Internationalen Hygieneausstellung, 1911.

Secondary Sources

Adams, Carole. *Women Clerks in Wilhelmine Germany: Issues of Class and Gender*. Cambridge: Cambridge University Press, 1988.

Adams, Mark B. ed. *The Wellborn Science: Eugenics in Germany, France, Brazil, and Russia*. New York and Oxford: Oxford University Press, 1990.

Alexander, Jennifer Karns. *The Mantra of Efficiency: From Water Wheel to Social Control.* Baltimore: Johns Hopkins University Press, 2008.

Allen, Michael Thad. *The Business of Genocide: The SS, Slave Labor, and the Concentration Camps.* Chapel Hill: University of North Carolina Press, 2002.

Aly, Götz. *Hitler's Beneficiaries: Plunder, Racial War, and the Nazi Welfare State.* Translated by Jefferson Chase. London: Metropolitan/Holt, 2007.

Aly, Götz, and Susanne Heim. *Vordenker der Vernichtung. Auschwitz und die deutschen Pläne für eine neue europäische Ordnung.* Hamburg: Hoffmann und Campe, 1991.

Ash, Mitchell G. ed. *Wissen, Politik, und Öffentlichkeit. Von der Wiener Moderne bis zur Gegenwart.* Wien: WUV, 2002.

Assmann, Aleida, Frank Hiddemann, and Eckhard Schwarzenberger, eds. *Firma Topf & Söhne: Hersteller der Öfen für Auschwitz. Ein Fabrikgelände als Erinnerungsort?* Frankfurt: Campus, 2002.

Ayaß, Wolfgang. *"Asoziale" im Nationalsozialismus.* Stuttgart: Klett-Cotta, 1995.

Backes, Uwe, Eckhard Jesse, and Rainer Zitelmann, eds. *Der Schatten der Vergangenheit.* Frankfurt/Berlin: Propyläen, 1990.

Bahners, Patrick, and Alexander Camman, eds. *Bundesrepublik und DDR. Die Debatte um Hans-Ulrich Wehlers "Deutsche Gesellschaftsgeschichte".* München: C. H. Beck, 2009.

Bahro, Berno. *Der SS-Sport. Organisiation—Funktion—Bedeutung.* Paderborn: Schöningh, 2013.

Bajohr Frank, and Michael Wildt, eds. *Volksgemeinschaft. Neue Forschungen zur Gesellschaft des Nationalsozialismus.* Frankfurt: S. Fischer, 2009.

Bajohr, Frank. "Dynamik und Disparität. Die nationalsozialistische Rüstungsmobilisierung und die 'Volksgemeinschaft.'" In *Volksgemeinschaft,* edited by Bajohr and Wildt, 78–93. Frankfurt: S. Fischer, 2009.

– *Parvenüs und Profiteure. Korruption in der NS-Zeit.* Frankfurt: Büchergilde, 2001.

Bankier, David. *Probing the Depth of German Antisemitism: German Society and the Persecution of Jews, 1933–1945.* New York: Berghahn Books, 2000.

Baranowski, Shelley. *Strength through Joy: Consumerism and Mass Tourism in the Third Reich.* Cambridge: Cambridge University Press, 2004.

Barrett, Michael Baker. "Soldiers, Sportsmen, and Politicians. Military Sport in Germany, 1924-1935." PhD diss., University of Massachusetts, 1977.

Beck, Herta. *Leistung und Volksgemeinschaft. Der Sportarzt und Sozialhygieniker Hans Hoske, 1900–1970.* Husum: Matthiesen Verlag, 1991.

Becker, Frank. "Rationalisierung–Körperkultur–Neuer Mensch. Arbeitsphysiologie und Sport in der Weimarer Republik." In *Arbeit,*

Leistung, edited by Plesser and Thamer, 149–70. Stuttgart: Franz Steiner, 2012.

– *Den Sport gestalten. Carl Diems Leben 1882–1962*. 4 vols. Duisburg: Universitätsverlag Rhein-Ruhr, 2009–2011.

– "Revolution des Körpers. Der Sport in Gesellschaftsentwürfen der klassischen Moderne." In *Der neue Mensch*, edited by Gerstner, Könczöl and Hentwig, 87–104. Frankfurt: Peter Lang, 2006.

– *Amerikanismus in Weimar. Sportsymbole und politische Kultur*. Wiesbaden: DUV, 1993.

Beddies, Thomas. *"Du hast die Pflicht gesund zu sein." Der Gesundheitsdienst der Hitlerjugend 1933–1945*. Berlin: be.bra. Wissenschaft, 2010.

Behrendt, Michael C. "Accidents Happen: François Ewald. The 'Antirevolutionary' Foucault, and the Intellectual Politics of the French Welfare State." *Journal of Modern History* 82 (2010): 585–624.

Berg, Christa. *Handbuch der deutschen Bildungsgeschichte*. Vol. 4 of *1870–1918: Von der Reichsgründung bis zum Ende des ersten Weltkriegs*. München: C. H. Beck, 1991.

Berghoff, Hartmut. "Did Hitler create a new society? Continuity and change in German social history before and after 1933." In *Weimar and Nazi Germany*, edited by Panayi, 74–104. Harlow: Longman, 2001.

Bergien, Rüdiger. *Die bellizistische Republik. Wehrkonsens und "Wehrhaftmachung" in Deutschland, 1918–1933*. München: Oldenbourg, 2012.

Bernett, Hajo. *Sportunterricht an der nationalsozialistischen Schule. Der Schulsport an den höheren Schulen Preußens 1933–1940*. Sankt Augustin: Hans Richarz, 1985.

– *Der Weg des Sports in die nationalsozialistische Diktatur. Die Entstehung des Deutschen (Nationalsozialistischen) Reichsbund für Leibesübungen*. Schorndorf: Hofmann, 1983.

–, ed. *Nationalsozialistische Leibeserziehung. Eine Dokumentation ihrer Theorie und Organisation*. Schorndorf: Karl Hofmann, 1966.

– "Nationalsozialistischer Volkssport bei 'Kraft durch Freude.'" *Stadion* 5 (1979): 89–146.

Berryman, John W., and Roberta J. Park, eds. *Sport and Exercise Science: Essays in the History of Medicine*. Urbana: University of Illinois Press, 1992.

Bessel, Richard. *Fascist Italy and Nazi Germany: Comparisons and Contrasts*. Cambridge: Cambridge University Press, 1996.

– *Germany after the First World War*. Oxford: Clarendon Press, 1995.

Beyer, Erich. "Sport in der Weimarer Republik." In Vol 3.2 of *Geschichte der Leibesübungen*, edited by Ueberhorst, 657–700. Berlin: Bartels and Wernitz, 1982.

Blanke, Richard. *Orphans of Versailles: The Germans in Western Poland, 1918–39.* Lexington: University of Kentucky Press, 1993.

Bodó, Béla. "The Medical Examination and Biological Selection of University Students in Nazi Germany." *Bulletin of the History of Medicine* 76 (2002): 719–48.

Boemeke, Manfred F., Roger Cickering, and Stig Förster, eds. *Anticipating Total War. The German and American Experiences, 1871–1914.* Cambridge: Cambridge University Press, 1999.

Bönker, Dirk. *Militarism in a Global Age. Naval Ambitions in Germany and the United States before World War I.* Ithaca: Cornell University Press, 2012.

Bolte, Karl Martin. *Sozialer Aufstieg und Abstieg. Eine Untersuchung über Berufsprestige und Berufsmobilität.* Stuttgart: Ferdinand Enke, 1959.

Borut, Jacob. "Jews in German Sports during the Weimar Republic." In *Emancipation through Muscles,* edited by Brenner and Reuveni, 77–92. Lincoln: University of Nebraska Press, 2006.

Bourdieu, Pierre. *Distinction. A Social Critique of the Judgment of Taste.* Translated by Richard Nice. Cambridge: Harvard University Press, 1984.

Brenner, Michael, and Gideon Reuveni. eds. *Emancipation through Muscles: Jews and Sports in Europe.* Lincoln: University of Nebraska Press, 2006.

Brinkschulte, Eva. *Körperertüchtigung(en). Sportmedizin zwischen Leistungsoptimierung und Gesundheitsförderung.* Habiltation: FU Berlin, 2002.

Bröckling, Ulrich. *Das unternehmerische Selbst. Soziologie einer Subjektivierungsform.* Frankfurt: Suhrkamp, 2007.

– "Menschenökonomie und Humankapital. Eine Kritik der bio-politischen Ökonomie." *Mittelweg 36* 12, no. 1 (2003): 3–22.

–, Susanne Krasmann, and Thomas Lemke. eds. *Gouvernementalität der Gegenwart. Studien zur Ökonomisierung des Sozialen.* Frankfurt: Suhrkamp, 2000.

Broszat, Martin. "Resistenz und Widerstand. Eine Zwischenbilanz des Forschungsprojekts 'Widerstand und Verfolgung in Bayern 1933-1945.'" In *Nach Hitler,* edited by Graml and Henke, 68–91. München: Oldenbourg, 1987.

– *Zweihundert Jahre deutsche Polenpolitik.* 2nd rev. ed. Frankfurt: Suhrkamp, 1978.

– "Soziale Motivation und Führer-Bindung des Nationalsozialismus." *Vierteljahreshefte für Zeitgeschichte* 18 (1970): 382–409.

Browning, Christopher. *Ordinary Men: Reserve Police Battalion 101 and the Final Solution in Poland.* New York: Harper Collins, 1992.

Bruch, Rüdiger vom, and Brigitte Kaderas, eds. *Wissenschaften und Wissenschaftspolitik. Bestandsaufnahmen zu Formationen, Brüchen und*

Kontinuitäten im Deutschland des 20. Jahrhunderts. Stuttgart: Franz Steiner, 2002.

Bryant, Thomas. *Friedrich Burgdörfer (1890–1967). Eine diskursbiographische Studie zur deutschen Demographie im 20. Jahrhundert*. Stuttgart: Franz Steiner, 2010.

Buddrus, Michael. *Totale Erziehung für den totalen Krieg. Hitlerjugend und nationalsozialistische Jugendpolitik*. München: K. G. Saur, 2003.

Budraß, Lutz. *Flugzeugindustrie und Luftrüstung in Deutschland 1918 –1945*. Düsseldorf: Droste, 1998.

Buggeln, Marc, and Michael Wildt, eds. *Arbeit im Nationalsozialismus*. Berlin: De Gruyter, 2014.

Burleigh, Michael, ed. *Confronting the Nazi Past: New Debates on Modern German History*. London: Palgrave MacMillan, 1996.

Buss, Wolfgang. "Die Entwicklung des deutschen Hochschulsports vom Beginn der Weimarer Republik bis zum Ende des NS-Staates. Umbruch, Neuanfang, oder Kontinuität?" PhD diss., Göttingen, 1975.

Cachay, Klaus, Steffen Bahlke, and Helmut Mehl. *"Echte Sportler"–"Gute Soldaten." Die Sportsozialisation des Nationalsozialismus im Spiegel von Feldpostbriefen*. Weinheim and München: Juventa, 2000.

Campbell, Joan, *Joy in Work, German Work: The National Debate, 1800–1945*. Princeton: Princeton University Press, 1989.

Canning, Kathleen. *Gender History in Practice: Historical Perspectives on Bodies, Class, and Citizenship*. Ithaca and London: Cornell University Press, 2006.

– *Languages of Labor and Gender: Female Factory Work in Germany, 1850–1914*. Ithaca: Cornell University Press, 1996.

Carden-Coyne, Ana. *Reconstructing the Body: Classicism, Modernism, and the First World War*. Oxford: Oxford University Press, 2009.

Chickering, Roger. *"We Men Who Feel Most German": A Cultural Study of the Pan-German League*. Boston: Allen & Unwin, 1984.

Chu, Winson. "Volksgemeinschaften unter sich. German Minorities and Regionalism in Poland, 1918-39." In *German History from the Margins*, edited by Gregor, Roemer and Roseman, 104–26. Bloomington: Indiana University Press, 2006.

Cocks, Geoffrey, *The State of Health: Illness in Nazi Germany*. Oxford: Oxford University Press, 2012.

– *Psycho Therapy in the Third Reich. The Göring Institute*. 2nd ed. New Brunswick: Transactions, 1997.

Cohen, Deborah. *The War Come Home: Disabled Veterans in Britain and Germany, 1914–1939*. Berkeley: University of California Press, 2001.

Conrad, Sebastian, *Globalisierung und Nation im deutschen Kaiserreich*. München: C. H. Beck, 2006.

Court, Jürgen. *Deutsche Sportwissenschaft in der Weimarer Republik und im Nationalsozialismus.* 2 vols. Berlin: LIT Verlag, 2008 and 2014.

– Sportanthropometrie und Sportpsychologie in der Weimarer Republik," *Sportwissenschaft* 32 (2002): 401–14.

Cowan, Michael. *Cult of the Will: Nervousness and German Modernity.* University Park: Pennsylvania State University Press, 2008.

Cowan, Michael, and Kai Marcel Sicks, eds. *Leibhaftige Moderne. Körper in Kunst und Massenmedien 1918–1933.* Bielefeld: Transcript, 2005.

Crew, David, ed. *Nazism and German Society, 1933-1945.* London and New York: Routledge, 1994.

Czech, Michaela. *Frauen und Sport im nationalsozialistischen Deutschland. Eine Untersuchung zur weiblichen Sportrealität in einem patriarchalischen Herrschaftssystem.* Berlin: Tischler, 1994.

Dickinson, Edward Ross. "Biopolitics, Fascism, Democracy. Some Reflections on Our Discourse about Modernity." *Central European History* 37, no. 1 (2004): 1–47.

– "Citizenship, Vocational Training, and Reaction: Continuation Schooling and the Prussian 'Youth Cultivation' Decree of 1911." *European History Quarterly* 29 (1999): 109–47.

– *The Politics of German Child Welfare from the Empire to the Federal Republic.* Cambridge: Harvard University Press, 1996.

Dinçkal, Noyan. *Sportlandschaften. Sport, Raum und (Massen-)Kultur in Deutschland 1880–1930.* Göttingen: Vandenhoeck & Ruprecht, 2013.

– "Das gesunde Maß an Schädigung. Die Inszenierung von Sport als Wissenschaft während der Dresdner Hygiene-Ausstellung 1911." *Historische Anthropologie* 17 (2009): 17–37.

– "Der Körper als Argument. Die Deutsche Hochschule für Leibesübungen und die Produktion wissenschaftlicher Gewissheiten über den Nutzen des Sports." In *Sport auf dem Weg in die Moderne,* edited by Krüger, 173–97. Berlin: LIT Verlag, 2009.

– "Medikomechanik. Maschinengymnastik zwischen orthopädischer Apparatebehandlung und geselligem Muskeltraining, 1880-1918/19." *Technikgeschichte* 74, no. 3 (2007): 227–50.

Dogliani, Patrizia. "Sport and Fascism." *Journal of Modern Italian Studies* 5, no. 3 (2000): 326–48.

Dowe, Dieter, Karlheinz Kuba, and Manfred Wilke, eds. *FDBG-Lexikon. Funktion, Struktur, Kader und Entwicklung einer Massenorganisation der SED (1945–1990).* Berlin: Friedrich-Ebert-Stiftung, 2009. Accessed 3 July 2012. http://library.fes.de/FDGB-Lexikon/rahmen/lexikon_frame.html.

Ebbinghaus, Angelika, and Klaus Dörner, eds. *Vernichten und Heilen. Der Nürnberger Ärzteprozess und seine Folgen*. Berlin. Aufbau, 2001.

Ebbinghaus, Angelika, Klaus Dörner, and Karl Heinz Roth. "Kriegswunden. Die kriegschirurgischen Experimente in den Konzentrationslagern und ihre Hintergründe." In *Vernichten und Heilen*, edited by Ebbinghaus and Dörner, 177–218. Berlin: Aufbau, 2001.

Echternkamp, Jörg, ed. *Germany and the Second World War.* Vol 9.1 of *Politicization, Disintegration, and the Struggle for Survival*. Oxford: Clarendon Press, 2008.

– "At War, Abroad and at Home: The Essential Features of German Society in the Second World War." In Vol. 9.1 of *Germany and the Second World War*, edited by Echternkamp, 1–109. Oxford: Clarendon Press, 2008.

– *Das Deutsche Reich und der Zweite Welkrieg. Vol. 9.2 of Die Deutsche Kriegsgesellschaft 1939-1945.* München: DVA, 2005.

Eckart, Wolfgang U., ed. *Man, Medicine, and the State: The Human Body as an Object of Medical Research in the 20th Century*. Stuttgart: Franz Steiner, 2006.

Eghigian, Greg. *Disability, Insurance, and the Birth of the Social Entitlement State in Germany*. Ann Arbor: University of Michigan Press, 2000.

Ehmer, Josef, ed. *"Arbeit": Geschichte, Gegenwart, Zukunft*. Leipzig: Akad. Verl.-Anst., 2002.

Eichberg, Henning. *Leistung, Spannung, Geschwindigkeit. Sport und Tanz im gesellschaftlichen Wandel des 18./19. Jahrhunderts*. Stuttgart: Klett Cotta, 1978.

Eisenberg, Christiane. *'English Sports' und deutsche Bürger. Eine Gesellschaftsgeschichte 1800–1939*. Paderborn: Ferdinand Schöningh, 1999.

– "Massensport in der Weimarer Republik. Ein statistischer Überblick." *Archiv für Sozialgeschichte* 33 (1993): 137–77.

Eley, Geoff, and Keith Nield. *The Future of Class in History: What's Left of the Social?* Ann Arbor: University of Michigan Press, 2007.

Eley, Geoff. *Reshaping the German Right: Radical Nationalism and Political Change After Bismarck*, 1980. Reprint, Ann Arbor: University of Michigan Press, 1991.

Erenberg, Lewis. *The Greatest Fight of Our Generation. Louis vs. Schmeling.* Oxford: Oxford University Press, 2006.

Etzemüller Thomas. *Ein immerwährender Untergang. Der apokalyptische Bevölkerungsdiskurs im 20. Jahrhundert*. Bielefeld: Transcript, 2007.

Fasbender, Sebastian. *Zwischen Arbeitersport und Arbeitssport. Werksport an Rhein und Ruhr 1921–1938*. Göttingen: Cuvillier, 1997.

Federspiel, Ruth. *Soziale Mobilität im Berlin des zwanzigsten Jahrhunderts. Frauen und Männer in Berlin-Neukölln 1905–1957*. Berlin: de Gruyter, 1999.

Felsch, Philipp. *Laborlandschaften. Physiologische Alpenreisen im 19. Jahrhundert*. Göttingen: Wallstein, 2007.

– "Volkssport. Zur Ökonomie der körperlichen Leistungsprüfung im Nationalsozialismus." *SportZeit* 1, no. 3 (2001): 5–29.
Flachowsky, Sören. "'Das Institut erfreut sich in den Kreisen der Industrie des Ruhrbezirks ganz besonderer Beliebtheit.' Das Kaiser-Wilhelm-Institut für Arbeitsphysiologie und die Montanindustrie 1913–1945." In *Arbeit, Leistung,* edited by Plesser and Thamer, 357–424. Stuttgart: Franz Steiner, 2012.
Fleischhacker, Jochen, "Menschen und Güterökonomie. Anmerkungen zu Rudolf Goldscheid's demoökonomischem Gesellschaftsentwurf." In *Wissen, Politik, und Öffentlichkeit,* edited by Ash, 207–29. Wien: WUV, 2002.
Föllmer, Moritz. *Individuality and Modernity in Berlin: Self and Society from Weimar to the Wall.* Cambridge: Cambridge University Press, 2013.
– "Was Nazism Collectivistic? Redefining the Individual in Berlin, 1930-1945." *Journal of Modern History* 82, no. 1 (2010): 61–100.
Foucault, Michel. *The History of Sexuality*: *Vol. 1.* London: Penguin, 2008.
Frese, Matthias. "Vom 'NS-Musterbetrieb' zum 'Kriegsmusterbetrieb'. Zum Verhältnis von deutscher Arbeitsfront und Großindustrie." In *Der zweite Weltkrieg,* edited by Michalka, 382–401. München: Piper, 1997.
– *Betriebspolitik im Dritten Reich. Deutsche Arbeitsfront, Unternehmer und Staatsbürokratie in der westdeutschen Großindustrie.* Paderborn: Ferdinand Schöningh, 1991.
Frevert, Ute. *Women in German History: From Bourgeois Emancipation to Sexual Liberation.* Oxford and New York: Berg, 1989.
– *Krankheit als politisches Problem. Soziale Unterschichten in Preussen zwischen medizinischer Polizei und staatlicher Sozialversicherung.* Göttingen: Vandenhoeck & Ruprecht, 1984.
Frohman, Larry. *Poor Relief and Welfare in Germany from the Reformation to World War I.* Cambridge: Cambridge University Press, 2008.
– "Prevention, Welfare and Citizenship: The War on Tuberculosis and Infant Mortality in Germany, 1900-1930." *Central European History* 39 (2006): 431–81.
Garski-Hoffmann, Petra, André Kaiser, Steffen Seischab, and Reinhard Tietzen. *Nürtingen 1918–1950. Weimarer Republik, Nationalsozialismus, Nachkriegszeit.* Nürtingen: Sindlinger-Burchartz, 2011.
Garski-Hoffmann, Petra. "Ausländische Zwangsarbeiter." In *Nürtingen 1918–1950,* edited by Garski-Hoffmann et al., 300–18. Nürtingen: Sindlinger-Burchartz, 2011.
Geary, Dick. "Working Class Identities in the Third Reich." In *Nazism, War, and Genocide,* edited by Gregor, 42–55. Exeter: University of Exeter Press, 2005.
Gems, Gerald G. "Welfare Capitalism and Blue-Collar Sport: The Legacy of Labor Unrest." *Rethinking History* 5, no. 1 (2001): 43–58.

Gerstner, Alexandra, Barbara Könczöl, and Janina Hentwig, eds. *Der Neue Mensch. Utopien, Leitbilder und Reformkonzepte zwischen den Weltkriegen.* Frankfurt: Peter Lang, 2006.

Geuter, Ulrich. *The Professionalization of German Psychology in Nazi Germany.* Cambridge: Cambridge University Press, 1992.

Geyer, Michael, and Sheila Fitzpatrick, eds. *Beyond Totalitarianism: Stalinism and Nazism Compared.* Cambridge: Cambridge University Press, 2009.

Geyer, Michael. "Restorative Elites, German Society and the Nazi Pursuit of War." In *Fascist Italy and Nazi Germany,* edited by Bessel, 134–64. Cambridge: Cambridge University Press, 1996.

Gillingham, John. "The 'Deproletarianization' of German Society: Vocational Training in the Third Reich." *Journal of Social History* 19 (1986): 423–32.

Gilman, Sander, and Claudia Schmölders, eds. *Gesichter der Weimarer Republik. Eine physiognomische Kulturgeschichte.* Köln: DuMont, 2000.

Goldhagen, Daniel. *Hitler's Willing Executioners. Ordinary Germans and the Holocaust.* New York: Vintage, 1997.

Goltermann, Svenja. *Körper der Nation. Habitusformierung und die Politik des Turnens.* Göttingen: Vandenhoeck & Ruprecht, 1998.

Graml, Hermann, and Klaus-Dietmar Henke, eds. *Nach Hitler. Der schwierige Umgang mit unserer Geschichte.* München: Oldenbourg, 1987.

Grant, Susan. *Physical Culture and Sport in Soviet Society: Propaganda, Acculturation, and Transformation in the 1920s and 1930s.* London and New York: Routledge, 2013.

Graumann, Carl Friedrich, ed. *Psychologie im Nationalsozialismus.* Berlin: Springer, 1985.

Grazia, Victoria de. *The Culture of Consent: Mass Organization of Leisure in Fascist Italy.* Cambridge: Cambridge University Press, 1981.

Gregor, Neil, Niels H. Roemer, and Mark Roseman, eds. *German History from the Margins.* Bloomington: Indiana University Press, 2006.

Gregor, Neil, ed. *Nazism, War, and Genocide.* Exeter: University of Exeter Press, 2005.

– *Stern und Hakenkreuz. Daimler-Benz im Dritten Reich.* Berlin: Propyläen, 1998.

Grüttner, Michael. *Studenten im Dritten Reich.* Paderborn: Schöningh, 1995.

Gundlach, Horst. ed. *Arbeiten zur Psychologiegeschichte.* Göttingen: Hogrefe, 1994.

Gunga, Hanns Christian. *Nathan Zuntz: His Life and Work in the Fields of High Altitude Physiology and Aviation Medicine.* Amsterdam and London: Academic Press, 2009.

Guttsman, Wilhelm L. *Worker's Culture in Weimar Germany: Between Tradition and Commitment.* New York: Berg, 1990.

Hachtmann Rüdiger. "Arbeit und Arbeitsfront: Ideologie und Praxis." In *Arbeit im Nationalsozialismus*, edited by Buggeln and Wildt, 87–106. Berlin: De Gruyter, 2014.

– *Ein Koloß auf tönernen Füßen. Das Gutachten des Wirtschaftsprüfers Karl Eicke über die Deutsche Arbeitsfront vom 31. Juli 1936*. München: Oldenbourg, 2006.

– *Industriearbeit im "Dritten Reich." Untersuchungen zu den Lohn- und Arbeitsbedingungen in Deutschland*. Göttingen: Vandenhoeck & Ruprecht, 1989.

Hagner, Michael. "Verwundete Gesichter, verletzte Gehirne. Zur Deformation des Kopfes im Ersten Weltkrieg." In *Gesichter der Weimarer Republik*, edited by Gilman and Schmölders, 78–95. Köln: DuMont, 2000.

Hahn, Judith. *Grawitz, Genzken, Gebhardt. Drei Karrieren im Sanitätsdienst der SS*. Münster: Klemm & Oelschlaeger, 2008.

Hancock, Eleanor. "Employment in Wartime. The Experience of German Women during the Second World War." *War and Society* 12, no. 2 (1994): 43–68.

Harney, Klaus. "Fortbildungsschulen." In Vol. 4 of *Handbuch der deutschen Bildungsgeschichte*, edited by Berg, 380–8. München: C. H. Beck, 1991.

Hartmann, Heinrich. *Der Volkskörper bei der Musterung. Militärstatistik und Demographie in Europa vor dem Ersten Weltkrieg*. Göttingen: Wallstein Verlag, 2011.

Harvey, Elizabeth. *Women and the Nazi East: Agents and Witnesses of Germanization*. New Haven and London: Yale University Press, 2005.

– *Youth and the Welfare State in Weimar Germany*. Oxford: Clarendon, 1993.

Hau, Michael. "Constitutional Therapy and Clinical Racial Hygiene in Weimar and Nazi Germany." *Journal of the History of Medicine and Allied Sciences*. doi: 10.1093/jhmas/jrv034.

– "Volksertüchtigung, Wehrbereitschaft und Volkskraft. Debatten vor und nach 1914." *Limbus. Australisches Jahrbuch für germanistische Literatur- und Kulturwissenschaft* 7 (2014): 181–96.

– "Sports in the Human Economy. '*Leibesübungen*,' Medicine, Psychology, and Performance Enhancement during the Weimar Republic." *Central European History* 41 (2008): 381–412.

– *The Cult of Health and Beauty in Germany: A Social History 1890–1930*. Chicago: University of Chicago Press, 2003.

– "The Holistic Gaze in German Medicine, 1890-1930," *Bulletin of the History of Medicine* 74 (2000): 495–524.

Havemann, Nils. *Fussball unterm Hakenkreuz. Der DFB zwischen Sport, Politik und Kommerz*. Frankfurt: Campus, 2005.

Hayes, Peter. *Industry and Ideology: IG Farben in the Nazi Era*. Cambridge: Cambridge University Press, 2001.

Heim, Susanne. *Kalorien, Kautschuk, und Karrieren: Pflanzenzüchtung und landwirtschaftliche Forschung in Kaiser-Wilhelm-Instituten, 1933–1945.* Göttingen: Wallstein, 2003.

Herbert, Ulrich. *Hitler's Foreign Workers: Enforced Foreign Labor in Germany under the Third Reich.* Translated by William Templer. Cambridge: Cambridge University Press, 1997.

– *Best. Biographische Studien über Radikalismus, Weltanschaung und Vernunft 1903–1989.* 2nd ed. Bonn: Dietz, 1996.

– "'The Real Mystery in Germany.' The German Working Class during the Nazi Dictatorship." In *Confronting the Nazi Past,* edited by Burleigh, 23–36. London: Palgrave MacMillan, 1996.

– "'Die guten und die schlechten Zeiten.' Überlegungen zur diachronen Analyse lebensgeschichtlicher Interviews." In *"Die Jahre weiß man nicht,"* edited by Niethammer, 67–96. Bonn: J. H. W. Dietz Nachf, 1983.

Herzog, Dagmar. *Sex after Fascism: Memory and Morality in Twentieth Century Germany.* Princeton: Princeton University Press, 2007.

Heuel, Eberhard. *Der umworbene Stand. Die ideologische Integration der Arbeiter im Nationalsozialismus.* Frankfurt/New York: Campus, 1989.

Hinrichs, Peter. *Um die Seele des Arbeiters. Arbeitspsychologie, Industrie- und Berufssoziologie in Deutschland, 1871–1945.* Köln: Pahl Rugenstein, 1981.

Hoberman, John. *Testosterone Dreams: Rejuvenation, Aphrodisia, Doping.* Berkeley: University of California Press, 2005.

– *Mortal Engines. The Science of Performance and the Dehumanization of Sport.* New York: Free Press, 1992.

– "The Early Development of Sports Medicine in Germany." In *Sport and Exercise Science,* edited by Berryman and Park, 233–82. Urbana: University of Illinois Press, 1992.

Hörath, Julia. "'Arbeitsscheue Volksgenossen'. Leistungsbereitschaft als Kriterium der Inklusion und Exklusion." in *Arbeit im Nationalsozialismus,* edited by Buggeln and Wildt, 308–28. Berlin: De Gruyter, 2014.

Hoffmann, David L., and Annette F. Timm. "Utopian Biopolitics. Reproductive Policies, Gender Roles, and Sexuality in Nazi Germany and the Soviet Union." In *Beyond Totalitarianism,* edited by Geyer and Fitzpatrick, 87–129. Cambridge: Cambridge University Press, 2009.

Holt, Richard. *Sport and Society in Modern France.* London: McMillan, 1981.

Hong, Young-Sun. *Welfare, Modernity, and the Weimar State, 1919–1933.* Princeton: Princeton University Press, 1998.

Hürter, Johannes. *Wilhelm Groener. Reichswehrminister am Ende der Weimarer Republik.* München: Oldenbourg, 1993.

Jahnke, Karl Heinz, and Michael Buddrus, eds. *Deutsche Jugend 1933–1945. Eine Dokumentation.* Hamburg: VSA-Verlag, 1989.

Jensen, Erik N. *Body by Weimar: Athletes, Gender, and German Modernity.* Oxford: Oxford University Press, 2010.
Joch, Winfried. *Politische Leibeserziehung und ihre Theorie im nationalsozialistischen Deutschland.* Frankfurt: Lang, 1976.
Johnson, Molly Wilkinson. *Training Socialist Citizens: Sports and the State in East Germany.* Leiden: Brill, 2008.
Jones, Eugene Larry. "The German National Union of Commercial Employees from 1928 to 1933." *Journal of Modern History* 48, no. 3 (1976): 462–82.
Kaden, Helma, and Helmut Westphal. "Der Missbrauch des Sports zur Formierung der faschistischen V. Kolonne in Polen (1934-1938)." *Theorie und Praxis der Körperkultur* 21 (1972): 581–5.
Kater, Michael. "The Reich Vocational Contest and Students of Higher Learning in Nazi Germany." *Central European History* 7 (1974): 225–61.
Katzer, Nikolaus. "Körperkult und Bewegungszwang. Zur gesellschaftlichen Dynamik des frühen sowjetischen Sportsystems." In *Sport auf dem Weg in die Moderne,* edited by Krüger, 257–83. Berlin: LIT Verlag, 2009.
Kershaw, Ian. "'Volksgemeinschaft.' Potential und Grenzen eines neuen Forschungkonzepts." *Vierteljahreshefte für Zeitgeschichte* 59 (2011): 1–17.
– *The End: Hitler's Germany 1944–1945.* London: Allen Lane, 2011.
– *Popular Opinion and Political Dissent in the Third Reich: Bavaria 1933–1945.* Oxford: Clarendon, 1983.
Keys, Barbara. "The Body as Political Space: Comparing Physical Education under Nazism and Stalinism." *German History* 27, no. 3 (2009): 395–413.
– *Globalizing Sport: National Rivalry and International Community in the 1930s.* Cambridge: Harvard University Press, 2006.
Kienitz, Sabine. *Beschädigte Helden. Kriegsinvalidität und Körperbilder 1914–1923.* Paderborn: Ferdinand Schöningh, 2008.
Killen, Andreas. *Berlin Electropolis: Shock, Nerves, and German Modernity.* Berkeley: University of California Press, 2006.
Klein, Marie Luise. "Betriebssport in der Bundesrepublik Deutschland." In *Arbeitnehmerinitiativen,* edited by Pfister, 121–30. Sankt Augustin: Academia, 1999.
Klemperer, Victor. *LTI. Notizbuch eines Philologen.* 20th ed. Leipzig: Reclam, 2005.
Klönne, Arno. *Jugend im Dritten Reich. Die Hitlerjugend und ihre Gegner.* Köln: Papyrossa, 2003.
Knox, MacGregor. *Common Destiny: Dictatorship, Foreign Policy, and War in Fascist Italy and Nazi Germany.* Cambridge: Cambridge University Press, 2000.
König, Wolfgang. *Volkswagen, Volksempfänger, Volksgemeinschaft. "Volksprodukte" im Dritten Reich: Vom Scheitern einer nationalsozialistischen Konsumgesellschaft.* Paderborn: Ferdinand Schöningh, 2004.

Koonz, Claudia. *The Nazi Conscience*. Cambridge: Harvard University Press, 2005.

– *Mothers in the Fatherland: Women, the Family, and Nazi Politics*. New York: St. Martin's Press, 1987.

Kramer, Nicole. *Volksgenossinnen an der Heimatfront. Mobilisierung, Verhalten, Erinnerung*. Göttingen: Vandenhoeck & Ruprecht, 2011.

Krüger, Arnd. *Theodor Lewald. Sportführer ins Dritte Reich*. Berlin: Bartels & Wernitz, 1975.

Krüger, Michael. *Der deutsche Sport auf dem Weg in die Moderne. Carl Diem und seine Zeit*. Berlin: LIT Verlag, 2009.

–, ed. *"mens sana in coprore sano." Gymnastik, Turnen, Spiel und Sport als Gegenstand der Bildungspolitik vom 18. bis zum 20. Jahrhundert*. Hamburg: Czwalina, 2008.

– *Körperkultur und Nationsbildung: Die Geschichte des Turnens in der Reichsgründungsära—eine Detailstudie über die Deutschen*. Schorndorf: Hofmann, 1996.

Kühne, Thomas. *Kameradschaft. Die Soldaten des nationalsozialistischen Krieges und das 20. Jahrhundert*. Göttingen: Vandenhoeck & Ruprecht, 2005.

Labisch, Alfons, and Reinhard Spree, eds. *Medizinische Deutungsmacht im sozialen Wandel*. Bonn: Psychiatrie-Verlag, 1989.

Lämmer, Manfred, ed. *Deutschland in der Olympischen Bewegung. Eine Zwischenbilanz*. Frankfurt: NOK, 1999.

Langenfeld, Hans. "Die ersten beiden Jahrzehnte." In *Deutschland in der Olympischen Bewegung*, edited by Lämmer, 41–83. Frankfurt: NOK, 1999.

Langewiesche, Dieter. *Liberalismus in Deutschland*. Frankfurt: Suhrkamp, 1988.

– "The Impact of the German Labor Movement on Workers' Culture." *Journal of Modern History* 59 (1987): 506–23.

Large, David Clay. *Nazi Games: The Olympics of 1936*. New York: Norton, 2007.

Lebovic, Nitzan. The Philosophy of Life and Death. Ludwig Klages and the Rise of Nazi Biopolitics. New York: Palgrave Macmillan, 2013.

Lehnstaedt, Stephan. *Okkupation im Osten. Besatzeralltag in Warschau und Minsk 1939–1944*. München: Oldenbourg, 2010.

Lemke, Thomas. *Gouvernementalität und Biopolitik*. 2nd ed. Wiesbaden: VS-Verlag, 2008.

– Susanne Krasmann, and Ulrich Bröckling. "Gouvernementalität, Neoliberalismus und Selbsttechnologien." In *Gouvernementalität der Gegenwart*, edited by Bröckling et al., 7–40. Frankfurt: Suhrkamp, 2000.

Lerner, Paul. *Hysterical Men: War, Psychiatry, and the Politics of Trauma in Germany*. Ithaca: Cornell University Press, 2003.

Lidtke, Vernon. *The Alternative Culture: Socialist Labor in Imperial Germany.* New York and Oxford: Oxford University Press, 1985.

Linton, Derek S. "Preparing German Youth for War." In *Anticipating Total War,* edited by Boemeke, Chickering, and Förster, 167–87. Cambridge: Cambridge University Press, 1999.

– *"Who Has the Youth, Has the Future": The Campaign to Save Young Workers in Imperial Germany.* Cambridge: Cambridge University Press, 1991.

Lück, Helmut. "'Und halte Lust und Leid und Leben auf meiner ausgestreckten Hand.' Zu Leben und Werk von Robert Werner Schulte." In *Arbeiten zur Psychologiegeschichte,* edited by Gundlach, 39–48. Göttingen: Hogrefe, 1994.

Lüdtke, Alf. "'Deutsche Qualitätsarbeit'-ihre Bedeutung für das Mitmachen von Arbeitern und Unternehmern im Nationalsozialismus." In *Firma Topf & Söhne,* edited by Assmann et al., 123–38. Frankfurt: Campus, 2002.

– "German Work and German Workers. The Impact of Symbols on the Exclusion of Jews in Nazi Germany. Reflections on an Open Question." In *Depth of German Antisemitism,* edited by Bankier, 296–311. New York: Berghahn Books, 2000.

–, ed. *The History of Everyday Life: Reconstructing Historical Experiences and Ways of Life.* Princeton: Princeton University Press, 1995.

– "What Happened to the 'Fiery Red Glow.'" In *History of Everyday Life,* edited by Lüdtke, 198–251. Princeton: Princeton University Press. 1995.

– "The 'Honour of Labour': Industrial Workers and the Power of Symbols under National Socialism." In *Nazism and German Society,* edited by Crew, 67–109. London and New York: Routledge, 1994.

Luh, Andreas. *Betriebssport zwischen Arbeitgeberinteressen und Arbeitnehmerbedürfnissen. Eine historische Analyse vom Kaiserreich bis zur Gegenwart.* Aachen: Meyer & Meyer, 1998.

Mackenzie, Michael. "The Athlete as Machine: A Figure of Modernity in Weimar Germany." In *Leibhaftige Moderne,* edited by Cowan and Sicks, 48–62. Bielefeld: Transcript, 2005.

Madajczyk, Czeslaw. *Die Okkupationspolitik Nazideutschlands in Polen 1939–1945.* Translated by Berthold Puchert. Köln: Pahl-Rugenstein, 1988.

Mai, Gunther. "Arbeiterschaft zwischen Sozialismus, Nationalismus und Nationalsozialismus." In *Schatten der Vergangenheit,* edited by Backes et al., 195–217. Frankfurt/Berlin: Propyläen 1990.

Mallmann, Klaus-Michael, and Gerhard Paul. *Herrschaft und Alltag. Ein Industrierevier im Dritten Reich. Widerstand und Verweigerung im Saarland.* Vol. 2. Bonn: J. H. W. Dietz, 1991.

Mason, Timothy. *Nazism, Fascism and the Working Class*. Edited by Jane Caplan. Cambridge: Cambridge University Press, 1995.
– *Social Policy in the Third Reich: The Working Class and the 'National Community.'* Oxford: Berg, 1993.
– "The Workers' Opposition in Nazi Germany." *History Workshop Journal* 11 (1981): 120–37.
–, ed. *Arbeiterklasse und Volksgemeinschaft*. Opladen: Westdeutscher Verlag, 1975.
Maubach, Franka. *Die Stellung halten. Kriegserfahrungen und Lebensgeschichten von Wehrmachtshelferinnen*. Göttingen: Vandenhoeck & Ruprecht, 2009.
Mertens, Lothar. *"Nur politisch Würdige." Die DFG-Forschungsförderung im Dritten Reich 1933–1937*. Berlin: Akademie Verlag, 2004.
Meschnig, Alexander. *Der Wille zur Bewegung. Militärischer Traum und totalitäres Programm. Eine Mentalitätsgeschichte vom Ersten Weltkrieg zum Nationalsozialismus*. Bielefeld: Transcript, 2008.
Meskill, David. *Optimizing the German Workforce: Labor Administration from Bismarck to the Economic Miracle*. New York: Berghahn Books, 2010.
– "Characterological Psychology and the German Political Economy in the Weimar Period (1919-1933)." *History of Psychology* 7, no. 1 (2004): 3–19.
Métraux, Alexandré. "Die angewandte Psychologie vor und nach 1933 in Deutschland." In *Psychologie im Nationalsozialismus*, edited by Graumann, 222–62. Berlin: Springer, 1985.
Michalka, Wolfgang, ed. *Der zweite Weltkrieg. Analysen, Grundzüge, Forschungsbilanz*. München: Piper, 1997.
Michl, Susanne. *Im Dienste des "Volkskörpers." Deutsche und französiche Ärzte im Ersten Weltkrieg*. Göttingen: Vandenhoeck & Ruprecht, 2007.
Mörath, Verena. *Die Trimm-Aktionen des deutschen Sportbundes zur Bewegungs- und Sportförderung in der BRD 1970–1994* (Veröffentlichungsreihe der Forschungsgruppe Public Health. Forschungsschwerpunkt Arbeit, Sozialstruktur und Sozialstaat). Berlin: Wissenschaftszentrum für Sozialforschung, 2005.
Morsch, Günter. *Arbeit und Brot. Studien zur Lage, Stimmung, Einstellung und Verhalten der deutschen Arbeiterschaft 1933–1936/37*. Frankfurt: Peter Lang, 1993.
Nagel, Anne C. *Hitler's Bildungsreformer. Das Reichsministerium für Wissenschaft, Erziehung und Volksbildung*. Frankfurt: S. Fischer, 2012.
Neitzel, Sönke, and Harald Welzer. *Soldaten On Fighting, Killing, and Dying: The Secret WW II Transcripts of German POWS*. Melbourne: Scribe, 2011.
Neumann, Alexander. "Das KWIA und der Kampf gegen die Ermüdung." In *Arbeit, Leistung*, edited by Plesser and Thamer, 171–95. Stuttgart: Franz Steiner, 2012.

Niemann, Hans Werner. "'Volksgemeinschaft' als Konsumgemeinschaft?" In *'Volksgemeinschaft,'* edited by Schmiechen-Ackermann, 87–109. Paderborn: Ferdinand Schöningh, 2012.

Niethammer, Lutz, ed. *"Die Jahre weiß man nicht wo, wo man die heute hinsetzen soll." Faschismuserfahrungen im Ruhrgebiet. Lebensgeschichte und Sozialkultur im Ruhrgebiet 1930–1960.* Bonn: J. H. W. Dietz Nachf., 1983.

Nolan, Mary. "Rationalization, Racism, and Resistenz: Recent Studies of Work and the Working Class in Nazi Germany." *International Labor and Working-Class History* 48 (1995): 131–51.

– *Visions of Modernity: American Business and the Modernization of Germany.* New York: Oxford, 1994.

Nolte, Paul. "Leistung -ein bürgerliches, kein faschistisches Prinzip." Accessed 6 October 2012. http://lesesaal.faz.net/wehler/exp_forum.php?rid=9.

Nolzen, Armin. "The NSDAP, the War, and German Society." In Vol. 9.1 of *Germany and the Second World War,* edited by Echternkamp, 111–206. Oxford: Clarendon Press, 2008.

Osten, Philipp. *Die Modellanstalt. Über den Aufbau einer "modernen Krüppelfürsorge" 1905–1933.* Frankfurt: Mabuse, 2004.

Panayi, Panikos, ed. *Weimar and Nazi Germany: Continuities and Discontinuities.* Harlow: Longman, 2001.

Patel, Kiran Klaus. *Soldiers of Labor: Labor Service in Nazi Germany and New Deal America, 1933–1945.* Cambridge: Cambridge University Press, 2005.

Patzel-Mattern, Katja. *Ökonomische Effizienz und sozialer Ausgleich. Die industrielle Psychotechnik in der Weimarer Republik.* Stuttgart: Franz Steiner Verlag, 2010.

Peiffer, Lorenz. "Der Ausschluss der deutschen Juden 1933 aus deutschen Turn- und Sportvereinen und das Beschweigen nach 1945. Alte und neue Perspektiven deutscher Sporthistoriografie." *Zeitschrift für Geschichtswissenschaft* 59, no. 3 (2011): 217–29.

– *Sport im Nationalsozialismus: Zum aktuellen Stand der sporthistorischen Forschung. Eine kommentierte Bibliographie.* Göttingen: Die Werkstatt, 2009.

–, and Dietrich Schulze-Marmeling, eds. *Hakenkreuz und rundes Leder. Fußball im Nationalsozialismus,* Göttingen: Die Werkstatt, 2008.

– "'Auf zur Gefolgschaft und zur Tat!': Deutsche Turnerschaft und Nationalsozialismus –zwischen Selbstgleichschaltung und Selbstbehauptung." *IWK: Internationale wissenschaftliche Korrespondenz zur Geschichte der deutschen Arbeiterbewegung* 35 (1999): 530–48.

– *Die deutsche Turnerschaft. Ihre politische Stellung in der Zeit der Weimarer Republik und des Nationalsozialismus.* Ahrensburg: Czwalina, 1976.

Peukert, Detlev. *The Weimar Republic: The Crisis of Classical Modernity*. Translated by Richard Deveson. New York: Hill and Wang, 1987.

– *Grenzen der Sozialdisziplinierung. Aufstieg und Krise der deutschen Jugendfürsorge, 1878–1932*. Köln: Bund-Verlag, 1986.

–, and Jürgen Reulecke, eds. *Die Reihen fast geschlossen. Beiträge zur Geschichte des Alltags unterm Nationalsozialismus*. Wuppertal: Peter Hammer, 1981.

Pfister, Gertrud. "Neue Frauen und weibliche Schwäche. Geschlechterarrangements und Sportdiskurse in der Weimarer Republik." In *Sport auf dem Weg in die Moderne*, edited by Krüger, 285–310. Berlin: LIT Verlag, 2009.

– *Zwischen Arbeitnehmerinitiativen und Unternehmensinteressen. Zur Geschichte des Betriebssports in Deutschland*. Sankt Augustin: Academia Verlag, 1999.

– "The Medical Discourse on Female Physical Culture in Germany in the 19th and early 20th Centuries." *Journal of Sport History* 17 (1990): 183–98.

Planert, Ute. "Der dreifache Körper des Volkes. Sexualität, Biopolitik und die Wissenschaften vom Leben." *Geschichte und Gesellschaft* 26 (2000): 539–76.

Platz, Johannes, Lutz Raphael, and Ruth Rosenberger. "Anwendungsorientierte Betriebspsychologie und Eignungsdiagnostik." In *Wissenschaften und Wissenschaftspolitik*, edited by vom Bruch und Kaderas, 291–309. Stuttgart: Franz Steiner, 2002.

Plesser, Theo, and Hans-Ulrich Thamer, eds. *Arbeit, Leistung, Ernährung. Vom Kaiser-Wilhelm-Institut für Arbeitsphysiologie in Berlin zum Max-Planck-Institut für molekulare Physiologie und Leibniz Institut für Arbeitsforschung in Dortmund*. Stuttgart: Franz Steiner, 2012.

Poore, Carol. *Disability in Twentieth-Century German Culture*. Ann Arbor: University of Michigan Press, 2007.

Poovey, Mary. *Uneven Developments: The Ideological Work of Gender in Mid-Victorian England*. Chicago: University of Chicago Press, 1988.

Prange, Klaus. "Der Zentralausschuß und die Finanzierung von Leibesübungen, Spiel und Sport." *Sportwissenschaft* 24 (1994): 29–48.

– "Der Zentralausschuß zur Förderung der Volks- und Jugendspiele (1891-1922)." *Stadion* 17 (1991): 193–206.

Presner, Todd Samuel. *Muscular Judaism: The Jewish Body and the Politics of Regeneration*. London and New York: Routledge, 2007.

Price, Matthew. "Bodies and Souls. The Rehabilitation of Maimed Soldiers in Germany and France During the First World War." PhD diss., Stanford University, 1998.

Przyrembel, Alexandra. *"Rassenschande." Reinheitsmythen und Vernichtungslegitimation im Nationalsozialismus*. Göttingen: Vandenhoeck & Ruprecht, 2003.

Rabinbach, Anson. *The Human Motor: Energy, Fatigue, and the Origins of Modernity*. New York: Basic Books, 1990.

Raupach, Andrea. *Ignaz Kaup (1870–1944). Hygieniker zwischen Sozial- und Rassenhygiene*. PhD diss., Mainz, 1989.

Read, John. "Physical Culture and Sport in the early Soviet Period." *Australian Slavonic and East European Studies* 10 (1996): 59–84.

Reeg, Karl-Peter. *Friedrich Georg Christian Bartels (1892–1968). Ein Beitrag zur Entwicklung der Leistungsmedizin im Nationalsozialismus*. Husum: Matthiesen Verlag, 1988.

Reith, Reinhold. "Leistungsgesellschaft? Diskussionen über Leistungslohn in historischer Perspektive." In *Arbeit*, edited by Ehmer, 115–36. Leipzig: Akad. Verl.-Anst., 2002.

Repp, Kevin. *Reformers, Critics, and the Path of German Modernity: Anti-Politics and the Search for Alternatives, 1890–1914*. Cambridge: Harvard University Press, 2001.

Reulecke, Jürgen. "Die Fahne mit dem goldenen Zahnrad: Der Leistungskampf der deutschen Betriebe." In *Reihen fast geschlossen*, edited by Peukert and Reulecke, 245–69. Wuppertal: Peter Hammer, 1981.

Roelcke, Volker. "Programm und Praxis der psychiatrischen Genetik an der Deutschen Forschungsanstalt für Psychiatrie unter Ernst Rüdin." In *Rassenforschung an Kaiser-Wilhelm-Instituten*, edited by Schmuhl, 38–67. Göttingen: Wallstein, 2003.

Rose, Nikolas. *Inventing Our Selves: Psychology, Power, and Personhood*. Cambridge: Cambridge University Press, 1996.

Rossol, Nadine. *Performing the Nation in Interwar Germany: Sport, Spectacle and Political Symbolism, 1926–1936*. New York: Palgrave Macmillan, 2010.

Rowley, Alison. "Sport in the Service of the State: Images of Physical Culture and Soviet Women, 1917-1941." *The International Journal of the History of Sport* 23, no. 8 (2006): 1314–40.

Rupke, Nicolaas, ed. *Science, Politics, and the Public Good*. London: Macmillan, 1988.

Sarasin, Philipp. *Geschichtswissenschaft und Diskursanalyse*. Frankfurt: Suhrkamp, 2003.

–, and Jakob Tanner. *Physiologie und industrielle Gesellschaft. Studien zur Verwissenschaftlichung des Körpers im 19. und 20. Jahrhundert*. Frankfurt: Suhrkamp, 1998.

Sattler, Friederike. "Arbeitsmobilisierung" and "Sozialistischer Wettbewerb." In *FDBG-Lexikon*, edited by Dowe et al. Berlin: Friedrich-Ebert-Stiftung, 2009. Accessed July 3, 2012. http://library.fes.de/FDGB-Lexikon/rahmen/lexikon_frame.html.

Schaar, Thorsten. *Vom Hitlerjungen zum Reichsjugendführer der NSDAP. Eine nationalsozialistische Karriere*. PhD diss., Univeristät Rostock, 1998.

Schäfer, Hans Dietrich. *Das gespaltene Bewußtsein. Vom Dritten Reich bis zu den langen Fünfziger Jahren*. Göttingen: Wallstein, 2009.

Schäfer, Josef. "Ministerialrat Dr. med. Arthur Mallwitz 1880-1968. Ein Leben für Sport, Sportmedizin und Gesundheitsfürsorge." PhD diss., Bonn, 2003.

Schäfer, Ralf. *Militarismus, Nationalismus, Antisemitismus: Carl Diem und die Politisierung des bürgerlichen Sports im Kaiserreich*. Berlin: Metropol, 2011.

–"Der Zentralausschuß für Volks- und Jugendspiele und seine Stellung in der deutschen Sportgeschichte." In *"mens sana in corpore sano,"* edited by Krüger, 41–55. Hamburg: Czwalina, 2008.

Schenk, Dieter. *Hans Frank. Hitler's Kronjurist und Generalgouverneur*. Frankfurt: S. Fischer, 2006.

Schmidt, Ulf. Karl Brandt. *The Nazi Doctor: Medicine and Power in the Third Reich*. London: Hambledon Continuum, 2007.

– *Justice at Nuremberg: Leo Alexander and the Nazi Doctor's Trial*. New York: Palgrave, 2004.

– *Medical Films, Ethics, and Euthanasia in Nazi Germany*. Husum: Matthiesen, 2002.

Schmiechen-Ackermann, Detlef, ed. *"Volksgemeinschaft": Mythos, wirkungsmächtige soziale Verheißung oder soziale Realität im "Dritten Reich"?* Paderborn, Ferdinand Schöningh, 2012.

Schmuhl, Hans Walter, ed. *Rassenforschung an Kaiser-Wilhelm-Instituten vor und nach 1933*. Göttingen: Wallstein, 2003.

Schneider, Christian and Cordelia Stillke and Bernd Leineweber. *Das Erbe der Napola: Versuch einer Generationengeschichte des Nationalsozialismus*. Hamburg: Hamburger Edition, 1996.

Schneider, Michael. *Unterm Hakenkreuz. Arbeiter und Arbeiterbewegung 1933–1939*. Bonn: J. H. W. Dietz, 1999.

Schneider William H. *Rockefeller Philanthropy and Modern Biomedicine: International Initiatives from World War I to the Cold War*. Bloomington: Indiana University Press, 2002.

Schoenbaum, David. *Hitler's Social Revolution: Class and Status in Nazi Germany, 1933–1939*. New York and London: W. W. Norton, 1980.

Schottdorf, Gertrud. *Arbeits- und Leistungsmedizin in der Weimarer Republik*. Husum: Matthiesen, 1995.

Schwartz, Michael. *Sozialistische Eugenik. Eugenische Sozialtechnologien in Debatten und Politik der deutschen Sozialdemokratie 1890–1933*. Bonn: Dietz, 1995.

Seischab, Steffen. "Nürtingen im zweiten Weltkrieg." In *Nürtingen 1918–1950*, edited by Garski-Hoffmann et al., 319–52. Nürtingen: Sindlinger-Burchartz, 2001.

Siegel, Tilla. "Whatever was the Attitude of German Workers? Reflections on Recent Interpretations." In *Fascist Italy and Nazi Germany*, edited by Bessel, 61–77. Cambridge: Cambridge University Press, 1996.

–, and Thomas von Freyberg. *Industrielle Rationalisierung unter dem Nationalsozialismus*. Frankfurt and New York: Campus, 1991.

– *Leistung und Lohn in der nationalsozialistischen Ordnung der Arbeit*. Opladen: Westdeutscher Verlag, 1989.

Siegelbaum, Lewis. *Stakhanovism and the Politics of Productivity in the USSR, 1935–1941*. Cambridge: Cambridge University Press, 1988.

Smelser, Ronald. *Robert Ley: Hitler's Labor Front Leader*. Oxford: Berg, 1988.

Spode, Hasso. "Fordism, Mass Tourism and the Third Reich: The 'Strength through Joy' Seaside resort as an Index Fossil." *Journal of Social History* 38, no. 1 (2004): 127–55.

Spoerer, Mark. "Die soziale Differenzierung der ausländischen Zivilarbeiter, Kriegsgefangenen und Häftlinge im Deutschen Reich." In Vol. 9.2 of *Das Deutsche Reich und der Zweite Weltkrieg*, edited by Echternkamp, 485–576. München: DVA, 2005.

Springmann, Veronika. "Fußball im Konzentrationslager." In *Hakenkreuz und rundes Leder*, edited by Peiffer and Schulze-Marmeling, 498–503. Göttingen: Die Werkstatt, 2008.

Steinbacher, Sybille. "Differenz der Geschlechter? Chancen und Schranken für die Volksgenossinnen." In *Volksgemeinschaft*, edited by Bajohr and Wildt, 94–104. Frankfurt: S. Fischer, 2009.

Steiner, André. *The Plans that Failed*. New York: Berghahn, 2010.

Steinhöfer, Dieter. *Hans von Tschammer und Osten. Reichssportführer im Dritten Reich*. Berlin: Bartels & Wernitz, 1973.

Steinkamp, Peter. "Pervitin (Metamphetamine) test, use, and misuse in the German Wehrmacht." In *Man, Medicine, and the State*, edited by Eckart, 61–72. Stuttgart: Franz Steiner, 2006.

Stiller, Eike. "Fußball in der organisierten Arbeitersportbewegung." In *Hakenkreuz und rundes Leder*, edited by Peiffer and Schulze-Marmeling, 166–77. Göttingen: Die Werkstatt, 2008.

Süß, Winfried."*Volkskörper" im Krieg. Gesundheitspolitik, Gesundheitsverhältnisse und Krankenmord im nationalsozialistischen Deutschland, 1939–1945*. München: Oldenbourg, 2003.

Tauber, Peter. *Vom Schützengraben auf den grünen Rasen. Der erste Weltkrieg und die Entwicklung des Sports in Deutschland*. Berlin: LIT Verlag, 2008.

Teichler, Hans Joachim. *Internationale Sportpolitik im Dritten Reich*. Schorndorf: Hofmann, 1991.

–, and Gerhard Hauk, eds. *Illustrierte Geschichte des Arbeitersports*. Berlin: Dietz, 1987.

Tooze, Adam. *The Wages of Destruction: The Making and Breaking of the Nazi Economy*. London: Allen Lane, 2006.

Treitel, Corinna. "Max Rubner and the Biopolitics of Rational Nutrition." *Central European History* 41 (2008): 1–25.

Tumblety, Joan. *Remaking the Male Body: Masculinity and the Uses of Physical Culture in Interwar and Vichy France*. Oxford: Oxford University Press, 2013.

Ueberhorst, Horst. *Geschichte der Leibesübungen. Leibesübungen und Sport in Deutschland vom Ersten Weltkrieg bis zur Gegenwart*. Berlin: Bartels und Wernitz, 1982.

– *Carl Krümmel und die nationalsozialistische Leibeserziehung*. Berlin: Bartels & Wernitz, 1976.

Uhlmann, Angelika. "'Der Sport ist der praktische Arzt am Krankenlager des deutschen Volkes.' Wolfgang Kohlrausch und die Geschichte der deutschen Sportmedizin." PhD diss., Freiburg, 2004.

Urban, Thomas. *Schwarze Adler, weiße Adler. Deutsche und polnische Fußballer im Räderwerk der Politik*. Göttingen: Die Werkstatt, 2011.

Vatin, François. "Arbeit und Ermüdung. Entstehung und Scheitern der Psychophysiologie der Arbeit." In *Physiologie und industrielle Gesellschaft*, edited by Sarasin and Tanner, 347–68. Frankfurt: Suhrkamp, 1998.

Wassong, Stephan. *Playgrounds und Spielplätze. Die Spielbewegung in den USA und Deutschland 1870–1930*. Aachen: Meyer & Meyer, 2007.

Wedemeyer-Kolwe, Bernd. *Vom "Versehrtenturnen" zum Deutschen Behindertensportverband (DBS). Eine Geschichte des deutschen Behindertensports*. Hildesheim: Arete Verlag, 2011.

– "Aussonderung oder Förderung? Die 'Körpererziehung' der Behinderten im 'Dritten Reich.'" In "mens sana in corpore sano," edited by Krüger, 127–42. Hamburg: Czwalina, 2008.

Wehler, Hans-Ulrich. *Deutsche Gesellschaftsgeschichte*. 5 vols. München: C. H: Beck, 2005–8.

Weindling, Paul. *Health, Race, and German Politics between National Unification and Nazism, 1870 - 1945*. Cambridge: Cambridge University Press, 1989.

– "Hygienepolitik als sozialintegrative Strategie im späten deutschen Kaiserreich." In *Medizinische Deutungsmacht*, edited by Labisch and Spree, 37–55. Bonn: Psychiatrie-Verlag, 1989.

– "The Rockefeller Foundation and German Biomedical Sciences, 1920-1940: From Educational Philanthropy to International Science Policy." In *Science, Politics, and the Public Good*, edited by Rupke, 119–40. London: Macmillan, 1988.

Weipert. Matthias. *"Mehrung der Volkskraft." Die Debatte über Bevölkerung, Modernisierung und Nation 1890–1933*. Paderborn: Ferdinand Schöningh, 2006.

Weiss, Sheila Faith. "The Race Hygiene Movement in Germany, 1904-1945." In *The Wellborn Science,* edited by Adams, 8–68. Oxford: Oxford University Press, 1990.

Werner, Wolfgang Franz. *"Bleib übrig!": Deutsche Arbeiter in der nationalsozialistischen Kriegswirtschaft*. Düsseldorf: Schwann, 1983.

Wesp, Gabriela. *Frisch, Fromm, Fröhlich, Frau. Frauen und Sport in der Weimarer Republik*. Frankfurt: Ulrike Helmer, 1998.

Wetzell Richard F. "Kriminalbiologische Forschungen an der DFA für Psychiatrie." In *Rassenforschung an Kaiser-Wilhelm-Instituten,* edited by Schmuhl, 68–98. Göttingen: Wallstein, 2003.

– *Inventing the Criminal: A History of German Criminology, 1880–1945*. Chapel Hill: University of North Carolina Press, 2000.

Weyrather, Irmgard. "'Deutsche Arbeit'—Arbeitskult im Nationalsozialismus." *Zeitschrift für Religions- und Geistesgeschichte* 56, no. 1 (2004): 18–36.

Wiesen, Jonathan S. *Creating the Nazi Marketplace: Commerce and Consumption in the Third Reich*. Cambridge: Cambridge University Press, 2011.

Wildt, Michael. "Der Begriff der Arbeit bei Hitler." In *Arbeit im Nationalsozialismus,* edited by Buggeln and Wildt, 3–24. Berlin: De Gruyter, 2014.

– "'Volksgemeinschaft': Eine Antwort auf Ian Kershaw." *Zeithistorische Forschungen/Studies in Contemporary History* Online-Ausgabe 8, no. 1 (2011): 102-9. http://www.zeithistorische-forschungen.de/16126041-Wildt-1-2011.

Wolsing, Theo. *Untersuchungen zur Berufsausbildung im Dritten Reich*. Kastllaun: Aloys Henn, 1977.

Zitelmann, Rainer. *Hitler: The Politics of Seduction*. Translated by Helmut Bogler. London: London House, 1999.

Zollitsch, Wolfgang. *Arbeiter zwischen Weltwirtschaftskrise und Nationalsozialismus. Ein Beitrag zur Sozialgeschichte der Jahre 1928 bis 1936*. Göttingen: Vandenhoeck & Ruprecht, 1990.

Zweiniger-Bargielowska, Ina. *Managing the Body: Beauty, Health, and Fitness in Britain, 1880–1939*. Oxford: Oxford University Press, 2011.

– "Building a British Superman: Physical Culture in Interwar Britain." *Journal of Contemporary History* 41 (2006): 595–610.

Index

German and European Studies

General Editor: Jennifer J. Jenkins

1 Emanuel Adler, Beverly Crawford, Federica Bicchi, and Rafaella Del Sarto, *The Convergence of Civilizations: Constructing a Mediterranean Region*
2 James Retallack, *The German Right, 1860–1920: Political Limits of the Authoritarian Imagination*
3 Silvija Jestrovic, *Theatre of Estrangement: Theory, Practice, Ideology*
4 Susan Gross Solomon, ed., *Doing Medicine Together: Germany and Russia between the Wars*
5 Laurence McFalls, ed., *Max Weber's 'Objectivity' Revisited*
6 Robin Ostow, ed., *(Re)Visualizing National History: Museums and National Identities in Europe in the New Millennium*
7 David Blackbourn and James Retallack, eds., *Localism, Landscape, and the Ambiguities of Place: German-Speaking Central Europe, 1860–1930*
8 John Zilcosky, ed., *Writing Travel: The Poetics and Politics of the Modern Journey*
9 Angelica Fenner, *Race under Reconstruction in German Cinema: Robert Stemmle's Toxi*
10 Martina Kessel and Patrick Merziger, eds., *The Politics of Humour in the Twentieth Century: Inclusion, Exclusion, and Communities of Laughter*
11 Jeffrey K. Wilson, *The German Forest: Nature, Identity, and the Contestation of a National Symbol, 1871–1914*
12 David G. John, *Bennewitz, Goethe,* Faust: *German and Intercultural Stagings*
13 Jennifer Ruth Hosek, *Sun, Sex, and Socialism: Cuba in the German Imaginary*
14 Steven M. Schroeder, *To Forget It All and Begin Again: Reconciliation in Occupied Germany, 1944–1954*

15 Kenneth S. Calhoon, *Affecting Grace: Theatre, Subject, and the Shakespearean Paradox in German Literature from Lessing to Kleist*
16 Martina Kolb, *Nietzsche, Freud, Benn, and the Azure Spell of Liguria*
17 Hoi-eun Kim, *Doctors of Empire: Medical and Cultural Encounters between Imperial Germany and Meiji Japan*
18 J. Laurence Hare, *Excavating Nations: Archaeology, Museums, and the German-Danish Borderlands*
19 Jacques Kornberg, *Pope Pius XII's Dilemma: Facing Atrocities and Genocide in World War II*
20 Patrick O'Neill, *Transforming Kafka: Translation Effects*
21 John K. Noyes, *Herder: Aesthetics against Imperialism*
22 James Retallack, *Germany's Second Reich: Portraits and Pathways*
23 Laurie Marhoefer, *Sex and the Weimar Republic: German Homosexual Emancipation and the Rise of the Nazis*
24 Bettina Brandt and Daniel Purdy, eds. *China and the German Enlightenment*
25 Michael Hau, *Performance Anxiety: Sport and Work in Germany from the Empire to Nazism*

www.ingramcontent.com/pod-product-compliance
Lightning Source LLC
LaVergne TN
LVHW090147080826
844660LV00013B/708/J

* 9 7 8 1 4 4 2 6 3 0 6 2 8 *